Goa

THE ROUGH GUIDE

There are more than one hundred Rough Guide titles
covering destinations from Amsterdam to Zimbabwe

Forthcoming titles include
Bangkok • Barbados • Edinburgh
Japan • Jordan • Syria

Rough Guide Reference Series
Classical Music • The Internet • Jazz • Opera • Reggae
Rock Music • World Music

Rough Guide Phrasebooks
Czech • French • German • Greek • Hindi & Urdu • Indonesian • Italian
Mandarin Chinese • Mexican Spanish • Polish • Portuguese • Russian
Spanish • Thai • Turkish • Vietnamese

Rough Guides on the Internet
http://www.roughguides.com
http://www.hotwired.com/rough

Rough Guide Credits

Text Editor:	Sarah McAlister
Series Editor:	Mark Ellingham
Editorial:	Martin Dunford, Jonathan Buckley, Samantha Cook, Jo Mead, Kate Berens, Amanda Tomlin, Ann-Marie Shaw, Paul Gray, Vivienne Heller, Sarah Dallas, Chris Schüler, Helena Smith, Kirk Marlow, Julia Kelly, Caroline Osborne, (UK); Andrew Rosenberg (US)
Online Editors:	Alan Spicer (UK); Geronimo Madrid (US)
Production:	Susanne Hillen, Andy Hilliard, Judy Pang, Link Hall, Nicola Williamson, Helen Ostick
Cartography:	Melissa Flack, David Callier, Maxine Burke
Finance:	John Fisher, Celia Crowley, Catherine Gillespie
Marketing & Publicity:	Richard Trillo, Simon Carloss, Niki Smith (UK); Jean-Marie Kelly, SoRelle Braun (US)
Administration:	Tania Hummel, Alexander Mark Rogers

Acknowledgements

David would like to thank the following for their help, advice and hospitality in February 1997: Ajit Sukhija (Panjim), Shelly and Theresa (Candolim), and Christe and Ermina D'Costa (Benaulim). Thanks, too, to Simon Lewis for sharpening the Hampi account, and to Lis, Naom, Stuart, Sarah Mop, Floss and James Top Stanley for sundry food and transport tips.

At Rough Guides in London, thank you to Sarah McAlister and Kate Berens for eagle-eyed editing, Sam Kirby (once again) for deciphering my messy maps, Helen Ostick for lightning-fast setting and Elaine Pollard for proofreading.

This edition published September 1997 by Rough Guides Ltd, 1 Mercer Street, London WC2H 9QJ.

Distributed by the Penguin Group:

Penguin Books Ltd, 27 Wrights Lane, London W8 5TZ.

Penguin Books USA Inc, 375 Hudson Street, New York 10014, USA.

Penguin Books Australia Ltd, 487 Maroondah Highway, PO Box 257, Ringwood, Victoria 3134, Australia.

Penguin Books Canada Ltd, 10 Alcorn Avenue, Toronto, Ontario, Canada M4V 1E4.

Penguin Books (NZ) Ltd, 182–190 Wairau Road, Auckland 10, New Zealand.

Printed in England by Clays Ltd, St Ives PLC

Typography and **original design** by Jonathan Dear and The Crowd Roars.

Illustrations throughout by Edward Briant.

Goa

THE ROUGH GUIDE

Written and researched by
David Abram

THE ROUGH GUIDES

Help us update

We've gone to a lot of trouble to ensure that this second edition of the *Rough Guide to Goa* is accurate and up-to-date. However, things inevitably change, and if you feel we've got it wrong or left something out, we'd like to know: any suggestions, comments or corrections would be much appreciated. We'll credit all contributions and send a copy of the next edition – or any other *Rough Guide* if you prefer – for the best correspondence.

Please mark letters "Rough Guide to Goa" and send to:
Rough Guides, 1 Mercer St, London WC2H 9QJ or
Rough Guides, 375 Hudson St, 9th floor, New York, NY 10014.

E-mail should be sent to:
mail@roughguides.co.uk

Online updates about Rough Guide titles can be found on our website at http://www.roughguides.com

The Author

Born in Cardiff, Wales, David Abram first travelled to Goa in 1984 during a gap year between school and university at Warwick (where he read French), but saw little more of the state on this occasion than the underside of a few palm trees. A decade later – after teaching English in Portugal and Greece, and dabbling in anthropology on a Native American reservation in Montana – he returned to India as a Rough Guide author, realizing then that Goa would make an ideal subject for a book. Rough Guides agreed, and this, in conjunction with updating trips for the *India* guide, has allowed him to study the undersides of many more palm trees since.

When not writing or researching guide books, David spends as much time as possible at home in Barrow Gurney, near Bristol, playing his clarinet and dreaming up other excuses for foreign travel.

Readers' letters

Many thanks to all the readers of India and the first edition of Goa who took the trouble to write with updates, criticisms and suggestions for this book, in particular: Mrs J Austin, Fiona Beard, Andy Brown, Annette Burns, Mark Harding, Karin Larsen, Richard Lawson, John and Jenny May, Monica Mukherji, Lisa Naylor, B. R. Pearson, RHS, Julie Sadler, R. Scott, H. Smith, R. Smith, Ivan Soares, Steve Steward, Lyn & Colin V.

Rough Guides

Travel Guides • Phrasebooks • Music and Reference Guides

We set out to do something different when the first Rough Guide was published in 1982. Mark Ellingham, just out of University, was travelling in Greece. He brought along the popular guides of the day, but found they were all lacking in some way. They were either strong on ruins and museums but went on for pages without mentioning a beach or taverna. Or they were so conscious of the need to save money that they lost sight of Greece's cultural and historical significance. Also, none of the books told him anything about Greece's contemporary life – its politics, its culture, its people, and how they lived.

So with no job in prospect, Mark decided to write his own guidebook, one which aimed to provide practical information that was second to none, detailing the best beaches and the hottest clubs and restaurants, while also giving hard hitting accounts of every sight, both famous and obscure, and providing up-to-the-minute information on contemporary culture. It was a guide that encouraged independent travellers to find the best of Greece, and was a great success, getting shortlisted for the Thomas Cook travel guide award, and encouraging Mark, along with three friends, to expand the series.

The Rough Guide list grew rapidly and the letters flooded in, indicating a much broader readership than had been anticipated, but one which uniformly appreciated the Rough Guides' mix of practical detail and humour, irreverence and enthusiasm. Things haven't changed. The same four friends who began the series are still the caretakers of the Rough Guide mission today: to provide the most reliable, up-to-date and entertaining information to independent-minded travellers of all ages, on all budgets.

We now publish 100 titles and have offices in London and New York. The travel guides are written and researched by a dedicated team of more than 100 authors, based in Britain, Europe, the USA and Australia. We have also created a unique series of phrasebooks to accompany the travel series, along with the acclaimed series of music guides, and a best-selling pocket guide to the Internet and World Wide Web. We also publish comprehensive travel information on our two websites: http://www.hotwired.com/rough and http://www.roughguides.com

Contents

Part Three Contexts   231

List of maps

MAP SYMBOLS

━━━	Railway	▣	Restaurant
═50═	Highway	ⓘ	Tourist Office
═══	Road	⊠	Post Office
-----	Path	♨	Mosque
— — —	Ferry route	▲	Hindu Temple
～～～	Waterway	⇂	Waterfall
━━--	Chapter division boundary	▨	Building
━-━--	State border	➕	Church
━━ ═ ═	District boundary	₊₊₊	Christian Cemetery
✈	Airport	▨	Park
★	Taxi, Rickshaw, Bus	⋮	Beach
⚓	Lighthouse	▨	Rocks
↓	Viewpoint	⚽	Football Pitch
◉	Hotel		

Introducing Goa

F amous for its white sand beaches, mesmeric sunsets and for the easy-going nature of its inhabitants, the small Indian state of **Goa**, just over a hundred kilometres from north to south, has been renowned as one of Asia's most irresistible destinations since the Portuguese navigator Vasco da Gama sailed down the Malabar coast in 1498, in search of "Christians and spices". He found neither, but the fort he established further south at Cochin resulted, twelve years later, in the erstwhile Muslim port and its hinterland becoming a Portuguese colony, which it remained until 1961. A decade later, the overland trail reached the Konkan coast, bringing with it the annual influx of backpackers that would soon make the state synonymous with hedonistic hippy holidays.

Since then, Goa has largely shaken off its reputation as a drop-out zone, but the tens of thousands of visitors who flock here each year still do so primarily to relax on the region's beautiful **beaches**. Lapped by the balmy waters of the Arabian Sea, around two dozen stretches of soft, white sand indent the Goan coast, from spectacular 25km sweeps to secluded palm-backed coves. The level of development on them varies wildly, and while most are these days lined with shack cafés and new hotels, it's still possible to sidestep the tourist scene. Indeed, the fabled strands showcased in glossy holiday brochures are only a small part of the picture.

A short foray from the coast will take you into the state's real heart, the densely populated alluvial strip **inland** – a lush patchwork of paddy fields, coconut plantations, whitewashed churches and gently meandering rivers, where the pace of life has altered little for centuries. Further east, the jungle-covered **hills** of the Western Ghats separate Goa from the rest of India, scattered with tiny thatch-roofed settlements and isolated communities of forest-dwelling farmers who are direct descendants of the region's aboriginal peoples.

The product of 450 years of **Portuguese domination**, Goa is a unique blend of east and west that is at once exotic and strangely familiar: Christmas and Carnival are celebrated as enthusiastically by the thirty percent Christian minority as the Diwali and Durga festivals are by the mainly Konkani-speaking Hindus. The state's separate identity is discernible in numerous other ways too, most visibly in its Latin-influenced architecture, but also in a fish- and meat-rich cuisine that would be anathema to most Indians. Another marked difference is the prevalence of **alcohol**. Beer is cheap, and six thousand or more bars around the state are licensed to serve it, along with the more traditional tipples of *feni*, the local hootch, and *toddi*, a derivative of palm sap.

Thanks to the fecund tropical climate of the region, and the well-watered soil of its seaward side, Goan farmers grow a wide array of **crops**, ranging from rice, the main staple, to cashew, areca (the source of betel nuts) and fruits for export. On the coast itself, coconut cultivation and **fishing** (both inshore, with small boats, canoes and hand nets, and offshore with modern trawlers) are still the main sources of income. The relatively recent discovery of iron in the hills to the east has also generated considerable revenue, and the economy is further fuelled by the stream of remittance cheques sent home by expatriate Goans working in Bombay and the Gulf states. The consequent higher standard of living has, inevitably, stimulated a massive influx of **immigrants** from elsewhere in India, who today comprise around a third of the total population.

Goa's other big money-spinner is, of course, **tourism**. Lured here in the 1960s by the locals' apparently permissive stance on drink, drugs and nudity – not to mention abundant cheap food and accommodation – the first foreigners to take advantage of the new state's pristine beaches were **"hippies"**. As the region's fame spread, however, the unconventional minority was gradually squeezed out, leaving the more accessible stretches of coastline near Panjim free for development for **mainstream tourism**. Coastal villages that were ramshackle fishing settlements less than a generation ago have metamorphosed into ritzy western-style resorts, complete with concrete hotel campuses, swimming pools and rows of parasols that vie for room on the dunes with old wooden outriggers and palm-thatch huts. The "alternative" contingent has meanwhile fled up the coast, ditching Pink Floyd along the way in favour of hard-edged, chest-thumping techno music. The legendary **full-moon parties** have survived, though, despite numerous police crackdowns, and continue to attract thousands of revellers, especially around the Christmas/New Year period.

Three decades of tourism and industrial development have inevitably taken their toll on the environment, and **green issues** nowadays feature prominently on the political agenda. In recent years, much anger has been directed towards a handful of purpose-built luxury hotels, which have been accused of ignoring environmental laws and tapping scarce supplies of ground water, chopping down coconut trees and even displacing villagers. We have tried to reflect such concerns in the guide, indicating which hotels have been

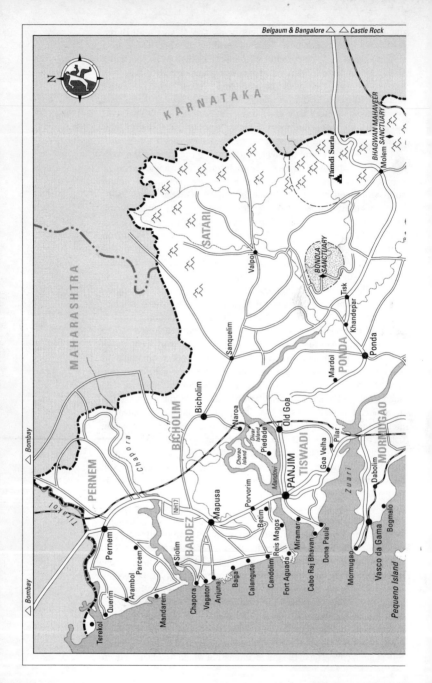

MAP OF GOA

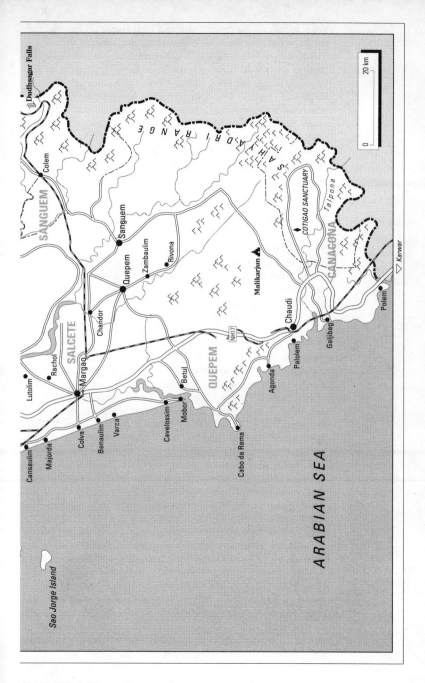

taken to task by the green lobby, and what you can do to minimize the impact of your presence in this part of the world.

If you've never travelled in Asia before, Goa may come as something of a shock. Its beaches certainly conform to the glossy holiday brochure image, but once outside the tourist spots many first-time visitors are surprised to find themselves in workaday rural India, where bullock carts far outnumber cars, rice is planted by hand, and where the majority of villagers draw their water from a communal well, subsisting on an average annual wage that is far lower than the cost of a flight from Europe. Don't, however, let this deter you from venturing off the beaten track in Goa. The little-frequented corners of the state are likely to yield some of the most memorable moments of your trip, combining beautiful scenery with the chance to encounter a way of life that is worlds away from the headlong commercialism of the beach resorts.

Where to go

Which **beach** you opt for when you arrive largely depends on what sort of holiday you have in mind. Heavily developed resorts such as **Calangute** and **Baga**, in the north, and **Colva** (and to a lesser extent **Benaulim**), in the south, offer more "walk-in" accommodation, shopping and tourist facilities than elsewhere. Even if you don't fancy crowded bars and purpose-built hotels, it can be worth heading for these centres at first, as finding places to stay in less commercialized corners is often difficult. **Anjuna**, **Vagator** and **Chapora**, where accommodation is generally more basic and harder to come by, are the beaches to aim for if you've come to Goa to party. To get a taste of what most of the state must have been like twenty or thirty years ago, however, you'll have to travel further afield – to **Arambol**, a sleepy fishing village and hippy hang-out in the far north; or to **Agonda** and **Palolem**, near the Karnatakan border, where tourism has yet to make much impact.

Foremost among worthwhile attractions away from the coast are the ruins of the Portuguese capital at **Old Goa**, nine kilometres from Panjim – a sprawl of Catholic cathedrals, convents and churches that draws crowds of Christian pilgrims from all over India. Another popular day excursion is to Anjuna's Wednesday **flea-market**, a sociable place to shop for souvenirs and the latest rave gear. Further inland, the thickly wooded countryside around **Ponda** harbours numerous temples, where you can check out Goa's peculiar brand of Hindu architecture. The *taluka* (district) of Salcete, and its main market town, **Margao**, is also littered with wonderful Portuguese mansions, churches and seminaries, whose gabled baroque facades nose tantalizingly above the tropical treeline. In addition, wildlife enthusiasts may be tempted into the interior to visit the nature reserves at **Molem**, in the far east of Central Goa, and **Cotigao** in the south, which harbour fragile populations of rare animals.

With so many tempting beaches, markets, monuments and nature reserves within the state, it's no surprise that few visitors venture across the Goan border into neighbouring Karnataka. But beyond the shelter of the Western Ghat mountains, the parched plateau lands of the Deccan Trap sprawl east over the apex of peninsula India, dotted with a string of industrial cities, and, of more interest to visitors, the decaying remnants of older capitals. Among these is one of the most spectacular archeological sites in South India, the ghost city of **Hampi**. Strewn over a vast area of boulder hills, the capital of the formidable Vijayanagar dynasty was razed by Muslim invaders in 1565, and today, weed-choked palaces, temples and discarded statues are virtually all that remains of this once opulent metropolis. However, a visit here will give you a vivid insight into the extravagant art and culture of pre-colonial Hindu India, while the ten-hour journey to the ruins can be an adventure in itself.

For this reason, we've included a detailed account of Hampi in chapter four, **Around Goa**, which also features the highlights along the **Konkan coast**, the lush alluvial strip running south from Goa in the shadow of the Sahyadri Hills. Previously accessible only by a winding pot-holed highway, this region can now be painlessly reached by train from Goa on the new superfast Konkan Railway. The high point of any trip through coastal Karnataka has to be the ramshackle Hindu pilgrimage town of **Gokarn**, site of several ancient shrines and a crop of unspoilt beaches. India's highest waterfall, spectacular **Jog Falls**, 154km from Goa, also lies within relatively easy reach of the coast, hidden deep in the jungle-draped Sahyadri range. It's possible to string these two together in a trip of three to four days, but with a week to spare you'll be able to spend time exploring rarely visited fishing villages and forest areas along the way, experiencing at first hand an India that's a far cry from the tourist enclaves of Goa.

When to visit

The best **time to come** to Goa is during the dry, relatively cool winter months between late October and early March. At other times, either the sun is too hot for comfort, or the monsoon rains make life miserable for everyone except the fishers and hoteliers, who get to sit around all day snoozing and playing backgammon. During peak season, from mid-December to the end of January, the weather is perfect, with the temperature gauge rarely nudging above a manageable 32°C. Finding a room or a house to rent at that time, however – particularly over the Christmas and New Year fortnight when the tariffs double, or triple – can be a real hassle.

Part 1

The Basics

Getting there from Britain and Ireland

Direct flights to Goa from the UK – recently introduced by European charter airlines to serve the booming package tour trade – are the quickest, cheapest and most convenient way to reach Goa, as there are no direct scheduled services. The state's only airport, Dabolim, is also a far more relaxed point of arrival than Bombay – the other main gateway to southern India, where you have to change onto a domestic flight. The one drawback with flying direct is that charter tickets only allow short stays, usually of two to three weeks. So if you're planning a stay of a couple of months or more, you may have to opt for an indirect flight, with a night or two in Bombay to arrange onward transport to Goa.

At present, three **charter** airlines leave Britain for Goa each week, stopping in the Middle East for an hour en route to re-fuel. *Monarch* and *Britannia* fly out of London **Gatwick** on Saturdays, and *Caledonian* on Thursdays and Fridays, with extra departures on Thursdays from **Manchester** with *Monarch*. The flight time, including refuelling, is around eleven and a half hours.

CAA regulations prohibit the sale of flight-only **tickets** to Goa from outside India, but there's nothing to stop you from purchasing an all-in package holiday (see p.4) and ditching the accommodation part of the deal once you've arrived. This can work out much cheaper than a scheduled flight via Bombay, especially if you manage to pick up a last-minute bargain. Note that the Indian government does not as a rule allow holders of Indian passports to travel on charter flights to Goa.

BA and *Air India* fly direct **scheduled services** every day from London to Bombay, with *Air Singapore* covering the route twice weekly. A range of other airlines, including *KLM, Gulf* and *Emirates*, fly with brief stopovers in their own countries. Flying time is around eleven hours, and return fares are quoted at around £600 in low season, although you can normally find cheaper deals through **discount agents**, who sell off excess seats for airlines at prices as low as £360, or less. Try the agents listed on p.5, or check the Sunday newspapers' travel sections, free Antipodean publications (eg *TNT* or *Southern Cross*) outside the mainline London train stations, and weekly listings magazines such as *Time Out*.

Once you have arrived in Bombay, you can catch a connecting flight to Goa (pre-booked in the UK or not), or make your way there by cata-maran, train or bus – see pp.13–17 for details of onward travel from Bombay.

Flights from Ireland

There are no direct flights to either Goa or Bombay from **Ireland**. However, *British Airways* fly from Dublin to Bombay via London, and *Swissair* via Zürich. At around £600, *Swissair* represents the best deal in high season out of Dublin. Alternatively, try a combination of *Air France* and *Air Inter* via Paris, or, if you're on a tight budget, travel to London and pick up a cheap flight from there (see above).

At £500 return, *Aeroflot's* daily flight from Shannon to Delhi is the rock-bottom route to

Airlines

The following airlines operate scheduled **flights to Bombay** from the UK, usually with a short stopover in their home country if this lies en route to India.

Aeroflot, Sun Alliance House, Dawson St, Dublin 2 (☎ 01/679 1453).

Air France, Colet Court, 100 Hammersmith Rd, W6 (☎ 0181/759 2311); 29–30 Dawson St, Dublin 2 (☎ 01/844 5633).

Air India, Mathisen Way, Colnbrook, Slough SL3 (☎ 0181/745 1000).

Air Lanka, 205 Holland Park Ave, London W11 4XB (☎ 0171/930 4688).

Alitalia, 27–28 Piccadilly, London W1P 9PF (☎ 0171/602 7111).

Biman Bangladesh Airlines, 17 Conduit St, London W1R 9TD (☎ 0171/629 0252).

British Airways, 156 Regent St, London W1R 5TA; 19–21 St Mary's Gate, Market St, Manchester M1 1PU; 32 Frederick St, Edinburgh EH2 2JR; 9 Fountain Centre, College St, Belfast BT1 6ET (all enquiries ☎ 0345/222111).

Egyptair, 296 Regent St, London W1R 6PH (☎ 0171/580 5477).

Emirates Airlines, Gloucester Park, Cromwell Rd, London SW7 (☎ 0171/808 0033).

Gulf Air, 10 Albemarle St, London W1X 3HE (☎ 0171/408 1717).

KLM Royal Dutch Airlines, 190 Great South West Rd, Bedfont TW14 (☎ 0990/750900); 58 Mulgrave St, Dun Laoghaire, Ireland (☎ 01/284 3823).

Kuwait Airlines, 16 Baker St, London W1M 2AD (☎ 0171/412 0006).

Lufthansa, Old Bond St, London W1X 4EM (☎ 0345/737747).

Pakistan International Airways, 1–15 King St, London W6 9LA (☎ 0181/741 8066).

Singapore Airlines, 580–586 Chiswick High Rd, London W4 5RP (☎ 0181/563 6767).

Swissair, 10 Wardour St, London W1 (☎ 0171/434 7200); 3rd Floor, 54 Dawson St, Dublin 2 (☎ 01/677 8173).

Syrian Arab Airlines, 27 Albemarle St, London W1X 3FA (☎ 0171/493 2851).

Charter airlines in the UK

The following British charter airlines fly to Goa from the UK, with a brief re-fuelling stopover in one of the Gulf states en route.

Britannia, Luton Airport, Luton, Beds LU2 9ND (☎ 01582/424155).

Caledonian Airlines, Caledonian House, Gatwick Airport, Crawley, West Sussex RH6 0LF (☎ 01293/536321).

Monarch Airlines, Luton Airport, Luton, Beds LU2 9ND (☎ 01582/400000).

India, although there has been a lot of concern recently about the safety record of this airline. Moreover, the flight can involve long late-night or multi-day stopovers in Moscow. *Aeroflot* is also notorious for overbooking passengers on return flights (this is especially likely to happen at peak periods), so confirm your return seat as soon as possible.

Package holidays

The advent of direct charter flights and the comparatively low cost of food and accommodation in Goa have made it among the most affordable winter **package holiday** destinations in the world for sun-starved northern Europeans. Depending on the kind of hotel you choose, a fortnight's break could set you back anywhere between £350 and £1900. Prices also vary according to the time of year, soaring from mid-December to mid-January, and bottoming out from late March to early May when the charters stop. However, even during the peak Christmas–New Year period, last-minute bargains regularly appear in travel agents' windows, as tour operators scramble to sell off unbooked holidays.

In addition to standard accommodation and half-board deals, most companies offer optional extras, ranging from **excursions** around the state to longer trips elsewhere in India, including Bombay, Kerala, Agra (to see the Taj Mahal) and Rajasthan. Several operators also include

Discount flight agents in Britain and Ireland

Campus Travel, 52 Grosvenor Gardens, London SW1W 0AG (☎0171/730 3402); 541 Bristol Rd, Birmingham B29 6AU (☎0121/414 1848); 39 Queen's Rd, Bristol BS8 1QE (☎0117/929 2494); 5 Emmanuel St, Cambridge CB1 1NE (☎01223/324283); 166 Deansgate, Manchester M3 3FE (☎0161/273 1721); 105–106 St Aldates, Oxford OX1 1DD (☎01865/242067); 53 Forest Rd, Edinburgh EH1 2QP (☎0131/668 3303). *Student/youth travel specialists, with branches also in YHA shops and on campuses all over Britain.*

Cheap Flights, http://www.cheapflights.co.uk. An on-line catalogue of discount flight agents specializing in cheap air fares to Goa, among hundreds of destinations worldwide. Particularly good for last-minute bargains.

Global Travel, 10 Maddox St, London W1R 9PN (☎0171/629 5123). *Discount flights to Bombay and other Indian destinations, but no student fares.*

Standtrend Travel, 3 Woodside Ave, London N12 8AN (☎ & fax 0181/445 0041). *Highly knowledgeable South Asia flight specialist offering flight-only deals to Goa, as well as bargain last-minute package deals.*

STA Travel, 74 Old Brompton Rd, London SW7 3LQ and 117 Euston Rd, London NW1 2SX (☎0171/937 9962); 25 Queen's Rd, Bristol BS8 1QE (☎0117/929 3399); 38 Sidney St, Cambridge CB2 3HQ (☎01223/66966); 75 Deansgate, Manchester M3 5EJ (☎0161/834 0668); 88 Vicar Lane, Leeds LS1 7JH (☎0113/244 9212); Cardiff University Union, Park Place, Cardiff CF1 3QN (☎01222/382350). *Discount fares, with particularly good deals for students and young people.*

Trailfinders, 42–50 Earls Court Rd, London W8 6FT (☎0171/938 3366); 194 Kensington High St, London W8 7RG (☎0171/938 3939); 58 Deansgate, Manchester M3 2FF (☎0161/839 6969). *One of the best-informed and most efficient agents dealing with Asia; good for RTW tickets, too.*

Travel Bug, 597 Cheetham Hill Rd, Manchester M8 5EJ (☎0161/721 4000). *Discount long-haul ticket specialists offering overland packages, plenty of RTW options and Indian Airlines domestic flight passes.*

USIT, Aston Quay, O'Connell Bridge, Dublin 2 (☎01/679 8833); 10–11 Market Parade, Cork (☎021/270900); Fountain Centre, College St, Belfast (☎01232/324073). *Student travel specialists.*

Goa as part of a more extensive tour of South India, while others use the state as a venue for **special interest holidays**. Among the more popular of these are bird-watching, sailboarding and scuba diving; a couple of firms will even organize your wedding, complete with bullock-cart carriage and a locally tailored dress.

Holidays may be booked directly from the tour companies or through travel agents; discounted packages are only sold by travel agents. As few retailers deal with all the different operators, it's a good idea to phone around for a range of quotes, and check out the travel pages of daily newspapers and weekend supplements. Another good tip is to avoid half-board or all-inclusive holidays: it is much cheaper, and more enjoyable, to eat out than stay in your hotel.

It is also worth pointing out that there exists in Goa a vehement **local opposition to tourism** in general, and to package tourism in particular, both because of its impact on Goan culture and because of the drain so many extra visitors inevitably place on the area's fragile ecology. This resentment is rarely, if ever, directed at tourists themselves. Instead, it is reserved for the developers and officials who sidestep environmental laws to build large water-guzzling resorts. So before you book your holiday, read the rundown of green issues given in Contexts (see p.245), and look up the listing of any hotel you may be considering in the guide: if somewhere has been accused of infringing environmental legislation, we've said so.

Specialist tour operators in Britain

Abercrombie and Kent, Sloane Square House, Holbein Place, London SW1W 8NS (☎0171/730 9600). *Upmarket sightseeing tours for small groups or individuals in chauffeur-driven air-conditioned cars, from around £1300.*

Bales, Bales House, Junction Rd, Dorking, Surrey RH4 3EJ (☎01306/885991). *Their 16-day escorted tour of South India costs around £2100, with an optional unaccompanied 7-day extension to Goa (£795 extra).*

Butterfield's Indian Railway Tours, Burton Fleming, Driffield, Yorks YO25 0PQ (☎01262/470230). *Goa features briefly on the unique "South India Railway Tour" (£1095), conducted in special train carriages.*

Cox and Kings, Gorden House, 10 Greencoat Place, London (☎0171/873 5000). *Resolutely upmarket tailor-made tours to India, offering 7- and 14-night stays in the Fort Aguada Beach Resort from £1000, and 5-night extensions for £545.*

Discover India, 29 Fairview Crescent, Rayners Lane, Harrow, Middx HA2 9UB (☎0181/429 3300). *Tailor-made trips to Goa in all price groups.*

Distant Dreams, *Cosmos*, Tourama House, 17 Homesdale Rd, Bromley, Kent BR2 9LX (☎0181/464 3444). *Formula beach vacations in large resort complexes from around £620; also extensions to other destinations in South India, including the Maldives.*

Explore Worldwide, 1 Frederick St, Aldershot, Hants GU11 1LQ (☎01252/319448). *The 16-day architectural "Treasures of Central India" option (£1030) winds up in Goa after a tour of the Deccan's main monuments.*

Global Link, Colette House, 52–55 Piccadilly, London W1V 9AA (☎0171/409 7766). *Gourmet food tours, standard and tailor-made sightseeing.*

Hayes and Jarvis, 152 King St, London W6 0QU (☎0181/748 5050). *A range of beach holidays, mostly in flashy resorts, from £440.*

Highlife Holidays, 79 Cricklewood Broadway, London NW2 3JR (☎0181/452 3388). *Sightseeing tours with beach extensions from around £500 a week.*

The Imaginative Traveller, 14 Barley Mow Passage, London W4 4PH (☎0181/742 3049). *Three days in Goa tacked on to the end of a 20-day trip around South India (£1000), or a 7-night "Tropical Paradise" tour with luxury accommodation at the Fort Aguada Beach Resort (£750).*

Inspirations, Victoria House, Victoria Rd, Horley, Surrey RH6 7AD (☎01293/822244). *Beach holidays for £400–2000 – and special interest alternatives that include bird-watching, scuba diving and sailboarding. The largest UK operator in Goa.*

Kuoni Travel, Kuoni House, Dorking, Surrey RH5 4AZ (☎01306/740500). *Standard resort-based packages (from £500–1050), or longer tours of India.*

Manos, 168–172 Old Street, London EC1V 9BP (☎0171/216 8070). *A wide range of packages from £500–1700, in modest guest houses or star resort hotels.*

Pettits India, 14 Lonsdale Gardens, Tunbridge Wells, Kent TN1 1NU (☎01892/515966). *Pricey five-star holidays in the Fort Aguada Beach Resort: direct flights and accommodation for £700–1100 for 7 nights.*

Somak Holidays, Somak House, Harrovian Village, Bessborough Rd, Harrow, Middx HA1 3EX (☎0181/423 3000). *An extensive range of good-value beach holidays from £400, plus optional excursions to Bombay and Kerala.*

Sun World, *Iberotravel*, 29/31 Elmfield Rd, Bromley, Kent BR1 1LT (☎01132/555222). *Budget and luxury beach holidays, including "Jungle Camp" trips to the interior and 7-night deals for between £400 and £500.*

Thomson Worldwide, Greater London House, Hampstead Rd, London NW1 (☎0171/707 9000). *Fourteen-night packages in five-star resorts from £490–1250.*

Tropical Places, Freshfield House, Lewes Rd, Forest Row, East Sussex RH18 5ES (☎01342/825123). *Excellent-value 2- to 5-star packages from around £540.*

Getting there from North America

There are no direct flights to Goa from the US or Canada. Travellers either have to fly into Delhi or Madras and then pick up a thrice-weekly domestic flight into Goa on *Indian Airlines*, or fly via Bombay and connect with *Indian Airlines, Damania, East-West, Jet* or *Modiluft* for the one-hour journey to Goa – all have daily services. *Air India* also flies once daily into Goa from Bombay, Delhi and Cochin; four times weekly from Bangalore and Madras and twice weekly from Ahmedabad.

Goa's busiest season is December to February and flights book quickly. Often, a tour operator with a good package deal can get you the most for your dollar.

No matter which way you look at it or where exactly you're flying from, you're in for a long trip. Most airlines fly via their hub city in Europe or Asia before continuing to either Bombay or Delhi, and picking up a regional carrier to Goa.

Air India offers the best option to Goa: low-season fares from New York start at $1730 and high season at $2208. These and other prices quoted are for midweek travel. Flying on weekends adds $50 to $100 to the return fare. *KLM* quotes a year-round New York to Goa fare of $2902.

Regardless of where you buy your ticket, **fares** are dependent on season. These may vary from airline to airline and from year to year. Roughly, **high season** is from mid-June to mid-September and around Christmas and New Year; **low season** from mid-January to mid-May, with the 'shoulder' season sandwiched between these dates.

If India is only one stop on a longer journey, you might want to consider buying a **Round-the-World (RTW) ticket**. Some travel agents can sell you an "off-the-shelf" RTW ticket that will have you touching down in about half a dozen cities (Delhi is on many itineraries); others will have to assemble one for you, which can be more tailored to your needs but is apt to be more expensive. RTW tickets including India and Europe can be found for as little as $1299 (low season) or $1450 (high season).

Shopping for tickets

Airline **tickets** are sold through many channels, and there's no magic rule for predicting which will be cheapest. Whatever the airlines are offering, however, any number of specialist travel agents set out to better. These are the outfits you'll see advertising in the Sunday newspaper travel sections. If you're in a city with a fair-sized immigrant population, it might also be worth your while checking out one of the ethnic newspapers available, in New York at least, in English.

You can normally cut costs by going through a **specialist flight agent** – either a **consolidator**, who buys up blocks of tickets from the airlines and sells them at a discount, or a **discount agent**, who wheels and deals in blocks of tickets offloaded by the airlines, and often offers special student and youth fares and a range of other travel-related services such as travel insurance, rail passes, car rentals, tours and the like. Remember that these companies make their money by dealing in bulk – don't expect them to answer lots of questions. Some agents specialize in **charter flights**, which may be cheaper than

Airlines in the USA and Canada

Aeroflot	☎ 888/552-9264.	**Kuwait Air**	☎ 1800/458-9248.
Air Canada	☎ 1800/776-3000.	**Lufthansa**	☎ 1800/645-3880
Air France	☎ 1800/237-2747	in Canada call	☎ 1800/555-1212
in Canada	☎ 1800/667-2747.	for local toll-free number.	
Air India	☎ 1800/223-2420	**Malaysian Airlines**	☎ 1800/552-9264.
in Canada call	☎ 1800/555-1212	**Northwest Airlines**	☎ 1800/447-4747.
for local toll-free number.		**PIA (Pakistan Inter-**	☎ 1800/221-2552
British Airways	☎ 1800/247-9297	**national Airlines)**	or 212/370-9158.
in Canada	☎ 1800/243-6822.	**Royal Jordanian**	
Cathay Pacific	☎ 1800/233-2742	**Airlines**	☎ 212/949-0050.
in Canada call	☎ 1800/555-1212	**Singapore Airlines**	☎ 1800/742-3333.
for local toll-free number.		**Thai International**	☎ 1800/426-5204
Gulf Air	☎ 888/FLY GULF	in Canada	☎ 1800/668-8103.
	or 1800/553-2824.	**United Airlines**	☎ 1800/241-6522.
KLM	☎ 1800/374-7747		
in Canada	☎ 514/939-4000.		

anything available on a scheduled flight, but departure dates are fixed and withdrawal penalties are high (check the refund policy). If you travel a lot, **discount travel clubs** are another option – the annual membership fee may be worth it for benefits such as cut-price air tickets and car rental.

Don't automatically assume that tickets purchased through a travel specialist will be cheapest – once you get a quote, check with the airlines and you may turn up an even better deal. Be advised also that the pool of travel companies is swimming with sharks – exercise caution and never deal with a company that demands cash upfront or refuses to accept payment by credit card. Also bear in mind that the lower priced tickets will often come with restrictions (length of stay, advance booking requirements, etc) and that penalties for changing your plans can be stiff.

From Eastern and Central USA

Flying **east** from the USA, you'll stop over somewhere in Europe (depending on the carrier's hub city) and probably again somewhere in the Gulf.

Discount travel companies in the USA and Canada

Air Brokers International, 150 Post St, Suite 620, San Francisco, CA 94102 (☎ 1800/883-3273). *Consolidator.*

Council Travel, 205 East 42nd St, New York, NY 10017 (☎ 212/822-2700 or 1800/743-1823). *Nationwide US student travel organization.*

FlyTime, 45 West 34th St, Suite 305, New York, NY 10001 (☎ 212/760-3737). *Consolidator specializing in tickets to India.*

Hariworld Travel, 25 West 45th St, Suite 1003, New York, NY 10036 (☎ 212/957-3000). *Biggest Indian consolidator; agent for Indrail Passes.*

High Time Travel, 303 5th Ave, Suite 204, New York, NY 10016 (☎ 212/684-7700). *Consolidator specializing in tickets to India.*

Moment's Notice, 7301 New Utrecht Ave, Brooklyn, NY 11204 (☎ 718/234-6295). *Discount Travel Club*

STA Travel, 10 Downing St, New York, NY 10014 (☎ 1800/777-0112 or 212/627-3111). *Specialists in student travel.*

Travel Cuts, 187 College St, Toronto, ON M5T 1P7 (☎ 1800/667-2887 or 888/238-2887 or 416/979-2406). *Student and general discount travel organization.*

UniTravel, 1177 North Warson Rd, St Louis, MO 63132 (☎ 1800/325-2222). *Consolidator.*

Figure on at least 18 hours' total travelling time from the East Coast. *Air India* has the only direct flights to India (from New York); on all other airlines you'll change planes in their hub city.

Air India and *PIA* discount their tickets heavily through a few specialist New York consolidators (see box). Marked-down tickets on European carriers – notably *British Airways, Air France* and *Lufthansa* – are frequently sold by other discount agents. Other airlines flying between the eastern USA and India include *KLM, Aeroflot, Gulf Air, Kuwait Airways* and *Egypt Air*. Or you can simply hop on any of the many airlines that fly to London and pick up a flight to India from there.

North American tour operators

Absolute Asia, 180 Varick St, New York, NY 10014 (☎212/627-1950). *Customizes independent tours to and including Goa.*

Adventure Center, 1311 63rd St, Suite 200, Emeryville, CA 94608 (☎1800/227-8747). *Offer "Goa and the Deep South", a 23-day camping trip including Goa, Bombay and Madras for $905–940 for land cost. Their"Treasures of Central India", a 15-day hotel-accommodated tour, that also includes Goa in its itinerary, is priced at $1175–1240 for the land package.*

Archeological Tours, 271 Madison Ave, Suite 904, New York, NY 10016 (☎212/986-3054). *Offer a 24-day scholar-led tour of the south. The in-depth tour of sacred and historical sights starts in Bombay, heads east, then along the coast (Madras, Bangalore), up to Hampi and eventually Goa. Land cost is $4540; land and air from New York $5480; plus $427 for internal flights.*

Cox and Kings, 511 Lexington Ave, Suite 355, New York, NY 10017 (☎1800/999-1758). *Their "Southern Trader" is a 20-day escorted tour including Bombay, Hyderabad, Bangalore, Mysore, Madras, Cochin and Goa for $3845. They'll also customize or add on Goa to any Indian itinerary.*

Geographic Expeditions (formerly InnerAsia), 2627 Lombard St, San Francisco, CA 94123 (☎1800/777-8183). *Will customize a sea-kayaking tour to Goa, or add a visit onto one of their other India packages.*

Himalayan Travel, 110 Prospect St, Stamford, CT 06901 (☎1800/225-2380). *Offer a 19-day escorted "Images of the Deep South" tour, which includes 6 days in Goa, for a land cost of $1695. They also arrange independent tours to Goa, depending on the clients' needs.*

Journeys, 4011 Jackson Rd, Ann Arbor, Michigan, MI 48103 (☎1800/255-8735). *Will customize Goa packages.*

Journeyworld International, 119 West 57th St, Suite 1620, New York, NY 10019-2303 (☎1800/635-3900 or 212/247-6091). *Specialize in individual cultural tours to India and Nepal but will add a few days in Goa to their itineraries if a client so wishes.*

Mastermark Tours, 13910 Champion Forest Drive, Suite 111, Houston, TX 77069 (☎1800/356-5858 or 281/440-3833). *Offer escorted general interest tours to India. Their 27-day "Extensive India and Nepal" tour includes two days in Goa. Air and land price is $6195 per person (departing from New York) and includes 4/5 star hotels, breakfast and dinner, air-conditioned transportation and sightseeing, baggage handling, taxes and service charges.*

Mercury Travels Ltd, 509 Madison Ave, Suite 1906, New York, NY10022 (☎1800/223-1474). *Specialize in customized tours, and will put together a package to, or including, Goa.*

Rama Tours, 6 North Michigan Ave, Suite 1420, Chicago, IL 60602 (☎1800/TEL-RAMA). *A full service operator to India, offering either individual packages to Goa, or Goa as part of more than one city tours. They have a 6-day Bombay/Goa plan for $685 (land price). The Bombay–Goa air fare is $130 with this operator.*

Safaricentre, 3201 North Sepulveda Bd, Manhattan Beach, CA 90266 (☎1800/223-6046). *Specialize in adventure and nature packages. They are also agents for Exodus, specialists in biking and hiking tours.*

Worldwide Adventures, 36 Finch Ave West, Toronto, Ontario, M2N 2G9 (☎1800/387-1483). *Specialists in trekking, cycling, etc holidays to Asia. Although it does not figure in their fixed tours, they will customize a package to Goa.*

Prices are most competitive out of **New York**, where the cheapest low-season consolidated fares to Delhi or Bombay hover around $1000 in low season and rise to $1500 in high season.

From **Washington** or **Miami**, figure on $1200 in low season to $1500 in high season; from **Chicago** $1220 to $1520; and from **Dallas/Fort Worth** $1290 to $1550. Again, most carriers will quote you fares to Bombay, then a return domestic flight at $100–130 to Goa.

From the West Coast

From the **West Coast**, it takes about as long to fly eastward or westward – a minimum of 22 hours' total travelling time – and if you're booking through a consolidator there may not be much difference in price, either. *Cathay Pacific*, *Malaysian Airlines* and *Singapore Airlines* are the main carriers flying over the Pacific to Bombay (which is closer to Goa), with *Thai International* and *United Airlines* flying to Delhi, each via their respective hubs. *Air India* doesn't do the trans-Pacific route, but can book passengers on *Northwest* to any of several Asian capitals and then fly them the rest of the way. For eastbound routings, see above.

From **LA** or **San Francisco**, you're looking at a minimum of $1200 to fly to Delhi or Bombay in low season, and up to $1500 in high season, with an add-on of $50–65 for a one-way domestic flight to Goa.

From Canada

The only direct flight from **Canada** to India is on the Toronto–Delhi routing with *Air India*, via London, taking around 20 hours; all other routings involve a plane change and more layover time. *Air Canada* flies from all major Canadian cities to London, where passengers can join a London–Delhi flight. Other airlines offering services to India, via their capitals, include *British Airways*, *Cathay Pacific*, *Lufthansa* and *KLM*.

From **Montréal** or **Toronto**, discounted low/high-season fares to Delhi or Bombay are around CDN$1545/1760; from **Vancouver** (via the Pacific) CDN$1520/1855. Add on around CDN$140 for the flight to Goa.

Packages and organized tours

Including Goa on a package tour of India can be a good – but brief – way of sampling what the province has to offer, in conjunction with other major sights. A tour company can shield you from the subcontinent's many little frustrations, enabling you to cover more ground than if you were going it alone. Of course, you'll have to be prepared to forego independence and spontaneity, and accept that there will be only fleeting and predominantly mercenary encounters with local people.

The tours listed above focus on Goa, taking in temples and beaches. Tour prices are always wildly out of line with the cost of living in India, and whether you take one will depend on which is tighter, your budget or your schedule. Excluding air fare, a two-week tour is likely to cost at least $1000; a three-week luxury trip can cost as much as $3000 or more.

Getting there from Australia and New Zealand

There are no direct flights to Goa from Australia or New Zealand, and all services fly via an Asian hub city into Delhi, Bombay or Madras, where you can pick up a connecting domestic flight, or travel overland to Goa.

All fares quoted below are for travel during the **low season** (February–November); flying at **peak times** (throughout December and January) can add substantially to these prices.

From **eastern Australia**, *Qantas* combines with *Air India* to fly four times a week to **Delhi**, and once a week to **Bombay**, both via Singapore. Twice a week, *Qantas* and *British Airways* operate a service to **Madras**, again via Singapore. *Malaysian Airlines, Singapore Airlines* and *Thai International* also fly to Delhi, via Kuala Lumpur, Singapore or Bangkok respectively.

Fares from the eastern states with *Qantas* start around A$1500, while fares with *Malaysian, Singapore* or *Thai International* start at A$1410. **Agents** such as *STA* or Indian specialists (see box on p.12) can often better these fares by combining sectors: for example, Sydney to Hong Kong with *Ansett*, then flying on to Bombay with *Swiss Air*, for a total fare of A$1349 for a three-month ticket. Fares from **Perth** are generally around A$100–200 less. **Add-on flights** from Bombay to Goa on *Indian Airlines* cost A$85 one-way, A$170 return, if pre-booked.

From **New Zealand**, the cheapest **fares** to India from Auckland are around NZ$1720, though flying with the major airlines will take this nearer the NZ$2000 mark; fares from Wellington generally cost an extra NZ$100 or so. **Routes** are similar to those from Australia: *Air New Zealand* joins forces with *Air India* to fly to Bombay or Delhi via Singapore, Hong Kong or

---

Airlines in Australia and New Zealand

Air New Zealand, 5 Elizabeth St, Sydney (local-call rate ☎13 2476); Level 18, 1 Queen St, Auckland (☎09/366 2400).

Ansett Australia, 501 Swanson St, Melbourne (☎03/9623 3333).

British Airways, Level 26, 201 Kent St, Sydney (☎02/9258 3300); 154 Queen St, Auckland (☎09/356 8690).

Malaysian Airlines, 16 Spring St, Sydney (local-call rate ☎13 2627); Level 12, Swanson Centre, 12–26 Swanson St, Auckland (☎09/373 2741).

Qantas, 70 Hunter St, Sydney (local-call rate ☎13 1211); Qantas House, 154 Queen St, Auckland (☎09/357 8900).

Singapore Airlines, 17–19 Bridge St, Sydney (local-call rate ☎13 1011); Lower Ground Floor, West Plaza Building, corner of Customs and Albert streets, Auckland (☎09/379 3209).

Swissair, 33 Pitt St, Sydney (☎02/9232 1744).

Thai International Airways, 75–77 Pitt St, Sydney (☎02/9844 0999, toll-free ☎1800/422 020); Kensington Swan Building, 22 Fanshawe St, Auckland (☎09/377 3886).

Travel agents and operators in Australia and New Zealand

Adventure World, *Australia* 73 Walker St, North Sydney, plus branches in Brisbane and Perth (☎02/9956 7766, toll-free ☎1800/221 931). *New Zealand* 101 Great South Rd, Remuera, Auckland (☎09/524 5118).

Anywhere Travel, 345 Anzac Parade, Kingsford, Sydney (☎02/9663 0411).

Brisbane Discount Travel, 260 Queen St, Brisbane (☎07/3229 9211).

Budget Travel, 16 Fort St, Auckland, plus other branches around the city (☎09/366 0061, toll-free ☎0800/808 040).

Flight Centres, *Australia* Level 11, 33 Berry St, North Sydney (☎02/9241 2422); Bourke St, Melbourne (☎03/9650 2899); plus other branches nationwide. *New Zealand* National Bank Towers, 205–225 Queen St, Auckland (☎09/309 6171); Shop 1M, National Mutual Arcade, 152 Hereford St, Christchurch (☎03/379 7145); 50–52 Willis St, Wellington (☎04/472 8101); other branches countrywide.

India Travel Centre, 81 York St, Sydney (☎02/9299 1111).

India Nepal Travel Centre, 17 Castlereagh St, Sydney (☎02/9223 6000).

Northern Gateway, 22 Cavenagh St, Darwin (☎08/8941 1394).

STA Travel, *Australia* 702–730 Harris St, Ultimo, Sydney; 256 Flinders St, Melbourne; other offices in state capitals and major universities (nearest branch ☎13 1776; telesales ☎1300/360 960). *New Zealand* Travellers' Centre, 10 High St, Auckland (☎09/309 0458); 233 Cuba St, Wellington (☎04/385 0561); 90 Cashel St, Christchurch (☎03/379 9098); other offices in Dunedin, Palmerston North, Hamilton and major universities. (World Wide Web site: www.statravelaus.com.au; email traveller@statravelaus.com.au).

Thomas Cook, *Australia* 321 Kent St, Sydney; 257 Collins St, Melbourne; branches in other state capitals (all branches local-call rate ☎13 1771; or call Thomas Cook Direct, toll-free ☎1800/064 824). *New Zealand* 96–98 Anzac Ave, Auckland (☎09/379 3920).

Bangkok; *Singapore Airlines* also fly via Singapore, while *Thai International* goes via Bangkok. Pre-booked return flights from Bombay to Goa on *Indian Airlines* are NZ$207 (see also p.14).

Many **Round-The-World routes** take in Delhi or Bombay, with fares starting from around A$2200/NZ$2800. If your preferred RTW ticket doesn't include India, it costs around A$675/NZ$880 for an add-on three-month excursion fare to Delhi from Kuala Lumpur, Singapore or Bangkok.

Organized tours

If your schedule is tight, an **organized tour** can enable you to cover more ground in a shorter time – at a price. Excluding air fare, a 2-week tour is likely to **cost** at least A$1500; for example, a 15-day itinerary with *Explore Worldwide* (book through *Adventure World* – see box above), starting from Bombay and taking in Goa, Ajanta and Ellora, Hyderabad and Hampi, with the emphasis on history and culture, costs A$1565 (not including return air fare from Australia).

Getting there from Bombay

With any domestic air ticket in India, it's essential to **re-confirm your flight at least 72 hours before departure**. Fail to do this, and you're likely to find yourself at the end of a long waiting list, or worse. Passengers travelling on *Indian Airlines*, in particular, should re-confirm both their Bombay–Goa and Goa–Bombay legs well in advance, either through a travel agent, or with the domestic carrier direct.

Although increasing numbers of visitors fly to Goa direct from Europe, the vast majority – even those who only come for short periods – are obliged to travel via Bombay, 600km north. The journey is comfortably undertaken by plane or catamaran, although if you have more time than money, you may prefer to catch a train or bus.

Domestic flights and long-distance train and bus services also connect Goa with several **other major cities in India**, including Delhi, Madras and Bangalore. Few short-stay visitors approach the state this way, although a journey across the subcontinent by public transport is a memorable experience that is well worth considering. Should you choose to travel to Goa overland, we recommend you check out the *Rough Guide to India*.

By plane

At present, three **airlines** operate daily services to Goa from Bombay's domestic airport, **Santa Cruz** – *Indian Airlines*, *Jet* and *Skyline NEPC*. If you can afford it, this is the most painless way to go: the journey takes only one hour, and costs around Rs1925 (£39/$59) if you pay in Indian rupees. Most major international carriers have agreements with one or more of their domestic counterparts in India, so it is possible to book your onward domestic flight at the same time as you pay for your international ticket. This can work

out a little more expensive, with agents charging anything from £40–75 one-way, but at least you're guaranteed a seat. If you wait until you arrive in Bombay to book your Goa flight, you could well end up hanging around for several days, as competition for tickets is fierce, especially around Christmas and New Year.

By train

Time was when the train journey to Goa from Bombay, winding south across the Deccan via Pune, took nearly twenty-four hours. Now, thanks to the high-speed **Konkan Railway** (see p.34), travelling time has been slashed to ten hours, and will drop even lower, to six or seven hours by 1998. With fares undercutting even buses, it's hard to see how the other forms of surface transport will be able to hold their own over the coming years.

While the Konkan Railway undoubtedly offers a quick and cheap route to Goa from Bombay, it has a couple of drawbacks. The first is that, as on all Indian trains, you have to **reserve your seat in advance**. Computerized booking has made this a lot easier in recent years but you still have to go to the station yourself, preferably well ahead of your intended departure date. UK and other

Tickets for travel on the Konkan Railway between Bombay and Goa may be pre-booked in the UK through **SD Enterprises**, 103 Wembley Park Drive, Wembley, Middx HA9 8HG (☎0181/903 3411; Mon–Fri 9am–5.30pm, Sat 9am–2pm).

foreign passport holders may book their tickets at two fast-track tourist ticketing facilities, both in downtown Bombay. The first lies on the upper floor of the Western Railways booking office in **Churchgate Station** (Mon–Fri 9.30am–4.30pm, Sat 9.30am–2.30pm), next door to the Government of India Tourist Office; the second at the Central Railway booking office, to the rear of **Victoria Terminus** (Mon–Sat 9am–1pm & 1.30–4pm; counter no. 22, or no. 21 on Sun). Both counters have access to special "Tourist Quotas", which are released the day before departure if the train leaves in the day, or the morning of the departure if the train leaves after 5pm. The one catch is that you have to pay for tourist quota tickets in foreign currency (travellers' cheques will do), unless you can produce a recent encashment certificate. Change is always given in rupees.

Fares for the 640km trip are Rs180 for second-class "three-tier" accommodation (which has three pull-down bunks on each side of the compartments), and Rs580 for the more comfortable "two-tier" air-conditioned compartments (the latter service, with two bunks on each side, only runs three times per week).

The other drawback with the Konkan Railway is that its trains leave from the inconveniently situated **Kurla Station**, way north of downtown Bombay, near Santa Cruz domestic airport. You can either get there by cab, or jump on a local train from Victoria Terminus (a hassle if you're weighed down with luggage).

When this book went to press, the Konkan Railway was only running as far as **Sawatwadi**,

a small station on the Goa–Maharashtra border, from where buses were laid on for the onward trip to Panjim. By the end of 1997, however, you should be able to travel to within a stone's throw of Panjim, and south through Margao to Chaudi and beyond. The number of services should also be increased from one to five per day.

By catamaran

Damania's long-awaited **catamaran** service between Bombay and Goa was inaugurated in November 1994. The Scandinavian-built vessel, whose aeroplane-style reclining seats are sealed inside glacial air-conditioned cabins, takes seven hours to reach Panjim, leaving Bombay at 10am on Tuesdays and Thursdays, and 10.30pm on Saturdays and Sundays. Seats in economy class (lower deck) cost Rs1050–1250, depending on the time of year; a ticket in business class (upper deck, with headphones and a choice of meals) will set you back upwards of Rs1250; and there's a "no-show" penalty of Rs200 if you fail to turn up. The trip itself is pretty boring as the catamaran sails up to 40km offshore, and many passengers suffer from sea sickness because of being enclosed in a cabin. Considering this, together with the cost and journey time, you're better off travelling on the Konkan Railway.

Tickets for the catamaran are sold through most reputable travel agents in Bombay (see box above), and through *Frank Damania Shipping's* main office at the Passenger Terminal, Shed No. 2, New Ferry Wharf, Mallet Bunder Rd, Mazagao Docks (☎ 022/374 3737–9, fax 374 3740) – a fif-

A SURVIVAL GUIDE TO BOMBAY

The Maharashtran capital of Bombay is, admittedly, no holiday resort – with its chronic shortage of space, pollution problems and the jarring extremes of wealth and poverty – but it definitely has excitements of its own.

What follows is a very brief guide to getting into the city, and some pointers on what to do when you're there. For a full treatment, check out the *Rough Guide to India*.

ARRIVAL AND INFORMATION

Bombay's **international airport**, Sahar, lies north of the city, an hour and a half or more by road from the centre but only a fifteen-minute trip from the **domestic airport**, Santa Cruz. If you're **transferring between the two**, either take the *EAT* bus (hourly, 4am–1am; Rs25), jump on the free shuttle "fly-bus" (every 30min from outside the terminal building), or catch a **taxi**. You can avoid haggling over the fare by paying in advance at the taxi counter on Sahar's arrivals concourse; the price is marginally more expensive than the equivalent meter rate, but at least you'll be taken the most direct route. Money can be changed at the *State Bank of India*'s 24-hour **exchange facility** in the arrivals hall. If you're on an afternoon or evening flight – when most hotels tend to be full – it's worth using the **accommodation booking desk**.

The easiest way to **get into the city centre**, 26km south, is by taxi (again, pay in advance). However, if you're on a tight budget and happy to carry your bags around, catch the *EAS* bus from the car park outside the arrivals terminal (Rs50), which heads down the west side of the peninsula and drops passengers at the *Air India* building on Nariman Point, and near the Gateway of India, Colaba; the latter stop is closer to most of the hotels.

The best source of **information** in Bombay is the excellent India Government Tourist Office, 123 M Karve Rd (Mon–Fri 8.30am–6pm, Sat 8.30am–2pm; ☎ 022/203 3144), opposite Churchgate station's east exit. The staff here are exceptionally helpful and hand out a range of maps and leaflets on Bombay; they are also a useful source of advice for onward travel to Goa. In addition, there are 24-hour tourist information counters at Sahar (☎ 022/832 5331) and Santa Cruz (☎ 022/614 9200) airports, and at VT train station (☎ 022/262 2859).

ACCOMMODATION

Finding a **room** at the right price when you arrive in Bombay can be a real problem. Tariffs are inflated and the best places fill up by noon, so phone ahead as soon as (or preferably well before) you arrive. Note that rooms in mid- and top-of-the-range hotels can be booked through the accommodation counter in Sahar airport (see above).

Those who just want to crawl off the plane and straight into bed generally make a beeline for one of the many hotels scattered around the suburbs near the airports; try *Airlines International*, Plot No. 4, Prabhat Colony, Santa Cruz East, near the domestic airport (☎ 022/614 3069), the *Rang Mahal*, Station Rd, Santa Cruz West (☎ 022/649 0303), or any of the more upmarket places listed at the airports' accommodation desks. Otherwise, **Colaba**, in the south of the city, is the district to head for, with dozens of options at all prices. Offering large, clean rooms for under Rs200, the *Lawrence Hotel*, 3rd Floor, 33 Rope Walk Lane (☎ 022/284 3618), is far and away the best budget option in the centre, while both the *Salvation Army*, Red Shield House, 30 Mereweather Rd, behind the *Taj Hotel* (☎ 022/284 1824), and *YMCA*, 18 Madam Cama Rd (☎ 022/202 0445), have clean budget rooms and dorm accommodation. Good choices for rooms under Rs750 include the *Kerawala Chambers*, 3rd and 4th Floors, 25 PJ Ramchandani Marg (☎ 022/282 1089), the *Gulf*, 4/36 Kamal Mansion, Arthur Bunder Rd (☎ 022/283 3742) and *Whalley's*, Jaiji Mansion, 41 Mereweather Rd (☎ 022/283 4286).

Close to **VT**, the *Oasis*, 272 SBS Marg (☎ 022/269 7886), *Prince* 34 Walchand Hirachand Rd, near Red Gate (☎ 022/261 2809), and *Lords*, 301 Ali Mazban Path (☎ 022/261 0077), are basic establishments with most rooms under Rs350; *Welcome*, 257 SBS Marg (☎ 022/261 2196), provides a degree of luxury for around Rs750. Over in the **Marine Drive** area, the *Chateau Windsor*, 86 VN Rd (☎ 022/204 3376) is the best of the bunch, with comfortable rooms for around Rs800. If it's full try *Norman's*, around the corner at 127 Marine Drive (☎ 022/203 4234).

Continues over

Continued from over

THE CITY AND SIGHTS

Bombay is a sprawling metropolis of more than thirteen million people, but its centre – crammed on to a narrow spit of land that curls like a drooping finger into the Arabian Sea – is fairly compact and easy to find your way around on foot or by short taxi rides.

Colaba, at the far southern end of the peninsula, is Bombay's main tourist enclave, comprising a dozen or so blocks of dilapidated colonial tenement buildings that spread east from its busy thoroughfare, **Shahid Bhagat Singh Marg** (known as the "**Colaba Causeway**"). In spite of being a trendy hangout for the city's rich young things, the area has retained the distinctly sleazy feel of the bustling port it used to be, with dodgy moneychangers, drug dealers and pimps hissing at passers-by from doorways.

At the northeast corner of Colaba, Bombay's most famous landmark, the **Gateway of India**, is a honey-coloured arch built in 1924 to commemorate the visit of King George V and Queen Mary nine years earlier, although it is more often remembered as the place the British chose to stage their final departure from the subcontinent in 1948. Directly behind the Gateway is India's ritziest hotel, the **Taj Intercontinental**, the preserve of visiting diplomats, Arab sheikhs and the city's jet set. Lesser mortals are allowed in to sample the opulent restaurants and coffee shops.

A five-minute walk from the hotel, the **Prince of Wales museum** (Tues–Sun 10.15am–6pm; Rs3), houses a superb collection of Indian painting and sculpture from 3500 BC to the British Raj. Among the many highlights are fragments of stonework from the now defunct ancient Buddhist *stupa* at Bharhut, and the vast array of Indian miniature paintings on the first floor. The building itself – a blend of Gujarati-Hindu, Islamic and English municipal styles – is also something of a historical monument, epitomizing the hybrid Indo-Saracenic school of architecture.

The commercial heart of Bombay, known as **Fort**, lies immediately north of Colaba. Featuring the cream of the city's Raj-era buildings – including **Victoria Terminus (VT)** and the onion-domed **GPO** – its hectic streets stream with roaring traffic and office *wallahs* in crisp cotton clothes. In the eye of the storm stands the small

and simple **St Thomas' Cathedral** – reckoned to be the oldest English structure in Bombay. Its polished brass and wood interior has altered little in three hundred years, with memorial plaques to colonial parishoners who met an untimely death here in battle or from disease.

Bombay's central **bazaars**, a ten-minute ride from VT, are the city at its most intense: an anarchic jumble of narrow streets that you could feasibly wander around for weeks without ever seeing the same shopfront twice. The best place to start a foray into this area is **Crawford Market** (officially Mahatma Phule Market), ten minutes' walk north of VT, where you can find anything from onion *bhajis* to budgerigars.

EATING

In keeping with its cosmopolitan credentials, Bombay is bursting with interesting places to eat. **Shahid Bhagat Singh Marg** (or "Colaba Causeway"), leading off from Wellington Circle in Colaba, has a wide range of eateries: the *Delhi Durbar* dishes up an array of rich and moderately priced, spicy Mughlai food. Across the street is Bombay's most popular tourist bar-restaurant, *Leopold's*, where you can tuck into pizzas and other Western-style food, washed down with draught beer. The *Café Mondegar*, next to the *Regal* cinema on Colaba Causeway, is the other main tourist hang-out, serving a good range of light meals, with a CD juke box and murals by a famous Goan cartoonist. For a filling and inexpensive South Indian meal, you won't do better than the *Majestic*, near the *Regal* cinema, whose good-value *thalis* and fiery snacks are a big hit with budget travellers. **Shivaji Marg**, perpendicular to Shahid Bhagat Singh Marg, features the city's best and most authentic Chinese restaurant, *Nanking*, with lots of delicious – and pricey – Cantonese and seafood specialities. Nearby Tulloch Rd, running directly behind the *Taj*, is home to *Bademiya*, the legendary *kebab wallah* who serves cheap, delicious, flame-grilled mutton, chicken or fish in hot *rotis* on the pavement. *Chetana*, 34 K Dubash Marg opposite the Jehanngir Art Gallery, is absolutely the last word in fine Indian vegetarian cuisine, and a great place for a splurge; it's expensive, but not extravagantly so.

teen-minute cab ride north from Colaba. Before making any hard travel plans, **check the departure times** with a travel agent, as these have tended to change annually over the past few years.

By bus

The Bombay–Goa **bus** journey ranks among the very worst in India. Don't believe travel agents who assure you it takes thirteen hours. Clapped-out buses and appalling road surfaces along the sinuous coast make eighteen hours a more realistic estimate. With the Konkan Railway now up and running, you'd have to be a real masochist to choose to travel this way, although occasionally seats get fully booked on the train, leaving the bus as the only cheap option.

Tickets start at around Rs220 for a push-back seat on a beaten-up *Kadamba* (Goan) or *MSRTC*

(Maharashtran) bus. These services are in demand in high season, so book in advance at the *Kadamba* kiosks just north of Victoria Terminus. Private buses also run to Goa, costing around Rs270 for a noisy front-engine *Tata*, to Rs550 for a place on a top-of-the-range imported air-conditioned bus with pneumatic suspension, video and toilet. Tickets should again be booked as far ahead as possible, ideally through one of the travel agents listed on p.14, though it's sometimes worth turning up at the car park opposite the *Metro Cinema*, Azad Maidan, where most of the private buses leave from, on the off chance of a last-minute cancellation. Make sure, in any case, that you are given both your seat and the bus registration numbers, and confirm the exact time and place of departure with the travel agent, as these frequently vary between companies.

Visas and red tape

Gone are the days when Commonwealth nationals could arrive visa-less in India and stay as long as they pleased: nowadays everybody needs a visa, except Nepalis and Bhutanis.

Multiple-entry **tourist visas** for all nationalities are issued either for three months from the date of entry into India (£13/$40/CDN$20) – the date

of entry must be within ninety days of issue of the visa – or for six months from the date of issue, not of entry (£26/$60/CDN$40).

The best place to get a visa is in your country of residence, from the **embassies and high commissions** listed overleaf. In the three UK branches (Mon–Fri 9.30am–1pm), applications currently take between one hour and ninety minutes to be processed; turn up as early in the day as possible to collect an appointment ticket, which will tell you when you have to return to submit your form, along with three colour passport-sized photographs. In the US, visas are usually available on the same day if you apply in person by noon, but check your nearest embassy, high commission or consulate to be sure.

Tourist visas are also available **by post**. Allow a minimum of fifteen working days in the UK, and check in advance the cost of the postage and packaging. In the US this takes five days if you mail your application, accompanied by 2 passport photos, by Federal Express. An alternative, if you're short of time or live a long way from the embassy, is to pay a **visa agency** to obtain the

Indian diplomatic representatives abroad

Australia Embassy: 3–5 Moonah Place, Yarralumla, Canberra, ACT 2600 (☎ 02/6273 3999). Consulates: 25 Bligh St, Sydney, NSW 2000 (☎ 02/9223 9500); 13 Munro St, Coburg, VIC 3058 (☎ 03/9384 0141); The India Centre, 49 Bennett St, Perth, WA 6004 (☎ 08/9221 1485).

Canada High Commission: 10 Springfield Rd, Ottawa, ON K1M 1C9 (☎ 613/744-3751). Consulates: 2 Bloor St West, Suite 500, Toronto, ON M4W 3E2 (☎ 416/960 0752); 325 Howe St, 2nd Floor, Vancouver, BC V6C 1Z7 (☎ 604/662-8811).

Ireland Embassy: 6 Leeson Park, Dublin 6 (☎ 01/497 0843).

New Zealand Embassy: 10th floor, 180 Molesworth St (PO Box 4045), Wellington 1 (☎ 04/473 6390).

UK Embassy: India House, Aldwych, London WC2B 4NA (☎ 0171/836 8484, fax 836 4331). Consulates: 20 Augusta St, Jewellery Quarter, Hockley, Birmingham B18 6JL (☎ & fax 0121/212 2782); St Andrew's House, 141 West Nile St, Glasgow G1 2RN (☎ 0141/331 0777, fax 333 1116).

USA Embassy of India (Consular Section): 2107 Massachusetts Ave Northwest, Washington DC 20008 (☎ 202/939-7000). Consulates: 3 East 64th St, New York, NY 10021-7097 (☎ 212/774-0600 or 0610); 540 Arguello Blvd, San Francisco, CA 94118 (☎ 415/668-0662); 455 North City Front Plaza, NBC Tower Building, Suite 850, Chicago, IL 60611 (☎ 312/595-0405); Suite 600, 6th floor, 3 Post Oak Central, 1990 Post Oak Blvd, Houston, Texas 77056 (☎ 713/626-2148 or 2355).

---

visa on your behalf. This service costs £15–20, plus the cost of the visa. In the UK the cheapest company is *Trailfinders Visa Service*, 194 Kensington High Street, London W8 (☎ 0171/938 3848); otherwise try *The Visa Service*, 2 Northdown Street, King's Cross, London N1 (0171/833 2709), or *Visa Express*, 31 Corsham Street, London W1 (☎ 0171/252 4822). Most companies recommend you apply at least a week before your departure date, especially during peak season (October–February), but *Visa Express* will deliver in only 24 hours.

Contrary to what you might hear on the travellers' grape vine, or read in some guide books, it is no longer possible to **extend tourist visas** in India (unless you have a very good reason to do so, such as illness). If you want to stay for longer than six months, you have to leave the country and apply for a new visa; most people do this in Colombo, Sri Lanka, or Kathmandu, Nepal.

For details of **other visas** – foreigners of Indian origin, business travellers and even students of yoga can get five-year visas – contact your nearest Indian embassy.

Travel insurance

In the light of the potential health risks involved in a trip to Goa – see p.20 – travel insurance is too important to ignore. In addition to covering medical expenses and emergency flights, it also insures your money and belongings against loss or theft. Flights paid for with a major credit or charge card offer some automatic cover, but usually only while travelling to and from your destination. Some package tours, too, may include insurance, but package operators more commonly offer an insurance deal as an extra: it might be worth checking against alternative policies, though differences in price and cover are likely to be slight.

Always check the fine print of a policy. A 24-hour medical emergency contact number is a must, and one of the rare policies that pays your medical bills directly is far better than one that reimburses you on your return home. The per-article limit for loss or theft should cover your most valuable possession (a camera, for example) but, conversely, don't pay for cover you don't need – such as too much baggage or a huge sum for personal liability. Make sure, too, that you are covered for all the things you intend to do. Activities like climbing are usually specifically excluded, but can be added for a supplement.

Frequent travellers may benefit from **annual insurance policies**, but these usually put an upper limit on the duration of any single trip, likely to be ninety days at most.

Among **UK insurers**, *Worldwide Travel Insurance Ltd*, at Elm Lane Office, Elm Lane, Tonbridge, Kent TN10 3XS (☎01732/773366) are about the cheapest, offering a month's cover for around £36. Other companies with competitive rates, especially for young people, include: *Endsleigh*, 97–107 Southampton Row, London WC1B 4AG (☎0171/436 4451), and *Columbus Travel Insurance* (☎0171/375 0011). You should also phone for a quote from *Campus*, *STA* and *Trailfinders*, who all sell good-value, flexible policies through their travel agency branches throughout the UK.

Travellers from the **US** should carefully check their current insurance policies before taking out a new one. You may discover that you are already covered for medical and other losses while abroad. Holders of *ISIC* cards are entitled to be reimbursed for $3000-worth of accident coverage and 60 days of in-patient benefits of up to $100 a day for the period the card is valid. If you do want a specific travel insurance policy, there are numerous kinds to choose from: short-term combination policies covering everything from baggage loss to broken legs are the best bet and will either cost around $75 for ten days' injury and evacuation, plus $2.50 per day for baggage, or be calculated according to the cost of your holiday. Companies you might try include: *STA Travel* ☎1800/777-0112 or 212/627-3111; *Travel Guard*, 1145 Clark St, Stevens Point, WI 54481 (☎715/345-0505 or 1800/826-1300); *Access America International*, PO Box 90310, Richmond, Virginia, VA23230 (☎1800/284-8300); and *Travel Assistance International* (☎1800/821-2828).

In **Australia**, policies issued by *STA Travel* (☎1300/360 960) and *Cover-More* (☎02/9202-8000, toll-free 1800/251 881) cater for the needs of travellers on all budgets; a typical policy will cost A$160–180 for one month.

Making a claim

If you need to **make a claim**, you must have a **police report** in the case of theft or loss. Your policy document will include the relevant form, which should be taken to the nearest police post to be signed and stamped as soon after the loss as possible. Expect to have to pay a little *baksheesh* for the privilege; Rs100 should more than suffice.

Claims for **medical expenses** require supporting evidence of treatment in the form of bills, though with some policies, doctors and hospitals will be able to bill your insurers direct. Keep photocopies of everything you send to the insurer and don't allow months to elapse before informing them. Write immediately and tell them what's happened; you can usually claim later.

Health

Goa is arguably the most salubrious state in India, and very few travellers fall seriously ill while they are there. However, it can be all too easy during lengthy, healthy spells on the beach to forget that you are still in South Asia, and that normally innocuous things such as salad, a rare steak or a drink mixed with untreated water can pose very real health risks. It is therefore important to be aware of potential pitfalls in advance, and steer clear of them at all costs.

Precautions

Although standards of sanitation in Goa are generally high – particularly in international-style resort hotels – a few common-sense **precautions** are in order, bearing in mind that things such as bacteria multiply far more quickly in a tropical climate, and that you will have little immunity to Indian germs.

When it comes to **food**, remember that tourist restaurants and Western dishes are every bit, if not more, likely to cause you grief than local cafés and meals. Be particularly wary of prepared dishes that have to be reheated – ask yourself how long they've been on display in the heat. Anything boiled, fried or grilled (and thus sterilized) in your presence is usually all right, though meat can sometimes be dodgy; anything that has been left out for any length of time is definitely suspect. Raw unpeeled fruit and vegetables should always be viewed with suspicion, and you should avoid salads unless you know they have been soaked in an iodine or potassium permanganate solution. Fruit-sellers on the beaches sometimes handle peeled food with their left hands (see p.47), so make sure you douse your slice of pineapple or melon with safe water before eating it.

Be vigilant about **personal hygiene**. Wash your hands often, especially before eating, keep all cuts clean, treat them with iodine or antiseptic, and cover them to prevent infection. Be fussier about sharing things like drinks and cigarettes than you might be at home; never share a razor or toothbrush. It is also inadvisable to go around barefoot and best to wear flip-flop sandals even in the shower.

Among items you might wish to carry with you – though all are available in Goa itself, at a fraction of what you might pay at home – are antiseptic cream, plasters, lints and sealed ban

---

In Britain, travellers who call the **"Health Line"** run by **MASTA** – the Medical Advisory Service for Travellers Abroad – on ☎0891/224100 receive the latest detailed health advice by return post. MASTA is based at the London School of Hygiene and Tropical Medicine, Keppel St, London WC1E 7HT (☎0171/631 4408). Calls are charged at 49p per minute during peak periods, and 39p per minute at other times.

What about the water?

One of the chief concerns of many prospective visitors to Goa is whether the water is safe to drink: it isn't, though unfamiliarity with Indian micro-organisms is generally more of a problem rather than any great virulence in the water itself. The fact is, if you are in the region for a while, your stomach will have to get used to local bugs, and you may well get a slight dose of diarrhoea at some point. By exercising reasonable caution, however, you can minimize the risk of going down with anything more serious.

Untreated water is difficult to avoid completely: it is used to make *lassi* and ice (which appears in drinks without being asked for), and utensils are washed up with it. **Bottled water**, often known by the brand name *Bisleri*, is available virtually everywhere in the state. Always check that the seal is intact, as refilling bottles is not unheard of.

If you're concerned about the long-term environmental impact of so many discarded water bottles kicking around, or plan to go somewhere with no access to mineral water – which really only applies to travellers venturing well off the beaten track – find an appropriate method of **treating water**. Boiling for a minimum of five minutes is sufficient to kill micro-organisms but is not always practical and does not remove unpleasant tastes. **Chemical sterilization** is cheap and convenient, but dirty water remains dirty and still contains organic matter. You can safely and quickly sterilize water using chlorine or iodine tablets, although these leave an unpleasant after-taste (which can be masked with lemon or lime juice) and are not always effective in preventing such diseases as amoebic dysentery and giardia. Tincture of iodine is better; add a couple of drops to one litre of water and leave to stand for twenty minutes. Pregnant women, babies and people with thyroid problems should avoid using iodine sterilizing tablets or iodine-based purifiers, or use an additional iodine-removal **filter**. The various kinds of filter only remove visible impurities and the larger pathogenic organisms (most bacteria and cysts). However fine the filter, it will not remove viruses, dissolved chemicals, pesticides, herbicides, etc.

Purification, a two-stage process involving both filtration and sterilization, gives the most complete treatment. Portable water purifiers range from pocket-size units weighing 60 grams to ones up to 800 grams. Among the best water purifiers on the market are those made in the UK by *Pre-Mac*; for suppliers, contact:

All Water Systems Ltd, Unit 12, Western Parkway Business Centre, Lower Ballymount Rd, Dublin 12, Ireland (☎ 01/456 4933).

Outbound Products, 1580 Zephyr Ave, Box 56148, Hayward CA 9454, USA (☎ 1800/663-9262); 8585 Fraser St, Vancouver, BC V5X 3Y1, Canada (☎ 604/321-5464).

Pre-Mac (Kent) Ltd, 40 Holden Park Rd, Southborough, Tunbridge Wells, Kent TN4 0ER, England (☎ 01892/534361).

dages, a course of *Flagyl* antibiotics and a box of Immodium (*Lomotil*) for emergency diarrhoea treatment, rehydration sachets, insect repellent and something like *Anthisan* for soothing bites, and paracetamol or aspirin.

Advice on avoiding **mosquitoes** is offered under "Malaria" below. If you do get bites or itches try not to scratch them: it's hard, but infection and tropical ulcers can result if you do. Tiger Balm and even dried soap may relieve the itching.

Vaccinations

No inoculations are legally required for entry into India, but meningitis, typhoid and hepatitis A jabs are recommended, and it's worth ensuring that you are up to date with tetanus, polio and other boosters.

Hepatitis A is not the worst disease you can catch in Goa, but the frequency with which it strikes travellers makes a strong case for immunization. Transmitted through contaminated food and water, or through saliva, it can lay a victim low for several months with exhaustion, fever and diarrhoea. The new *Havrix* vaccine has been shown to be very effective and lasts for up to ten years – unlike gamma globulin, the traditional serum against hepatitis, which offers little protection and wears off after three months.

Symptoms by which you can recognize hepatitis include yellowing of the whites of the eyes, general malaise, orange urine (though dehydration could also cause that) and light-coloured stools. If you think you have it, steer clear of alcohol, try to avoid passing it on, and get lots of rest. More serious is **hepatitis B**, passed on like AIDS through blood or sexual contact. There is a vaccine, but it is only recommended for those planning to work in a medical environment. Otherwise, your chances of getting hepatitis B are low.

Typhoid is also spread through contaminated food or water, but is rare in Goa outside the monsoon. It produces a persistent high fever with malaise, headaches and abdominal pains, followed by diarrhoea. Vaccination can be by injection (the old two-jab or newer single-shot variety, with one inoculation for a booster), giving three years' cover, or orally – tablets are more expensive but easier on the arm.

Cholera, spread the same way as hepatitis A and typhoid, causes sudden attacks of watery diarrhoea with cramps and debilitation. Again, this disease rarely occurs in Goa, breaking out in isolated epidemics. If you get it, take copious

Dogs

Stray dogs hang around everywhere in Goa, especially on the beaches and outside café-shacks, where they scavenge scraps. Stay in a village for any time and one is bound to latch on to you, but it's a good idea to avoid stroking them, no matter how in need of love they look. Quite apart from the rabies risk, most carry a plethora of parasites and skin diseases. Leaving your temporary pet, whose ribs will have disappeared after weeks of being well fed, can also be a wrench.

amounts of water with rehydration salts and seek medical treatment; there is a vaccination but it offers very little protection. Most medical authorities now recommend vaccination against **meningitis** too. Spread by airborne bacteria (through coughs and sneezes for example), it is a very unpleasant disease that attacks the lining of the brain and can be fatal.

You should have a **tetanus** (or lockjaw) booster every ten years whether you travel or not. It is picked up through contaminated open wounds – if you cut yourself on something dirty and are not covered, get a booster as soon as you can. Assuming that you were vaccinated against **polio** in childhood, only one (oral) booster is needed during your adult life. Immunizations against mumps, measles, TB, and rubella are a good idea for anyone who wasn't vaccinated as a child and hasn't had the diseases.

Rabies is widespread in Goa, and the best advice is to give dogs and monkeys a wide berth, indeed not play with animals at all, no matter how cute they might look. A bite, a scratch or even a lick from an infected animal could spread the disease; immediately wash any wound gently with soap or detergent, and apply alcohol or iodine if possible. Find out what you can about the animal and swap addresses with the owner (if there is one) just in case. If the animal might be infected, act immediately to get treatment – rabies is invariably fatal once symptoms appear. There is a vaccine, but it is expensive, serves only to shorten the course of treatment you need anyway, and is only effective for a maximum of three months.

Malaria

Protection against malaria is essential. The disease, caused by a parasite in the saliva of *Anopheles* mosquitoes, is endemic everywhere in Goa and particularly virulent during, and immediately after, the monsoons (late June–September). It has a variable incubation period of a few days to several weeks, so you can become ill long after being bitten.

It is vital to take **preventative tablets** (prophylactics) according to a strict routine, and to cover the period before and after your trip. The basic drug used is chloroquine (trade names include *Nivaquin*, *Avloclor* and *Resochin*), usually two tablets weekly, but Goa has chloroquine-resistant strains, and you'll need to supplement it with

Children

The main problem for **children**, especially small ones, is their extra vulnerability. Even more than their parents, they need protecting from the sun, unsafe drinking water, heat and unfamiliar food. Remember too that diarrhoea, perhaps just a nuisance to you, could be dangerous for a child: rehydration salts are vital if your child goes down with it. Make sure too, if possible, that your child is aware of the dangers of rabies: keep children away from animals, and consider a rabies jab.

daily proguanil (*Paludrine*) or weekly *Maloprim*. A new weekly drug, mefloquine (*Lariam*), was supposed to replace all these, but during its first year on the market many travellers complained of serious side-effects, notably acute depression, and few doctors these days recommend it. Australian authorities now prescribe the antibiotic tetracycline instead.

If you go down with malaria, you'll probably know. The fever, shivering and headaches are like severe flu and come in waves, usually beginning in the early evening. Malaria is not infectious, but can be dangerous and sometimes even fatal if not treated quickly. If you can, go to a doctor for a blood test to confirm the strain; if this isn't possible, take two 600mg quinine tablets three times daily for seven days, then three *Fansidar* tablets. If you can't get quinine, take ordinary chloroquine (10mg per kilo body weight up to 600mg maximum, usually four tablets), then half as much eight hours later. If you improve, repeat the second dose on the next two days; if not, your malaria is chloroquine-resistant, so see a doctor or obtain and take three *Fansidar*.

Side effects of anti-malaria drugs may include itching, rashes, hair loss and even sight problems, and it's probably not advisable to use them for prolonged periods; on a trip of three months or less, it is just common sense. Chloroquine and quinine are safe during pregnancy, but *Maloprim*, *Fansidar*, mefloquine and tetracycline should be avoided then. Note that the doses we quote apply to adults: children will need lower ones.

The most effective way to ensure you don't contract malaria, however, is to **avoid mosquito bites**. Try to sleep under a net – one which can hang from a single point is best (you can usually find a way to tie a string across your room to

hang it from), burn mosquito coils (available in most general stores) or use repellent (an Indian brand called *Odomos* is widely available and effective, and *Avon Skin So Soft* bath oil is regarded by some as the best repellent of all). Mosquito "buzzers" are a lot less effective. Though active from dusk till dawn, female *Anophelēs* mosquitoes prefer to bite in the evening, so be especially careful at that time. Wear long sleeves, skirts and trousers, avoid dark colours, which attract mosquitoes, and put repellent on all exposed skin.

Another reason to avoid getting bitten is that mosquitoes spread **Japanese encephalitis**. There have been several outbreaks of this fatal disease in Goa in recent years, all of them during or shortly after the monsoons (August–October). Symptoms are similar to malaria.

Intestinal troubles

Diarrhoea is the most common bane of travellers. When mild and not accompanied by other major symptoms, it may just be your stomach reacting to unfamiliar food. Accompanied by cramps and vomiting, it could well be food poisoning. In either case, it will probably pass of its own accord in 24–48 hours without treatment. In the meantime, it is essential to replace the fluids and salts you're losing, so take lots of water with **oral rehydration salts** (commonly referred to as ORS, or called *Electrolyte* in Goa). If you can't get them, use half a teaspoon of salt and three of sugar in a litre of water. It's a good idea to avoid greasy food, heavy spices, caffeine and most fruit and dairy products; but some say bananas and pawpaws are good, as is coconut water, while curd or a soup made from Marmite or Vegemite (if you happen to have some with you) are forms of protein that can be easily absorbed by your body when you have the runs. We advise against drugs like *Lomotil* or *Immodium*, which simply plug you up – they undermine the body's efforts to rid itself of infection – but they can be a temporary stopgap if you have to travel. If symptoms persist more than a few days, a course of antibiotics may be necessary; this should be seen as a last resort, following medical advice.

It's a good idea to look at what comes out when you go to the toilet. If your diarrhoea contains blood or mucus, the cause may be dysentery or giardia. With a fever, it could well be caused by **bacillic dysentery**, and may clear up without treatment. If you're sure you need it, a course of antibiotics such as tetracycline should sort you out, but they also destroy "gut flora" in your intestines (which help protect you – curd can replenish them to some extent), and if you start a course, be sure to finish it, even after the symptoms have gone. Similar symptoms without fever indicate **amoebic dysentery**, which is much more serious, and can damage your gut if untreated. The usual cure is a course of metronidazole (*Flagyl*), an antibiotic which may itself make you feel ill, and should not be taken with alcohol. Similar symptoms, plus rotten-egg belches and farts, indicate **giardia**, for which the treatment is again metronidazole. If you suspect that you have any of these, seek medical help, and only start on the metronidazole if there is definitely blood in your diarrhoea and it is impossible to see a doctor.

Finally, bear in mind that oral drugs, such as malaria pills and contraceptive pills, are likely to be largely ineffective if taken while suffering from diarrhoea.

Bites and creepy-crawlies

Worms may enter your body through skin (especially the soles of your feet), or food. An itchy anus is a common symptom, and you may even see them in your stools. They are easy to treat with worming tablets from any pharmacy.

Biting insects and similar animals other than mosquitoes may also aggravate you. The obvious ones are **bed bugs** – look for signs of squashed ones around cheap hotel beds. An infested mattress can be left in the hot sun all day to get rid of them, but they often live in the frame or even in walls or floors. Head and body **lice** can also be a nuisance but medicated soap and shampoo (preferably brought with you from home) usually see them off. Avoid scratching bites, which can lead to infection. Bites from ticks and lice can spread **typhus**, characterized by fever, muscle aches, headaches and eventually red eyes and a measles-like rash. If you think you have it, seek treatment (tetracycline is usually prescribed).

Some of the illnesses and parasites you can pick up in India may not show themselves immediately. If you become ill within a year of returning home, tell whoever treats you where you have been.

Heat trouble

The sun and the heat can cause a few unexpected problems. Many people get a bout of **prickly heat** rash before they've acclimatized. It's an infection of the sweat ducts caused by excessive perspiration that doesn't dry off. A cool shower, zinc oxide powder (sold in Goa) and loose cotton clothes should help. **Dehydration** is another possible problem, so make sure you're drinking enough liquid, and drink rehydration salts when hot and/or tired. The main danger sign is irregular urination (only once a day, for instance), but dark urine also probably means you should drink more.

It is vital not to underestimate the burning power of the Goan **sun**, which will fry any exposed skin not protected with a high-factor block. Take particular care during your first week or two, and on days when there is a lot of high cloud around, which can make the sun seem deceptively benign. Many people also fall asleep on the beach and awake to find themselves in the full glare of the sun with their skin burnt to a cinder. In addition, a light hat is a good idea, especially if you're doing a lot of walking.

Finally, be aware that overheating can cause **heatstroke**, which is potentially fatal. Signs are a very high body temperature without a feeling of fever, but accompanied by headaches and disorientation. Lowering the body temperature (with a tepid shower, for example) is the first step in treatment.

HIV and AIDS

AIDS is still a relatively unknown quantity in India, and often regarded as a foreign problem, but indications are that HIV levels are already high among prostitutes, and the same presumably applies to intravenous drug users. You are also, of course, at risk from your fellow travellers. It is therefore extremely unwise to contemplate casual sex without a condom. Take some with you (Indian ones may be less reliable; also, be aware that heat affects the durability of condoms), and insist on using them.

Should you need an injection or a transfusion in Goa, make sure that new, sterile equipment is used; any blood you receive should be from voluntary rather than commercial donor banks. If you have a shave from a barber, make sure he uses a clean blade, and don't submit to processes such as ear-piercing, acupuncture or tattooing unless you can be sure that the equipment is sterile.

Getting medical help

Pharmacies can usually advise on minor medical problems, and most doctors in Goa speak English. Basic medicaments are made to Indian Pharmacopoeia (IP) standards, and most medicines are available without prescription (always check the sell-by date). **Hospitals** vary in standard. **Private clinics** tend to be better than state-run ones, but may not have the same facilities. The hospitals in Panjim and Vasco da Gama are pretty good, although they sometimes require patients to buy necessities such as plaster casts and vaccines, and to pay for X-rays, before procedures are carried out. However, charges are usually so low that for minor treatment the expense may well be lower than the initial "excess" on your insurance. Addresses of clinics and hospitals can be found in our "Listings" sections for major towns in this book.

Accidents and emergencies

Goa has witnessed a disturbing spate of fatal, or near-fatal, **accidents** involving tourists over the past few years, most of them connected with motorcycles. It is therefore essential when travelling by rented transport to know where to go if either you, or someone you are with, gets badly injured, as few hospitals in the state have the sophisticated equipment or specialist doctors needed to speedily diagnose serious injuries. Making straight for the right clinic instead of the wrong casualty department can save your life.

The only place in Goa with a modern brain scanner – essential for treating **head injuries** – is the Salgonkar Medical Research Centre in Vasco da Gama (☎0834/512524). If you think you may have broken a bone, however, Dr Bale's 24-hour surgery in Porvorim, 4km north of Panjim on the main Mapusa road (NH17), is a safer bet.

Emergency telephone numbers for **ambulances** and local hospitals are given in the "Listings" sections where available. In the majority of cases, however, you'll get to hospital a lot quicker by flagging down a car or finding a taxi to take you.

Information and maps

The Indian government maintains a number of tourist offices abroad, where you can pick up a range of pamphlets. Their main purpose is to advertise rather than inform, but they can be extremely helpful and knowledgeable.

Other sources of information include travel agents and the larger package tour companies operating in Goa. These are in business for themselves, of course, so their advice may not always be totally unbiased.

In Goa itself, both the national and state government run **tourist information offices**, providing general travel advice and handing out an array of printed material, from handy state maps to glossy leaflets on specific destinations. Government tourist offices are open Monday to

Indian Government Tourist Offices abroad

Australia Level 1, 17 Castlereagh St, Sydney, NSW 2000 (☎ 02/9232 1600, fax 9223 3003; email goito@tpgi.com.au).

Canada 60 Bloor St West, Suite 1003, Toronto, Ontario M4W 3B8 (☎ 416/ 962-3787).

UK 7 Cork St, London W1X 1PB (☎ 0171/ 437 3677).

USA 3550 Wiltshire Bd, Suite 204, Los Angeles, CA 90010 (☎ 213/380-8855); 30 Rockefeller Plaza, Room 15, North Mezzanine, New York, NY 10112 (☎ 212/586-4901 or 4902).

Friday 9.30am–5pm and Saturday 9.30am–1pm; the main branch of the Indian government's tourist office is on Church Square in Panjim (see p.65). This place operates independently of the information counters and bureaux run by the state tourism department, *Goa Tourism*, and local tourism-development corporation, GTDC, who collectively offer a wide range of travel facilities, including guided tours, car rental and their own hotels.

Maps

The first, and only, truly **accurate map** of Goa appeared in 1995, with the publication of John Callanan's excellent *Goa Beach Guide (Roger Lascelles*; £3.95). Combining detailed coverage of the state's road network with scale plans of all the resorts, it is indispensable if you're planning to travel any distance by rented motorcycle or

Websites

Carry out a search for "Goa" on the Internet and your search engine will return a surprisingly long list of hits. Ranging from sites for Goa Trance aficionados (see p.146) to hippy nonsense home pages in Danish and Dutch, most are of limited interest to the average tourist. However, the following are worth a browse before you travel:

Goa Interactive

http://www.goa-interactive.com
Currently the most comprehensive site, featuring everything from hard facts and figures, news, views and weather reports, to articles on temples, the freedom movement and folk dances. It also gives (commercially biased) advice on accommodation and eating.

Goa State Tourism

http://www.inetindia.com/travel/state/goa
Goa Tourism's homepage features colour snaps of the famous beaches, but little else that you won't find covered more comprehensively in this book. It does, however, offer handy links to other more interesting sites.

Blue Surf Goa

http://www.indiaexpress.com/goa/
Billed as a "one-stop information bank on Goa", this site is only likely to appeal to business and upmarket travellers.

Goenkar: Goa Community Site

http://www.goenkar.com/
Pitched at the Goan expatriate community, with lively cartoons, news, editorials from state newspapers, readers' letters, and numerous hot links.

Goacom

http://www.goacom.com
Another commercial site, so its hotel and restaurant reviews are far from impartial, although the travel information can be helpful.

India Express

http://www.indiaexpress.com/
Check out the latest articles, and archive material dating back a couple of years, from the regional issue of India's largest newspaper (special features on Goa, from the *Herald*, appear at http://www.indiaexpress.com.goa/gomantak).

City.Net Goa

http://www.city.net/countries/india/goa/
Part of the Travel Channel/Condé Nast Traveler website, this url accesses tourist and travel information for Goa, and has useful links to other sites.

car. As yet, few shops in Goa stock it, so get hold of one before you leave from the outlets listed below.

Visitors who stick to the resorts, however, generally manage well enough with the ubiquitous government-published *Tourist Map* (Rs7), available at most information offices and counters, and perfectly adequate for jaunts along the coast. It features all the major roads, byways and sights, although the information can be vexingly inaccurate at times, particularly if you venture off the beaten track.

In addition, there are a number of other state maps on the market that include insets of city and town plans. However, as these tend to be far from reliable, we recommend you use the more carefully researched street plans contained in this book. Go-ahead *Findoll Communications* publish a series of glossy colour maps of resorts in Bardez, including Candolim, Calangute, Baga,

Anjuna, Chapora and Vagator, sold with an accompanying yellow pages booklet. They are detailed and accurate enough, but unfortunately omit the names of any hotels, restaurants and other businesses that refused to pay the subscription necessary for inclusion.

Getting good **maps of India** in India itself can be difficult; the government forbids the sale of detailed maps of border areas, which include the entire coastline. So if you're planning to venture into Karnataka or Maharashtra, or are travelling to Goa from Bombay, it makes sense to bring one with you. The most detailed map of the country available throughout Europe, the US and Australia is *Nelles Verlag* 1:1,500,000 *Map of South India*, which features colour contours and is a handy route-planning aid. *Bartholomew's* 1:4,000,000 *Map of South Asia* is the international best-seller for the subcontinent; *Lascelle's* version, on the same scale, is also worth considering.

Book and map outlets

Australia & New Zealand: *Bowyangs*, 372 Little Bourke St, Melbourne, Vic 3000 (☎03/9670 4383); *Hema*, 239 George St, Brisbane, QLD 4000 (☎07/221 4330); *The Map Shop*, 16a Peel St, Adelaide, SA 5000 (☎08/8231 2033); *Perth Map Centre*, 891 Hay St, Perth, WA 6000 (☎09/9322 5733); *Speciality Maps*, 58 Albert Street, Auckland (☎09/307 2107); *Travel Bookshop*, 20 Bridge St, Sydney, NSW 2000 (☎02/9241 3554).

Canada: *Open Air Books and Maps*, 25 Toronto St, Toronto ON M5R 2C1 (☎416/363-0719); *Ulysses Travel Bookshop*, 4176 St-Denis, Montréal (☎514/843-9447); *World Wide Books and Maps*, 736 Granville St, Vancouver BC V6C IG3 (☎604/687-3320).

Ireland: *Eason's Bookshop*, 40 O'Connell St, Dublin 1 (☎01/873 3811); *Fred Hanna's Bookshop*, 27–29 Nassau St, Dublin 2 (☎01/677 4754); *Hodges Figgis Bookshop*, 56–58 Dawson St, Dublin 2 (☎01/677 4754).

UK: *Books from India*, 45 Museum St, London WC1A 1LY (☎0171/405 3784); *John Smith and Sons*, 57–61 St Vincent St, Glasgow G2 5TB (☎0141/221 7472); *National Map Centre*, 22–24 Caxton St, London SW1H 0QU (☎0171/222 4945); *Stanfords*, 12–14 Long Acre, London WC2E 9LP (☎0171/836 1321; mail order service), 52 Grosvenor Gardens, London SW1W (☎0171/730 1314) and 156 Regent's St, London W1R (0171/434 4744) ; *Thomas Nelson and Sons*, 51 York Place, Edinburgh EH1 3JD (☎0131/557 3011). The *Goa Beach Guide* may also be ordered through any UK branch of *Waterstone's*.

USA: *The Complete Traveler Bookstore*, 199 Madison Ave, New York NY 10016 (☎212/685-9007) and 3207 Fillmore St, San Francisco CA 94123 (☎415/923-1511); *Elliot Bay Book Company*, 101 South Main St, Seattle WA 98104 (☎206/624-6600); *Rand McNally*, 444 North Michigan Ave, Chicago IL 60611 (☎312/321-1751), 150 East 52nd St, New York NY 10022 (☎212/758-7488) and 595 Market St, San Francisco CA 94105 (☎415/777-3131); *Traveler's Bookstore*, 22 West 52nd St, New York NY 10019 (☎212/664-0995).

Costs, money and banks

India is, unquestionably, one of the least expensive countries for travellers in the world, and although the cost of living in Goa is far higher than most other parts of the country, a little foreign currency still goes a long way.

With provisions for tourists ranging from luxury five-star resorts to palm-leaf shacks, **what you spend** depends entirely on you: where you stay, how you get around, what you eat and what you buy. On a budget of as little as £5/$8 per day, you'll manage if you stick to the cheapest of everything and don't move about too much; double that, and you can permit yourself the odd splurge meal, the occasional mid-range hotel, and a few souvenirs. If you're happy spending £15–20/$20–30 per day, however, you can really pamper yourself; to spend much more than that, you'd have to be staying in the best hotels and eating in top restaurants.

Accommodation ranges from £1.50/$2 per night upwards (see p.34), while a mid-range seafood meal in an ordinary beach café is unlikely to cost even that much. How you **travel around** makes a big difference: public transport costs pennies, but a day on a rented motorcycle or a long-distance taxi ride can set you back what you might expect to spend on several days' accommodation. Costs also vary considerably between resorts: basically, the more touristy the area, the higher the prices. A snack in or around Fort Aguada and Candolim, for example, could come to the same as a slap-up South Indian

meal in Panjim or Margao, while the price of a pineapple in Mapusa market inflates ten-fold between there and Calangute beach.

Some independent travellers tend to indulge in pernickety penny-pinching, which Goans find rather pathetic – they know how much an air ticket costs, and have a fair idea of what you can earn at home. Bargain where appropriate, but don't begrudge a few rupees to someone who's worked hard for them: consider what their services would cost at home, and how much more valuable the money is to them than it is to you. Even if you get "ripped off" on every rickshaw journey you make, it will only add at most one percent to the overall cost of your trip. Remember too, that any pound or dollar you spend in Goa goes that much further, and luxuries you can't afford at home become possible here: sometimes it's worth spending more simply because you get more for it. At the same time, don't pay well over the odds for something if you know what the going rate is. Thoughtless extravagance can, particularly in remote areas, contribute to inflation, putting even basic goods and services beyond the reach of local people at certain times of year.

Indian money

India's unit of currency is the **rupee**, usually abbreviated "Rs" and divided into a hundred paise. Almost all money is paper, with notes of 1, 2, 5, 10, 20, 50, 100 and 500 rupees. **Coins** start at 1 paisa, then range up through 5, 10, 20, 25 and 50 paise, and 1, 2 and 5 rupees. The exchange rate at the time of publication is around 59Rs/35Rs to £1/$1.

Banknotes, especially lower denominations, can get into a terrible state, but don't accept torn ones; nobody else will be prepared to take them, so you will be left saddled with the things. You can change them at large branches of big banks such as the *State Bank of India*, or slip them into the middle of a wad when paying for something (which is probably how they'll have been passed to you).

Large denominations can also be a problem, as **change** is often in short supply, particularly in small towns and villages. Many Indian people cannot afford to keep much lying around, and you shouldn't necessarily expect shopkeepers or rickshaw *wallahs* to have it (and they may – as may you – try to hold onto it if they do). Paying for your groceries with a Rs100 bill will probably entail waiting for the grocer's errand boy to go off on a quest around town trying to change it. Keeping a wad of Rs5 or Rs10 notes handy isn't a bad idea (you can get bundles of fifty stapled together in banks; holes from the staples don't count as rips, so long as they don't reach the edge of the note).

Travellers' cheques and credit cards

Take along a mixture of cash and travellers' cheques to cover all eventualities, and keep a few small denominations for the odd foreign-currency purchase. US dollars are the easiest **currency** to convert, with pounds sterling a close second. Major hard currencies such as Australian dollars, Deutschmarks, Dutch guilder, Japanese yen or French francs can all be changed easily in tourist areas. If you enter the country with US$10,000 or the equivalent, you are supposed to fill in a currency-declaration form.

Travellers' cheques aren't as liquid as cash and are changed at a slightly lower rate than bills in banks, but they are obviously more secure. Not all banks and foreign-exchange desks, however, accept them, and those that do can be quirky about exactly which ones they will change – well-known brands such as *Thomas Cook*, *American Express* or *Visa* are your best bet.

A **credit card** is a handy back-up, as an increasing number of hotels, restaurants, large shops and airlines now take plastic; *American Express*, *Access/Mastercard*, *Visa* and *Diners Club* are the most commonly accepted. If you have a selection of cards, take them all; you'll get much the same exchange rate as you would in a bank, and bills can take a surprisingly long time to be charged to your account at home. The *Bank of Baroda* issues rupees against a *Visa* card at all its branches, while *Amex* will issue rupees or travellers' cheques to card-holders against a cheque at their offices.

It is illegal to carry rupees into or out of India, and you won't get them at a particularly good rate in the West anyhow (though you might in Thailand, Malaysia or Singapore). The janitors in Dabolim airport have cottoned on to this, and devised a lucrative sideline by offering large-denomination foreign coins, given to them by tourists as tips, in exchange for your excess rupees.

Changing money

Changing money in Goan banks tends to be a time-consuming business, involving lots of form-filling and queuing at different counters, so change substantial amounts at any one time. Main branches in towns and major resorts are the most efficient. Elsewhere, the *State Bank of India* is your best bet, while most branches of the *Bank of Baroda* are good for *Visa*.

Outside **banking hours** (Mon–Fri 10am–2pm, Sat 10am–noon), large hotels change money for residents (albeit at a lower rate), and there's a small *State Bank of India* counter at Dabolim airport that opens at flight times. However, the best

---

Travellers' cheques and credit cards: addresses

If either your credit card or travellers' cheques are lost or stolen, contact one of the local offices below or, better still, telephone the 24-hour emergency number given to you when first issued.

American Express
Panjim *Menezes Air Travel*, 204 Rua de Ourem (☎ & fax 0832/225081).
Bombay Oriental Building, 276 Dr DN Marg, Colaba (☎022/204 8291).

Thomas Cook
Panjim Alcon Chambers, Devanand Bandodkar Rd (☎0832/221312, fax 221313).

Bombay Dr DN Marg, near Flora Fountain, Fort (☎022/204 8556).

Visa
Panjim *Bank of Baroda*, Azad Maidan; *Andhra Bank*, opposite *Ashok Samrat* cinema.
Bombay *Andhra Bank*, 18 Homi St, near Flora Fountain, Fort.

all-round places to change foreign notes and travellers' cheques are the branches of **private exchange companies** that have recently sprung up in Panjim and the main coastal resorts. These tend to be fast and efficient, and change at roughly bank rates. Otherwise, a number of reputable **travel agents** are licensed to change money. Failing that, there's always the **black market**: most taxi drivers will change large banknotes, although you'll have to haggle over the rate.

Wherever you change money, though, hold on to **exchange receipts**, or "encashment certificates"; they will be required if you want to change back any excess rupees when you leave the country, or buy things like air tickets with rupees, and if you need a tax clearance form. Note that the *State Bank of India* now charges for these.

Wiring money to Goa is a lot easier than it used to be. Indian banks with branches abroad, such as the *State Bank of India* and the *Bank of Baroda*, can (in theory) wire money by telex from those branches to ones in Goa in two working days. *Thomas Cook* takes around the same time, and is less prone to technical hitches. They will transfer cash paid into any of their overseas branches to their office in Panjim (see box above), for a typical fee of around 3 percent of the total amount.

Baksheesh

The most common form of *baksheesh* – basically slipping someone money on the quiet in exchange for some kind of service – is **tipping**: this can encompass anything from help finding a room or carrying your luggage, to cracking open a coconut on the beach. Large amounts are not expected – ten rupees should satisfy all the aforementioned. Taxi drivers and staff at cheaper hotels and restaurants do not necessarily expect tips but always appreciate them, of course, and they can keep people sweet for the next time you call. Some may take liberties in demanding *baksheesh*, but it's often better just to acquiesce rather than spoil your mood and cause offence over trifling sums.

More expensive than plain tipping is paying people to **bend the rules**, many of which seem to have been invented for precisely that purpose. The prime culprits here are the police, who invariably take bribes rather than arrest or officially fine people for petty offences (such as driving without an international licence). Being caught with drugs is more serious. For some pointers on how to deal with the rapacious Goan cops, see "Police, trouble and personal security" on p.45.

The last kind of *baksheesh* is **alms giving**. In a country without social security, this is an important custom. People with disabilities and mutilations are the traditional recipients, and it seems right to join locals in giving small change to them, especially when visiting temples. Kids demanding money, pens or the like are a different case, pressing their demands only on tourists. In return for a service it is fair enough, but to yield to any request encourages them to go and pester others. Think twice before you do so.

Getting around

Before Independence, the many rivers that drain Goa's coastal plain made getting around a stop-and-start affair. Nowadays, however, bridges have largely superseded the old estuary ferries, and the state is latticed with metalled roads. Served by streams of clapped-out buses, these connect all the major settlements and resorts on the coast with the three towns of the interior. To get away from your fellow tourists, though, you'll want to get off the main roads and spend some time exploring rural Goa. The best way to do this is to rent some form of transport, although the state's only train line runs from Vasco da Gama to link up with the Bombay–Bangalore line in neighbouring Karnataka, and allows you to penetrate the dense jungle-covered terrain of the Western Ghats.

The main public transport **routes** and **timings** are listed at the end of each chapter in "Travel Details".

Buses

Cheap, frequent and running just about everywhere accessible by road, **buses** are by far the most popular mode of transport in Goa, and you're bound at some point to catch one, if only to get into town or to the next resort. Visitors not yet initiated into the joys of Indian public transport are unlikely to forget the experience.

If you're lucky or catch the bus near the beginning of its route, you might get a seat. Otherwise,

be prepared for an uncomfortable crush as more and more passengers squeeze themselves and bags of shopping (some of it still alive) up the centre aisle. **Private buses** are particularly notorious for overloading. Conductors dangle out of the side doors chanting their destination with the rapidity of horse-racing commentators, as if they're working to some kind of performance-related pay scheme.

One consolation for the crush is that **fares** are so low as to be virtually free by Western standards. The one-and-a-half-hour journey from Panjim to Margao for example, costs less than Rs10 (around 20p/30c). Travelling by bus is also a great way to experience the Goans' Goa. Bumping along at often breakneck speeds with distorted Konkani pop music blaring through the sound system, you could find yourself sitting next to a neatly dressed office *wallah* on his way home from work, or a Kunbi fisherwoman with her basket of fish fresh off the family boat. And if the hairy driving starts to get to you, have faith in the protective deities that always sit in shrines near the driver's seat, decked with garlands of flowers: multicoloured Hindu gods or radiant Madonnas, depending on the religion of the bus owner.

Tickets are generally sold by conductors on the bus itself – keep some small change handy for this – although the state transport company, **Kadamba** (aka KSRTC), sells them from hatches in the main bus stands. Bus **information** for specific destinations is given in the relevant account in the Guide section of this book.

Motorbikes, mopeds and cycles

It is hard to overstate the sense of freedom that breezing around the open roads of Goa on a **motorcycle** can bring. On a rented bike you can reach the state's remote beaches and cover long distances with relative ease. The downside, of course, is that two-wheelers can be perilous. In 1993–94, one person a day died on the Goan roads; many were tourists. Before driving away, therefore, ensure the lights and brakes are in good shape, and be especially vigilant at night: many roads are poor and unlit, and stray cows and bullock carts can appear from nowhere.

Motorcycles are available at most of the coastal resorts. Officially, you need an **international driver's licence** to rent and ride anything more powerful than a 50cc moped. Owners and rental companies rarely enforce this, but some local police use the rule to extract exorbitant *baksheesh* from tourists. If you don't have a licence with you, the only way around the problem is to avoid big towns such as Panjim, Margao and Mapusa (or Anjuna on Wednesday – market day), and to carry only small sums of money when driving. If you are arrested for not having the right papers, it's no big deal, though police officers may try to convince you otherwise; keep cool, and be prepared to negotiate. It is also a good idea to get some evidence that the bike is rented and insured before heading off.

Rates vary according to both season and vehicle; most owners also insist on a hefty deposit and/or passport as security. The cheapest bike, a 50cc **moped**, costs Rs70–100 per day. These are fine for buzzing to the beach and back, but to travel further you need gears and a bit more power. Other options include the stylish Enfield Bullet 350cc that is, nevertheless, heavy, unwieldy and – at upwards of Rs250 per day – the most expensive bike to rent. A more sensible choice for first-timers is the reliable Honda Kinetic 100cc, which has automatic gears and costs Rs100–150 per day. For all-round performance and manoeuvrability, though, you can't beat the fast and light Yamaha RD100cc, which is economical on fuel and generally well suited to the windy Goan roads. These go for Rs125–200. Finally, the one vehicle to avoid, at all costs, is the notoriously unreliable Indian-made Rajdoot.

Two-stroke **fuel** is sold at service stations (known locally as "petrol pumps") in Panjim, Mapusa and Margao, and at regular intervals along the national highways. In smaller settlements, including a number of resorts such as Anjuna and Colva, you can only buy fuel by the *Bisleri* bottle in general stores or through backstreet suppliers, details of which are given throughout the Guide. Most villages also have a **motorcycle-repair** specialist (aka a "puncture *wallah*"), although in theory the person you rented your machine from should foot the bill for routine maintenance (including punctures, blown bulbs and any mechanical failures). Damage to the bike incurred during a road traffic accident, of

It is essential if you rent a motorcycle in Goa to know where the best **accident and emergency units** are located. Details of these appear in "Health" on p.25.

course, has to be paid for by you. It is important you agree on such details with the owner before driving away.

Cycling

Indian-made "sit-up-and-beg" Hero **bicycles** – ideal for a gentle jaunt along the hard sand but fiendishly hard work over longer distances – may be rented in most towns and resorts. Rs30–50 per day is the going rate, and you could be asked to leave a deposit, or even your passport, as **security**. In Panjim (see p.66), they are rented out at standard Indian (ie non-tourist) rates of Rs2 per hour; you may, however, find the capital's anarchic traffic a little too nerve-wracking for comfort. Before peddling off, try the cycle out for size, and make sure the back wheel lock works.

Bringing a bike from abroad requires no special paperwork, and most airlines allow you to take cycles at no extra cost. However, spare parts and accessories are invariably of different sizes and standards in Goa, and you may have to improvise. Bring basic spares and tools, and a pump. Panniers are the obvious thing for carrying your gear, but inconvenient when not attached to your bike, and you might consider sacrificing ideal load-bearing and streamlining technology for a backpack you can lash down on the rear carrier.

Taxis and car rental

It is much more usual for tourists in Goa to be driven than to drive: car rental firms generally operate on the basis of supplying chauffeur-driven vehicles, while taxis are available at cheap daily rates.

Japanese six-seater Maruti mini-vans are the most common type of **taxi** nowadays, but you'll also come across plenty of Hindustan Ambassadors – the classic Indian automobile based on the old British Morris Oxford. In larger towns, taxis queue at ranks; elsewhere, they tend to hang around outside the upmarket hotels. **Rates**, even for short journeys, are always negotiable (there are no metered taxis in Goa), so ask a member of staff in your hotel reception what the correct fare should be before setting off.

For longer sightseeing trips, you can either engage a taxi *wallah* yourself, or arrange a car in advance through your hotel, local tourist office, or the GTDC, Trinora Apartments, Panjim (☎0832/226515). In addition, a couple of international **rental chains** operate in Goa: *Hertz*, opposite Dom Bosco High School, Market Area, Panjim (☎0832/224304 or 223758), and *Budget Rent-a-Car*, c/o *Sai Service*, Mapusa Rd, Porvorim, on the north side of the Mandovi bridge near Panjim (☎0832/217755). Most firms charge by the kilometre (around Rs5/km for a non-a/c Maruti), or according to a sliding time/distance scale, with extra charges for night stopovers (usually of around Rs100); the driver sleeps in the car. What you pay also depends on the make of car, the cheapest being a Maruti Premier, and the most expensive being an air-conditioned Contessa, with an Ambassador falling roughly between the two. Typical prices for a 12-hour/110-kilometre trip range from Rs750/£13 to Rs1550/£26. It costs less if you pay for the car in Goa rather than your home country, as rates in India are roughly thirty percent less than the UK or USA.

Self-drive

Self-drive is also now available in Goa, though the service seems to be intended more for middle-class Indians out to impress their friends and relatives than tourists ("They'll never know it's rented!"). You will, in any case, be a lot safer if you leave the driving to someone more at home with the state's racetrack rules of the road. If you're willing to risk it, try *Budget* or *Hertz* (the latter have a counter at Dabolim airport: see p.160). Rates for 24hr/150km range from around Rs700 for a no-frills Maruti to Rs1100 for an air-conditioned Ambassador. Note that you need an international driver's licence to drive in Goa.

Motorcycle taxis and auto-rickshaws

Goa's unique pillion-passenger **motorcycle taxis**, often referred to as "pilots", are ideal for nipping between beaches or into town from the resorts. Bona fide operators ride black bikes (usually Enfields) with yellow mudguards and white number plates. Fares should be settled in advance, and rarely amount to more than Rs40 for about a twenty-minute trip. Apart from buses, this is the cheapest form of public transport in Goa.

That most Indian of vehicles, the **auto-rickshaw** is the front half of a motor scooter with a couple of seats mounted on the back. Cheaper than taxis, better at zipping in and out of traffic, and usually metered (though you'll have to insist), auto-rickshaws are a little unstable and their drivers often rather reckless, but that's all part of the fun.

In Goa, auto-rickshaws are painted black and yellow, and licensed rickshaw *wallahs* obliged to wear a regulation-issue khaki-coloured jacket. However, the fares are far from uniform, and you'll have to haggle before you arrive at a reasonable rate. As a rule of thumb, Rs15 should take you just about anywhere in Panjim, Margao and Mapusa. For longer rides, motorcycle taxis are much quicker and better value.

Ferries

If auto-rickshaws are the quintessentially Indian mode of transport, flat-bottomed **ferries** are their Goan equivalent. Crammed with cars, buses, commuters on scooters, fisherwomen and clumps of bewildered tourists, these rusting blue-painted hulks provide an essential service, crossing the coastal backwaters where bridges have not yet been built. They're also incredibly cheap, and run from the crack of dawn to late in the evening.

Among the most frequented river crossings in Goa are: Panjim to Betim, across the Mandovi (every 15min), Old Goa to Divar Island (every 15min); Divar to Naroa (every 20–30min), Siolim to Chopdem, across the Chapora River for Arambol and Pernem (every 15min), Querim to Terekol, over the Tiracol River (every 30min), and Cavelossim in southern Salcete to Assolna (every 20–30min), for Cape Rama and Quepem. A **launch** also chugs across Mormugao Bay between Vasco da Gama's harbour and Dona Paula (4 daily). However, this and most other services are frequently disrupted during the monsoons, between July and September, when the rivers flood.

Trains

Many travellers arriving in Goa from Bombay or South India do so by **train**, but if you fly direct and do not venture outside the state you may well never need to catch one. The only line, a recently upgraded broad-gauge track, runs east from Mormugao harbour, near Vasco da Gama, to join up with the main Bombay–Bangalore network. Along the way, it winds through Margao and the Ghats to the Karnatakan border, passing directly over Dudhsagar Falls en route. Deep in a roadless region, these spectacular cascades are most easily accessible by rail, although train services have been severely disrupted over the past few years by work on the line (see p.76). It is therefore a good idea to check the temporary timetables at *Indian Railways*' counter in Panjim's *Kadamba* bus stand, or at Vasco da Gama station, Goa's principal railhead, beforehand. **Bookings** can be made at either of these places, and at Margao station, although you won't need a reservation for Dudhsagar. Note that reservations on *Indrail* passes can only be made at Vasco da Gama station.

In addition to the trans-Ghat railway, the new **Konkan Railway** cuts straight through the state from north to south, past a string of hitherto remote villages and rural towns. Apart from rendering Goa accessible from Bombay in only eight hours, this line allows you to reach the formerly remote south of the state, notably Chaudi and Palolem, direct from Panjim and Margao.

Tours and cruises

GTDC operate guided bus **tours** out of Panjim and major coastal resorts to sights around the state. The itineraries, however, cover too much ground in too little time, and are somewhat rushed for most people. Those offered as **optional excursions** by package tour companies and large hotels, on the other hand, tend to be conducted at a more civilized pace, although they're very expensive by Goan standards. Details of tour options from different towns and resorts appear throughout the Guide section.

Backwater **cruises** along the Mandovi River from Panjim are a kind of aquatic equivalent of GTDC's bus tours. Once again, these tend to be more popular among domestic than foreign tourists, although the only "sights" to speak of, given that most take place after dark, are the troupes of dancers and musicians who accompany the cruises with Konkani folk tunes and hits from Hindi films. A more detailed rundown of launch trips from Panjim features on p.65.

Accommodation

There are a vast number of beds for tourists in Goa, and most of the year you can rely on turning up pretty much anywhere and finding a room – if not in a hotel, then in a private house.

Only in December and January, the state's high season, are you likely to experience problems. At this time, it is worth arriving at each new place early in the day, and taking whatever is available in the hope that you will be able to exchange it for something better later on.

Inexpensive rooms

Budget accommodation in Goa, catering mainly for backpacking tourists, ranges from grim concrete cells to cosy family-run guesthouses. Naturally, the further off the beaten track you get, the cheaper the accommodation; it's most expensive in Panjim, where prices are typically between 25 and 50 percent higher than elsewhere. In the more popular resorts such as Calangute and Baga, room rates may double in peak season. At other times, however, Rs200 should buy you a decent double room with a fan,

Accommodation price codes

All **accommodation prices** in this book are coded using the symbols below. In principle, the prices given are for the least expensive double rooms in each establishment in high season (mid-Dec to mid-Jan). Out of season, tariffs drop by as much as 50 percent, especially if you negotiate for a stay of a week or more. Where mid-range hotels have one or two budget options, we give a spread of price codes to show the cost of the cheapest and most expensive rooms. Local taxes have been included in each case, unless specifically stated otherwise.

① up to Rs100. Very basic rooms in family houses.

② Rs100–150. No frills, except perhaps a fan.

③ Rs150–225. The bottom of the attached bathroom bracket – usually a smallish room with a fan and running water.

④ Rs225–350. Modest but comfortable guesthouse accommodation.

⑤ Rs350–500. Swish by Indian standards, with bathroom en suite and a quiet fan.

⑥ Rs500–750. Mid-range hotel accommodation.

⑦ Rs750–1200. Immaculate Western-style hotel room, satellite TV and air-conditioning. Some four-star hotels fall into this bracket.

⑧ Rs1200–2200. Luxurious centrally air-conditioned rooms that come with most mod cons, including access to a pool.

⑨ Rs2200 and up. Top-notch five-star style: ritzy rooms, a choice of restaurants, coffee shop, sports facilities, pool, lawns, shopping and in-house travel agent.

window and attached shower-toilet. Cold taps and "bucket baths" are the order of the day – not really a problem in the Goan climate – and it's always wise to check the state of the bathroom and toilet before parting with any money.

In more remote villages, accommodation usually consists of bare mud-floored rooms in modest family houses. Washing water generally comes from the well, and toilets are small outhouses that the local pigs keep clean by eating human waste products, alleviating the need for sewers. Conditions like these may be more rudimentary than what you're used to, but they are usual for most Goans, and, more importantly, place a much lighter burden on the fragile coastal ecology than do water-intensive Western-style hotels.

Mid-range hotels

Mid-range hotels in the Western mould, with reception areas, room service and a restaurant, nowadays account for the bulk of Goa's accommodation. Rooms in such places are frequently booked up en bloc by European package companies, forcing up their tariffs to exorbitant levels. However, a large number still rely mainly on walk-in customers, and have kept their prices competitive. A spacious room, freshly made bed,

fan, your own spotless (usually "sit-down") toilet, balcony and hot and cold running water can cost as little as Rs400 (around £7.50). Extras that bump up the price include satellite TV, carpets, and, above all, **air conditioning**. Abbreviated in this book (and in Goa itself) as a/c, air conditioning is not necessarily the advantage you might expect – in some hotels you can find yourself paying double for a system that is so dust-choked, wheezy and noisy as to preclude any possibility of sleep – but providing it is what seems to entitle a hotel to consider itself mid-range.

GTDC, the state tourism corporation, also runs its own chain of "resorts" and "hostels", similar to standard mid-range hotels, but providing cheaper dormitory accommodation alongside pricier air-conditioned rooms. They are generally good value, though frequently rather run-down.

Upmarket hotels

Most of Goa's **upmarket hotels** fall into one of two categories: slick modern establishments pitched at business travellers and wealthy Westerners, or luxury international-style resort complexes catering primarily for package tourists. While the former are confined to the state capital, Panjim, the latter crop up in all but the most remote coastal villages – much to the chagrin of local environmentalists.

Inevitably, the star resorts are nearly always situated on or within easy walking distance of a beach, usually amid well-watered lawns and with their own restaurants, coffee shops and sports facilities. If you haven't booked your room through a package firm, though, you'll pay through the nose for it. **Rates** for walk-in customers, though very reasonable compared with similar places in Europe, the States and Australia, are staggeringly expensive by Indian standards, starting at around Rs2000.

Long-term rentals

Houses are often rented by the month, or season. If you can get two or three people to share costs, and want to drop roots in a village or coastal resort, this is an option worth considering. However, the best places in settlements such as Anjuna, Chapora and Arambol – the established hangouts of long-staying travellers – tend to be snapped up well in advance of the season by visitors who return to the same house year after year. Seasonal lets also tend to be unfurnished, and you'll probably have to shell out on matresses, locks and cooking equipment; these can be resold before you leave.

To arrange rental, find a village where you want to stay and ask around. Rents vary from village to village, but you can usually pick something up in October or November for Rs3500–5000 per month. Obviously, the more money you can pay up front and the longer you intend to stay, the less the house should cost. It also pays to haggle, particularly towards the beginning or end of the season.

Eating and drinking

In keeping with the Konkani proverb "*prodham bhookt, magi mookt*" ("you can't think until you've eaten well"), food and drink are taken very seriously in Goa. They are also prepared and consumed at a typically laid-back pace, and you can expect to spend at least a couple of hours each day lounging at a table, whether in a sand-blown beach bar or on a palm-shaded restaurant terrace. Indeed, meal times may well provide some of the most memorable moments of your trip: there can be few better ways to savour those legendary sunsets, for example, than over a freshly grilled sharkfish steak, washed down with a bottle of ice-cool beer or a long *feni*.

Nor are such gastronomic delights likely to dent your budget. The overwhelming majority of eateries in Goa are simple palm-thatch **beach shacks**, where a slap-up fish supper will set you back around Rs150 (£2.50 or $4.30). Service can be unbelievably slow and fixtures rudimentary, but the food is usually fresh and tasty. More established resorts like Calangute, Candolim and Colva boast a clutch of swankier beach shacks – complete with tablecloths, candles and expensive sound systems. Shack owners are supposed pay a hefty annual licence fee to Goa Tourism for the privilege of trading on the beaches, but as this lies beyond the pocket of many local families, particularly in more remote resorts, a large number set up illegally. This means they can be closed down at any time – a fate shack-*wallahs* avoid by slipping *baksheesh* to the local police. Further pressure is brought to bear by neighbouring star hotels. Aware that the beach shacks undercut their restaurants by half or more (and invariably serve fresher, tastier food), some hotel owners have been known to employ heavies, and even the police, to intimidate or close down popular beach cafés. At the very least, the staff in your hotel will probably try to dissuade you from eating on the beach, telling you the shacks are unhygienic.

Most **upmarket restaurants** tend to be air-conditioned, marble-lined halls or poolside terraces in four- or five-star hotels, with a wide range of imaginatively presented dishes; expect to pay in excess of Rs250 (£4/$7) for an attentively served three-course meal. Finally, Panjim and the larger resorts harbour several restaurants that specialize in regional Indian cuisines and Chinese and Tibetan food. Once again, these tend to be a cut above your average beach café, with uniformed waiters and air conditioning.

Goan food

If you come across a group of locals eating in a village café or roadside *dhaba* (food stall), chances are they'll be tucking into a pile of **fish curry and rice**. Goa's national dish, eaten twice each day by most of its population, consists of a runny red-chilli sauce flavoured with dried fish or prawns, and served with a heap of fluffy white rice, a couple of small fried sardines and a blob of hot pickle. Cheap and filling, this is mixed into a manageable mush and shovelled down with your fingers: a technique that generally takes Westerners some time (and several messy faces) to master.

Outside the state, Goa is known primarily for its distinctive **meat** specialities. Derived from the region's hybrid Hindu, Muslim and Latin-Catholic heritage, these tend to be flavoured with the same stock ingredients of coconut oil and milk, blended with onions and a long list of spices, including Kashmiri red chillies. The most famous of all Goan dishes, though, has to be **pork vin-daloo**, whose very name epitomizes the way Konkani culture has, over time, absorbed and adapted the customs of its colonial overlords. The dish, misleadingly synonymous in Western countries with any "ultra-hot curry", evolved from a Portuguese pork stew that was originally seasoned with wine (*vinho*) vinegar and garlic (*alho*). To this *vinhdalho* sauce, the Goans added palm sap (*toddi*) vinegar and their characteristic sprinkling of spices. Pork was prohibited by the Muslims, but made a comeback under the Portuguese and now forms an integral part of the Goan diet, particularly on festive occasions such as Christmas, when Christian families prepare **sorpatel**: a rich stew made from the shoulders, neck, kidneys and ears of the pig. Another Portuguese-inspired pork speciality is **leitao**, or suckling pig, which is roasted and stuffed with chopped heart, liver, green chillies and parsley.

Goa is also one of the few places in India where beef is regularly eaten, although you're more likely to be offered chicken simmered in **xacuti** (pronounced "sha-*koo*-tee") sauce. This eye-wateringly hot preparation, traditionally made to revive weary rice planters during the monsoon, was originally vegetarian (in Konkani, *sha* means "vegetable", and *kootee* "cut into small pieces"), but is nowadays more often used to spice up meat of various kinds.

Not surprisingly, **seafood** features prominently in coastal areas. Among the varieties of **fish** you'll encounter are shark, kingfish, *pomfret* (a kind of flounder), mackerel and sardines. These are lightly grilled over wood fires, fried, or baked in clay ovens (*tandoors*), often with a red hot paste smeared into slits on their sides. The same sauce, known as **rechad**, is used to cook squid (*ambot tik*). Shrimps, however, are more traditionally baked in pies with rice-flour crusts (*apas de camarão*), while crab and lobster are steamed or boiled and served whole.

Finding **authentic Goan food** can be surprisingly difficult as it is essentially home cooking: no tourist restaurant can hope to match the attention to detail lavished on special feast day dishes by Goan housewives. However, an increasing number of restaurants tack a couple of token local specialities onto their menus, albeit ones that have been adapted for the sensitive Western palate, and these are worth a try.

The choicest seafood is beyond the reach of most Goans' pockets as the tourist industry has forced up prices, so the best places to eat fish are the resorts. For no-nonsense fish steak and fries, the state's ubiquitous palm-thatch beach cafés offer unbeatable value. Meals in these rough-and-ready places cost a fraction of what you'll pay in a hotel restaurant, and they are invariably fresh and safe, in spite of the signs posted outside many of the star resorts advising residents to steer clear of them – more because they poach custom than poison punters.

Rice and breads

In tourist restaurants, meat and seafood are generally served with fries and salad, but locally grown short-grain "red" **rice** is the main staple in the villages. In addition, the Portuguese introduced soft wheat-flour **bread rolls**, still made early each morning in local bakeries. Restaurateurs mistakenly assume foreign visitors prefer Western-style spongy square loaves, so if you want to try the infinitely tastier indigenous variety, make a point of asking for **pao** (or *poee* in Konkani).

Another delicious Goan bread to look out for is *sanna*, made from a batter of coconut milk and finely ground rice flour that is leavened with fermenting palm sap (*toddi*). These crumpet-like rolls are steamed and served with pork and other meat dishes because they are great for soaking up spicy Goan gravies.

Desserts and breakfasts

No serious splurge is considered complete without a slice of the state's favourite dessert, **bebinca**. A festive speciality prepared for Christmas, this ten-layered cake, made with a rich mixture of coconut milk, sugar and egg yolks, is crammed with cholesterol, but an absolute must for fans of solid old-fashioned puddings. The same is true of **batica**, another sweet and stodgy coconut cake that is particularly mouthwatering when served straight out of the oven with a dollop of ice cream.

Breakfast usually consists of oily omelettes, but you could ask for an **alebele**, a pancake stuffed with fresh coconut and syrup. A healthy tropical fruit salad, steeped in coconut milk and home-made set yoghurt (*curd*), is another great way to start the day. The crepe-like *masala dosa*, filled with spicy potato and nut, makes a great blow-out breakfast, although most early-rising Goans prefer to start the day with a lighter *idli* (steamed rice cake) or *wada* (doughnut-shaped deep-fried lentil cake) dipped in fiery *sambar* sauce and *subje* (white coconut chutney).

Indian food

If you get fed up with Goan-style fish and fries, **Indian food** is a good option. Most mid-range and upmarket restaurants serve a representative cross section of the subcontinent's regional cuisines, and the towns are scattered with smaller snack bars that cater for Goa's sizeable immigrant community. Vegetarians, in particular, will find these **udipi restaurants** a welcome sight, although the dishes they serve tend to be much spicier than those on offer at "curry houses" in Western countries.

Curry is actually something of a misnomer. The word, which in India is used to describe one particular aromatic herb (the *corri* leaf), denotes a wide range of dishes, each made with its own characteristic blend of spices, or *masala*. In most cases, they are served on oval side plates with a separate pile of white rice and a small pot of *chatni* and *raita*, a cool, soothing sauce made from yoghurt, and flavoured with coriander and cucumber.

The majority of **vegetarian dishes** come from the mainly Hindu regions of Maharashtra and Gujarat and tend to be rice-based or feature fresh vegetables in a spicy sauce. **Mughlai cooking**, mostly non-vegetarian, is very rich, using expensive ingredients such as pure *ghee* (clarified butter), almonds, sultanas and saffron. The other popular northern style, refined to an art form by the notoriously sybaritic Punjabis, is **tandoori**. The name refers to the deep clay oven (*tandoor*) in which the food is cooked. *Tandoori* chicken is marinated in yoghurt, herbs and spices before cooking. Boneless pieces of meat, marinated and cooked in the same way, are known as *tikka*, and may be served in a medium-strength *masala*, or in a thick butter sauce. They are generally accompanied by *rotis* or *nan* breads, also baked in the *tandoor*.

South Indian dishes, served at top speed in dozens of snack bars in Panjim, Margao and Mapusa, are Goa's most popular kind of fast food. Cheap, tasty and filling, they are also **pure vegetarian**. Arguably the most quintessential

South Indian snack is the *masala dosa*, a large crispy pancake stuffed with a spicy potato concoction.

Non-Indian food

Chinese food is served in most multi-cuisine restaurants, although, with the exception of two joints in Panjim (see p.72 & 74), it tends to be cooked by local chefs and is not what you might call authentic. Still, rice and noodle dishes make a pleasant change, and are easier on the digestive system if you're having stomach problems.

Western food is also widely available in the resorts. Expensive international-standard hotels often lay on buffets and fussy à la carte menus prepared by foreign-trained chefs. However, a growing number of beach restaurants also rustle up passable imitations of pizzas, pasta, lasagne, stroganoff and even full English breakfasts, using local ingredients.

Fruit

Lovers of tropical **fruit** will find plenty to get their teeth into in Goa. Lying on the beach, you'll be approached at regular intervals by fruit *wallahs* carrying baskets of bananas, watermelons, oranges, pineapples and, from late March onwards, succulent mangoes. Once you've fixed a price, the fruit is peeled and sliced with a machete. It's safe to eat, but you may want to sluice it over with sterilized water to be doubly sure, especially if the vendor has touched it with his or her left hand (see p.47).

Fresh **coconuts** are the healthiest fruit of all. Their milk and meat are chock-full of vitamins, and a fair-sized nut will tide you over between breakfast and supper time if you're marooned on the beach. Itinerant vendors usually carry a couple, but in more off-track areas you're better off asking a *toddi* tapper to cut you one straight from the tree. Goans prefer to eat young green nuts, whose flesh is softer and milk sweeter. The top is hacked off and two holes punctured with the tip of a machete: you can drink the milk through these or with a straw. Afterwards, the fruit *wallah* or *toddi* tapper will crack the nut open so you can scoop out the meat.

Among the less familiar fruit, the *chickoo*, which looks like a kiwi and tastes a bit like a pear, is worth a mention, as is the watermelon-sized jackfruit, whose green exterior encloses

sweet, slightly rubbery segments, each containing a seed. *Papayas* are also sold at most markets, and green custard apples crop up in fruit sellers' baskets, although you'll probably need to be shown how to peel away their knobbly skins to expose the sweet yellow fruit inside.

Drinking

With bottled water, tea and coffee widely available, you may have no need of **soft drinks**. These have long been surprisingly controversial in India. Coca Cola and Pepsi have recently made comebacks, after being banned from the country for seventeen years – a policy originally instigated to prevent the expatriation of profits by foreign companies. Since the return of the cola giants, militant Hindu groups have threatened to make them the focus of a new boycott campaign against multinational consumer goods. The absence of Coke and Pepsi also spawned a host of Indian copies such as Campa (inocuous), Thumbs Up (almost undrinkable), Gold Spot (sickly sweet fizzy orange), and Limca (rumoured to have connections with Italian companies, and to include additives banned there). All contain a lot of sugar, but little else: adverts for Indian soft drinks have been known to boast "Absolutely no natural ingredients!".

You may choose to quench your thirst with straight **water** (treated, boiled or bottled; see also p.21), or brands of sweetened **fruit juice**: Frooti is debatably the best of these. If the carton looks at all mangled, though, it is best not to touch it as it may have been recycled. Duke's mango drink, which comes in a clear glass bottle like Coca Cola, is also worth a try, and most refreshing when mixed with soda.

Goa's greatest cold drink, however, has to be **lassi** – a mixture of curd and water that is drunk with sugar, salted or mixed with fruit. It varies widely from smooth and delicious to insipid and watery, and is sold at virtually every café, restaurant and canteen in the state. In addition, freshly made **milkshakes** are commonly available at establishments with blenders. They'll also sell you what they call a **fruit juice**, but which is usually fruit, water and sugar (or salt) liquidized and strained. With all such drinks, as appetizing as they may seem, you should exercise great caution before deciding to drink them: try to find out where the water came from first.

Feni

Distilling was first introduced to Goa more than four hundred years ago by Catholic missionaries. While the priests stewed up grape skins to make Portuguese firewater (*aguadente*), however, the locals improvised with more readily available substances such as coconut sap and cashew-fruit juice. The result, refined over the years to a rocket fuel concoction known as **feni** (from the Kontaki verb root *fen*, meaning "to froth"), has become the common man's tipple: a crystal-clear spirit that is, according to one aficionado, "to the Goan life what the sky is to a bird: a medium of limitless wonder and potential".

The most common variety of *feni* is made from coconut sap, or **toddi**. Three times each day, the *toddi* tapper shimmies up his individually numbered trees, which he normally rents from the local landlord on a share-crop basis, to release plastic seals bound around new shoots at the heart of the palm. The *toddi* then dribbles into a terracotta pot. At this stage it is slightly sweet, but by the end of the day the liquid becomes cloudy as it starts to ferment. **Urrack**, produced by boiling up the freshly fermented *toddi* and straining it through cotton, is rarely drunk. More often, it is distilled a second time, sometimes with cummin or ginger added as flavouring.

The juice used to make the stronger and more expensive **cashew feni** is sqeezed from the yellow fruit of the *caja* tree, brought to Goa from Brazil three hundred years ago by the Portuguese and now the source of the state's principal cash crop, **cashew nuts**. The extraction work was traditionally done by treading the pulp in large wooden barrels; nowadays, though, mechanical presses are more common. Once extracted, the juice is distilled in exactly the same way as its coconut cousin. However, cashew *feni* has a distinctly different taste, sometimes compared to Mexican tequila.

Both types of *feni* may be drunk neat, but you'll find them a lot more palatable diluted with water, soda or a soft drink (Limca and a twist of lemon works wonders with coconut *feni*). A couple of tourist bars in the major resorts also offer pleasant *feni* cocktails (one hotel even advertises cashew *feni* "slammer" nights). If you overindulge, though, brace yourself for the Mother of All Hangovers the following morning: Goa's national drink, whatever you disguise it with, is rough stuff.

Alcohol

Drinking **alcohol** is not the shameful activity it is in most other parts of India. Indeed, the easy availability and low cost/tax-free status of beers and spirits in Goa contribute in no small part to the state's popularity with domestic tourists: busloads of bar crawlers from neighbouring Karnataka and Maharashtra pour in on Saturdays and Sundays to take advantage of the liberal liquor laws. The flip side, however, is that the more frequented beaches tend to be plagued by gangs of drunks at weekends and public holidays; the state also has more than 60,000 registered alcoholics – way above the national average.

Beer is consumed in vast quantities. The biggest-selling brand is Kingfisher, but Arlem and Kings are also drinkable. The slightly bitter and unpleasant aftertaste in all Indian beers is caused by glycerine, a preservative which you can remove by pressing your middle finger over the mouth of the bottle and turning it upside down in a glass of water: when you remove your finger under water, the glycerine, which is heavier, will flow out of the bottle into the glass.

Few visitors acquire a taste for the traditional Goan tipple, **feni**, but locally produced spirits, known by the acronym IMFL (Indian-made Foreign Liquors) are generally palatable when mixed with soda or some kind of soft drink. Dozens of types of whisky are sold in bars, alongside Indian gin, vodka, rum and brandy; stick to big-name brands (as advertised on hoardings) and you shouldn't go far wrong.

In addition to spirits, Goa produces several varieties of **wine**, including a popular sparkling medium dry known as *Vinho Espumoso*, or *Vinicola*. You can buy this and other brands in large general stores in Panjim, Mapusa and Margao, and in most upscale restaurants. None approaches the quality of their Portuguese forebears, but the ubiquitous Goan **port** is passable and highly potent.

A FOOD GLOSSARY

Goan dishes and cooking terms

ambot tik	squid
ananas	pineapple
apa de camarao	prawn pie with a crisp rice-flour crust
balchao	a preserve of rich red-chilli sauce
bangra	a common mackerel-like fish
bazlele	fried
bharli vaangi	stuffed aubergines (eggplant)
bibo upkari	cashews cooked with spices
cabedala	pungent pork dish
cafreal	spicy fried chicken or fish
caja	cashew nut
caldo verde	Portuguese potato and cabbage soup
caranguejo	crab
chanyacho ros	dried peas prepared with dry-roasted coconut and whole spices
chourisso	small red pork sausages flavoured with *feni*, *toddi* vinegar and chillies; known as *l lingiss* in Konkani
feijoada	butter-bean stew that often comes with chunks of *chourisso*
gur	coconut sugar
keli	banana
kishmar	dried and powdered shrimp
koolee	crab
leitao	roast suckling pig; originally a speciality of Coimbra, Portugal
nal	coconut
neeshtay	fish
neeshtaychi corri	fish curry water
pilau	Basmati rice stewed in stock and flavoured with whole spices and saffron
peelo	sharkfish
pomfret	a tasty flat fish like flounder

rechad	a hot red-chilli paste, mainly used to flavour fish
rechado	stuffed with *rechad*
showd	lobster
sorpatel	pickled pork seasoned with hot spices; eaten at Christmas and marriage feasts
sungta	prawns
taanoo	rice
tamari bhaji	a red-spinach dish with onions, chillies and grated coconut
tel	cooking oil
toddi	palm sap vinegar or wine
toraso	swordfish
vindaloo	pork or chicken marinated in an extra-hot and sour curry sauce
visun	kingfish
wagio	tiger prawns
xacuti	a fiery sauce for meat made with lemon juice, nuts, coconut milk and lots of red chillies

Dishes from other regions

biriyani	rice with saffron or turmeric, whole spices and meat (sometimes vegetables), and often a hard-boiled egg; mild.
cutlet	minced meat or vegetables fried in the form of a flat cake
jalfrezi	with tomatoes and green chilli; medium hot
jeera	cummin; a *masala* so described will usually be medium hot
keema	minced lamb
korma	braised in yoghurt sauce with almonds; mild
malai kofta	balls of minced vegetables in a rich spicy sauce
pilau	rice lightly spiced and pre-fried

Continues over

Continued from over

rogan josh	red lamb curry; a classic *Mughlai* dish; medium hot
sambar	tangy vegetable and lentil soup with asafoetida and tamarind
subje	white-coconut chutney served with most South Indian dishes
tarka dal	split orange lentils cooked in a *masala* of turmeric, fried garlic and onions

Breads and pancakes

batura	soft deep-fried white bread that traditionally accompanies *channa* (chick peas)
chapati	unleavened bread made with mixed white and wholewheat flour, dry-baked on a flat griddle
dosa	crispy rice pancake
idli	steamed rice cake usually served with *sambar*
*kunechi poee	pitta-like unleavened bread, often baked or dry-fried in the shape of a butterfly
nan	white leavened bread baked in a clay oven (*tandoor*)
*pao, or poee	soft and crusty Portuguese-style white bread rolls
papadam	crisp, thin chick-pea-flour cracker, deep-fried or grilled
paratha	wholewheat bread made with butter and griddle-fried; tastes like a chewy pancake and is often stuffed with vegetables or meat

puri	soft white-dough bread that puffs up and crispens when deep-fried in oil
roti	a loosely used term; often just another name for *chapati*, though it should be thicker, chewier, and baked in a *tandoor*
*sanna	traditional crumpet-like bread rolls made with rice flour, sugar and partially fermented *toddi*
uttapam	griddle-fried rice-batter pancake, speckled with holes and soft in the middle; often prepared using onions
wada or *vada*	deep-fried doughnuts made from lentil flour

*Goan terminology; all other bread and pancake terms above refer to North or South Indian cuisine

Cakes and desserts

alebele	pancakes stuffed with grated fresh coconut
bebinca	a ten-layer Christmas cake made with egg yolks, coconut milk and sugar
bolinhas	small, round and syrupy rice-flour cakes
culculs	tiny shell-shaped biscuits
dodol	fudge-like balls of semolina flavoured with roasted coconuts, cashews and raw cane sugar (*jaggery*)
mangada	mango jam
neuros	half-moon-shaped stuffed pastries

Mail, phones and media

There is no need to be out of touch with the rest of the world while you're in Goa. The mail service is pretty reliable (if a little slow), and international phone calls are surprisingly easy. In addition, there are a number of decent English-language newspapers, and more people and places than you might imagine have access to English-language satellite TV.

Mail services

Mail can take anything from six days to three weeks to get to or from Goa, depending on where you are and the country you are mailing; ten days is about the norm. Most **post offices** are open Monday to Friday 10am–5pm and Saturday 10am–noon, but town GPOs keep longer hours (Mon–Sat 9.30am–1pm & 2–5.30pm). **Stamps** are not expensive, but you'll have to stick them on yourself as they tend not to be self-adhesive (every post office keeps a pot of evil-smelling glue for this purpose). You can also buy stamps at some big hotels. Aerogrammes and postcards cost the same to anywhere in the world. Ideally, you should also have mail franked in front of you; stamps are sometimes peeled off and resold by unscrupulous clerks.

Poste restante services throughout the state are pretty reliable, though exactly how long individual offices hang on to letters is largely at their own discretion; for periods of longer than a month, it makes sense to ensure your mail is marked with your expected date of arrival. Letters are filed alphabetically; in larger offices, you sort through them yourself. To avoid misfiling, your name should be printed clearly, with the surname in large capitals and underlined, but it is still a good idea to check under your first name too, just in case. Have letters addressed to you c/o Poste Restante, GPO (if it's the main post office you want), and the name of the town and state. Don't forget to take ID with you to claim your mail. The *American Express* office in Panjim also keeps mail for holders of their charge card or travellers' cheques (see p.74). Having **parcels** sent to you in Goa is not a good idea, as they often go astray. If you do have one sent, get it registered.

Sending a parcel from Goa can be a performance. First take it to a tailor and agree a price to have it wrapped in cheap cotton cloth (which you may have to buy yourself), stitched up and sealed with wax. Next, take it to the post office, fill in and attach the relevant customs forms (it's best to tick the box marked "gift" and give its value as less than Rs1000 or "no commercial value", to avoid bureaucratic entanglements), buy your stamps, see them franked and dispatch it. Parcels should not be more than a metre long, nor weigh more than 20kg. Surface mail is incredibly cheap, and takes an average of six months to arrive – it may take half, or four times that, however. It's a good way to dump excess baggage and souvenirs, but don't send anything fragile this way.

As in Britain, North America and Australasia, books and magazines can be sent more cheaply, unsealed or wrapped around the middle, as **printed papers** ("book post"). Remember that all packages from India are likely to be suspect at home, and searched or X-rayed: don't send anything dodgy.

Phones

Privately run **phone offices** with international direct-dialling facilities are very widespread. Advertising themselves with the acronyms **STD/ISD** (standard trunk dialling/international

International codes

From India:	To India:
UK ☎ 00 44	☎ 00 91
Irish Republic ☎ 00 353	☎ 00 91
US and Canada ☎ 00 1	☎ 011 91
Australia ☎ 00 61	☎ 0011 91
New Zealand ☎ 00 64	☎ 00 91

subscriber dialling), they are extremely quick and easy to use; some stay open late into the evening. Both national and international calls are dialled direct, and you pay the bill after you've made the call. Prices are often higher at small private places than in official telecommunications offices, particularly in tourist resorts. Calling from hotels is usually the most expensive option.

Home country direct services are now available from any STD/ISD phone to the UK, the USA, Canada, Ireland, Australia, New Zealand and a growing number of other countries. These allow you to make a collect or telephone credit card call to that country via an operator there. If you can't find a phone with home country direct buttons, you can use any phone toll-free, by dialling 000, your country code, and 17 (except Canada which is 000-167).

To **call Goa** (India) from abroad, dial the international access code, followed by 91 for India, the local code minus the initial zero, then the number you want.

Local phone numbers

To reduce congestion on the overloaded Indian telephone system, many larger businesses and hotels use several phone numbers, with only the final digit changing. In such cases we've denoted the range of numbers with a dash: ☎ 123456–9. If you don't get through on the first number (☎ 123456), work your way through the sequence until you do (☎ 123457, 123458, 123459).

The media

Goa has three English-language daily **newspapers**: the *Navhind Times*, which tends to support the political establishment of the day, and the more independent *Herald* and *Gomantak Times*. These locally published broadsheets all dish up a uniformly dry diet of regional and national news, with very limited coverage of foreign affairs. If you want to read about what's happening in the rest of the world, the international pages of **Indian newspapers** such as the *Times of India*, *Indian Express* or, better still, the *Independent*, are more informative. Alternatively, look for a **foreign paper or magazine**: the *Herald Tribune*, *Time*, *Newsweek*, *Le Monde*, *Der Spiegel*, the *Guardian*, and a range of British tabloids are sold in Panjim's two bookshops (see p.75), and at tourist shops in the major resorts several days after publication.

Anyone keen to learn more about Goan current affairs should also look out for the excellent **monthly magazine**, *Goa Today*, which spotlights local issues and features extracts of Goan fiction. Back issues covering a wide range of different topics are available through the *Goa Today* office, 3rd Floor, Shivkripa Apartments, near Dom Bosco High School, Panjim (☎ 0832/226132).

BBC World Service radio can be picked up on short wave on 15.31MHz (19.6m) between about 8.30am and 10.30pm (Indian time). If reception is poor, alternative frequencies include 17.79MHz (16.9m), 15.56MHz (19.3m) and 11.96MHz (25.1m).

The Indian government-run **TV** company, *Doordarshan*, which broadcasts a sober diet of edifying programmes, has found itself unable to compete with the onslaught of mass access to **satellite TV** in Goa, with illegal use of cables ensuring that one satellite dish can serve dozens of homes at an affordable price. The main broadcaster in English is Rupert Murdoch's *Star TV* network, which incorporates the BBC World Service, the Hindi-film oriented *Zee TV*, and a couple of American soap and chat channels.

Police, trouble and personal security

While the vast majority of visitors to Goa never encounter any trouble, tourist-related crime is definitely more prevalent than in any other parts of the country. Theft is the most common problem – usually of articles left unattended on the beach. Don't assume your valuables are safe in a padlocked house or hotel room,

either. Break-ins, particularly on party nights, are on the increase in the main resorts.

Most people carry their passports and travellers' cheques in concealed money belts, but guesthouses and hotels will often have some kind of **safe-deposit facility** where you can store your valuables. Don't, however, be tempted to

---

Child prostitution in Goa

Fears that Goa is fast becoming a playground for paedophiles were realized in 1996, when one local priest and a foreign tourist were prosecuted for child sex offences. Several other cases are awaiting trial, and evidence of organized paedophile rings with networks abroad is currently being accumulated by Interpol with the help of local police.

An undercover investigation was recently undertaken in India by NAWO (the National Alliance of Women's Movements), and revealed that around half of the prostitutes in Goa were girls between the ages of eleven and fifteen. Many claimed they were driven into the trade by poverty; others were sold by their parents to clear debts. The same research also showed that child prostitution was not merely confined to the traditional red-light districts, but had spilled onto Goa's beaches in recent years. So far, however, there have been very few convictions, mainly because of the ease with which offenders are able to bribe their way out of trouble, or jump bail. Until 1997, foreign paedophiles also knew that they were immune from prosecution in their home countries for offences committed against children in India. However, a new law was recently passed in the UK to facilitate the repatriation of convicted sex offenders, and it is hoped this will prove an effective deterrent.

Because child prostitution centres on the coastal resorts, you may come into direct contact with it during your holiday, and wonder

what course of action to take if you do. It's never easy to be one hundred percent sure that what you're seeing is actually child prostitution, but if you see a foreign man, or men, with Indian girls or boys on the beach, and if their behaviour towards the children is more attentive than seems normal, alert the local police. You may also be tempted to photograph the suspect, but bear in mind that by taking the law into your own hands in this way you may be putting yourself and your travelling companions at risk.

An international response to the problem of child sex tourism is being co-ordinated in the UK by the Coalition on Child Prostitution and Tourism, Unit 4, The Stableyard, Broomgrove Road, London SW9 9TL (☎0171/924 9555, fax 738 4110). Their advice to anyone who thinks they might have witnessed child prostitution in Goa is to contact the local police immediately, and to telephone the UK's National Criminal Intelligence Service (☎0171/238 8174), who run a confidential hotline. You may also wish to inform your tour company of your experience (letters to government offices from large charter operators carry a lot of clout in Goa), and write to Goa's Deputy Chief Minister, Mr Wilfred D'Souza, who was quoted in *The Hindustan Times* of March 1997 as claiming that "since those involved in (child) prostitution are not Goans, the State bears no responsibility for what is happening on Goa's beaches".

use the *Bank of Baroda*'s safe-deposit service in Anjuna, Calangute and Mapusa, as stuff has reputedly gone missing from these places in the past. It's also a good idea to always keep a separate record of the numbers of your travellers' cheques, together with a note of which ones you've cashed, and the papers and telephone numbers necessary for replacing them if they are stolen.

Police

The Goan **police** – recognizable by their blue berets, white shirts and khaki pants – have become a major hassle for tourists over the past few years. **Corruption**, which originally crept in as a reaction to low pay and late salaries but has since evolved into a form of institutionalized racketeering, is the root of the problem. Indeed, the pickings in India's premier tourist state are rumoured to be so rich that officers routinely pay large backhanders to be posted here. Over the past few years, some have even turned to old-fashioned robbery, the most publicized case being that of one Constable Digambar Naik, who was suspended for stealing £500 from a British tourist at Dabolim airport.

However, the way foreigners most often find themselves on the wrong side of the law is by driving around without a valid international driver's licence (see p.35). Even if you have one, though, the cop that waved you over will probably find another excuse to extract Rs100 or so *baksheesh*, usually for the absence of insurance papers or a helmet. The simple solution is to avoid police posts like the plague, which means travelling through towns such as Panjim, Mapusa and Margao, and to the Anjuna flea market, by public transport or on foot.

The most common cause of serious trouble is **drugs**. Many travellers mistakenly imagine that, because of Goa's free and easy reputation, drug use is legal. But possession of even a tiny amount of cannabis is a criminal offence, punishable by large fines or prison sentences of up to ten years. In the past, minor crimes were usually cleared up on the spot with out-of-court settlements. These days, however, you can expect to be relieved of all your cash and valuables, and required to leave the state within 24 hours, if you're lucky – the grim Fort Aguada prison accommodates several Westerners who weren't.

Nudism

Nudism is illegal in Goa, mainly because visitors in the past all too often ignored local sensibilities, forgetting or wilfully ignoring the fact that the state is part of India. In case tourists miss the "NO NUDISM" signs posted at the entrances to most beaches, police regularly patrol the busier resorts to ensure that decorum is maintained. If you are tempted to drop your togs, check that there are no families within eyeshot. No one is likely to object openly, but when you consider that wet Y-fronts and *saris* are about as risqué as beachwear gets for most Indians, you'll understand why men in G-strings and topless women cause such a stir (see below for more on Goan sensibilities).

Cultural hints and etiquette

Cultural differences extend to all sorts of little things. While allowances will usually be made for foreigners, visitors unacquainted with Goan customs may need a little preparation to avoid causing offence or making fools of themselves. The list of dos and don'ts here is hardly exhaustive: when in doubt, watch what the Goan people around you are doing.

Dress

The most common cultural blunder committed by foreign visitors to Goa concerns **dress**. People accustomed to the liberal ways of Western holiday resorts often assume it's fine to stroll around town in beachwear: it isn't, as the numerous stares and giggles that follow tourists who walk through Panjim, Margao or Mapusa shirtless or in a bikini top demonstrate. Ignoring local norms in this way will rarely cause offence, but you'll be regarded as very peculiar. This is particularly true for women (see "Women Travellers", p.53), who should keep legs and breasts well covered in all public places. It's OK for men to wear shorts, but swimming togs are only for the beach, and you shouldn't strip off your shirt, no matter how hot it is. None of this applies to the beach, of course, except in the most remote coastal villages, where local people may not necessarily be used to Western sunbathing habits (see also p.53).

Eating and the right-hand rule

Another minefield of potential faux-pas has to do with **eating**. In Goa (although not, as a rule, in tourist restaurants), this is traditionally done with the fingers, and requires a bit of practice to get absolutely right. Rule one is: eat with your right hand only. In Goa, as right across Asia, the left hand is for wiping your bottom, cleaning your feet and other unsavoury functions (you also put on and take off your shoes with your left hand), while the right hand is for eating, shaking hands and so on.

This rule extends beyond food too. In general, do not pass anything to anyone with your left hand, or point at anyone with it either; and Goans won't be impressed if you put it in your mouth. In general, you should accept things given to you with your right hand – though using both hands is a sign of respect.

The other rule to beware of when eating or drinking is that your lips should not touch other people's food. When drinking out of a cup or bottle to be shared with others, don't let it touch your lips, but rather pour it directly into your mouth. This custom can be difficult to get the hang of, but it protects you from things like hepatitis. It is also customary to wash your hands before and after eating.

Visiting temples and churches

Non-Hindus are welcome to visit Goan **temples**, but you're expected to observe a few simple conventions. The most important of these is to dress appropriately: women should keep their shoulders and legs covered, while men should wear long trousers or *lunghis*. Always remove your shoes at the entrance to the main hall (not the courtyard), and never step inside the doorway to the shrine, which is strictly off limits to

everyone except the *pujaris*. Photography is nearly always prohibited inside the temple, but OK around the courtyard. Finally, if there is a passage (*pradakshena*) encircling the shrine, walk around it in a clockwise direction.

It's also always a good idea to dress respectably when visiting **churches**, and to leave a small donation for the upkeep of the building when you leave.

Other possible gaffes

Kissing and embracing are regarded in Goa as part of sex: do not do them in public. It is not even a good idea for couples to hold hands. Be aware, too, of your **feet**. When entering a private home – especially a Hindu one – you should normally remove your shoes (follow your host's example); when sitting, avoid pointing the soles of your feet at anyone. Accidental contact with one's foot is always followed by an apology.

Finally, always ask someone's permission before taking their **photograph**, particularly in or around temples. If you photograph a hawker, flower-seller or any other low-income itinerant vendor on the beach, it is not impolite to offer them a tip.

Meeting people

Like most Indians, Goans are generally very garrulous and enjoy getting to know their visitors. You'll often be quizzed about your background, family, job and income by locals. Questions like these can seem baffling or intrusive to begin with, but such topics are not considered "personal", and it is completely normal to ask people about them. Asking the same things back will not be taken amiss – far from it. Being curious does not have the "nosey" stigma in Goa that it does in the West.

Things that Goans are likely to find strange about you are lack of religion (you could adopt one), travelling alone, being part of an unmarried couple (letting people think you are married can make life easier), and staying in cheap hotels when, as a tourist, you are obviously rich. You will probably end up having to explain the same things many times to many different people; on the other hand, you can ask questions too, so you could take it as an opportunity to ask things you want to know about Goa.

Festivals and holidays

Goa abounds with all kinds of festivals and holidays – Hindu and Christian, national and local – and the chances of your visit coinciding with one are good. Religious celebrations range from exuberant *Zatras*, when Hindu deities are paraded around their temple compounds in huge wooden chariots, to modest *festas*, celebrating the patron saint of a village church. Secular events are less common, although Carnival, which involves a cast of thousands, is the state's largest cultural event. Christmas also enjoys a high profile: travellers from all over South Asia converge on Goa for the Yuletide revelries, when local people traditionally consume prodigious quantities of pork, sweets and *feni* – the hallmark of most Goan festivals.

While Christian events follow the Gregorian calendar introduced by the Portuguese, the dates of Hindu celebrations vary from year to year according to the lunar cycle, with key rituals reserved for the full-moon (*purnima*) or new-moon (*ama*) periods. However, ascertaining exactly when any given temple is holding its *Zatra* can be difficult. If you're keen to see a major Hindu festival, ask for precise dates at the GTDC tourist office in Panjim, as it arranges transport to most major events for pilgrims.

FESTIVALS AND PUBLIC HOLIDAYS

JANUARY TO MID-MARCH

Festa dos Reis (Jan 6). Christians flock to Remedios Hill, Quelim (near Cansaulim, Salcete) for the state's main Epiphany celebration, during which three young boys, decked in brocaded silk and wearing crowns, ride to the hilltop chapel on white horses. Similar processions take place in the Franciscan church at Reis Magos, near Panjim (see p.119), and at Chandor (see p.177).

Bandeira festival (mid-Jan). Emigrant workers from Divar island (see p.96) return home for the local patron saint's day, and march through the village waving the flags of their adopted countries and firing pea shooters.

Republic Day (Jan 26). India's national day is marked with military parades and political speeches. Public holiday.

Ramadan (Jan). The start of a month when Muslims may not eat, drink or smoke from sunrise to sunset, and should abstain from sex.

Id-ul-Fitr (Jan/Feb). Muslims feast to celebrate the end of Ramadan.

Carnival (Feb/March). Three days of *feni*-induced mayhem centring on Panjim (see p.73) marking the run up to Lent.

Shigmo (Feb/March). Goa's version of the Hindu Holi festival – held over the full-moon period to mark the onset of spring – includes processions of floats, music and dance, in addition to the usual throwing of paint bombs; these can permanently stain clothing, so don't go out in your Sunday best.

Shivratri (Feb/March). Anniversary of Shiva's creation dance (*tandav*), and his wedding day. Big *pujas* are held at Shiva temples all over the state, and many Hindus get high on *bhang* – a milk and sugar preparation laced with ground cannabis leaves.

Continued. . .

MID-MARCH TO MAY

Easter (March/April). Christ's Resurrection is celebrated with fasting, feasting, and High Mass held in chapels and churches across Goa.

Procession of the Saints (March/April). Twenty-six life-size effigies of saints, martyrs, popes, kings, queens and cardinals are paraded around Goa Velha on the first Monday of Easter week. This solemn religious event is accompanied by a lively fun fair.

Our Lady of Miracles (Milagros) (April/May). Mapusa's main church (see p.117) is the venue for a big *tamasha*, or fair, held sixteen days after Good Friday and connected with the Hindu goddess Lairaya, whose worshippers also flock here to pay their respects.

Igitun Chalne (May). Dhoti-clad devotees of Lairaya enter trances and walk over hot coals in fulfillment of thanksgiving vows. This famous fire-walking ritual only takes place in Sirigao, Bicholim *taluka*.

Music Festival (May). Local rock, pop and jazz bands strut their stuff at the Kala Academy, Panjim.

JUNE–AUGUST

Sanjuan (June 24). The feast day of Saint John, or Sao Joao (corrupted in Konkani to "Sanjuan"), is celebrated all over Goa, but is particularly important in the coastal villages of Cortalim, Arambol (see p.152) and Terekol (Pernem) (see p.154). Youngsters torch straw dummies of "Judeu", representing Saint John's baptism (and thus the death of sin). In addition, the day includes processions of revellers in striped pants, and lots of drunken diving into wells to retrieve bottles of *feni*.

Sangodd (June 29). Slap-up *sorpotel* (roast pig) suppers mark the *festa* of Saint Peter, the patron saint of fishers. Boats are tied together to make floating stages on which extravagantly costumed actors and musicians perform traditional dramas for audiences assembled on the river banks. The biggest events take place in the villages of Orda, Saipem and Candolim, Bardez *taluka*.

Independence Day (Aug 15). India's largest secular celebration, on the anniversary of her Independence from Britain in 1947. Public holiday.

Janmashtami (Aug). Ritual bathing in the Mandovi River off Divar island (see p.96), near Old Goa, to celebrate Krishna's birthday.

Ganesh Chaturthi (late June). Giant effigies of the elephant-headed Hindu deity Ganesh, god of peace and prosperity, are displayed in elaborately decorated household and neighbourhood shrines, then taken through the streets to the river or sea for holy dips.

SEPTEMBER–DECEMBER

Dusshhera (Sept/Oct). A nine-day Hindu festival (usually with a two-day public holiday) associated with Rama's victory over Ravana in the *Ramayana*, and the goddess Durga's over the buffalo-headed Mahishasura. Celebrations include the construction of large effigies, which are burnt on bonfires with fireworks, and performances of *Ram Lila* (the Life of Rama) by schoolchildren.

Mahatma Gandhi's Birthday (Oct 2). A sober commemoration of Independent India's founding father. Public holiday.

Fama (Oct). Colva's miracle-working "Menino Jesus" statue (see p.184), normally locked away in the village church, is exposed to large crowds of pilgrims from all over Goa on the second Monday of October.

Divali (Oct/Nov). Five-day "festival of lights" to celebrate Rama and Sita's homecoming – an episode in the *Ramayana*. The event features the lighting of oil lamps and firecrackers, the giving and receiving of sweets, and the hanging of paper lanterns outside Hindu houses.

Liberation Day (Dec 17). The anniversary of Nehru's expulsion of the Portuguese from Goa in 1961 is a low-key public holiday, with military parades and the occasional air force flypast.

Christmas (Dec 24/25). Goan emigrants return home for the state's most important festival, which is celebrated by both Hindus and Christians. *Missa de Galo*, Midnight Mass (literally "cockerel mass" because it sometimes carries on until dawn), marks the start of festivities. Meanwhile, tourist ravers party in Anjuna. Christmas Day is a Public holiday.

Shopping and souvenirs

The streets and lanes of Goa's coastal resorts are glutted with handicraft boutiques and makeshift market stalls that offer inexhaustible shopping possibilities. You'll also be approached at regular intervals on the beach by hawkers selling everything from tropical fruit and bamboo flutes to head massages and papier-mâché boxes. These migrant vendors travel to the region from other parts of India, spending on average six months camped by the sea before returning home, or heading off to the Himalayan hill stations for the summer. The stuff they sell is generally expensive by Indian standards, but seems amazingly cheap if you arrive directly from Europe.

Where to shop

Deservedly the most famous place to **shop** in Goa is the flea market in **Anjuna** (see p.139). Just about everyone with something to sell – whether a dog-eared paperback or a heavy silver ankle bracelet – makes their way on Wednesday morning to the palm-shaded market ground, which has to be among the most exotic shopping locations in the world. Its only drawback is that the prices tend to be high, but mostly because of the mad money some tourists are prepared to part with for trinkets.

If you miss the flea market, you'll find virtually the same assortment of stalls in **Mapusa** on Friday mornings (see p.117). This weekly bazaar

---

Hawkers

Hawkers are a feature of beach life in all but the most remote resorts these days, and you'll be pestered by a steady stream of them in the course of any day. The large majority are kids from Karnataka, flogging cheap cotton clothes, coconuts and cold drinks, but you'll also come across Kashmiris selling papier-mâché boxes, Rajasthani girls with sacks of dodgy silver jewellery, Tamil stone carvers, buskers, painted bulls led around by their turbaned, oboe-blowing owners, and, most distinctive of all, Lamani tribal women from the Gadag-Hubli-Hampi area, with their coin necklaces, cowrie-shell anklets and rainbow-coloured mirrorwork.

Initially, this parade can be a novel distraction. The hawkers are usually polite and pleasant to chat with; and it is, after all, convenient to have a slice of melon or fresh pineapple cut for you just when you fancy one. Eventually, though, the constant attention will start to wear your patience, and you'll find yourself experimenting with different ways to shake off the hawkers, who, given half the chance, will congregate in tight huddles around you. An "I've-been-here-a-while-already" tan helps, as does feigning sleep or burying yourself in a book.

Failing that, a stern shake of the head or wave of the hand should send the vendor on his or her way. Occasionally, however, one comes along who won't take no for an answer, in which case, you'll either have to buy something (which will inevitably attract every other hawker on the beach) or else start shouting – neither of which is likely to bring you much peace and quiet the following day.

The best ploy if you're going to spend much time on the same beach is to hook up with one or two hawkers, and always do "beesness" with them; that way, the others will more often than not leave you alone. And in case you start losing your temper, remember that the hawkers live off the few rupees mark-up they make on the stuff they sell; they're not here out of choice, but from economic necessity. Most are either landless peasants fleeing poverty in the countryside, or else refugees from exploitative labour on construction sites and brick works in the cities. They may also have a hard time working the beaches in Goa, regularly getting beaten up by the police (hawking is technically illegal in the state), or for not paying *baksheesh* to local shack owners.

THE BASICS

is also more typically Goan, with fish, fruit, vegetables and other fresh produce sold alongside tourist goods.

In addition, souvenirs are sold on the **beaches** by itinerant hawkers, a large percentage of whom seem barely old enough to walk let alone haggle. Conducted at an unhurried pace in the shade of an old fishing boat, buying and selling can be a sociable pastime, although make one purchase and you'll be bothered non-stop by bands of other hopeful hawkers.

The kind of **places not to shop** if you are bargain hunting are the posh handicraft boutiques, particularly those located in, or near, an upmarket hotel: you can pick the same stuff up at the flea market at fairer prices.

Bargaining

Wherever you shop (with the exception of general stores), you will almost always be expected to **haggle**. Bargaining is very much a matter of personal style, but should always be lighthearted, never acrimonious. There are no hard and fast rules – it's really a question of how much something is worth to you. It's a good plan, however, to have an idea of how much you want to pay.

Don't worry too much about initial prices. Some people suggest paying a half or less of the opening price, but it's a flexible guideline depending on the shop, the goods and the shopkeeper's impression of you. You may not be able to get the seller much below the first quote; on the other hand, you may end up paying as little as a tenth of it – this is particularly true of beach hawkers. If you bid too low, you may be hustled out of the shop for offering an "insulting" price (a typically Kashmiri ploy), but this is all part of the game, and you will no doubt be welcomed as an old friend if you return the next day.

Don't start haggling for something if in fact you know you don't want it, and never let any figure pass your lips that you are not prepared to pay. It's like bidding at an auction. Having mentioned a price, you are obliged to pay it. If the seller asks you how much you would pay for something, and you don't want it, then say so. And never go shopping with a tout, who will get a commission on anything you buy, which means a higher price to you.

What to buy

Just about the only thing souvenirs on sale in Goa these days have in common is that they nearly all come from India, manufactured for the tourist market in other parts of the country and imported by the traders who sell them. Nor do you often come across bona fide Goan goods, or articles that aren't available in some form back home. The one consolation is that everything costs a lot less than it does in London or New York.

Goan goods

Goans generally lack the competitive business edge of their Indian neighbours, and thus tend to leave souvenir selling to migrant vendors from out of state. This, in part, explains the dearth of authentically **Goan souvenirs** on offer in the resorts. You can, however, pick up some exportable local produce. The most ubiquitous speciality on offer is **cashew nuts** – the state's number one cash crop. They come in a variety of sizes, whether salted, dry-roasted, loose or packaged.

The other typically Goan souvenir is a bottle of **feni** (see p.40), widely available in bars and liquor stores, or through your guesthouse owner: the best stuff is distilled in the coastal villages and kept for local consumption. If feni doesn't appeal, a bottle of **port wine** might, although the novelty value and low cost are likely to be more of an incentive than quality: Goan port is drinkable, but it is not a patch on the real thing.

Karnatakan goods

Among the most distinctive souvenirs are those touted by the Lamanis, an ethnic group from **Karnataka**. Easily recognizable by their multi-coloured tribal garb, these hawkers are members of a semi-nomadic low-caste minority who traditionally lived by transporting salt across the Deccan Plateau. These days, the women and girls make most of the family money through the sale of **textiles** and cheap **jewellery**, carefully tailored for the tourist trade. Their rainbow cloth, woven with geometric designs and inlaid with cowrie shells or fragments of mirror and mica, is fashioned into shoulder bags, caps and money belts. Their jewellery, however, is more traditional, made with coral beads, old Indian coins, and low-grade silver. If you haggle hard and can put up with all the shouting and tugging that inevitably accompanies each purchase, you can usually pick up this Karnatakan stuff at bargain prices.

Kashmiri goods

Forced to leave their homeland after the ongoing political unrest there killed off most of the tourist traffic, the **Kashmiris** are the most assiduous traders in Goa. If you get dragged into one of their shops, chances are it's a **carpet** they really want to sell you. Kashmiri rugs are among the best in the world, and you can get yourself one at a decent price in Goa (though you can also get ripped off if you're not careful). A *pukka* Kashmiri carpet should have a label on the back stating that it is made in Kashmir, what it is made of (wool, silk or "silk touch" – wool combined with a little cotton and silk to give it a sheen), its size, density of knots per square inch (the more the better), and the name of the design. To tell if it really is silk, scrape the carpet with a knife and burn the fluff – real silk shrivels to nothing and has a distinctive smell. Even producing the knife should cause the seller of a bogus silk carpet to demur.

The surest way to make sure a carpet reaches home is to take it away and post it yourself; a seller may offer to post it to you and bill you later, which is fair enough, but be aware that your carpet will be sent immediately, whatever you say, and if you use a credit card, your account will also be billed immediately, whatever is said.

The Kashmiris' other specialities are **leather clothes**, Himalyan **curios** and lacquered **papier-mâché**, which they make into pots, fussy little boxes and even baubles for Christmas trees. The most relaxed places to check out the full range are the Anjuna flea market or Mapusa's Friday-morning market; venture into one of their little shops and you'll find it difficult to get out.

Other goods

The **Tibetans'** central Asian features look almost as foreign in Goa as those of their Western customers, but these laid-back Himalayan traders have carved out a niche for themselves in the resorts selling reproduction Buddhist **curios**. Their other stock in trade is **silver jewellery**, which is sold by weight. In principle, the price per gram is fixed (Tibetans claim they hate haggling), but in practice you can usually knock down the rate,

which also varies according to how elaborate the piece is, and how much turquoise, coral or lapis lazuli has been added to it. However, the prices of **Himalayan handicrafts**, the Tibetans' other line, are generally more flexible. Whatever they tell you, though, none of the prayer wheels, brass Buddhas, *tsampa* bowls or *thangkas* (religious paintings on cloth) are antiques, and few actually come from the mountains: most are made in refugee camps in Old Delhi.

Browsing Anjuna or Mapusa market, you'll come across the odd apprentice stone carver from South India, taking time out to flog miniature **devotional statues**. These make great souvenirs, but they don't always come cheap: even a small piece cut from malleable soapstone takes hours of painstaking work. However, they also do a brisk trade in more affordable *trompe l'oeil* pendants. Touted as lucky talismans, these usually take the form of small Shiva faces which, when turned upside down or flipped over, look the same. Also worth keeping an eye open for are **woodcarvings** of gods from the South Indian state of Kerala; ones of the elephant-headed deity Ganesh, god of peace and prosperity and the overcomer of obstacles, are always a favourite.

Handicrafts from the western Indian states of **Gujarat** and **Rajasthan** crop up in most souvenir shops. Beautiful block-printed and appliqué bed covers are this region's forte, along with miniature paintings and elaborate mirrorwork textiles. You may also be shown gemstones from Jaipur, and elaborate silver jewellery, although it's never easy to tell fakes from the genuine articles.

Anjuna's flea market is awash with clothes made and sold by the village's transient Western population. These look a lot less incongruous on a Goan beach than back home, but are popular with tourists keen to kit themselves out for the big beach parties. **Rave gear** in drug-inspired day-glo colours features prominently, as do dresses and shirts fashioned from Balinese batiks, and woven or mirrorwork waistcoats. Anjuna is also the place to pick up those trendy wrap-around Thai trousers you see everywhere, along with *tangas*, the G-strings beloved of posey racket-ball players.

Women travellers

Compared with other regions of India, Goa is an easy-going destination for women travellers: incidents of sexual harassment are relatively rare, and opportunites to meet local women frequent. At the same time, it is important to remember that significant cultural differences still exist, especially in those areas where tourism is a relatively recent phenomenon.

Problems, when they do occur, invariably stem from the fact that many Western travellers do a range of things that no self-respecting Goan woman would consider: from drinking alcohol or smoking in a bar-restaurant, to sleeping in a room with a man to whom they are not married. Without compromising your freedom too greatly, though, there are a few common-sense steps you can take to accommodate local feelings.

The most important and obvious is **dress**. Western visitors who wear clothes that expose shoulders, legs or cleavage do neither themselves nor their fellow travellers any favours. Opt, therefore, for loose-fitting clothes that keep these areas covered. When travelling alone on public transport, it is also a good idea to sit with other women (most buses have separate "ladies' seats" at the front). If you're with a man, a wedding ring also confers immediate respectability.

Appropriate behaviour for **the beach** is a trickier issue. The very idea of a woman lying semi-naked in full view of male strangers is anathema to Goans. However, local people in the coastal resorts have come to tolerate such bizarre behaviour over the past two or three decades, and swimsuits and bikinis are no longer deemed indecent, especially if worn with a sarong. **Topless bathing**, on the other hand, is definitely out of the question (see "Nudism", p.46), even though you'll doubtless encounter bare breasts on the more hippified beaches. One very good reason to keep your top on is that it confounds the expectations of men who descend on Goa in

Rape

Rape is probably less of a danger in Goa than in most Western countries, but the number of sexual assaults on women travellers has seen a marked increase over the past few seasons, to the extent that a pamphlet entitled "Rape Alert" was posted around the resorts in 1996–7 by women tourists urging fellow travellers to take care at night. Among the incidents that provoked this was the 1996 attack on a thirty-three-year-old British woman in Anjuna by two men, one of whom was her taxi driver. In another incident in March 1997 (also in Anjuna) two Swedish women were gang raped by seven or eight men on their way home from a beach party; their motorbike was stopped by assailants armed with sticks and knives, and a male companion forced at knife-point to witness the rape.

Wherever you're staying, therefore, take the same commonsense precautions as you would at home: keep to the main roads when travelling on foot or by bicycle, avoid dirt tracks and unfrequented beaches unless you're in a group, and when you're in your house after dark, ensure that all windows and doors are locked.

Anyone wishing to make contact with a **Goan womens' group** may do so by writing to *Bailancho Saad*, 304 Prema Building, Panjim. The group, a Panjim-based collective, campaigns on a range of issues, from development and sexual discrimination in the work place, to harassment, violence and unethical tourism.

well enough understood. If you shout "don't touch me!" in a crowded area, you're likely to find people on your side, and your assailant shamed. Touching up a Goan woman would be judged totally unacceptable behaviour, so there's no reason why you should put up with it, either.

On the positive side, spending time with **Goan women** can be a delight. The only obstacle to this, particularly in rural areas, is that few women speak English, and you won't run into many local women in cafés. However, public transport can be a good meeting ground, as can shops and guesthouses, which are often run by women. On the beach, you'll also find yourself frequently mobbed by women hawkers from Karnataka and Rajasthan. Such encounters are, of course, motivated primarily by commercial interest, but can be rewarding nonetheless.

large parties from outside the state expressly to ogle women, enticed by the prospect of public nudity.

Not surprisingly, the beaches are where you're most likely to experience **sexual harassment**, known in Goa as "Eve teasing". Your **reaction** to harassment is down to you. Verbal hassle is probably best ignored, but if you get touched it's best to react: the usual English responses will be

Directory

Goan resorts. Most are conscientious when it comes to using sterilized needles, but you should check first or you could run the risk of contracting HIV.

Cigarettes Various brands of cigarettes, including imported makes such as Rothmans and Benson and Hedges, are available in Goa. More expensive imported rolling tobacco, including Golden Virginia, Duma and Samson, are sold at Anjuna flea market and some stalls around Colva, although it is advisable to bring your own papers as the indigenous Capstans are thick and don't stick very well, while imported Rizlas are expensive. One of the great smells of India is the *bidi*, the cheapest smoke, made with low-grade tobacco wrapped in a eucalyptus leaf.

Airport departure tax As you depart from Dabolim airport, you are expected to pay a tax of either Rs300 – for international flights – or Rs150, for domestic flights, so hang on to some rupees for that purpose.

Body-piercing and tattoos Western body-piercers and tattooists ply their trade in several

Contraceptives Oral contraceptives are available over the counter at most pharmacies in Goa. Indian condoms are less reliable than those in the West, so stock up at duty-free.

Duty-free allowance Anyone over 17 can bring in one US quart (0.95 litre – but nobody's going to quibble about the other 5ml) of spirits, or a bottle of wine and 250ml spirits; plus 200 cigarettes, or 50 cigars, or 250g tobacco. You may be required to register anything valuable on a Tourist Baggage Re-export Form to make sure you take it home with you, and to fill in a currency declaration form if carrying more than US$10,000 or the equivalent.

Electricity Generally 220V 50Hz AC, though direct current supplies also exist, so check before plugging in. Most sockets are European-style double round-pin but sizes vary. British, Irish and Australasian plugs will need an adaptor, preferably a universal one; American and Canadian appliances need a transformer, too, unless multivoltage. Power cuts and voltage variations are very common.

Gay and lesbian life Homosexuality is not generally open in Goa, and anal intercourse is actually an offence under the Indian penal code, while laws against "obscene behaviour" are used to arrest gay men cruising or liaising anywhere that could be considered a public space; lesbianism is much more clandestine. It isn't surprising, therefore, that gay and lesbian life in the state is very low-key. The tourist scene is also very straight-oriented, although one or other of the beach cafés at Ozran Vagator (see p.147) usually becomes a hangout for gay visitors during the season.

Laundry In Goa, no one goes to the laundry: if they don't do their own, they send it out to a *dhobi wallah*. Wherever you are staying, there will either be an in-house *dhobi wallah*, or one very close by to call on. The *dhobi wallah* will take your dirty washing to a *dhobi ghat*, a public clothes-washing area (the bank of a river for example), where it is shown some old-fashioned discipline: separated, soaped and given a damn good thrashing to beat the dirt out of it. Then it is hung out to dry in the sun and, once dried, taken to the ironing sheds where every garment is endowed with razor-sharp creases and then matched to its rightful owner by hidden cryptic markings. Your clothes will come back from the *dhobi wallah* absolutely spotless, though this kind of violent treatment does take it out of them: buttons get lost and eventually the cloth starts to fray.

Massage The art of massage has been practised in India since ancient times, and male masseurs, carrying a bag of oils and a towel, regularly offer their services on the beach. Their trade does not have the seedy connotations it sometimes does in the West, although women should definitely think twice before accepting a rubdown; it wouldn't cause offence, but would raise a few eyebrows in any cafés within eyeshot.

Photography Beware of pointing your camera at anything that might be considered "strategic", especially Dabolim airport, and anything military,

---

Things to take

Many things are of course easy to find in Goa and cheaper than at home, but here is a miscellaneous and rather random list of items you should consider taking with you:

A padlock (to lock rooms in budget hotels)

A universal electric plug adaptor and a universal sink plug (few sinks or bathtubs have them)

A mosquito net

A roll of adhesive tape (for blocking up holes in mosquito nets)

A sheet sleeping bag

A small flashlight

Long-life batteries for personal stereos, torches or cameras (Indian ones wear out quickly)

Earplugs (for street noise in hotel rooms and music on buses)

High-factor sunblock

A pocket alarm clock (for any early-morning departures)

A multi-purpose penknife

A needle and some thread (dental floss is better for holding baggage together)

Plastic bags (to sort your baggage, make it easier to pack and unpack, and keep out damp and dust)

Tampons (those available in Goa are not so wonderful)

Multi-vitamin and mineral tablets

A stick of glue (for fixing stamps to letters and postcards)

A motorcycle helmet with a visor or goggles (if you plan to rent a bike)

A sealable water bottle

even bridges, stations and main roads. Remember, too, that some people prefer not to be photographed, so it is wise to ask before you take a snapshot of them – and only common courtesy after all. Camera film is widely available in Goa (but check the date on the box), and it's pretty easy to get films developed, though they don't always come out as well as they might at home. Prices are broadly similar to those in the West, with the exception of slide film, which is harder to get hold of and considerably more expensive.

Time Goa is GMT+5hr 30min all year round. This makes it 5hr 30min ahead of London, 10hr 30min ahead of New York, 15hr 30min ahead of LA, and 4hr 30min behind Sydney; however, summer time in those places will vary the difference by an hour.

Toilets Toilets in most mid-range and upmarket hotels are of the standard Western-style "sit-down" type, and generally clean. In some budget guesthouses and bars, however, Asian loos are the norm – these involve getting used to the squatting posture. Paper, if used, should go into the bucket provided rather than down the loo. Indians instead use a pot of water and their left hand, a method you may prefer to adopt, but if you do use paper, keep some handy – it isn't usually supplied, and it might be an idea to stock up before going too far off the beaten track as it is not available everywhere. In most villages, "pig toilets" are more common. Believe it or not, these tend not to smell as bad as conventional ones. They are also more environmentally sound, as they use less water.

The Guide

CHAPTER 2
NORTH GOA

CHAPTER 4
AROUND GOA

CHAPTER 1
PANJIM &
CENTRAL GOA

CHAPTER 3
SOUTH GOA

N

Panjim and Central Goa

T
he wedge-shaped tract of land between the Mandovi and Zuari
rivers encompasses the whole gamut of Goan landscapes,
from the palm-fringed paddy fields of the coast, through the
wooded valleys of the interior, to the dense jungles and hills of the
Western Ghats.

Bounded in the east by the sinuous Cambarjua Canal, **Tiswadi**
taluka – the most densely populated district in the state – is technically an island linked to the rest of Goa by a network of concrete road
bridges and rusty river ferries. Known as the *Velhas Conquistas*
(**Old Conquests**), this was the first area to be colonized by the
Portuguese, whose grandiose former capital at **Old Goa** remains the
state's premier historical site. The ruined town's modern counter-
part, **Panjim** – officially known as Panaji – lies 10km west on the left
bank of the Mandovi, its colonial-style houses and grand civic buildings making for a worthwhile day away from the beach. A short
detour to **Pilar**'s seventeenth-century seminary and nearby
Talaulim's imposing parish church of Santana can also be rewarding. Other incentives to linger include the picturesque islands of
Chorao, site of Goa's only bird reserve, and **Divar**, whose main village, Piedade, harbours a crop of elegant Portuguese villas and a
stately hilltop church.

Hidden away in the hills of **Ponda** *taluka*, southeast of Panjim, is
Goa's largest concentration of **Hindu temples**. Built away from the
town in the fifteenth and sixteenth centuries to escape persecution

---

Accommodation price codes

All **accommodation prices** in this book are coded using the symbols
below. In principle, the prices given are for the **least expensive double
rooms in high season** (mid-Dec to mid-Jan). Local taxes have been included in each case, unless specifically stated otherwise.

① Up to Rs100	④ Rs225–350	⑦ Rs750–1200
② Rs100–150	⑤ Rs350–500	⑧ Rs1200–2200
③ Rs150–225	⑥ Rs500–750	⑨ Over Rs2200

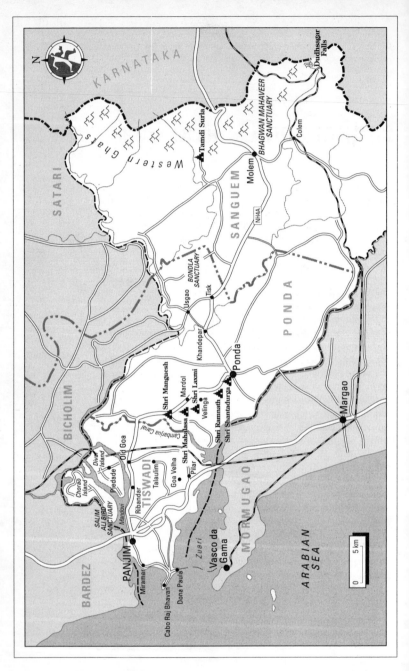

by the Portuguese, these architectural oddities, which fuse Hindu, Muslim, and European Renaissance styles, are often visited en route to the **spice plantations** dotted around the unprepossessing district headquarters, Ponda town, or as part of a longer tour to the wildlife reserves further east. Of these, the **Bhagwan Mahaveer Sanctuary** is much the most interesting. In addition to some stunning scenery, it boasts India's biggest waterfalls, **Dudhsagar**, and the last remaining medieval temple in Goa, the Mahadeva *mandir* at **Tamdi Surla**, in Sanguem *taluka*.

Panjim

Stacked around the sides of a lush terraced hillside at the mouth of the **Mandovi River**, PANJIM's skyline of sloping red-tiled roofs, whitewashed churches and mildewing concrete apartment blocks has more in common with Lisbon than Lucknow. The lingering European influence is most evident in the small squares and back lanes of the town's Latin quarters, **Fontainhas** and **Sao Tomé**. Here, Portuguese is still the lingua franca, the shopfronts sport names like Jose Pinto and de Souza, and the women wear knee-length dresses that would turn heads anywhere else in India.

Some visitors see no more of Panjim than its busy bus terminal, which is a pity. You can completely bypass the town when you arrive in Goa by jumping off the train or bus at Margao (for the south), or Mapusa (for the northern beach resorts), or by heading to the coast from the airport, but it's definitely worth spending time here – if only a couple of hours en route to the ruined former capital at Old Goa, 10km east, or the Hindu temples, further east around Ponda. Sights are thin on the ground, but the palm-lined squares and atmospheric old quarters, with their picturesque Neoclassical houses and Catholic churches, make a pleasant backdrop for aimless wandering.

Some history

The earliest mention of **Panjim** crops up in a Kadamba inscription, dated 1107, in which the settlement, then a handful of fishers' huts surrounded by dunes and swampland, is referred to as **Pahajani**, "land that does not flood". Recently, one eminent philologist contested the name may be derived from the Urdu *panch ima afsugani* – later corrupted by the Portuguese to *ponji* – meaning "five enchanted castles", a reference to the five hilltop **forts** erected here by **Muslim invaders** during the fourteenth century. Boasting fifty-five cannons, these were installed to guard the mouth of the Mandovi River, along with a grand fortified waterfront palace erected by Yusuf 'Adil Shah, the first Sultan of Bijapur. However, the defences failed to repel the Portuguese, who took the forts prior to the main assault on Ela (Old Goa), after which the site was used as a military embarkation point and customs post.

For more background to the Muslim era and Portuguese conquest of Goa, see "History" in Contexts on p.61.

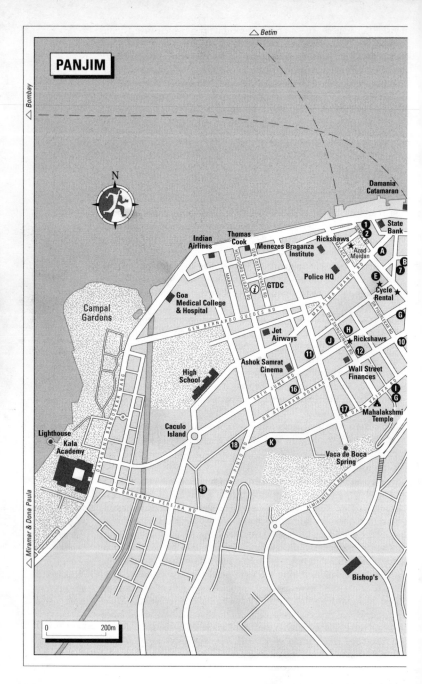

PANJIM

△ Betim

△ Bombay

△ Miramar & Dona Paula

N

Damania
Catamaran

State
Bank

1
2

Rickshaws

Azad
Maidan

A

B
7

Indian
Airlines

Thomas
Cook

Menezes Braganza
Institute

Police HQ

E

Cycle
Rental

GTDC

Goa
Medical College
& Hospital

G

Jet
Airways

H

Rickshaws

J

12

10

11

Ashok Samrat
Cinema

Wall Street
Finances

I

G

High
School

16

Mahalakshmi
Temple

17

Caculo
Island

18

K

Vaca de Boca
Spring

Lighthouse

Kala
Academy

19

Bishop's

Campal
Gardens

0   200m

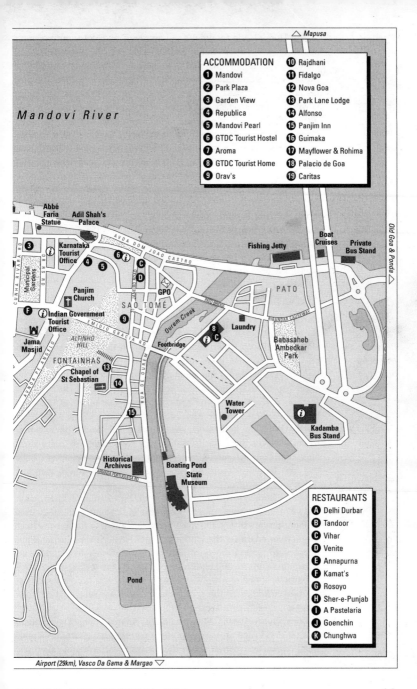

ACCOMMODATION
1. Mandovi
2. Park Plaza
3. Garden View
4. Republica
5. Mandovi Pearl
6. GTDC Tourist Hostel
7. Aroma
8. GTDC Tourist Home
9. Orav's
10. Rajdhani
11. Fidalgo
12. Nova Goa
13. Park Lane Lodge
14. Alfonso
15. Panjim Inn
16. Guimaka
17. Mayflower & Rohima
18. Palacio de Goa
19. Caritas

Mandovi River

Abbé Faria Statue

Adil Shah's Palace

AVDA DOM JOAO CASTRO

Boat Cruises

Private Bus Stand

Fishing Jetty

Karnataka Tourist Office

CUNHA RIVARA RD

DR. ATMARAM BORKAR RD

Municipal Gardens

Panjim Church

GPO

SAO TOMÉ

PATO

Old Goa & Ponda ▷

Indian Government Tourist Office

EMIDIO GRACIA RD

Ourem Creek

NEW PATTO BRIDGE

Laundry

Babasaheb Ambedkar Park

Jama Masjid

ALTINHO HILL

AVDA PE AGNELO

Footbridge

RUA DE OUREM

FONTAINHAS

Chapel of St Sebastian

Water Tower

Kadamba Bus Stand

Historical Archives

Boating Pond State Museum

Pond

RESTAURANTS
A. Delhi Durbar
B. Tandoor
C. Vihar
D. Venite
E. Annapurna
F. Kamat's
G. Rosoyo
H. Sher-e-Punjab
I. A Pastelaria
J. Goenchin
K. Chunghwa

Airport (29km), Vasco Da Gama & Margao ▽

Panjim

The Dominicans founded a college here in 1584, and convents and *hidalgos'* (nobleman's) houses sprang up in the seventeenth century, but Panjim remained little more than a scruffy colonial outpost of sailors and Kunbi fishing families until the lethal malaria epidemic of 1759. Leaving Old Goa to the mosquitoes, the then Governor converted Panjim's waterfront Muslim palace into a splendid residence, and during the early nineteenth century the town eventually eclipsed its predecessor upriver. Governor **Dom Manuel Port'e Castro** (1826–35), dubbed Panjim's "Founding Father", was largely responsible; he initiated the large-scale land drainage and construction project when the town acquired most of its grand civic buildings, squares, schools and roads. **Nova Goa**, as it was then known, became the territory's capital in 1843. Given its (more politically correct) Mahathi name, **Panaji**, in 1961, the city expanded rapidly after Independence, yet never reached the unmanageable proportions of other Indian state capitals: compared with Bombay or Bangalore, its uncongested streets today seem easy-going and pleasantly parochial.

Arrival

European charter planes and domestic flights from Bombay, Bangalore, Cochin, Delhi, Madras and Trivandrum arrive at Goa's **Dabolim airport**, 29km south of Panjim on the outskirts of Vasco da Gama. Pre-paid taxis into town from here (45min; Rs270), booked at the counter immediately outside the arrivals hall, can be shared by up to five people. *Kadamba* transfer buses (Rs20) meet *Indian Airlines* domestic flights, dropping passengers at the main bus stand and outside the *Indian Airlines* office on Dr D Bandodkar Road, in the northwest of town. The least expensive way to get from the airport is to walk to the roundabout on the nearby main road (turn left out of the terminal building), and pick up a local bus into Panjim – more hassle than it's worth if you're weighed down with luggage.

Dabolim airport is featured on p.160.

Long-distance government **buses** pull into Panjim at the town's busy *Kadamba* bus terminal, 1km east of the centre in the district of Pato; private interstate buses arrive a short way further north at the new stand under the Mandovi road bridge. It takes around ten minutes to walk from here across Ourem Creek to Fontainhas, where there are several budget hotels. If you plan to stay in the more modern west end of town, flag down a motorcycle taxi or jump into an auto-rickshaw at the rank outside the *Kadamba* station concourse.

Local buses from Calangute, Baga, Anjuna, Chapora, Mapusa, Margao and Vasco also arrive at the *Kadamba* interstate bus stand. Destinations are written above the relevant platform and called out with machine-gun rapidity by conductors.

Tours and cruises

GTDC and several private companies run a range of **bus tours** around the state. Pitched primarily at domestic visitors, they tend to be conducted at breakneck pace, cramming a dozen or so stops into a long day and leaving you far too little time to enjoy the sights. The only one really worth considering is the two-day "Dudhsagar Special", which covers Old Goa, several temples, Bondla and the Dudhsagar falls, with an overnight stay at Molem (daily; depart 10am, return 6pm the next day; Rs300). For booking and information, go the GTDC *Tourist Hostel*, near the Secretariat (☎0832/227103), or the GTDC *Tourist Home* in Pato (☎0832/45715) – the main departure point.

A good way to while away an idle hour is an evening **river cruise** along the Mandovi. GTDC runs two return trips every day from the old fishing jetty, directly beneath the Mandovi road bridge: the first at 6pm, and the second at 7.15pm. Aim for the earlier one, as it usually catches the last of the sunset. Snacks and drinks are available, and the Rs55 price includes a display of Konkani and Portuguese dance accompanied by folk singers in traditional Goan costume, and sometimes a live Hindi cover band. Two-hour "Full Moon" cruises also leave daily at 8.30pm, regardless of the lunar phase. Operating in direct competition to GTDC are *Emerald Waters'* cruises from the quay outside the *Hotel Mandovi*. In addition to evening departures (daily depart 5.45pm, 7pm, 8.15pm & 9.30pm; Rs100), also with live folk music and dance, and a bar, they offer longer sightseeing trips during the day. The "Rome of the Orient Special" (Mon, Wed, Thurs & Sat depart 1pm, return 5pm; Rs150) heads up the Mandovi River to Old Goa via Ribandar, with a guided tour of the monuments and free cocktails. Another cruise sails across Mormugao Harbour to Grande Island (Sun depart 10am, return 5pm; Rs600), where the launch pulls in for a few hours of swimming on a deserted beach. Finally, the "Backwater Cruise" (Tues depart 10am, return 5pm; Rs500) takes you upriver from Old Goa and down the Cambarjua Canal to the rarely visited St Estevam Island.

Bookings for the GTDC cruises can be made through their agents, *Goa Sea Travels*, opposite the *Tourist Hostel*. *Emerald Waters'* ticket counter is opposite the *Mandovi Hotel*. Alternatively, buy your ticket at the counters behind the jetty, underneath the Mandovi bridge.

Information

The Government of Goa's handy **information** counter, inside the concourse at the main *Kadamba* bus stand (Mon–Sat 9–11.30am & 1.30–5pm, Sun 9am–2pm; ☎0832/232169), keeps lists of all train and interstate bus timings, and can help you find accommodation. The equally efficient Indian Government **tourist office** is across town on Church Square (Mon–Fri 9.30am–6pm, Sat 9.30am–1pm; ☎0832/223412). Alternatively, try Goa Tourism's information desk inside the reception of the GTDC *Tourist Home* hotel in Pato (☎0832/45715 or 47972), on the east side of Ourem Creek near the bus stand. All three sell good state **maps** (Rs7) that are invaluable if you plan to do any motorcycling.

City transport

The most convenient way of **getting around** Panjim is by **auto-rickshaw**, with virtually no journey within the city costing more than around Rs15; either flag one down at the roadside or head for one of the ranks dotted around the city (see map). Even cheaper are motorcycle taxis (aka "pilots"), distinguished by their yellow mudguards; the fare from the *Kadamba* bus stand to Fontainhas is Rs10.

The only city **buses** likely to be of use to visitors run to Dona Paula from the main bus stand, via several stops along the esplanade (including the Secretariat) and Miramar beachfront; the journey from the centre out to Dona Paula costs Rs5. If you feel up to taking on Panjim's anarchic traffic, rent a **bicycle** by the hour (Mon–Sat only) from the stall up the lane opposite the GPO, or from the *Daud M Agar* bike shop, in front of the National Theatre (see map).

More information on local transport in Goa appears in Basics on p.31.

Cars with drivers are available for local sightseeing through GTDC, Trionora Apartments, Dr Alvares Costa Rd (☎0832/226515), or the India Government tourist office on Church Square, from Rs370–550 for a halfday (4hr) and Rs545–950 for a full day (8hr), or Rs4.30–9.50/km for longer hauls. **Self-drive** is available for around Rs600 for 24 hours from *Budget Rent-a-Car*, c/o *Sai Service*, Mapusa Rd, Porvorim, on the north side of Mandovi bridge (☎0832/217755).

Accommodation

The town centre is well stocked with **accommodation**, and finding a place to stay is only a problem during the festival of St Francis (November 24–December 3), and during peak season (from mid-December to mid-January), when tariffs double. At other times, hotels try to fill rooms by offering substantial discounts. The best inexpensive options are in Fontainhas, down by Ourem Creek, and in the back streets behind the esplanade. Standards are generally good, and even the cheapest rooms should have a window, a fan, running water and clean sheets. The rest of the hotels are mostly bland places in the more modern, west end of town.

Note that **check-out times** in Panjim vary wildly. Find out what yours is as soon as you arrive, or your hard-earned lie-in could end up costing you an extra day's room rent. All the hotels below are keyed to the map on pp.62–63.

Inexpensive

Alfonso, St Sebastian Chapel Square, Fontainhas; ☎0832/222359. Modest, old-fashioned family house in a picturesque backstreet, with large, mostly en-suite rooms and some self-catering facilities. Pleasant enough but a little overpriced, and unsociable 8am check-out. Single occupancy rates available. ⑤.

GTDC Tourist Home, around the corner from the bus stand, Pato; ☎0832/227972. Government-run hostel with dowdy dormitories and double rooms – fine for a night if you can't face hunting around town. Also does limited money-changing. ①–③.

Guimaka, near *Ashok Samrat* cinema; ☎0832/22369. No-frills guesthouse in the centre of the shopping district. Attached or non-attached rooms, and a relaxing courtyard. ②–③.

Mandovi Pearl, PO Box 329, behind GTDC *Tourist Hostel*; ☎0832/43928. Idiosyncratic lodge, close to the riverfront, run by a garrulous landlord for salesmen and budget travellers. The rooms are roughish but reasonably good value. ④.

Orav's, 31 Janeiro Rd; ☎0832/46128. Modern building in the old quarter, with good-sized, comfortable rooms and small balconies on front side overlooking the rooftops. ④.

Park Lane Lodge, near Chapel of St Sebastian; ☎0832/220238 or 227154. Spotless and characterful but cramped family guesthouse in old colonial style house. Pepper and coffee plants add atmosphere to a narrow communal terrace, and there's a TV lounge upstairs; also safe deposit facilities and good off-season discounts. Recommended. ④.

Republica, near GTDC *Tourist Hostel*; ☎0832/224630. Rock-bottom budget travellers' lodge with fairly clean rooms, attached shower-toilets and river views from a large wooden verandah. ④.

Moderate

Aroma, Cunha Rivara Rd; ☎0832/43519 or 228308–12, fax 224330. Very central and long-established hotel with a popular *tandoori* restaurant. Some rooms look onto Church Square. ④–⑤.

Caritas Holiday Home, south of the Caculo Island intersection, St Inez; ☎0832/220496, fax 220921. Shiny new place west of the town centre (near the museum), with spotless rooms but little character. ④.

Garden View, opposite Municipal Gardens; ☎0832/47844, fax 44168. Large, modern, impeccably clean and well-managed hotel. The more expensive front rooms overlook the square. Some a/c. Good value. ④–⑥.

GTDC Tourist Hostel, Avda Dom Joao Castro; ☎0832/223396. Very popular government-run hotel overlooking a busy thoroughfare and the river. The rooms are large and pleasant enough but no longer the bargain they used to be. Shops, a hair salon and tourist information in the lobby. ④–⑤.

Mayfair and **Rohma**, Dr Dada Vaidhya Rd; ☎0832/223317 or 230453. *Rohma* is the pricier and more comfortable of this popular pair of central, jointly managed hotels, pitched at middle class Indian tourists and business-men. ④–⑤.

Palacio de Goa, Gama Pinto Rd; ☎0832/221785 or 221786. Kitsch, five-storey Neoclassical facade and pleasant but plain rooms, with satellite TV, balconies and a recently revamped non-veg restaurant. ⑤.

Panjim Inn, E-212, 31 Janeiro Rd, Fontainhas; ☎0832/226523, fax 228136. Grand old Portuguese town house, now managed as an upmarket but homely hotel, with period furniture, individual balconies and a common verandah. An equally beautiful Hindu house across the road, recently acquired and renovated by the same owner, promises more of the same, with the added bonus of a leafy courtyard. Easily the best place in its class. ⑤–⑥.

Park Plaza, Azad Maidan; ☎0832/222601–5, fax 225635. A new hotel on a quiet square near the river. Close to the commercial centre, with all the usual amenities, including a restaurant, and courteous staff. ④–⑥.

Rajdhani, Dr Atmaram Borkar Rd; ☎0832/225362. Central, efficient and clean, with ceramic tile floors, single occupancy rates, and a good vegetarian restaurant downstairs. ⑤–⑥.

Expensive

Fidalgo, 18 June Rd; ☎0832/226291–9, fax 225061. Large, well-established place with all mod cons, including a pool, central a/c, money exchange, *Star TV* in all rooms, a health club, shopping arcade and an in-house travel agent. ⑧.

Mandovi, Dr D Bandodkar Rd; ☎0832/224405–9, fax 225451. Grand waterside hotel with river views from front rooms, central a/c, shops, in-house travel agent and a pool. The best in this category. ⑨.

Nova Goa, Dr Atmaram Borkar Rd; ☎0832/226231, fax 224958. Panjim's newest and least expensive top hotel. In the heart of the shopping area and with the usual comforts, plus bath tubs and a pool. ⑧.

The Town

Until recently, most visitors' first glimpse of Panjim was from the decks of the old Bombay steamer as it chugged into dock at the now-defunct ferry ramp. These days, however, despite the recent inauguration of the Konkan railway, and catamaran service from Bombay, the town is most usually approached by road – from the north via the huge ferro-concrete bridge that spans the Mandovi estuary, or from the south on the recently revamped NH7, which links the capital with the airport and railhead at Vasco da Gama. Either way, you'll have to pass through the suburb of **Pato**, home of the main *Kadamba* bus terminal, before crossing Ourem Creek to arrive in Panjim proper. West of **Fontainhas**, the picturesque Portuguese quarter, lies the commercial centre's grid of long straight streets fanning out west from Panjim's principal landmark, **Church Square**. Further north, the main thoroughfare, **Avenida Dom Joao Castro**, sweeps past the post office and **Secretariat** building before bending west along the waterfront towards the nearby beach resort of Miramar.

Panjim's few conventional sights are all grouped in the east end of town. A good route stringing them together heads along the esplanade from the Secretariat to the Menezes Braganza Institute, and then south to Church Square via Azad Maidan, winding up with an amble through the old quarters.

Church Square

The leafy rectangular park opposite the Government of India tourist office, known as **Church Square** or the **Municipal Garden**, forms the heart of Panjim. Originally called the Jardim de Garcia da Orta, after a famous sixteenth-century physician, it used to harbour a bust of

Portuguese explorer Vasco da Gama that was pulled down after Independence and replaced with India's national emblem: three Ashokean lions mounted on an abacus decorated with a wheel, symbolizing "strength and unity in diversity".

Presiding over the east side of the square is Panjim's most distinctive and photogenic landmark, the toothpaste-white Baroque facade of the **Church of Our Lady of the Immaculate Conception**. Standing at the head of a criss-crossing laterite walkway, between rows of slender palm trees, it was built in 1541, when the town was no more than a swamp-ridden fishing village, for the benefit of sailors arriving here from Lisbon. The weary mariners would stagger up from the quay to give thanks for their safe passage before proceeding to the capital at Old Goa – the original home of the enormous bell that hangs from the central gable. The second largest in the state, this was salvaged from the ruins of the Monastery of St Augustus on Holy Hill and installed here in a specially enlarged belfry, erected in 1871 at the same time as the steps.

Our Lady of the Immaculate Conception is open Mon–Sat 9am–1pm & 3.30–6pm, Sun 10.30am–1pm & 6.15–7pm.

The **interior** of the church is dominated by a splendid gilt **reredos** dedicated to Our Lady. On feast days, the original beams of the vaulted ceiling above it are festooned with strings of blue and white flowers to match the outside of the church.

For more on the ruins of the Monastery of St Augustus, see p.93.

North of Church Square

The road that runs north from the church brings you out at the riverside near Panjim's oldest surviving building. With its sloping tiled roofs, carved-stone coats of arms and wooden verandahs, the stalwart **Secretariat** looks typically colonial. Yet it was originally the summer palace of Goa's sixteenth-century Muslim ruler, the 'Adil Shah. Fortified with 55 cannons and a salt-water moat, its defences did not, however, deter the Portuguese. In 1510, Albuquerque's troops stormed the building, then converted it into a temporary rest house for the territory's governors, who used to overnight here en route to and from Europe. Following the viceroy's move from Old Goa in 1759, the palace, by this time known as the **Idalcaon's Palace** (from *Adil Khan*, a Portuguese corruption of 'Adil Shah), became the official viceregal residence, which it remained until the completion of the even grander mansion at Cabo, near Vasco da Gama, in 1918. Today, the Secretariat is the home of the Goan State Legislature, which explains the presence of so many shiny chauffeur-driven Ambassador cars, and the armed guards at the door. Plans are afoot, however, to move the secretariat across the river to Porvorim, and open this building to the general public as a museum.

One place you won't be prevented from visiting if you call in during office hours is the **Menezes Braganza Institute**, now the town's Central Library. Panjim's most impressive example of secular civic architecture stands behind the esplanade, 1km west of the Secretariat past the **Abbé de Faria statue** (see box on p.71). Among

The Menezes Braganza Institute is open Mon–Fri 9.30am–1.15pm & 2–5.30pm.

the colonial leftovers worth checking here are the panels of blue-and-yellow-painted ceramic tiles, known as **azulejos**, lining the lobby of the west (Malacca Road) entrance. These larger-than-life illustrations depict scenes from **Luis Vaz Camoes'** epic poem, *Os Luisiades*. The tone of the tableaux is intentionally patriotic (valiant Portuguese explorers being tossed on stormy seas and a nobleman standing defiantly before a dark-faced Indian sultan), but the tale was, in fact, intended as an invective *against* the Portuguese discoveries, which Camões rightly believed was milking his mother country dry and leaving its crown easy prey for the old enemy, Spain. In the **Antonio de Doronho Art Gallery** upstairs (same opening hours), you'll find another relic of the Portuguese era: a large Italian-style table used by the dreaded Inquisitors of Old Goa. It's displayed alongside other pieces of ornately carved antique furniture, coins and paintings by Goan artists.

For an account of the state archeological museum, see p.72.

Immediately south of the library building lies the parched grass square of **Azad Maidan**, fringed by tall trees and centred by a weed-choked pavilion of Corinthian pillars salvaged from the rubble of Old Goa. Built in 1847 to protect the huge brass statue of Alfonso de Albuquerque (now housed in the state archeological museum), the pavilion was made into a memorial to Goan freedom fighter Dr Tristão de Braganza Cunha after Independence.

Just west of the Secretariat stands Panjim's most striking statue. Glaring fixedly down from his pedestal, a long-haired, haggard-faced man is bent with his hands stretched over the supine body of a curvaceous woman, unconscious at his feet. Contrary to appearances, this peculiar portrait is not a scene from some lascivious nineteenth-century melodrama, but a memorial to one of Goa's more illustrious sons, the **Abbé de Faria** – priest, revolutionary, and the founding father of modern hypnotism (see box opposite).

Fontainhas and Sao Tomé

Panjim's oldest and most interesting district, **Fontainhas**, lies immediately west of Pato, overlooking the banks of the oily green Ourem Creek. The district, or ward (*vaddo*), was laid out on land reclaimed during the late eighteenth century by a Goan expatriate known as "the Mossmikar" because he had amassed his fortune in the African colony of Mozambique. From the footbridge that cuts between the bus stand and town centre, a dozen or so blocks of Neoclassical houses rise in a tangle of terracotta rooftops up the sides of **Altinho Hill**. Many have retained their traditional coat of ochre, pale yellow, green or blue – a legacy of the Portuguese insistence that every Goan building (except churches, which had to be kept white) should be colour-washed after the monsoons.

Altinho Hill may be climbed by following the steps up the alley next to Park Lane Lodge, which brings you to a great viewpoint over the city.

At the southern end of the neighbourhood, the pristine white-washed **Chapel of St Sebastian** is one of many Goan *igrejas* to remain faithful to the old colonial decree. It stands at the end of a

Abbé de Faria

José Custodio de Faria was born in Candolim, Bardez (see p.121), on May 20, 1756, the son of a down-at-heel seminarian and a local landowner's daughter. When this marriage ended in 1771, José's mother ran off to a nunnery, and his father took him to Lisbon, where the pair soon gained the patronage of the king, Dom José I. Faria senior eventually rose to become confessor to the king's daughter but fell out of favour in 1779, accused of whipping up sedition among Goan expats in Lisbon. José, too, was linked with the rebels and fled for Paris soon after.

While in the French capital, Faria developed an interest in the occult science of *magnétism*, or hypnosis. Aided by his exotic dark skin, ascetic dress and Goan-Brahmin credentials, the young priest started up a course in a school hall on the rue Clichy, attracting a large and predominantly female following; his "performances" enraged the clergy and scientific establishment, who spread rumours that Faria was taking advantage of his women students and patients. The final straw came when Jules Verne published a scathingly satirical play based on the Abbé's experiments and ruined his reputation. Faria died penniless in 1819 on the very day his now famous treatise on hypnosis, *De la cause du sommeil lucide* (On the Causes of Lucid Sleep), was published.

Faria's was the first to insist hypnotic trances were not produced by body fluids, but by suggestion, which opened up the notion of the unconscious mind. Largely forgotten in both Paris and his native Goa, his memory is most vividly preserved in Alexander Dumas' novel, *The Count of Monte Cristo*, in which he appears as a mad monk rotting away in the dungeons of the Château d'If off the coast of Marseille.

small square where Fontainhas' Portuguese-speaking locals hold a lively annual street *festa* to celebrate the Feast of Our Lady of Livrament in mid-November. The eerily lifelike crucifix inside the chapel formerly hung in the Palace of the Inquisition in Old Goa. Unusually, Christ's eyes are open – allegedly to inspire fear in those being interrogated by the Inquisitors. It was brought to Panjim in 1812, after the Inquisition had been suppressed in Goa, and installed in the 'Adil Shah's palace, finally coming to rest here a little over a century later when the viceroys had decamped to Cabo.

Sao Tomé ward is the other old quarter, lying north of Fontainhas on the far side of Emilio Gracia Road. This is the area to head for if you fancy a bar crawl: the narrow streets are dotted with dozens of hole-in-the-wall taverns, serving stiff measures of rocket-fuel *feni* under strip lights and the watchful gaze of colourful Madonnas. Drinks are cheap in these places, but you'll probably feel less conspicuous in the neighbourhood's best known hostelry, the *Hotel Venite* (see p.74), at the north end of 31 Janeiro Road.

South of Church Square

South of Church Square, the only landmark in a featureless jumble of concrete is the multicoloured **Mahalakshmi temple**, dating from the early eighteenth century and the first Hindu shrine established in Panjim during Portuguese rule. Behind it, a flight of stone steps climbs through shady woods to the top of **Altinho Hill**, where the grandest of Panjim's old colonial houses languish in overgrown gardens. Among the few not suffering from terminal neglect is the **Bishop's Palace**, where the Pope stayed during his 1989 visit to Goa. Its owners have clearly deemed it holy enough to merit a coat of whitewash.

The museum

Panjim's museum is open Tues–Sat 9.30am–1.15pm & 2–5.30pm.

Panjim's **state archeological museum** occupies a purpose-built complex on the east edge of town, a stone's throw southwest of the *Kadamba* bus stand. The collection consists mostly of pre-colonial artefacts, including village deities, *puja* utensils, a handful of *sati* and hero stones, fragments of temple sculpture and some fine **Jain bronzes** rescued by Customs and Excise officers from smugglers. Also of interest are the Christian icons and pieces of antique furniture displayed in a gallery devoted to **Western art**, and a series of **photographs** taken by a Portuguese colonial official around the turn of the century; among these are striking portraits of the contemporary rebel Rajput leader Dada Rane, and his heavily armed band of Goan freedom fighters.

Eating and drinking

Panjim is packed with good **places to eat**. Most are connected to a hotel (the *Hotel Venite* restaurant is the most popular with foreigners), but there are also plenty of smaller, family-run establishments tucked away in the backstreets of Sao Tomé, where a plate of fish curry and rice and a cold bottle of Kingfisher will set you back less than Rs50; vegetarians will do better at the numerous South Indian-style cafeterias that have sprung up in recent years. Two of these, the *Satkar* and the *Kamat*, open at around 7am for blow-out **breakfasts** – great if you have just staggered into town after an all-night bus journey. Beer, *feni* and other spirits are available in all but the purest "pure veg" places.

All cafés and restaurants are keyed to the map on pp.62–63.

A Pasteleria, Dr Dada Vaidya Rd. Panjim's best bakery does dozens of Western-style cakes, cookies and sticky buns, including brownies and fruit loaves. Takeaway only. Moderate.

Annapurna, Ormuz Rd. Traditional inexpensive South Indian *thalis* and snacks dished up by cotton-clad waiters in a large, clean, cool first-floor dining hall.

Chunghwa, *Hotel Samrat*, Dr Dada Vaidya Rd; ☎0832/224318. Authentic, upscale Cantonese restaurant with a/c, attentive service and a wide selection of moderately priced seafood, meat and veg dishes.

Delhi Durbar, behind the *Hotel Mandovi*. A provincial branch of the famous Bombay restaurant, and the best place in Panjim to sample traditional Mughlai

Carnival

Panjim's chaotic three-day **Carnival**, held during late February and early March, is the state's most famous festival. Introduced by the Portuguese as a means to let off steam before Lent, it has been celebrated with gusto in Goa since the eighteenth century, and now draws tens of thousands from around India and abroad. In recent years, however, the colourful parade forming its centrepiece has been the cause of **controversy**, as its organizers are accused of vulgarizing Goan culture for crude commercial gain.

The **origins** of Carnival date back to the hedonistic religious festivals of ancient Greece and Rome. The festival was later exported to the Spanish and Portuguese colonies, where black slaves infused it with a healthy dose of African panache. Known in Konkani as *Intruz* (a corruption of the Portuguese word *Entrudo*, from the Latin *Inroito*, meaning the start of Lent), Goa's carnival was grafted on to an indigenous tradition of local village festivals in which *khells*, or satirical folk plays, were – and still are – performed.

Following the centuries-old model, Panjim's Carnival is kicked off on *Sabato Gordo* (Fat Saturday) by the entry into the town of **King Momo**, who reads a decree ordering his subjects to forget their worries and "be happy". This unleashes three days of music, masked dance and general mayhem, accompanied by exuberant cross-dressing, mock battles fought with bags of sawdust or flour and water, known as **cocotes**, and **assaltos** or trick-or-treat-style raids on neighbours' kitchens.

Condemned by the Goan government as "colonial", the festivities were suspended following Independence but lately have enjoyed something of a revival, spurred on by injections of funds from local businesses, national liquor and cigarette manufacturers, and five-star hotel chains. Such **commercialism** angers many Goans, who claim it runs counter to the spirit of Carnival, which traditionally inverts and satirizes the prevailing power structures. Worse still, in many people's eyes, is the gradual **vulgarization** of the event, which has become closely associated in the popular Indian imagination with licentious behaviour, particularly among local women. The prime propagator of this myth are lurid feature films of the Hindi cinema that regularly include scenes of seduction and sexual intrigue set against a Goan Carnival backdrop. Nor, according to one Goan women's group, have such misconceptions been dispelled by official Carnival publicity, which actively promotes such unrepresentative images of women.

Over the past four or five years, other pressures have somewhat diminished the colours of Carnival, which has seen a marked decline in popularity. Foremost among these was the Church's pronouncement of 1993 that Catholic girls should not take part in the main parades. A ban on alcohol use by all participants rendered the processions even more lacklustre, as has the Municipality's insistence that floats should illustrate worthy, but essentially dull, themes, such as 1996's "Health For All By The Year 2000" – hardly a party winner.

In spite of the controversy, the main Saturday parade continues to draw large numbers of revellers to the Goan capital, while Goans all over the state avidly watch the event on television. However, if you plan to come to Panjim yourself, travel here for the day only, as hotels tend to be fully booked weeks in advance. It's also a good idea to bring plenty of film, and expect to get plastered in paint and sludge, hurled in balloon bombs by gangs of rowdy teenagers.

cuisine of mainly meat steeped in rich, spicy sauces. Patronized by an expense-account crowd, but you can eat well here for under Rs150.

Goenchin, off Dr Dada Vaidhya Rd. Glacial a/c and dim lighting, but unquestionably the best and most authentic Chinese food to be found in Goa. Expensive.

Kamat's, near Government Tourist Office, Municipal Gardens, 31 Janeiro Rd. Busy Indian fast-food cafeteria with formica booths and barefoot waiters. Their filling South Indian *thalis* consist of six dishes (including some delicious coconut-flavoured local specialities), or you can order piping hot *puri bhajis*, *dosas*, *wadas* and other snacks.

Nandan, ground floor of *Rajdhani* hotel, Dr Atmaram Borkar Rd. The classiest *thali* joint in town, with comfortable upholstered furniture and a/c. They offer a choice of Gujarati, Punjabi, South Indian or Chinese meals – all pure vegetarian.

Sher-e-Punjab, 18 June Rd, near the *Satkar*. North Indian food served up in a crowded city-centre restaurant. Their speciality – butter chicken – is delicious, and there's a reasonable veg menu.

Tandoor, *Hotel Aroma*, Cunha Rivara Rd. Inexpensive first-floor restaurant, overlooking the main square and serving the town's best *tandoori* meat and fish, with some veg and Chinese alternatives.

Venite, 31 Janeiro Rd. Deservedly popular hotel restaurant, serving great fresh seafood, including affordable lobster and crab, along with Western dishes, desserts, *feni* and cold beers. Wooden floors, balcony seats, candles and an eclectic cassette collection add to the ambience. Good breakfasts, too. Closed Sun.

Vihar, around the corner from *Venite*, on Avenida Dom Joao Castro. Spotlessly clean, bustling South Indian snack bar-cum-*thali* joint, offering cheap, freshly cooked food to a mixed clientele of middle-class domestic tourists and budget travellers. The best option if you're hankering for a real *masala dosa* or can't afford the *Venite*.

Listings

Airlines *Air India*, *Hotel Fidalgo*, 18 June Rd (☎0832/224081); *British Airways*, 2 Excelsior Chambers, MG Rd (☎ & fax 0832/228681); *Skyline NEPC* (also for *Gulf Air*, *Air France* and *Air Canada*), Bernard Guedes Rd (☎0832/220056); *Indian Airlines*, Dempo Building, Dr D Bandodkar Rd (☎0832/223831); *Jet*, Rizvi Chambers, office no. 102, Caetano Albuquerque Rd (☎0832/221476); *KLM* (also *PIA*), 18 June Rd, near *Titan* showroom (☎0832/226678).

American Express *Menezes Air Travel*, Rua de Ourem, near Pato Bridge (☎ & fax 0832/225081).

Banks Foreign exchange facilities include the *State Bank of India*, opposite the *Hotel Mandovi*, Avda Dom Joao Castro; the *Bank of Baroda* (where you can draw money on *Visa* cards), Azad Maidan; the *Andhra Bank*, opposite the *Ashok Samrat* cinema (also good for *Visa*); and the *Corporation Bank* on Church Square, around the corner from the government tourist office. The *Pheroze Framroze & Co Exchange Bureau*, Room 119, *Hotel Fidalgo*, 18 June Rd (Mon–Sat 9.30am–7pm, Sun 9.30am–1pm), also changes currency and travellers' cheques at standard bank rates, as does *Wall Street Finances*

Ltd on Dr Shirogoankar Road (Mon–Sat 9am–6pm), near the *Hotel Fidalgo*. Finally, *Thomas Cook* is out near the *Indian Airlines* office, at 8 Alcon Chambers, Devanand Bandodkar Rd (Mon–Sat 9am–6pm, and on Sun from Oct–March 10am–5pm; ☎0832/221312, fax 221313). In addition to the usual exchange facilities, this place also specializes in fast **international money transfers**.

Books The bookshops in both the *Hotel Fidalgo* and the *Hotel Mandovi* stock a reasonable range of English-language fiction in paperback, plus a selection of special interest titles and coffee-table tomes on Goa.

Hospital The region's largest hospital, the Goa Medical College, is 12km south of town on the Vasco road. For an ambulance, call ☎0832/46300 or 44566.

Laundry The hole-in-the-wall laundry on the south side of Pato Road, between the bus stand and Pato bridge (Mon–Sat 9.30am–8.30pm), cleans clothes within 24hr. The only place open on a Sunday is the pricey dry cleaner's in GTDC's *Tourist Hostel* on Avda Dom Joao Castro.

Music and dance Regular recitals of classical Indian music and dance are held at Panjim's school for the performing arts, the Kala Academy in Campal, at the far west end of town on Devanand Bandodkar Road. For details of forthcoming events, consult the boards in front of the auditorium or the listings page of local newspapers. The best place to shop for cassettes and CDs, both Indian and Western, is *VP Sinari's*, which has two branches: one opposite the Secretariat, and the other near the *Bombay Bazaar* mall on 18 June Rd. The *Kalpatru* music store, off the Calculo intersection at the west end of 18 June Rd, is also well stocked. For musical instruments, including excellent value Hoffner and Gibson copy guitars, mandolins and cases, as well as tabla, sitar and hand drums, call at *Pedro Fernandes & Cia*, 19 Avda Dom Joao Castro, next door to the *Vihar* restaurant, near the post office.

Pharmacies *Hindu Pharma* (☎0832/223176), near the tourist office on Church Square, stocks Ayurvedic, homeopathic and allopathic medicines. Alternatively, try *F Menezes*, opposite *Benetton*, on Avda Dom Joao Castro.

Police The Police Headquarters is on Malaca Rd, central Panjim. In emergencies, call ☎100.

Poste restante Panjim's reliable **poste restante** counter (Mon–Sat 9.30am–1pm & 2–5.30pm) is next door to the **GPO**, 200m west of Pato Bridge. Note that to get your stamps franked (the only way to ensure they won't get peeled off and resold by some unscrupulous clerk), you have to walk around the back of the building and ask at the office behind the second door on the right.

Travel agents *AERO Mundial*, Ground Floor, *Hotel Mandovi*, Dr D Bandodkar Rd (☎0832/223773); *Menezes Air Travel*, Rua de Ourem (☎ & fax 0832/222214); *TPH Travel*, Ground Floor, Padmavati Towers, 18 June Rd (☎0832/235365); *UVI Holidays*, Diamond Chambers, 18 June Rd (☎0832/226928, fax 223891); and *Rauraje Deshprabhu*, Cunha Rivara Rd (☎0832/221840). For air and *Damania* catamaran tickets, try *MGM International*, Mamai Camotim Building (near Secretariat), or *Tradewings Ltd*, Mascarenhas Buildings (near *Jolly Shoes*), Dr Akmaram Borkar Rd (☎0832/22243).

Visa extensions The Foreigners' Registration Office is at Police Headquarters (Mon–Fri 9.30am–1pm; ☎0832/226545).

Travelling to Mumbai (Bombay)

By far the quickest and most convenient way of **travelling to Mumbai (Bombay)** from Goa is to fly. *Indian Airlines, Skyline NEPC* and *Jet* operate scheduled flights from Dabolim airport (see p.160) to Bombay-Santa Cruz, costing between Rs1750 and Rs2100 one-way (or up to Rs2300/$76 if you purchase the ticket overseas – see p.13). The trip takes around an hour. Tickets can be hard to come by, so book as far in advance as possible through any of the travel agents listed above, or with the airline itself. If you already have a ticket, bear in mind domestic airlines require you to re-confirm your seat seventy-two hours before departure. Fail to do this, and you could well find yourself at the end of a long waiting list.

Until the imminent completion of the Konkan Railway (see below), *Damania Shipping*'s **catamaran** service, running between October and May, is the next best alternative to flying. Taking eight hours to reach Bombay, the Scandanavian-built vessel is new, fast and well fitted with aeroplane-style reclining seats, but affords a less-than-comfortable journey; even passengers with proven sea legs can find the sealed-in, glacially cold air-conditioned cabins a trial. Economy-class tickets on the lower deck cost Rs1100, and are available through *Damania*'s office in Panjim's fisheries building (☎0832/228711–4), on the riverfront near the *State Bank of India*, and through most reputable travel agents.

It is unlikely that the catamaran will be able hold its own against the **Konkan Railway**, which, when it's fully operational, will slash train travelling time between Goa and the Maharashtran capital from twenty-four to seven hours. When this book was researched, only one train per day covered the 640-km route, but if everything goes to plan, four more daily services will be added by the winter of 1997–8. With tickets costing a mere Rs178 in second class (or Rs559 for 2nd class with air conditioning), it's hard to see why anyone would want to take the catamaran or bus. The Konkan Railway company has also bought brand new rolling stock, so the carriages themselves are a lot cleaner and more comfortable than regular Indian Railways' trains. The one drawback is that the service terminates in the inconveniently situated Kurla station, in the north of Bombay, where you have to change on to an overground train for Victoria Terminus (VT), or catch a cab. **Reservations** should be made well in advance at Vasco or Margao train stations, or better still at the Konkan Railway Company's computerized booking office on the first floor of the *Kadamba* bus stand in Panjim (daily 9am–1pm & 3–5.30pm; ☎0832/512398).

Miramar

Panjim's esplanade continues west through the swish suburb of Campal, with its grand colonial residences (and their modern concrete counterparts), before swinging south towards the beach at **MIRAMAR**. If this were anywhere else but Goa, you might be tempted to spend an afternoon here, enjoying two kilometres of dark sand and views across Aguada Bay. As it is, the beach's noisy bus parties and over-zealous peanut *wallahs* make it far less attractive than most of the other resorts in easy reach of the capital. If all you want is a quick escape from Panjim to watch the sunset, however, the south end of Miramar beach, fifteen minutes' walk from the bus park, is fine. At this time of day, the only people you see are fishermen fixing their nets under the palm trees, and the odd café owner staring hopefully up the beach from an empty terrace.

Should you choose to **stay** in Miramar, the best option, by far, is GTDC's *Beach Resort* (☎0832/227754; ④), a campus of double-storey chalets set in a sandy garden directly behind the beach. The rooms are spacious, breezy and clean, and very good value if you don't mind being so far out of Panjim. A short way back up the main road towards Panjim, tucked down a suburban backstreet, the **youth hostel** (☎0832/225432; ①) offers much cheaper accommodation. Its rock-bottom dormitories are large, but get horrendously cramped and stuffy when there's a big block-booking of students.

Buses to Miramar leave every fifteen minutes from Panjim's *Kadamba* stand. You can also pick them up from the steamer jetty north of Church Square, and at various points along the waterfront. Travelling in the other direction, they stop just off Miramar's main roundabout, in front of the *Beach Resort*.

Dona Paula

Nestled 9km southwest of Panjim on the south side of the rocky, hammer-shaped headland that divides the Zuari and Mandovi estuaries, **DONA PAULA** takes its name from a viceroy's daughter who threw herself off the cliff here when refused permission to marry a local fisherman. Today, the views from the top of the peninsula over Miramar beach and Mormugao Bay are pleasant enough, but the village itself – a swanky suburb and upmarket beach resort – is characterless and commercialized, and not somewhere you'd choose to spend much time unless you're staying in one of the campus hotels that have mushroomed here in recent years.

Due to its proximity to Panjim, Dona Paula is a popular stop on GTDC bus tours of the area and tends to be heaving in season with crowds of visitors. Taking advantage of this transient trade, stalls laden with tasteless T-shirts and "I Love Goa" straw hats line the old fishing jetty, from where a small ferry shuttles across the bay to Mormugao harbour four times a day (20min). There's nothing much to see from the other side, but the trip is great fun, as the rusty old tub pitches and rolls past the container ships and sand dredgers moored at the mouth of the Zuari. The bluff behind Dona Paula's ferry jetty is crowned with a mock acropolis, below which stands Baroness von Leistner's whitewashed **sculpture**, *Image of India*, depicting a couple staring wistfully in opposite directions – the man towards the past and the woman to the nation's future.

Crouched on the westernmost tip of the headland, known as **Cabo Raj Bhavan**, is the official residence of the Governor of Goa, Daman and Diu. The site, a viceregal seat since 1918, was originally occupied by a Portuguese fort, erected in 1540 to guard the entrance to Goa harbour, whose cannons crossed fire with those of Aguada to the north and Mormugao to the south. These days, nothing remains of the old citadel. From the road beyond the *Institute of Oceanography*, you can, however, see the ruins of the small military **cemetery** the British built at the time of their brief occupation of the Cabo during the Napoleonic wars – a move intended to deter the French from invading Goa.

For more background on the Napoleonic wars in Goa, see "History" in Contexts on p.233.

Practicalities

Regular **buses** run from Panjim to Dona Paula until around 9pm, dropping passengers at the roundabout below the *Institute of Oceanography*, where you can usually pick up an auto-rickshaw into town. Mini-van **taxis** hang around outside the four main resort **hotels**, situated along the road to the jetty and 1km further east in the once sleepy hamlet of **Vainguinim**, where you'll find the five-star *Cidade de Goa* (☎0832/5221133, fax 223303; ⑧). With its two pools, shopping arcades, tennis courts, sauna, gym and watersports facilities, this is the village's premier resort complex. Overlooking a small and relatively inaccessible beach, it's sheltered on one side by a wooded headland, and on the other by an old laterite wall. Behind the *Cidade de Goa*, the more modest *Hotel Villa Sol* (☎0832/225852; ⑥) also has sea-facing air-conditioned rooms, a pool and sun terraces. Dona Paula's two remaining hotels are both on the opposite side of the bay above the jetty, and cater exclusively for package tourists. The secluded *Prainha* (☎0832/227221, fax 229959; ⑥) offers simple but comfortable chalets with balconies, and easy access to a quiet sandy cove to the north. The same is true of the *Dona Paula Beach Resort* (☎0832/227955; ⑥), the least expensive and most tastefully designed of the bunch, with ersatz Portuguese blocks around a central lawn, and some rooms with air conditioning and sea views. All of the places listed above have pricey à la carte **restaurants** that welcome non-residents.

Goa Velha

Blink during the breakneck journey between Panjim and Dabolim airport on the NH17, and you will probably miss **GOA VELHA**. Yet this run-of-the-mill roadside village, strewn across the paddy fields 9km southeast of the capital, was, until the emergence of Ela (Old Goa) during the fifteenth century, southwest India's wealthiest city and busiest port.

Goa Velha

The Procession of the Saints

The Procession of the Third Franciscan Order, better known as the **Procession of the Saints**, is one of the highlights of the state's religious calendar. Borne on the shoulders of local devotees, dozens of life-size effigies of saints, martyrs, popes, kings, queens and cardinals are paraded around the village on the first Monday of Easter week, watched by a huge crowd.

The tradition was instigated in the seventeenth century by the Franciscans as an attempt to reverse the decline in morals afflicting the colony at that time. Once the libertines and ruffians of Old Goa had clapped eyes on such striking symbols of piety and self-sacrifice, they would – or so it was hoped – give up their licentious lifestyles and embrace the teachings of Christ. How many conversions the Franciscans inspired is not recorded, but the event certainly caught on, and by the eighteenth century a total of 65 sumptuously attired statues, encrusted with gold and precious stones, took part in the procession. However, when the religious orders were suppressed in 1835, the event was banned and many statues destroyed. Not until the end of the nineteenth century was it finally revived, using money donated by the Franciscans.

Today, after delivering the Sermon of St Francis in the Church of St Andrew in Goa Velha, a priest orders a heavy black curtain to be drawn back, revealing the assembled effigies for the first time. Mounted on floats, the 26 figures are then carried into the square and around the village by members of **confrades**, "religious brotherhoods" formed out of the medieval trades guilds. Along the way, onlookers duck under the floats to receive the blessings of the saints. In their wake march representatives of the clergy, local villagers, school children chanting rosaries and, finally, members of the Third Franciscan Order. The procession draws to a close with a candle-lit mass outside the church, the statues arranged in a semicircle.

Although the parade itself is essentially a solemn affair, the **fun fair** that accompanies it certainly isn't. Togged out in their Sunday-best *shirtings*, *suitings* and silk dresses, bus loads of visitors descend on Goa Velha for the festival and for a glimpse of the 26 statues, displayed for the two days following the parade in St Andrew's Church.

On the north bank of the Zuari River, lie the remains of ancient **Govapuri**, or Gopakkapttana (later Gova), founded in 1054 by the Kadamba ruler Jayakeshi I. He moved his capital here from Chandrapura – now Chandor in Salcete *taluka* – to exercise more control over the movement of maritime traffic through the busy harbour. Import duties and taxes creamed off this lucrative trade (in Arabian horses, Chinese silks and southeast Asian spices) financed the construction of sumptuous palaces, temples and a well-planned city with its own charitable institutions. The period of prosperity survived two Kadamaba rebellions, brutally put down by their Chalukyan overlords, but not the arrival in Govapuri of the Sultan of Delhi's army in 1312, following which the Goan kings fled back to Chandrapura. Thereafter, the city witnessed a series of bloody sack-

For an account of Chandor, see p.177.

ings as it changed hands between the Muslim Bahmani dynasty and the Hindu Vijayanagars. It was finally left to rot in 1470, after the Zuari River silted up and receded, leaving the harbour high and dry.

Apart from a dusty blue sign commemorating Govapuri, erected on the side of the main road, and a lively **fish market** in the shade of the local bus shelter, there is nothing in Goa Velha likely to tempt you off the main road. The only time the village sees any real action is on the first Monday of Easter week, when its picturesque **Church of St Andrew**, on the main square, hosts the famous **Procession of the Saints** (see box).

Pilar

The **seminary** at **PILAR**, resting on the edge of a thickly wooded hill 12km southeast of Panjim, is one of the two theological colleges that survived out of the four founded by the Portuguese – the other is at **Rachol**. Established by the Capuchins in 1613, it was abandoned after the expulsion of the religious orders in 1835, but restored 22 years later by the Carmelites. Although it boasts a well-preserved seventeenth-century church and a small museum, the seminary, which is now run as a training college for Christian missionaries, makes a less than inspiring tourist destination and most of its visitors come on pilgrimages. However, if you are passing on the nearby NH17, the superb **views** over the Zuari estuary are worth a quick detour. Any of the Panjim–Cortalim–Vasco **buses** will drop you at the turn-off on the main road, from where it is possible to take a short cut through the modern wing of the seminary to a flight of old laterite steps that lead up the hill.

For details of the theological college at Rachol, see p.172.

The **Church of Our Lady of Pilar**, at the bottom of the car park, is entered through a stately whitewashed Baroque facade, whose gable is inscribed with the seminary's foundation date, 1613, picked out in blue. Deeply carved tombstones of Portuguese *hidalgos* line the floor of the entrance porch, which opens onto the **tomb of Father Angelo D'Souza**, head of Pilar seminary from 1918 until 1927, and regarded by Goan Christians as something of a saint. Ranged around a tiny garden, the cloisters inside are decorated with rather clumsily restored seventeenth-century **frescoes**. Look out, too, for a didactic pictorial depiction of the history of the world, drawn by a missionary in the 1940s for the "speedy and easy instruction of Indians, children and uneducated people".

The priming of young Goan priests for this proselytizing work continues in the large 1950s-style college at the top of the hill. Run by the Mission Society of St Francis Xavier, it occupies the site of an ancient Shiva temple, the Goveshwar *mandir*, from which the name Goa is believed to derive. A stone-lined **tank** nearby, which now supplies the seminary orchards, is among the only *in situ* remains of the Kadambas' former capital, Govapuri. Fragments of pottery and temple sculpture unearthed on the site are informatively displayed in a small **museum** on the first floor, along with a couple of palm-leaf manuscripts, a copy of the first Maharathi translation of the Gospels and a life-size model of a benign-faced, white-frocked padre converting an Indian couple in their grass hut.

The first floor of the building houses a **chapel** dominated by a set of stunning stained-glass windows, while the roof terrace a couple of storeys higher up affords fine panoramic views south over the Zuari River towards Vasco, and north across the lush rice fields and palm groves of Tiswadi *taluka*.

The only source of mineral water and snacks in Pilar is the tiny visitors' **café** at the bottom of the car park near the church.

Pilar

The museum of the Mission Society of St Francis Xavier is open daily 10am–5pm.

Talaulim

Lost deep in the heart of Tiswadi *taluka*, the ramshackle hamlet of **TALAULIM**, 4km north of Pilar, would feature on few maps were it not for the enormous **Church of St Anne** (Santana) that looms from its midst. Boasting arguably the most spectacular church facade outside Old Goa, it is fiendishly difficult to get to without your own transport, as **buses** from the capital are few and far between. With a car or motorcycle, however, you can tie Talaulim into a neat loop with Old Goa, Pilar and Panjim, 7km northwest.

The original church on the site was founded in the sixteenth century after reports that a vision of the Virgin Mary's mother, Saint Anne, had appeared before local villagers in the form of an old woman with a hat and walking stick. In 1695, a much grander replacement was erected, modelled on the Church of St Augustine in Old Goa, of which only a single ruined belfry now remains.

Years of neglect have taken their toll on this building, too, but it is still an impressive sight. Rising in five stages, the mighty whitewashed **facade** is composed of a Baroque gable (featuring a statue of Saint Anne as its centrepiece), flanked by a pair of square towers and positively bristling with pinnacles, shell motifs and balustrades. Sadly, much of the detail higher up is currently lost under a shroud of black mildew and weeds, although plans are afoot to restore the church.

Details of the Church of St Augustine in Old Goa appear on p.93.

Old Goa

Soaring high above the surrounding canopy of riverine palm groves, the colossal, cream-painted cathedral towers, belfries and domes of the former Portuguese capital, nowadays known as **OLD GOA**, are far and away the state's most impressive historical monuments, and collectively one of the finest crops of Renaissance architecture in the world. In its heyday, *Goa Dourada*, "Golden Goa", 10km east of

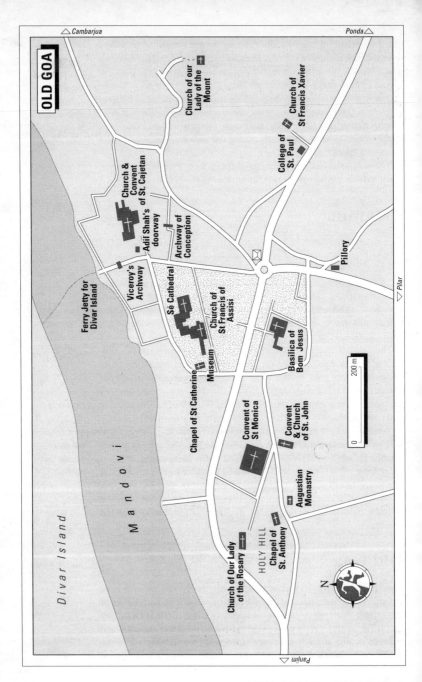

OLD GOA

△ Cambarjua

Ponda △

Church of our Lady of the Mount

Church of St Francis Xavier

College of St. Paul

Church & Convent of St. Cajetan

Adil Shah's doorway

Archway of Conception

Pillory

▽ Pilar

Viceroy's Archway

Sé Cathedral

Church of St Francis of Assisi

Ferry Jetty for Divar Island

Museum

Chapel of St Catherine

Basilica of Bom Jesus

200 m

0

Convent of St Monica

Convent & Church of St. John

M a n d o v i

Augustian Monastry

D i v a r   I s l a n d

HOLY HILL

Chapel of St. Anthony

Church of Our Lady of the Rosary

N

▽ Panjim

Panjim, was the largest, richest and most splendid city in Asia. With a population of around 300,000 in the 1500s (greater than either Lisbon or London at the time), it sprawled south from a grand civic centre and bustling port on the banks of the Mandovi River to within a stone's throw of the Zuari estuary, and west as far as Ribandar: a maze of narrow twisting streets, piazzas, ochre-washed villas and imposing Baroque churches.

Old Goa

These days you need a fertile imagination indeed to picture Old Goa as it must have looked in the sixteenth and seventeenth centuries. The vast suburbs have disappeared without trace, reduced to rubble and reclaimed by the jungle, leaving a mere dozen or so churches and convents marooned amid the *Archeological Survey of India*'s carefully manicured lawns. Granted World Heritage status by *UNESCO*, the site attracts busloads of foreign tourists from the coast and Christian pilgrims from around India in roughly equal numbers. While the former come primarily to admire the gigantic facades and gilt altars of Old Goa's beautifully preserved churches, the main attraction for the latter is the tomb of **Saint Francis Xavier**, the renowned sixteenth-century missionary, whose remains are enshrined in the **Basilica of Bom Jesus**.

If you're staying at one of the nearby resorts and are contemplating a day-trip inland, this is the most obvious and accessible option – in fact, Old Goa as yet has no hotels or restaurants (just snack bars and stalls around the bus stand), so a day-trip is the only feasible way to visit the site. Thirty minutes by road from the state capital, Old Goa is served by buses every fifteen minutes from Panjim's *Kadamba* bus stand (30min); alternatively, hop into an auto-rickshaw or rent a taxi. All the main package tour companies also offer Old Goa as an optional excursion, while GTDC slot its main highlights into several of their sightseeing tours, starting in Panjim, Mapusa, Vasco, Margao or Colva; further details and tickets for these are available at any GTDC hotel or information counter.

Some history

The earliest recorded occupation of **Old Goa** was at the beginning of the twelfth century, when the local Hindu king founded a *brahmin* colony, or *brahmapuri*. Known as **Ela**, the settlement later expanded under Vijayanagar, but was ransacked during the Muslim incursions of 1469. Having razed the former Hindu capital of Govapuri (now Goa Velha), the Bahmanis established a new port further north at Ela. This eventually became the second city of the ruler of Bijapur, **Yusuf 'Adil Shah**, following the break-up of the Bahmani kingdom towards the end of the fifteenth century. Encircled by fortified walls and a deep moat, Ela's grandest building was the 'Adil Shah's palace, whose lofty minarets once dominated the town, but of which only a lone-standing doorway now remains.

Goa Velha is covered on p.78.

Old Goa

Goa's fabled golden age began in 1510 with the appearance of the Portuguese. Commanded by **Alfonso de Albuquerque**, a squadron of warships moved in to mop up the remnants of a Muslim fleet it had previously engaged off Kerala, then seized the town to use it as a base for operations along the Malabar coast. The Portuguese were able to profit from the lucrative local trade in horses and spices, and as the wealth poured in, so did **immigrants** – by the end of the sixteenth century, some 2500 new arrivals every year replenished a population constantly depleted by disease. With them came **missionaries** from various religious Orders, encouraged by the colonial government as a "civilizing influence" on the natives. This process was hastened by the arrival in 1542 of **Francis Xavier**, and by the dreaded Holy Office, better known as the **Inquisition**, for whose trials and bloody *autos da fé* (acts of faith) the colony later became notorious.

For more on Francis Xavier, see pp.92–93.

Beneath the outward gloss of piety, however, Goa was fast developing a reputation for **decadence**. Accounts by European travellers of the day record that adultery, drunkenness and prostitution were rife, although ultimately natural and economic factors rather than vice were to bring about the city's **decline**. The original site was swampland, a perfect breeding ground for malaria-carrying mosquitoes. Bad drainage caused drinking water to become infected by raw sewage, and more than half the city's inhabitants died during the **epidemics** of 1543 and 1570, with a further 25,000 perishing in the first thirty years of the seventeenth century. To compound the health problems, the Mandovi started to silt up, preventing ships entering the harbour. Finally, after the Portuguese trade monopoly had been broken by the British, French and Dutch, **Viceroy Conde do Alvor** ordered the administrative capital to be shifted to Mormugao. This scheme was eventually dropped in favour of a move upriver to Panjim, but the damage to Old Goa had already been done, and most of the houses were demolished to provide masonry for the new capital. When the chronicler Abbé Cottineau de Kloguen passed through in 1827, he remarked with dismay that "nothing remains of the city but the sacred; the profane is entirely banished".

Mormugao is covered on p.162–3.

Arrival

Arriving by **bus**, you'll be dropped just south of main **square**, which is flanked by the **Basilica of Bom Jesus** to the south, with the **Sé Cathedral**, **Church of St Francis Assisi** and the **archeological museum** to the north. The main highlights all lie within comfortable walking distance of here and can be seen in three to four hours. The logical place to start any tour of the site is at its northeast corner, where the **Viceroy's Archway** marks the traditional entrance to the city from the Mandovi riverfront. Head south from here along the **Rua Direita**, Old Goa's principal thoroughfare, and you'll pass the chief monuments in more or less chronological order, winding up at

The architecture of Old Goa

Exuding the spirit of imperial self-confidence typical of its day, the architecture of Old Goa is resolutely European, inspired by contemporary Italian fashions rather than the indigenous traditions which it supplanted. The high point of the colony's building boom, in the early seventeenth century, coincided with the end of the Renaissance in Europe and the beginning of the **Baroque era**, whose style was characterized by twisting scrollwork, chubby winged cherubs, lashings of gilt and generally over-the-top ornamentation. In part, this shift was a reaction against the restrictive conventions of the past, but it also served the purposes of missionaries by providing awe-inspiring spectacles to impress new converts. You only have to step inside the Basilica of Bom Jesus to get some idea of the impact such splendour must have had on local people more used to modest monochrome stone temples.

The other architectural style represented at Old Goa is more particularly Portuguese. Named after its principal patron, King Mañuel (1495–1521), the **Mañueline movement** celebrated the achievements of the Portuguese discoveries by incorporating nautical motifs, such as anchors and ropes, into the buildings' design. Few examples of this style have survived, but for an idea, check out the main doorway of the Church of St Francis of Assisi, next to the museum, or the Church of Our Lady of the Rosary on Holy Hill.

Although many of Old Goa's churches feature decorative details carved from **basalt** (reputedly brought to Goa as ballast in the ships that sailed from Lisbon, but more probably quarried at Bassein, near Bombay), virtually all of Old Goa's churches were made of local **laterite**. As this porous red-brown stone eroded badly during the annual monsoons, a thick coat of lime whitewash, made from crushed clam shells, was traditionally applied over the top, and renewed after each rainy season. Nowadays, a far less appealing off-white paint is used, but the principle remains the same, as you'll see if you come here in early September, when the buildings are invariably covered with streaks of black mildew.

the Basilica, the spiritual hub of Old Goa. Enthusiasts may also wish to make an additional foray west to **Holy Hill**, site of some of the city's oldest and architecturally most important buildings, and to the hilltop **Church of Our Lady of the Mount**, which commands a fine view of the old city and its environs. However long you spend exploring the site, be sure to bring a sun hat and plenty of drinking water, as the heat and humidity can be ferocious.

The site

Throughout its most prosperous period in the sixteenth and early seventeenth centuries, Old Goa could only be reached by river. This remains the most spectacular approach to the site, although the vast majority of visitors now travel up the Mandovi from Panjim by road, crossing a three-kilometre-long causeway, the **Ponte de Linhares**, built by slaves in 1633 and reputedly still the longest bridge in South Asia.

The first thing that sea passengers would have seen when alighting at the landing stage was the pompous **Viceroy's Archway** in the city walls. Made from a mixture of red laterite and green granite, the gate was erected in 1599 by Viceroy Francisco da Gama as a memorial to the achievements of his grandfather, the famous explorer Vasco da Gama, whose statue and coat of arms feature on the river-facing side. On the opposite facade, a bible-carrying figure stands with its feet on the neck of a cringing native, symbolizing the victory of Christianity over "paganism".

Once under the archway, the new arrivals would head along the **Rua Direita** (so-named because it was allegedly the only straight street in town), towards the civic centre, passing the main bazaar, customs house, foundry and arsenal en route. Only sleepy palm groves line the road today, but when French adventurer François Pyrard walked down it after being shipwrecked in the Maldives in 1608, he was overwhelmed by the the the Rua Direita's cosmopolitan prosperity: "on both sides [are] many rich lapidaries, goldsmiths, and bankers, as well as the richest and best merchants and artisans in all Goa: Portuguese, Italians, Germans and other Europeans."

The Church and Convent of St Cajetan

The distinctive domed **Church of St Cajetan**, just south of the Viceroy's Archway, was erected between 1612 and 1661 by the Theatine Order. Sent to India by Pope Urban VIII, the priest-missionaries were refused entry to their original destination, the Sultanate of Galconda, and settled instead in Goa, where they built themselves this miniature replica of St Peter's in Rome, naming it after the founding father of their Order.

Like St Peter's, the church's **dome**, the only one remaining in Old Goa, is partially obscured from below by a grand Neoclassical **facade**, pierced by a Corinthian portico and flanked by a pair of square-turreted towers – the only concession made by the Italian architect to local Portuguese taste. Inside, the cross-plan of the building centres on a slab of stone that conceals a **well**, thought to be a remnant of the Hindu temple that formerly stood on the site. St Cajetan is also renowned for its fine **woodcarving**, notably the decoration of the pulpit, and the panels surrounding the high altar dedicated to *La Divina Providencia*. Behind this, a free-standing reredos rests on top of the **crypt** where the embalmed bodies of Portuguese governors were once kept in lead coffins before they were shipped back to Lisbon. Forgotten for over thirty years, the last batch (of three) was only removed in 1992 on the eve of the state visit to Goa of Portuguese President Mario Soares.

Adjoining this church is the **Convent of St Cajetan**, recently renovated and now used as a theological college for newly ordained priests. Immediately to its west, a lone-standing grey basalt **doorway**, raised on a plinth and reached by a flight of five steps, is all that remains of the once-grand Islamic **palace of 'Adil Shah**, ruler of Goa until the arrival of the Portuguese. Sections of the palace still stood when the governor decamped downriver to the swish suburb of Panelim in 1754, but these were eventually pulled down for use in the construction of Panjim. Ironically, the **Muslim doorway** may also have been made from plundered masonry: Historians believe the decorative work on the lintel to be Hindu, indicating that the stone must have come from an older temple erected nearby, although the scrollwork was clearly a later Portuguese addition.

The main square and Sé Cathedral

Old Goa's **main square** is an expanse of well-watered lawns, originally known as the **Terreiro de Gales** and once used for public hangings, cockfights and as a Portuguese military parade ground. These days, it's invariably teeming with bus parties who picnic under the shady trees. A stern notice warns visitors (or more particularly "couples") not to "commit unholy acts" in the grounds, under threat of imprisonment or a hefty Rs5000 fine. It is presumably to enforce this rule that the bizarrely named "Heritage Police", distinguished by their navy-blue uniforms, patrol the site from old-style canvas tents pitched nearby.

Dominating the square's north side is the mighty sixteenth-century **Sé Cathedral**, the episcopal seat of the Archdiocese of Goa and the largest church in Asia. Envisaged by its founder, Viceroy Redondo, as "a grandiose church worthy of the wealth, power and fame of the Portuguese who ruled the seas from the Atlantic to the Pacific", it took eighty years to build. Work on the interior was beset by financial problems and only completed in 1652, when Portuguese fortunes were already in decline. In callous colonial fashion, the shortfall was raised from the sale of land belonging to Goan Hindus who died without having converted to Christianity, while foundations were dug into the ruins of a mosque.

Although designed for the Dominican Order, the cathedral takes its cue from Jesuit architecture. However, one typically Goan inclusion were the two square **bell towers** flanking the main facade. The campanile still standing on the south side – the other collapsed after being struck by lightning in 1776 – houses the largest bell in Asia, the legendary *Sino do Ouro* or "**Golden Bell**", famed for its mellow tone. During the Inquisition, its tolling announced the start of Goa's gruesome *autos da fé*, held in the square in front of the Sé (now a lawn), to which suspected heretics would be led from the Palace of the Inquisition's dungeons opposite.

The main entrance opens onto an awe-inspiring **interior**, in which rows of huge pillars separate the broad barrel-vaulted nave from its side aisles. Ahead, the magnificent **reredos** rises above the main altar to the ceiling, contrasting sharply with plain white surroundings. Deeply carved and layered with gold leaf, it features six finely painted panels depicting scenes from the life and martyrdom of Saint Catherine, to whom the Sé is dedicated, suffused by light from the lofty side windows. The one on the top left shows her debating philosophy with foreign scholars. Opposite, she awaits execution for her heresy, before being beheaded in the bottom-left panel. Finally, in the bottom-right panel, her headless body is carried away by angels to Mount Sinai. The spiked wheel on which Saint Catherine was tortured (whence "Catherine Wheel" fireworks) is also depicted. In 1065 this became the symbol of the Order of Knights of Saint John, formed to protect the holy relics after Saint Catherine's corpse was disinterred in Alexandria, where she was executed, and taken to Sinai.

The small shrine nearest the altar on the north wall, known as the Chapel of St Anne, houses relics of the **Blessed Martyrs of Cuncolim**, whose plucky mission to convert the Muslim court of Moghul emperor Akbar resulted in their execution. Also much revered is the **Cruz dos Milagres**, or "Miraculous Cross", two chapels further down, which pilgrims petition to cure sickness. Housed behind an opulently carved wooden screen, the cross, which allegedly grew from a braid of palm leaves planted in a rock by a local priest, stood in a Goan village until an apparition of Christ appeared hanging from it in 1619. The chapel next to the entrance (also on the north side) contains another famous holy object: the **font** that Saint Francis Xavier used to baptize new converts.

The Church of Saint Francis of Assisi

The **Church of Saint Francis of Assisi**, sandwiched between the cathedral and archeological museum, dates from 1661 but stands on the site of an earlier convent church founded by Franciscans at the beginning of the sixteenth century. Elements of this first building were incorporated into the later one, probably to save money. They include the splendid Mañueline **doorway**, whose heavy ornamentation stands out like a sore thumb on an otherwise plain classical facade. Typical nautical themes include navigators' globes flanking the trefoil arch and a Greek cross above the royal coat of arms, which used to adorn the sails of Vasco da Gama and other Portuguese explorers' ships.

The **interior** of the church is no longer used for worship, and has a much older and more faded feel than its neighbours. Sculpted tombstones of Portuguese *hidalgos* pave the floor of the nave, while the walls and ceilings are plastered with frescoes and floral patterns rendered in delicate green, pink, yellow and gold. These latter designs are particularly well executed, perhaps because their Islamic style – derived from the Muslim-influenced art of Spain and Portugal – may have been familiar to local Goan artists. Less successful, but still of interest, are the painted wooden panels lining the chancel next to the high altar, which illustrate the life and teachings of Saint

Francis. As part of extensive renovation work currently being undertaken in this church, new, elaborately carved panels have been installed on the walls flanking the altar, crafted by local artisans using traditional motifs. Finally, the gilt reredos, which envelops the east wall of the church, centres on two large figures of Saint Francis and Jesus, beneath which are inscribed the vows of the Franciscan Order: "Poverty, Humility and Obedience".

The archeological museum

A wing of the old Franciscan monastery adjacent to the Church of St Francis of Assisi was converted in 1964 into Goa's main **archeological museum**, exhibiting a modest selection of pre-colonial sculpture, coins and manuscripts, as well as Portuguese artefacts. Presiding over the main entrance hall is a huge sixteenth-century bronze statue of Alfonso de Albuquerque, the military commander who conquered Goa in 1510. The statue stood in Old Goa but was later shifted to Panjim's municipal square, where it remained until Independence in 1961. A left turn takes you into the **Key Gallery**, whose exhibition of Hindu sculpture is dominated by the bronze figure of one-eyed sixteenth-century Portuguese poet Luis Vaz Camões, holding a copy of his epic *Os Lusiades* that was written during his sojourn in Goa. The statue used to form the focal point of the square outside the museum, between the Sé Cathedral and Basilica of Bom Jesus. However, the finest piece of sculpture is an intricately carved thirteenth-century standing icon of Vishnu flanked by his consort, Lakshmi, and the winged gryphon Garuda (directly in front of you as you enter). The images arching above the Preserver of the Universe's head are of his ten *avataras*, or incarnations. Also worth a close look are the nearby hero stones, carved as memorials to Hindu warriors who died bravely in battle. The best of these (right of the Vishnu sculpture) shows a king on his throne, surrounded by attendants, with the naval engagement in which he was killed depicted below.

Old Goa's archeological museum is open daily except Fri 10am–5pm.

Reached via the stairs at the far end of the Key Gallery, the **first floor** of the museum is given over mainly to a collection of sixty paintings of Portuguese governors. Beginning with the 1527 portrait of Dom João Castro and ending with the right-wing Portuguese dictator Salazar, who was in power at the time of Goa's liberation, most have seen some heavy-handed renovation and are of little artistic merit, although they provide a vivid account of formal dress over the centuries – much of it stiflingly unsuitable for the Goan climate.

The stairs at the far end of the room lead to the monastery cloisters, renovated in 1707 and now the main **sculpture gallery**. Alongside a handful of Islamic inscriptions and hero stones stand several *sati* stones dating from the Kadamba period. These marked the spot where a widow committed suicide by throwing herself on her husband's funeral pyre. *Sati* was outlawed during the British Raj but still occurs – albeit very rarely – in more traditional parts of India.

A memorial to a martyr of a different kind is encased in the northwest corner of the courtyard. The centrepiece of this small shrine is a carved stone pillar from Madras in which a fragment of the lance that reputedly skewered the apostle Saint Thomas (who first brought Christianity to India) was once embedded.

The Chapel of St Catherine

The small but historically significant **Chapel of St Catherine** stands on a stretch of sloping ground immediately west of the museum, hemmed in by palm groves and dense vegetation. An inscription etched on one of its bare laterite walls recalls that the present structure was built in the seventeenth century on the spot where Albuquerque first entered the Muslim city on St Catherine's Day in 1510. In fact, it replaced an older mud-and-straw church erected by the Portuguese commander as an act of thanksgiving soon after his victory. The building that superseded this was granted cathedral status by a Papal Bull of 1534, which it retained until the construction of the Sé. Architecturally, St Catherine's is important because its twin-towered facade provided the prototype for the Sé, and thus inaugurated a distinctively Goan style of church design.

The Basilica of Bom Jesus

Site of the world-famous mausoleum of Saint Francis Xavier, the **Basilica of Bom Jesus**, on the south side of the main square, is India's most revered and architecturally accomplished church, and the logical place to wind up a tour of Old Goa. Work on the building was completed in 1605, sixteen years after the Jesuits were first granted leave to construct a convent on the same spot. In 1964, it became the first church in South Asia to be promoted to a Minor Basilica, by order of Pope Pius XII, and today forms the main focus for Christian worship in the old colonial capital.

The design of the Basilica is believed to be derived from the Gesù, the Jesuits' headquarters in Rome, and, with its idiosyncratic blend of Neoclassical restraint and Baroque extravagance, is typical of the late Renaissance, with a sumptuous **facade**, the most ornate in Goa, culminating in the intricately carved and disproportionately large central pediment at the top. This is dominated by the IHS motif, standing for *Iaesus Hominum Salvator* ("Jesus the Saviour"), and a feature of all Jesuit churches. Unusually for Goa neither the facade, nor the rest of the building, is whitewashed, although plans are afoot to cover the soft red stone again as the monsoon rains have begun to blur some of the stonework. The erosion is particularly evident on the north wall, where you can admire the impressively sturdy buttresses that prop the Basilica up.

Spanned by a stark, lofty wooden ceiling, the **interior** is positively plain compared with the facade, but no less impressive, dominated by a massive gilt altarpiece, and a huge central statue of Saint

Ignatius Loyola, founder of the Jesuit Order, accompanied by the Infant Jesus. As you pass through the main doorway, look for two blue plaques attached to the pillars beneath the choir gallery, commemorating (in Latin and Portuguese) the inauguration of the Basilica in 1605. Midway down the nave on the north wall (opposite the sumptuously decorated main pulpit), stands a memorial to **Dom Jeronimo Mascarenhas**, whose will financed the construction of this church: its panels depict heroic episodes from his career as Captain of Cochin. Swathed in lush gold leaf, the gigantic **reredos**, filling the far end of the nave, remains the Basilica's most arresting feature, with spiralling scrollwork, extravagantly carved panels, statues and pilasters illuminated for maximum effect.

The Basilica's main claim to fame, however, is to be found in the south transept, the **mausoleum of Saint Francis Xavier** (immediately to the right as you leave the Basilica through the door on the right of the main altar). This was installed in 1698, a century and a half after his death, gifted to the Jesuits by the last of the Medicis, Cosimo III (1670–1723), Grand Duke of Tuscany, in exchange for the pillow on which the saint's head was laid to rest. It took Florentine sculptor **Giovanni Batista Saggini** a decade to design and was made from precious marble and coloured jaspers specially shipped from Italy. Set in the base are four superbly crafted **bronze panels** illustrating scenes from the life of the saint: preaching in the Moluccas; baptizing converts; swimming to escape the natives of Moro; and on his deathbed. The huge **silver casket** mounted on the plinth contains what is left of the body, although it was not part of the Medici endowment but was made earlier by Goan silversmiths in 1659. Its sides were originally encrusted with precious stones, but these have long disappeared.

From the tomb, a corridor leads behind the main altar to the **Sacristy**, renowned for its beautifully carved wooden door and stone door jamb. On display inside are several chests containing clerical regalia, along with one of Saint Francis Xavier's toes, which fell off the corpse in 1890. Stairs lead from here, via a room full of garish modern paintings of "**Goencho Sahib**", to a first-floor gallery where you get a good bird's-eye view of the casket and its contents.

Goa's **pillory** formerly stood smack in the centre of the city's main square but now occupies a quiet site southwest of the Basilica, overgrown with weeds in front of a mildew-covered concrete house. This pair of grey basalt columns, plundered from the ruins of a Hindu temple and mounted on a stepped plinth, once sported a set of iron rings to which petty criminals were bound, before being flogged and left to dangle for the edification of market goers.

Holy Hill (Monte Santo)

Anyone not totally churched out by this stage should head west up the lane leading from the bus stand to take in the cluster of monu-

Old Goa

For more on Saint Ignatius Loyola, see p.92.

The Sacristy is open daily except Fri 9am–noon & 2–5.30pm.

Old Goa

Saint Francis Xavier in Goa

Visit almost any church or Christian house in Goa, and you're certain to find an image of the state's patron saint, **Francis Xavier**, known locally with considerable affection as "**Goencho Sahib**". The "Apostle of the Indies" was born on April 6, 1506, the son of aristocrats in Navarre, Spain. In his late teens he left for Paris, where he studied for the priesthood at the Sorbonne. There he met fellow Basque nobleman and future mentor (Saint) **Ignatius Loyola** (1491–1556), who, after his ordination in 1534, recruited Xavier, along with five other young priests, to be founder members of the evangelical "Society of Jesus" (*Compana de Jesu*), later known as the **Jesuits**.

Around this time, reports were reaching the Lisbon court of the dissolute lifestyle being led by Portuguese expatriates in Goa. The king, Dom João III (1521–57), appealed to the Jesuits for help to reverse this moral decline, and when one of the original candidates fell ill, Francis Xavier was asked to lead the mission. He and his delegation arrived a year later, on May 6, 1542, and immediately set to work saving the souls of Goa's wayward colonials.

Xavier founded several churches, schools, a university and printing press, and ordained dozens of priests during his first five months. Then he sailed south to evangelize the lapsed Catholic Parava pearl fishers of the Malabar Coast, where **miracles** like curing the sick and raising the dead with a touch of his crucifix helped him notch up a staggering 30,000 conversions, before heading further east for Malacca and the Spice Islands.

Another brief spell in Goa was followed by two years in Japan, where Xavier tried unsuccessfully to convert the Shinto Buddhists. This was to be his last mission, for, on December 3, 1552, he died of a fever while trying to sneak into China. His body was buried on the deserted island of Sancian, near the mouth of the Canto River, coated with quicklime to hasten its decomposition. However, when the grave was reopened three months later, the corpse was in perfect condition. Reburied in Malacca, it was exhumed again after five months and found to be still incorrupt.

ments on **Holy Hill**. Nestled amid thick tropical vegetation, the first building encountered, to the left of the road, is the **Convent and Church of St John of God**, a late-seventeenth-century building abandoned after the supression of the religious orders in 1835. The **Convent of St Monica**, opposite, was at one time the only nunnery in the entire colony. Dating from 1601–27, it burned down in 1636, but was completely rebuilt the following year. These days, the triple-storeyed building looks the worse for wear, with weeds choking its buttressed walls and eroded Baroque stonework, but it is still occupied by nuns from the Mater Dei Institute. You can ask to be shown around the convent by ringing the bell at the main entrance; note the deeply carved Mañueline-style reliefs here. Inside, cloisters and a sunken courtyard enclose a small octagonal garden called the **Vale de Lirio**. Although in a poor state of disrepair, the convent's **church**, next door, is also worth a quick look, mainly for its fine pulpit and the blue-painted tilework near the altar – a peculiarly Portuguese art

The arrival of Xavier's body in Goa, in March 1554, was greeted by a vast and euphoric crowd. But the church would not formally acknowledge the miracle until a medical examination had been carried out by the viceroy's physician to ensure the corpse had not been artificially preserved. The medic declared the skin firm and the intestines intact, then asked a Jesuit priest to stick his finger into a hole in the chest. When the finger was withdrawn, it was smeared with blood that was "smelt and found to be absolutely untainted".

Saint Francis Xavier was eventually canonized in 1622 and his body installed in the **Basilica of Bom Jesus**, but not before bits of it had been removed by relic hunters – in 1614, his right arm was dispatched to the Pope in Rome (where it allegedly wrote its name on a pile of papers), a hand to Japan and parts of the intestines to southeast Asia. Other relics found their way into private homes, such as the Braganza-Perreira mansion in Chandor, whose family shrine boasts Saint Francis Xavier's diamond-encrusted fingernail. Much the most macabre mutilation, though, occurred in 1634 when a Portuguese noblewoman, Dona Isabel de Caron, bit off the little toe of the corpse's right foot. So much blood spurted into the woman's mouth that it left a trail all the way to her house and she was found out.

Once every ten years, the saint's body is carried in a three-hour ceremony from the Basilica of Bom Jesus to the Sé Cathedral, where visitors file past, touch and photograph it. During the last Exposition, from November 23, 1994 until January 7, 1995, an estimated two million pilgrims flocked for *darshan* (or ritual viewing) of the corpse, these days a shrivelled and somewhat unsavoury spectacle. The event, rumoured to be the last, was managed with military precision by the Goan Tourist Police, amid paranoid delusions that Pakistan's Inter Services Intelligence (ISI) were planning to steal the relic. However, the 48-day festival passed off without a hitch, and stallholders did a brisk trade in day-glo plastic Francis Xaviers, dashboard Madonnas and other religious kitsch.

---

form, rare in Goa, known as *azulejo*. The **cross** behind the high altar is believed to be miraculous: in 1636, it is said that the Christ figure opened its eyes and blood dribbled from its crown of thorns.

At one time the grandest building in the colony, Holy Hill's melancholic **Augustinian Monastery**, opposite St Monica's, now lies in ruins, though the partially collapsed belfry remains one of the city's most distinctive sights. The monastery was founded when the Augustinians first arrived in Goa in 1572, and was enlarged using a grant from the King of Portugal thirty years later. However, when the Orders were expelled, the monastery and church were deserted and soon became derelict. The spectacular facade finally collapsed in 1931, but its bell was salvaged from the rubble and installed in Panjim's Church of the Immaculate Conception, where it is still in use today.

Continue up the lane past the ruins and you'll soon arrive at the beautifully restored **Chapel of St Anthony**, commissioned in the fif-

Panjim's Church of the Immaculate Conception is described on p.69.

teenth century by Albuquerque and renovated by the Portuguese the year they were finally kicked out of Goa by Nehru. Saint Anthony is the patron saint of the Portuguese armed forces, which partly explains why the statue inside the chapel was granted the honorary rank of army captain. The painted figure used to be taken to the Treasury every year in a grand procession to collect its wages – a tradition discontinued by one of the governors, but quickly reinstated after he was nearly killed in an accident on St Anthony's Day.

To reach Holy Hill's most interesting monument, rejoin the path that runs in front of St Monica's church and follow it west as far as a small clearing. A plaque on the southwest corner of the **Church of Our Lady of the Rosary** records that from this vantage point above the Mandovi, Alfonso de Albuquerque followed the fortunes of the fateful battle of 1510. Erected by him soon after, in fulfilment of a victory vow, the original church was where Saint Francis Xavier preached on arrival here in 1542. Its successor, completed in 1549, is the oldest complete building in Old Goa, and the sole surviving church Goencho Sahib is likely to have visited in person, and it forms the state's best example of Mañueline architecture, with unusual rounded towers, tall windows and rope mouldings. Few visitors see the cruciform **interior**, which is only unlocked on feast days; it is unremarkable, except for the marble tomb of **Catarina a Piro**, believed to be the first European woman to set foot in the colony. A commoner, she eloped here to escape the scandal surrounding her romance with Portuguese nobleman Garcia de Sa, who later rose to be governor of Goa. Under pressure from no less than Francis Xavier, Garcia eventually married her, but only as she lay on her deathbed. Her finely carved tomb, set in the wall beside the high altar, incorporates a band of intricate Gujarati-style ornamentation, probably imported from the Portuguese trading post of Diu. Garcia's more modest gravestone lies in front of the main altar.

The Church of Our Lady of the Mount

Crowning a thickly wooded hilltop to the east of the city, the **Church of Our Lady of the Mount** is one of Old Goa's least accessible monuments, but one well worth making the effort to see. The best time to visit is towards the end of the day, when the **views** west over the tops of the city's Baroque facades and bell towers, silhouetted against the setting sun, are something to savour. The best way to **get there** is to follow the Cambarjua road, turning right up a narrow lane when you reach a small bar. This motorable track winds up the hill, petering out at a rough car park, from where a flight of old laterite steps runs the rest of the way (see map).

Our Lady of the Mount was one of three churches founded by Albuquerque after his victory over the Muslim ruler of Goa. The 'Adil Shah's army also mustered on this hilltop prior to their counter-assault on the city in 1510, as recorded by a plaque attached to the west wall of the church. Little of interest is to be found inside, but you could hunt around in front of the main altar for the tombstone bearing a skull and crossbones, which belongs not to a pirate, but to the Portuguese architect, **Antonio Alvares Pereira**, who designed the original church.

Chorao and Divar islands

Marooned amid mangrove swamps, shifting sandbanks and water-logged paddy fields in the Mandovi estuary, the islands of **Chorao** and **Divar** are very rarely visited by tourists in spite of their proximity to Panjim. But if you want to get a taste of rural Goa and haven't time to venture far from the coast, a trip across the river en route to or from Old Goa is worth considering. Passing through a string of tranquil farming hamlets in picturesque countryside, their peaceful (and mainly flat) lanes are perfect for **cycling**, at least for the time being: a new road and train line, complete with cuttings and huge concrete bridges, look set to shatter the serenity of the area.

Until then, however, the loop from the Ribandar ferry jetty to the Shri Saptakoteshwar temple at **Naroa**, and back across Divar to Old Goa, remains a pleasant way to pass an afternoon, taking a leisurely three to four hours by bicycle (or one and a half hours by motorbike). Alternatively, nip across the Mandovi River from Old Goa to **Piedade**, Divar's largest village, to visit the hilltop **Church of Our Lady of Compassion**, whose terrace affords stunning views south over the former capital and upriver to Panjim.

Chorao Island

Most of the western spur of sleepy **CHORAO ISLAND**, reached by ferry from Ribandar, 5km east of Panjim (every 15min, 6am–10pm; Rs2), has been turned into the **Dr Salim Ali Bird Sanctuary**. Fringed by a dense wall of mangrove swamps, the roadless reserve, which you can only get close to by boat, is home to a healthy and varied population of coastal birds, as well as flying foxes, jackals and the odd crocodile. The grey-brown mud flats around the sanctuary are also a good place to spot one of the region's more unusual fish, the bulbous-headed **mudskipper**, which, as its name implies, can often be seen leaping through the silt.

From the ferry crossing, the road heads north through a series of small Hindu settlements, some of them made of mud and thatch, to **Chorao village**: a picturesque scattering of Portuguese-style villas grouped below a whitewashed church. Bear right at the fork in the road here, and you'll eventually drop down the far side of the hill to the northern edge of the island. A **bridge**, surrounded by palm-fringed rice paddy, marks the border of Tiswadi and Bicholim *talukas*. To reach the Shri Saptakoteshwar temple at Naroa, turn

The Shri Saptakotesh-war temple at Naroa features on p.118.

right at the next junction and continue until you reach the main road, where you should turn left. A right turn here will take you downhill to the ferry crossing for Divar.

Divar Island

Encircled by the silt-laden waters of the Mandovi River, **DIVAR ISLAND** can only be reached by **ferry**: from the south via Old Goa (every 15min; free), or from the north at Naroa (every 20–30min; free). After crossing a broad flood plain, crisscrossed by drainage ditches and studded with wooded hillocks, both roads converge on the island's main settlement, **PIEDADE**, nestled at the foot of a hill in the shade of an old forest. The village, dominated from on high by its striking church, exudes a lazy, prosperous feel. Its leafy lanes harbour dozens of elegant and immaculately painted Portuguese villas, with typically Goan *balcoes* flanking their deep verandahs, and names like "Vivenda Fernandes" and "Saudades".

If you are wondering why most of Divar's inhabitants seem to be women, this is because a large number of its menfolk work abroad. Every January, however, the prodigal sons return home to take part in the **Bandeira Festival**, during which they parade around the village waving the flags of their adopted countries.

The Church of Our Lady of Compassion

Perched atop the hill above Piedade, the **Church of Our Lady of Compassion** occupies the site of an ancient Ganesh temple that was destroyed by Muslims in the late fifteenth century. Chunks of masonry from the Hindu building were incorporated into the first Christian structure erected here, reportedly seen by Albuquerque from his ship when he returned to Goa for the last time in 1515. It was enlarged ten years later, although the present building, designed by a Goan priest, dates from the early eighteenth century.

Tucked away to the south side of the church is a remnant of the illustrious Kadamba era, when this hilltop was a sacred Hindu site. A tiny walled **cemetery**, which the resident priest will unlock for you, encloses a chapel converted from the shrine of the former Ganesh temple. The deity was whisked away before the arrival of the Muslims, but the carving and painted plaster decoration on the ceiling is original, as is the fragment of ornate stone tracery in the window, carved about the same time as the foundation of the Tamdi Surla temple near Molem, in Sanguem *taluka*.

An account of the Tamdi Surla temple near Molem, in Sanguem taluka, features on p.109.

Its monuments aside, the best thing about Piedade, and reason enough to make the trip up here from Old Goa, are its superb panoramic **views**. Little wonder the region's ancient inhabitants rated this spot so highly. Sitting on the terraces of GTDC's recently laid-out **Children's Park**, south of the church, you can take in a wide sweep of scenery, from the shadow of the Western Ghats on the horizon, to the rice fields and tangled tributaries of the Mandovi River, flowing west past Panjim into the Arabian Sea. This is also a good place from which to admire the remains of Old Goa, whose gigantic belfries tower above the carpet of palm trees to the south.

Chorao and Divar islands

Ponda

Characterless, chaotic **PONDA**, 28km southeast of Panjim and 17km northeast of Margao, is Ponda *taluka*'s administrative headquarters and main market town, but not somewhere you're likely to want to hang around. Straddling the busy Panjim–Bangalore highway, the NH4, its ugly ferro-concrete centre is permanently choked with traffic, and may make you wonder why you ever left the coast. Of the few visitors who stop here, most do so en route to the nearby Hindu temples or wildlife reserves further east, or to take a look at Goa's best-preserved sixteenth-century Muslim monument, the **Safa Masjid**, 2km west on the Panjim road.

Until the road through the town was upgraded in the 1970s, Ponda was little more than a sleepy rural settlement, hemmed in by thickly forested hills and eclipsed by the port of **Durbhat**, 7km southwest on the Zuari River. Conquered by the Portuguese shortly after Albuquerque arrived in Goa at the beginning of the sixteenth century, its first real claim to fame was as the capital of Muslim rebel leader **Abdullah**, Prince of Bijapur, who plotted from here to overthrow his brother, Ibrahim 'Adil Shah, in 1555. The rebellion was nipped in the bud by the Bijapuri-Vijayanagar army, after which the town, along with its two **forts** (now in ruins), became a Muslim outpost on the edge of Christian Goa. It was only returned to the Portuguese by the Hindu King Sunda in 1791, following more than a century of Maharatha rule.

Ponda today is enjoying something of a boom, fuelled by its proximity to some of the state's largest **iron ore mines**. This prosperity has spawned a rash of small factories and industrial estates on the outskirts, as well as a rapid increase in size; swollen by a flood of immigrants from neighbouring Karnataka, the predominantly Hindu population has more than doubled over the past decade.

The Safa Masjid

Ponda's **Safa Masjid**, 2km west of the town centre in a district known as Shapur, is renowned less for its run-of-the-mill architecture than for being one of only two sixteenth-century Islamic monuments in Goa to survive the excesses of the Inquisition. Built in 1560 by the Bijapuri ruler Ibrahim 'Adil Shah, it presides over a complex that once included extensive formal gardens and a large palace, but which now lies in ruins beside the Panjim–Banagalore highway. If you are travelling by public transport, the easiest way to **get there** is by auto-rickshaw from Ponda's main bus stand.

Capped with a recent pointed terracotta tile roof, the Safa Masjid's rectangular **prayer hall** rests atop a high plinth, its whitewashed walls decorated with elegant Islamic arches. Surrounding the building are the stumps of several octagonal pillars where a covered courtyard once provided shade for worshippers. The interior, still in use, is plain except for the blind Bijapuri arches of the *mihrab*, or prayer wall, facing west towards Mecca.

The decoration around the sides of the **ablutions tank**, unusually situated to the south of the prayer hall rather than outside its main entrance, mirrors that of the mosque, suggesting that the two were contemporary. A superstition holds that it is dangerous to swim in the murky green water because of the hidden tunnels that are supposed to connect it with a smaller reservoir nearby – not that the soapy kids splashing around the shallows seem in the least deterred. Some locals also claim that the Safa Masjid is connected by secret underground passages to a ruined hilltop 2km north of here, although none has yet been discovered.

Practicalities

Ponda is served by regular **buses** from both Panjim (via Old Goa), and Margao, and lies on the main route east to Karnataka. The town's *Kadamba* bus stand is situated in the middle of town on the main square, next to the auto-rickshaw rank.

There are plenty of **places to stay** if you get stuck here. Best of the budget lodges is the *Padmavi* (no phone; ①) at the top of the square. For more comfort, try the *President* (☎0834/312287; ③–⑤), a short rickshaw ride up the Belgaum road, which has large, clean en-suite rooms, some with air conditioning. More upmarket is the three-star *Atash* (☎0834/312239, fax 313239; ⑥), 4km northwest on the NH4 at **Farmagudi**, whose comfortable air-conditioned rooms have satellite TV, and there's also a restaurant and car parking facilities. However, the best mid-range deal within striking distance of Ponda has to be GTDC's *Tourist Resort* (☎0834/312932; ③–④), also at Farmagudi (look for the signpost on the roundabout below the Shivaji memorial), whose en-suite chalets, stacked up the side of a steep hill overlooking the highway, are spacious, clean and reasonably priced. There's also a small terrace restaurant serving a standard menu of spicy mixed cuisine.

Decent **places to eat** in Ponda itself are few and far between, although the *Sanman* on the main square is fine for a pit stop, offering a good selection of inexpensive South Indian-style snacks. A five-minute walk up the main Belgaum road from the square, the no-nonsense *Gomantak* is deservedly more popular, with a cheap and exhaustive veg and non-veg menu that includes mountainous fish *thalis* and piping hot *channa batura*. If you fancy eating somewhere a little swankier, try the *Hotel President*'s dimly lit but air-conditioned restaurant, just up the lane, where tasty Chinese, Mughlai and vegetarian main courses cost around Rs50.

Ponda's main **service station** is 1km northeast of the square on the Belgaum road. The shop opposite stocks basic **motorbike spares**.

Around Ponda

Scattered among the lush valleys and forests **around Ponda** are a dozen or so **Hindu temples** founded during the seventeenth and eighteenth centuries, when this hilly region formed a Christian-free buffer zone between Portuguese Goa and the Hindu-dominated hinterland. Although the temples themselves are fairly modern by Indian standards, their deities are ancient and held in high esteem by both local people and the thousands of pilgrims from Maharashtra and Karnataka who travel here on special "tours" to see them.

For some background information on Hindu temples, see p.242.

The temples are concentrated in two main clusters: the first to the north of Ponda on the busy NH4, and the second deep in the countryside around 5km west of the town. You would have to be an avid

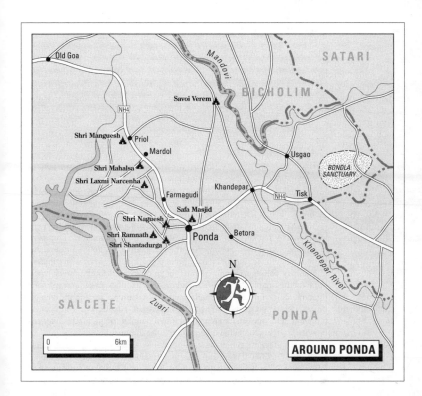

templo-phile indeed to see more than half a dozen in a day. Most people only manage the **Shri Manguesh** and **Shri Mahalsa** between the villages of **MARDOL** and **PRIOL**, which both lie a stone's throw from the main highway and are among the most interesting temples in the state. Any of the regular **buses** that run between Panjim and Margao

---

GOAN TEMPLES

Stick to the former Portuguese heartland of Bardez, Salcete and Tiswadi *talukas*, and you'd be forgiven for thinking Goa was exclusively Christian. It isn't, of course, as the innumerable brightly painted Hindu **temples** nestled amid the lush woodland and areca groves of more outlying areas confirm. The oldest-established and best-known **devuls** (from the Sanskrit word meaning "house of God") lie well away from the coastal resorts, but are worth hunting out. Apart from being some of South Asia's quirkiest sacred buildings, they are the main focus of religious life for the state's Hindu majority, offering the chance to experience at first hand traditions that have endured here for over 1500 years.

Goa's first temples were made of wood and mud brick, and later of stone, during the rule of the Kadamba dynasty, between the fifth and fifteenth century AD. Fragments of sculpture and masonry unearthed on the site of the ancient capital, Govapuri (see p.79), suggest these were as skillfully constructed as the famous monuments of the neighbouring Deccan region. However, only one, the richly carved Mahadeva temple at **Tamdi Surla** in east Goa (see p.109), has survived. The rest were systematically destroyed, first by Muslim invaders, and later by the Portuguese. To ensure that the deities themselves did not fall into the hands of iconoclasts, many were smuggled away from the Christian-dominated coastal area to remote villages in the interior, which explains why the greatest concentration of temples in Goa today is among the dense woodland and hidden valleys of Ponda *taluka*, southeast of Panjim.

Architecture

The **design** of Goan temples has altered dramatically over the centuries, yet without ever ditching the four fundamental features of Hindu architecture. Symbolizing the Divine Mountain from which the sacred River Ganges flows into the world, the **sanctuary tower**, or *shikhara*, rises directly above the **shrine room**, or *garbhagriha*, where the *devta* is housed. This inner sanctum is the most sacred part of the building: only the strictly vegetarian *pujaris* (priests) can cross its threshold, after performing acts of ritual purification. The main shrine, flanked by those of the two *pariwar devtas* (accessory deities) and surrounded by a **circumambulatory passage** (*pradakshena*), is approached through one or more pillared assembly halls, called **mandapas**, used for congregational worship and ritual recitals of music and dance. When the halls are full, the crowds spill outside on to the *prakara*, or **courtyard**. Finally, adjacent to most temples you will also find a stepped **water tank**, or *tirtha*, in which devout worshippers bathe before proceeding to the shrine.

In addition to these basic components, Goan temples boast some unusual features of their own – some necessitated by the local climate, or the availability of building materials, others the result of outside influ-

---

via Ponda drive past these. The others are further off the beaten track, although they are not hard to find on motorbikes: the locals will wave you in the right direction if you get lost. Ponda's auto-rickshaw *wallahs* also know the way, but expect to be charged for waiting time.

Around Ponda

ences. The impact of European/Portuguese architecture (inevitable given the fact that the majority of Goan temples were built during the colonial era, but ironic considering the Portuguese destroyed the originals) is most evident on the exterior of the buildings. Unlike conventional Hindu temple towers, which are curvilinear, Goan *shikharas*, taking their cue from St Cajetan's Church in Old Goa (see p.86), consist of octagonal drums crowned by tapering copper domes. Hidden inside the top of these is generally a pot of holy water called a **poornakalash**, drawn from a sacred Hindu river or spring. The sloping roofs of the *mandapas*, with their projecting eves and terracota tiles, are also distinctively Latin, while the glazed ceramic Chinese dragons often perched above them, originally imported from Macau, add to the colonial feel. Embellished with Baroque-style balustrades and pilasters, Islamic arches, and the occasional bulbous Moghul dome, the sides of larger temples also epitomize Goan architecture's flair for fusion.

Worth looking out for inside the main assembly halls are **woodcarvings** and panels of **sculpture** depicting mythological narratives, and the opulently embossed solid silver **doorways** around the entrance to the shrines, flanked by a pair of guardians, or **dwarpalas**. The most distinctively Goan feature of all, however, has to be the **lamp tower**, or *deepmal*, an addition introduced by the Maharathas, who ruled much of Goa during the seventeenth and eighteenth centuries. Also known as *deep stambhas*, literally "pillars of light", these five- to seven-storey whitewashed pagodas generally stand opposite the main entrance. Their many ledges and windows harbour tiny oil lamps that are illuminated during the *devta*'s weekly promenade, when the temple priests carry the god or goddess around the courtyard on their shoulders in a silver sedan chair known as a **palkhi**.

Near the *deepmal* you'll often come across a ornamental plant pot called a **tulsi vrindavan**. The straggly but sacred shrub growing inside it, *tulsi*, represents a former mistress of Vishnu whom his jealous consort Lakshmi turned into a plant after a fit of jealous pique. Hindus also regard a number of **trees** as auspicious, including the *peepal*, with its spatula-shaped leaves, and the majestic banyan, both of which can invariably be found in the temple courtyard, surrounded by circular pedestals, and bristling with red penants and small shrines.

Zatras

The most spectacular processions of the year occur during the annual **Zatra** celebrations, when the temple *devta*, together with his or her two principal accessory deities, is hauled around the precinct in a colossal and ornately carved octagonal wooden chariot, or **rath**. The grand promenades, which attract large crowds of locals but few foreign visitors, are accompanied by cacaphonic trumpet blasts and drumming from the temple musicians, whose instruments are stored in special galleries known as **sonddios**.

The Shri Manguesh temple

Shri Manguesh *mandir*, 9km north of Ponda near the village of Priol, is one of the largest, wealthiest and most frequently visited temples in Goa. Its principal deity, a stone Shivalingam, was first brought here in the sixteenth century from its previous hiding place on the south bank of the Zuari River at Curtolim, although the present building was erected over two hundred years later. During the time of the Inquisition, devotees from the Old Conquests area used to creep across the Cambarjua Canal under cover of darkness to worship here, knowing that torture, imprisonment or even execution awaited them if caught.

Amid lush forest at the foot of a steep hillside, the temple is now approached in a more leisurely fashion via a raised **walkway** through waterlogged paddy fields – land given to the temple by the local rajah in the eighteenth century. A flight of steps, lined by flower and incense *wallis*, leads to the main entrance, overlooking a large **water tank** whose ornamental brickwork is picked out with whitewash. The courtyard inside, hemmed in by ugly modern *argashallas* (pilgrims' hostels) and offices, is dominated by a seven-storey **deepmal**, the most impressive lamp tower in Goa.

The temple itself, painted ochre, blue and white, is a kitsch concoction of Moghul-style domes, Baroque balustrades and pilasters piled around the sides of a grand octagonal sanctuary tower. Its principal deity, Shiva in his beneficent form, Manguesh, presides over a silver shrine, flanked by a solid gold idol and lit by oil lamps.

Before you leave, be sure to check out the ancient stone *devtas* housed in the **subsiduary shrines** to the rear of the main building (from left to right: Lakshmi Narayan, Satiri and Mulkeshwar), and the gigantic ceremonial chariots (*raths*), put to use during the annual *Zatra* festival, which are stored in the northwest corner of the compound.

The Shri Mahalsa temple

Like Shri Manguesh, the **Shri Mahalsa temple**, 7km northwest of Ponda, originally stood in Salcete, but was destroyed in the sixteenth century during a siege by 'Adil Shah's Muslim army after a platoon of Portuguese soldiers had taken refuge in it. The deity survived, having previously been smuggled across the Zuari River to **Mardol**, where it was installed in a new temple. This has been rebuilt or renovated on several occasions since: the last time in 1993–95, when a shiny new *mandapa*, or pillared porch, was added and the courtyard paved with finest Karnatakan marble.

Crowned by rising tiers of red pyramidal roofs, the distinctly oriental Shri Mahalsa is noted for its fine **woodcarvings**, especially on the pillars supporting the eaves of the main *mandapa*, set above beautiful floral panels. Inside, an ornate ceiling spans deeply carved and brightly painted images of Vishnu's ten incarnations, or *avatars*. The presiding deity here is Vishnu's consort, the black-faced Goddess Mahalsa (aka Lakshmi, Goddess of wealth and prosperity), who peers out from her silver shrine, swathed in red and yellow silk.

Standing beside the seven-storey, pink- and white-painted *deepmal* in the courtyard is an unusual brass **lamp pillar**. The column, erected in 1978, symbolizes the Hindu *Axis Mundi*, Mount Kailash, which the gods placed on the back of Vishnu's second incarnation, the **tortoise** Kurma (featured at the base of the pillar) prior to his epic plunge into the Primordial Ocean. The dive was performed to rescue all the treasures of the world lost in the Great Flood. When Kurma reached the bottom of the sea, a cosmic serpent was coiled around the mountain and then pulled, churning the oceans and forcing their contents to the surface. Among the goodies that came to light were a jar of immortality-giving nectar, the *Amrit Samovar*, and Vishnu's consort, Lakshmi. The Preserver's winged vehicle (*vahana*), the half-man half-eagle **Garuda**, crowns the top of the pillar, whose oil lamps are lit every Sunday evening.

West of the temple, a flight of steps drops down to a laterite-lined **water tank**, overlooked by a large sacred *peepal* tree. The opposite (east) gateway, leading from the courtyard to the main road, is surmounted by a pagoda-roofed **musicians' gallery**, or *naubhat khanna*, where the instruments used during Shri Mahalsa's *pujas*, Sunday evening promenades and annual *Zatra* are stored.

Shri Mahalsa's pujas take place daily at 12.30pm & 8.30pm.

The Shri Lakshmi Narcenha temple

Crouched on the side of a steep, densely wooded hill, the secluded **Shri Lakshmi Narcenha** *mandir* at **Velinga**, 3km southwest of Mardol, is one of the more picturesque temples around Ponda. To find it, turn west where the main highway begins its climb up to Farmagudi, and follow the road for 1500m until it reaches Velinga village. The path to the temple starts at the top of the grassy square, in the centre of which stands a modern concrete shrine.

Transferred here from Salcete in 1567, the Lakshmi-Narcenha *devta* housed inside this temple, a conventional eighteenth-century structure surrounded by neat lawns and pilgrims' hostels, is Vishnu in his fourth incarnation as the man-lion Narashima, aka Narayan. However, his shrine and the brightly painted assembly hall leading to it (lined with images of Vishnu's various *avatars*) are of less interest than the beautiful **water tank** at the far end of the courtyard. Fed by an eternal spring, this is fringed by a lush curtain of coconut palms, and entered (from the opposite side) via a grand ceremonial gateway. Its stepped sides, used by locals as communal bathing- and *dhobi-ghats*, are ornamented with rows of Islamic-arched niches. The squat **tower** behind is a musicians' gallery.

The Shri Naguesh temple

From the main intersection at Farmagudi, dominated by a statue of the Maharatha leader **Shivaji**, a narrow back road winds sharply down the sides of a sheltered valley, carpeted with cashew trees and dense thickets of palms, to the **Shri Naguesh temple** at **Bandora**, 4km northwest of Ponda. If you are working your way north, note that this temple can also be approached via the road that starts opposite the Shri Shantadurga *mandir* near Quela (see below).

Established at the beginning of the fifteenth century and later renovated by the Maharathas, Shri Naguesh is older than most of its neighbours, although stylistically very much in the same mould, with the usual domed *shikhara*, or terracotta-tiled roofs, and gaudy Goan decor. Lying in its entrance porch is a stately black **Nandi** bull, vehicle of the temple's chief deity, Shiva, here known as Naguesh. Once inside, your eye is drawn to the multicoloured wood-carvings that run in a continuous frieze along the tops of the pillars. Famous all over Goa, these depict scenes from the Hindu epic *Ramayana*, in which the God Rama (Vishnu's seventh incarnation), with the help of Hanuman's monkey army, rescues his wife Sita from the clutches of arch demon Ravana. After the great battle, the couple are reunited back home in Ayodhya, as shown in one of the last panels. The silver-doored **sanctum** (*garbhagriha*), flanked by subsiduary shrines dedicated to Lakshmi-Narayan (left) and the elephant-headed Ganesh (right), houses a Shiva *devta*. If you're lucky, you may see it flooded with holy water – a costly ritual performed to cure sickness. Opening onto the courtyard are a couple of accessory shrines. The one on the south side harbours a *lingam* carved with the face of Shiva – a rare form of the god known as **Mukhaling**. The temple **tank**, whose murky green waters are teeming with fish, is also worth a look, if only to hunt for the donatory inscription (on the wall beside the steps) recording the foundation of the temple in 1413.

The Shri Shantadurga temple

Standing with its back to a wall of thick forest and its front facing a flat expanse of open rice fields, **Shri Shantadurga** is Goa's largest and most famous temple, and the principal port of call on the region's Hindu pilgrimage circuit. Western visitors, however, may find its heavily European-influenced architecture less than exotic, and barely worth the detour from Ponda, 4km northeast. If you are pushed for time, skip this one and head straight for the temples further north at Mardol and Priol, described above.

From the row of souvenir and cold drink stalls along the roadside, steps lead to Sri Shantadurga's main entrance and courtyard, enclosed by offices and blocks of modern pilgrims' hostels, and dominated by a brilliant-white six-storey **deepmal**. The russet- and cream-coloured temple, crowned with a huge domed sanctuary

tower, was erected by the Maharatha Chief Shivaji's grandson, Shahu
Raja, in 1738, some two centuries after its presiding deity had been
brought here from Quelossim in Mormugao *taluka*, a short way
inland from the north end of Colva Beach.

The **interior** of the building, dripping with marble and glass chandeliers, is dominated by an exquisitely worked **silver screen**,
embossed with a pair of guardian deities (*dwarpalas*). Behind this
sits the garlanded Shantadurga *devi*, flanked by images of Vishnu
and Shiva. According to Hindu mythology, Durga, another name for
Shiva's consort, Parvati, the Goddess of Peace, resolved a violent dis-
pute between her husband and rival God Vishnu, hence her position
between them in the shrine, and the prefix *Shanta*, meaning "peace",
that was henceforth added to her name.

After paying their respects to the Goddess, worshippers generally
file along the passage leading left to the subsiduary shrine where
Shantadurga sleeps. Also worth a look before you leave are the
devi's colossal *raths*; during the annual February *Zatra* festival held
here, these elaborately carved wooden chariots are pulled around the
precinct by teams of honoured devotees.

The Shri Ramnath temple

Thanks to the garishly outsize entrance hall tacked onto it in 1905,
the **Shri Ramnath temple**, 500m north up the lane from Shri
Shantadurga, is the ugly duckling of Ponda's monuments. The only
reason you'd want to call in here is to view the opulently decorated
silver screen in front of the main shrine, the most extravagant of its
kind in Goa. Brought from Lutolim in Salcete *taluka* in the sixteenth
century, the *lingam* housed behind it is worshipped by devotees of
the Shaivite and Vaishnavite sects of Hinduism, Shri Ramnath being
the form of Shiva propitiated by Lord Rama before he embarked on
his mission to save Sita from the clutches of the evil Ravana – a story
told in the Hindu epic, the *Ramayana*.

Khandepar

Hidden deep in dense woodland near the village of **KHANDEPAR**,
5km northeast of Ponda on the NH4, is a group of four tiny free-
standing **rock-cut cave temples**, gouged out of solid laterite some
time towards the end of the first millennium AD. They are among
Goa's oldest historical monuments but are also virtually impossible
to find without the help of a guide or knowledgeable local: ask someone to show you the way from the Khandepar crossroads, where the
buses from Ponda pull in.

Set back in the forest behind a slowly meandering tributary of the
Mandovi River, the four caves each consist of two simple cells hewn
from a single hillock. Their tiered roofs, now a jumble of weed-
choked blocks, are thought to have been added in the tenth or

Spice plantations

An essential ingredient in Goa's notoriously fiery cuisine, and prized for centuries by European palates as meat preservers and flavouring agents, **spices** were one of the region's principal exports long before Vasco da Gama left the Malabar Coast with a *caravela* full of pepper in 1499. Nowadays, they are grown, along with other cash crops such as cashews, tropical fruit and areca nuts, in several large **spice plantations** around Ponda.

Many of the big package tour companies these days offer pre-booked **excursions** to the spice farms, combining them with a visit to one or more of the Hindu temples nearby. The tours usually kick off with an introductory talk (and a stiff "peg" of locally distilled *feni*), followed by a stroll through the orchards. In keeping with a centuries-old system developed by strictly vegetarian Brahmin farmers, the plantations are divided into three tiers of terraces, stacked up a well-irrigated hillside. Planted at the top in the shade of flowering trees are spindly areca palms, coconuts, mangoes and jackfruit. Below these come breadfruit, star apples, banana trees, cinnamon and nutmeg; finally, at the bottom, are pineapple and cardamom.

Being herded around with a busload of fellow tourists may not be your idea of a perfect day out, but the spice plantation tours do offer a hassle-free way to sample the beautiful interior of Goa, which few visitors on package holidays get to see. However, if you'd prefer to arrange a visit independently, this can be done through Joseph Barreto, *Hotel Four Pillars*, Rua da Ourem, Panjim (☎0832/225240), who takes small groups to the *Pascal Farm*, near Khandepar, Ponda.

eleventh centuries, probably by the Kadambas, who converted them into Hindu temples. Prior to that, they were almost certainly Buddhist sanctuaries, occupied by a small community of monks. Scan the insides of the caves with a torch (watching out for snakes), and you can make out the carved pegs used for hanging robes and cooking utensils; the niches in the walls were for oil lamps. The outer cell of cave one also has lotus medallions carved onto its ceiling, a typically Kadamban motif that was added at roughly the same time as the stepped roofs.

The Bondla Sanctuary

Bondla is open daily except Thurs 9.30am– 5.30pm; tickets, sold at the gate, cost Rs4, with additional charges of Rs5 for cars, Rs5 for cameras and Rs10 for videos.

Of Goa's four nature reserves, the **BONDLA SANCTUARY**, 52km east of Panjim on the border of Ponda and Sanguem *talukas*, is the least appealing. Encompassing a mere eight square kilometres of mixed deciduous and evergreen forest, its centrepiece is a seedy **zoo** whose cramped enclosures are guaranteed to enrage any animal enthusiast hoping to see fauna in the wild. On the plus side, Bondla is set amid some magnificent **scenery**. Draped with lush jungle, a spectacular ridge of hills rises to the southeast, roamed by herds of *gaur* (Indian bison), black-faced *langur*, jackals, monkeys, wild boar, several species of deer, pythons, some gargantuan spiders and a handful of elusive leopards. The park is also a bird- and butterfly-spotter's paradise, boasting enough rare species to warrant a lengthy stop if you're on an ornithological tour of the region.

Approached from the west via the crossroad settlement of **Usgao**, the park gates open onto a surfaced road which drops down to a car park and café. Nearby, a small **Interpretation Centre** gives a run-down of Bondla's flora and fauna, and displays natural curiosities that include a whale skeleton. Most visitors proceed from here to the **zoological and botanical gardens**, lured by the promise of elephant rides and the chance to ogle a captive lion or tiger, although its mangy macaques and big cats cooped up in pens are distressing, and you'd be better to head along the lane leading south from the car park. Fording several streams, this road is impassable during the monsoons, but at other times is a safe and scenic short cut to the more inspiring Bhagwan Mahaveer Sanctuary (see below), and the railhead for the Dudhsagar waterfalls at Colem, 25km southeast.

The Interpretation Centre opens daily except Thurs 9.30am–1pm & 2–5.30pm.

The zoological and botanical gardens are open daily 11am–noon & 3–4pm.

Practicalities

The easiest way to get to the park is to take a bus from Panjim or Margao to Ponda, and then jump into a taxi or auto-rickshaw for the remaining 13km. Alternatively, catch any bus heading east on the NH4 from Panjim or Ponda towards Molem, and get off at Bondla's nearest roadhead, **Tisk**, 11km south, where you can pick up the Forest Department's special **minibus** service (Mon–Wed, Fri & Sat depart Tisk 11am & 7pm, Sun depart 10.30am & 7pm; Rs3).

Accommodation in Bondla is limited to the Forest Department's plain but pleasant *Tourist Cottages* (①–③), tucked away under the trees near the park gates, which has a dozen self-contained chalets, and some cheap dormitory beds. Rooms here can be hard to come by, especially on weekends and public holidays, so it is a good idea to make an advance **reservation** through the Forest Department's head office in Panjim, on the ground floor of Junta House (opposite the *Hotel Fidalgo*), Swami Vivekanand Road (☎0832/225926). The only other places to stay within striking distance are GTDC's *Tourist Resort* at Molem, 17km southeast, or at Ponda (see p.97).

Moderately priced Goan, Indian and Chinese **food** is available at *The Den* restaurant in Bondla, next door to the *Tourist Cottages*.

The Bhagwan Mahaveer Sanctuary

Bounded in the north by the mountains of the Karnatakan border, the **BHAGWAN MAHAVEER SANCTUARY** encompasses 240 square kilometres of semi-evergreen and moist deciduous woodland, peppered with clearings of parched yellow savannah grass and the occasional mud and palm-thatched tribal village. The thick tree cover harbours a diverse array of **wildlife**. However, unless you are prepared

The Bhagwan Mahaveer Sanctuary is freely accessible at all times.

(and equipped) to spend days trudging along unmarked forest trails, you will be lucky to see more action than the odd squirrel, as animal numbers were decimated by hunters and poachers during the colonial era. Since the creation of the sanctuary, many species have recovered, but the woods are still eerily quiet compared with reserves elsewhere in India.

Easily Bhagwan Mahaveer's most famous attraction, and an increasingly popular destination for package tour groups, are the **Dudhsagar waterfalls** in the far southeast corner of the park, which can only be reached by a memorable jeep or train journey through some amazing scenery. To get to Bondla's other well-known sight, you will definitely need your own transport. The **Mahadeva temple** at **Tamdi Surla**, Goa's best-preserved ancient monument, lies at the dead end of a windy back road, crouched at the foot of the Western Ghats. Also worth considering if you have your own car or motorcycle, and plan to spend a night or two in the park, is a visit to **Devil's Canyon**, a picturesque river gorge near Molem. Permission must first be obtained from the park warden, in the **Interpretation Centre**, 100m beyond the police check-post, who will unlock the barrier and give you directions. The canyon itself is a popular picnic spot, particularly during the monsoon season, even though its river is rumoured to be infested with ominously named mugger crocodiles.

The Interpretation Centre is open daily 9.30am–5.30pm.

This far-flung corner of Goa is also the homeland of the **Dhangars**, whose traditional livelihood of nomadic buffalo herding is currently under threat from deforestation, forcing many to take up settled agriculture or migrate to the towns. Alcoholism is also something of a problem among the Dhangars, and the sight of men lying comatose by the roadside clutching an empty bottle is all too common in more remote districts of the park.

Practicalities

The main jumping-off point for the Bhagwan Mahaveer Sanctuary is **Molem**, a fly-blown cluster of truckers' *dhabas*, *chai* stalls and liquor shops grouped around a dusty crossroads, 28km east of Ponda on the NH4. Only 10km from the Karnatakan border, this is also the site of a busy police and customs checkpoint, and the logical place to stock up on fuel if you are heading east by car or motorcycle; note that you are not technically allowed across the Goan border with a rented bike, although it is usually possible to *baksheesh* your way past the checkpoint. The nearest railhead is 5km south at the village of Colem. Track conversion work has closed this route for the past couple of years, but by the time this book is published services should once again be running from Vasco and Margao through Colem, and on across the Ghats into Karnataka. All **buses** bound for Belgaum, Hubli, Bangalore and Hospet (for Hampi), also stop at Molem, and there are several daily local services from Ponda. **Transport around the park** (which for most visitors means a return trip to Tamdi Surla, or to the train station) is limited to the handful of auto-rickshaws and jeeps that ply their trade on the Molem crossroads.

The only **accommodation** inside – or anywhere near – the sanctuary is GTDC's *Forest Resort* (☎0834/600238; ③–⑤) at Molem. A campus of semi-detached concrete chalets scattered under the trees, 200m beyond the police post, this roadside motel is spartan by Western standards, but clean and comfortable enough, with attached shower-toilets, running water, fans and verandahs in all of its rooms, several of which are air conditioned.

That the *Tourist Resort*'s dismal **restaurant** is also the best place in Molem to eat doesn't say much for the competition. Few items listed on the standard multi-cuisine menu are regularly available, while those that are all taste much the same (tongue-numbingly spicy) – not that travellers who stagger in here for a pit stop on the long bus journey to or from Bangalore seem bothered. Some consolation is available in the form of chilled beer and passable port wine.

Tamdi Surla

Six or seven hundred years ago, the Goan coast and its hinterland were scattered with scores of richly carved stone temples. Only one, though, came through the Muslim onslaught and religious bigotry of the Portuguese era unscathed. Erected in the twelfth or thirteenth century, the tiny **Mahadeva temple** at **TAMDI SURLA**, 12km north of Molem in the far northeastern corner of Sanguem *taluka*, owes its survival to its remote location in a tranquil clearing deep in the forest at the foot of the Western Ghats, which enfold the site in a sheer wall of impenetrable vegetation. To get there, head north from the Molem crossroads and bear right when you reach the fork in the road after 3km. The next right turn, 2km further north, is signposted. From here on, the route is winding but easy to follow and very scenic, passing through a string of picturesque villages and long stretches of woodland. If you are coming from Ponda on the NH4, note that it is quicker to approach Tamdi Surla via the hamlet of Sancordem: turn left off the highway 5km east of Tisk and carry on until you reach the fork mentioned earlier. Note that there is nowhere to eat or drink beyond Molem, so take your own provisions.

Why the Kadamba dynasty, who ruled Goa between the tenth and fourteenth centuries, chose this out-of-the-way spot remains a mystery: no traces of medieval settlement have been unearthed in the vicinity, nor did it lie near any major trade route. Yet the temple, dedicated to Shiva, was clearly important, built not from malleable local laterite but the finest weather-resistant grey-black basalt, carried across the mountains from the Deccan plateau and lavishly carved *in situ* by the region's most accomplished craftsmen. Their intricate handiwork, which adorns the interior and sides of the building, is still astonishingly fresh and stands as a poignant memorial to the Goa's lost Hindu architectural legacy.

Facing east – so that the rays of the rising sun light its deity at dawn – the temple is composed of a *mandapa*, or pillared porch, with three stepped entrances, a small *antaralhaya* (vestibule) and *garbhagriha* (shrine) surmounted by a three-tiered sanctuary tower, or **shikhara**. The tower's top section has collapsed, giving the temple a rather stumpy appearance, but the carving on its upper sections is still in good shape. As you walk around, check out the beautiful **bas-reliefs** that project from the sides. Punctuating the four cardinal points, these depict the gods of the Hindu trinity, Shiva (north), Vishnu (west) and Brahma (south), with their respective consorts featured in the panels above. Look out for the bands of delicate carving that pattern the sides of the porch, capped with an oddly incongruous roof of plain grey sloping slabs.

After a purifying dip in the river immediately east of the temple, reached via a flight of old stone *ghats*, or steps, worshippers would proceed to the main **mandapa**, or porch, for *darshan*, the ritual viewing of the deity. In its centre stands a headless Nandi bull, Shiva's *vahana*, or vehicle, surrounded by four matching columns, one of whose bases bears a relief of an elephant trampling a horse – thought to symbolize the military might of the Kadamba dynasty. The building's finest single piece of stonework, however, has to be the intricate lotus motif carved out of the *mandapa*'s **ceiling**. Flanked by four **accessory deities** that include a damaged dancing goddess (left) and an elephant-headed Ganesh (right), the pierced-stone **screen** surrounding the door of the vestibule comes a close second. The shrine itself houses a stone Shivalingam, mounted on a pedestal.

Dudhsagar waterfalls

Measuring a mighty six hundred metres from head to foot, the famous **waterfalls** at **DUDHSAGAR**, near the easternmost edge of Sanguem *taluka* on the Goa-Karnataka border, are the second highest in India, and a spectacular enough sight to entice a steady stream of visitors from the coast into the rugged Western Ghats. After pouring across the Deccan plateau, the headwaters of the Mandovi River form a foaming torrent that fans into three streams, then cascades down a near-vertical cliff face, streaked black and dripping with lush foliage, into a deep green pool. The Konkani name for the falls, which literally translated means "sea of milk", derives from clouds of mist kicked up at the bottom when the water levels are at their highest between October and December.

Overlooking a steep, crescent-shaped head of a valley carpeted with pristine tropical forest, Dudhsagar is set amid breathtaking **scenery**, making the rail journey there an unforgettable experience. Unfortunately, the line, which climbs above the tree canopy via a series of spectacular cuttings and stone bridges, has been closed for over two years while conversion work is carried out. Regular broad-gauge services should be running by the winter of 1997–98, but in the meantime, the only way of **getting to Dudhsagar** is by four-wheel-drive **Jeep** via Molem or Colem (see below).

On arrival at the falls themselves, spanned by an old viaduct, you'll probably be pestered by lads offering to show you the way to the river, and to protect you from the **monkeys** that scamper around the place trying to pilfer food from picnickers. The path is steep and slippery in places, but you won't need a guide to find it: just head back along the rails from the train platform and turn right when you reach the gap between the two **tunnels**. After a fifteen-minute scramble, the trail emerges at a shady **pool** hemmed in by large grey-brown boulders – an ideal spot for bathing. If you want to escape the large groups that congregate here, clamber over the rocks a little further downstream, where there are a number of more secluded places to swim and watch the amazing butterflies and kingfishers that flit past.

A more strenuous way to while away a few hours before catching the train or jeep back is the climb to the **head of the falls**. This arduous ninety-minute hike is relentlessly steep and impossible to follow without the help of a guide, but well worth the effort for the superb views from the top.

Dudhsagar practicalities
The best time to visit Dudhsagar is immediately after the monsoons, from October until mid-December, although the falls flow well into April. Until the new broad-gauge railway line is finished, the only way to get there is by four-wheel-drive **Jeep** from the railway junction village of **Colem** (reachable by taxi from the north coast resorts for around Rs1000). The cost of the onward thirty- to forty-minute Jeep trip from Colem to the falls, which takes you across rough forest tracks and two or three river fords, is around Rs200–250 per person; the drive ends with an enjoyable fifteen-minute hike, for which you'll need a sturdy pair of shoes. Finding a Jeep-*wallah* is easy; just turn up in Colem and look for the "Controller of Jeeps" near the station. However, if you're travelling alone or in a couple, you may have to wait around until the vehicle fills up, or else fork out Rs1800 or so to cover the cost of hiring the whole Jeep yourself. Note that it can be difficult to arrange transport of any kind from Molem crossroads, where regular taxis are in short supply.

For details of the two-day GTDC tour, see p.65.

In recent years, GTDC, a number of large resort hotels and some package holiday companies have also been offering Dudhsagar as an **excursion**. The all-in price of the trip, which starts at the crack of dawn and finishes around 8pm, usually includes the minibus or taxi fare to Colem, the Jeep trip to and from Dudhsagar (or the equivalent first-class train ticket when the new track is laid), guides and a packed lunch. If you rent a car, it is also possible to combine a visit to Dudhsagar with a detour to the Mahadeva temple at Tamdi Surla. When the train is operating, snacks and cold drinks, including mineral water, are available in Dudhsagar at GTDC's rough-and-ready **café**, next to the station, but it's still advisable to bring your own supplies.

The Mahadeva temple at Tamdi Surla is on p.109.

Travel details

By bus

Panjim to: Arambol (12 daily; 1hr 45min); Baga (every 30min; 45min); Calangute (every 30min; 40min); Candolim (every 30min; 30min); Chaudi (hourly; 2hr 15min); Dona Paula (every 15min; 20min); Goa Velha (every 15min; 30min); Mapusa (every 15min; 25min); Margao (every 15min; 55min); Miramar (every 15min; 15min); Molem (5 daily; 1hr 45min); Old Goa (every 15min; 20min); Pernem (6 daily; 1hr 15min); Pilar (every 15min; 30min); Ponda (hourly; 50min); Vasco da Gama (every 15min; 50min).

Ponda to: Margao (hourly; 40min); Molem (5 daily; 1hr).

By ferry

Divar to: Naroa (every 20min; 5min).

Old Goa to: Divar Island (every 15min; 5min).

Panjim to: Betim (every 15min; 5min).

Ribandar to: Chorao (every 15min; 5min).

By train

Note that the train frequencies and timings of services between Vasco, Margao and Dudhsagar may well have changed since this book went to print due to conversion work carried out on the line between Margao and Castle Rock, Karnataka. Before undertaking any rail journey along this route, therefore, check departure times with the Tourist Information counter in Panjim's Kadamba bus stand, or at any railway station. For details of **trains to Bombay** *from Goa on the new Konkan Railway, see p.13.*

Colem to: Dudhsagar (2 daily; 40min); Margao (2 daily; 1hr 40min); Vasco da Gama (2 daily; 2hr).

Dudhsagar falls to: Colem (2 daily; 40min); Margoa (2 daily; 2hr 15min); Vasco da Gama (2 daily; 2hr 45min).

Chapter 2

North Goa

B eyond the mouth of the Mandovi estuary, the Goan coast
sweeps **north** in a near-continuous string of beaches, broken
only by the odd salt-water creek, rocky headland and three
tidal rivers – two of which, the Chapora and Arondem, still have to be
crossed by ferry. The most-developed resorts in this district, known
as **Bardez** *taluka*, all lie within a half-hour drive of Panjim.
Occupying the middle and northern part of a seven-kilometre strip of
pearl-white sand, **Calangute** and **Baga** are the epicentres of the
tourist boom, with a glut of hastily erected hotels, restaurants and
handicraft shops. Once infamous colonies of hippies gathered in
these two villages during their annual winter migration from the
Himalayas; now both heave during high season with British charter
tourists, busloads of day-trippers from out-of-state and itinerant
Indian vendors hawking trinkets on the beach.

The "scene", meanwhile, has drifted further north. **Anjuna**, the
next sizeable village up the coast from Baga, is where most of the
Christmas–New Year full-moon parties take place. This picturesque
settlement, scattered around paddy fields behind a superb soft-sand
beach, is also renowned for its Wednesday **flea market**, where you
can buy anything from Tibetan prayer wheels to cutting-edge techno
tapes. Further north still, **Vagator** and **Chapora** are the preserve of
long-stay travellers who hole up in simple houses and huts until the
onset of summer drives them to cooler climes. Accommodation of
any kind is thinner on the ground once you cross the Chapora River

---

Accommodation price codes

All **accommodation prices** in this book are coded using the symbols
below. In principle, the prices given are for the **least expensive double
rooms in high season** (mid-Dec to mid-Jan). Local taxes have been included in each case, unless specifically stated otherwise.

① Up to Rs100	④ Rs225–350	⑦ Rs750–1200
② Rs100–150	⑤ Rs350–500	⑧ Rs1200–2200
③ Rs150–225	⑥ Rs500–750	⑨ Over Rs2200

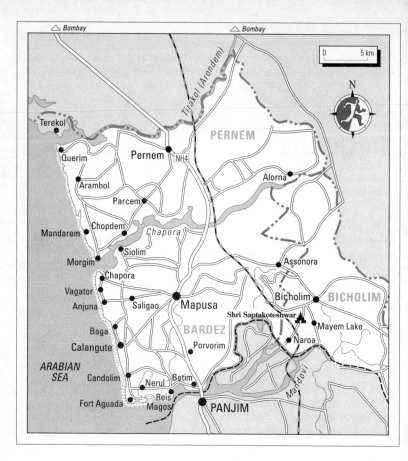

from Bardez into the mainly Hindu *taluka* of **Pernem**. The only place with anything resembling a tourist scene this far north is the Christian fishing community of **Arambol**, which hosts a small contingent of budget travellers and die-hard back-to-earthers.

The **interior** of north Goa – through Bardez and Pernem to Bicholim and Satari *talukas* – harbours few sights likely to entice you from the coast, although the vibrant Friday market at **Mapusa**, Bardez's largest town, is definitely worth a visit. Further off the beaten track but of historical interest are the Saptakoteshwar temple at **Naroa** and the Maharatha fort at **Terekol**, at the northernmost tip of the state. Neither of these monuments is essential, but getting to them via the winding back roads of the lush hinterland can be fun. If you are staying in one of the resorts around Calangute, the Portuguese fort at **Aguada**, whose imposing laterite battlements afford stunning views up the coast, warrants an excursion, while nearby **Reis Magos**, with its sixteenth-century bastion and church, is another historic site worth visiting en route to or from Panjim.

Most of the tourist traffic arriving in north Goa is siphoned off towards the coast through Mapusa. For short trips between towns and resorts, **motorcycle taxis** are the quickest and most convenient way to get around, although **buses** also run to all the villages along the coast, via the ferry crossings at **Siolim**, 7km north of Anjuna, and **Querim** (for Terekol). However, much the best way to travel to the quieter corners of the area is by rented motorcycle, available at all the main resorts.

For more general advice on renting motorcycles, see "Getting around" in Basics on p.31.

Mapusa

With a burgeoning population of 31,000, ramshackle **MAPUSA** (pronounced "Mapsa"), the district headquarters and main transport hub of Bardez *taluka*, is the state's third-largest town. If you arrive by road from Bombay and plan to stay in one of the north Goan resorts, you can jump off the bus here and pick up a local service straight to the coast, rather than continue to Panjim, 13km further south.

Arrival

Other than to shop, the only reason you may want to visit Mapusa is to arrange onward **transport**. All **buses** between Goa and Maharashtra pass through here, so you don't need to travel to Panjim to book a ticket to Bombay or Pune. Reservations for private buses can be made at the numerous agents' stalls at the bottom of the square, next to where the buses pull in; the *Kadamba* terminal – the departure point both for long-distance state buses and **local services** to Calangute, Baga, Anjuna, Vagator, Chapora and Arambol – is five minutes' walk down the main road, on the southwest edge of town. You can also get to the coast from Mapusa on one of the **motorcycle taxis** that wait in line at the bottom of the square. Rides to Calangute and Anjuna take twenty minutes and cost between Rs40 and Rs50. Taxis charge considerably more, but you can split the fare with up to five people.

As soon as you step off the bus, you'll be pestered by touts trying to get you to rent a motorbike. They'll tell you that rates here are lower than on the coast – they're not. Another reason to wait a while is that Mapusa's police set up roadblocks on the outskirts of town to collar motorbike-riding tourists without international licences or insurance documents.

Accommodation

With Candolim, Calangute, Baga and Anjuna only a short bus or taxi ride away, the only conceivable reason you might want to stay in Mapusa would be if you arrived here too late to pick up onward transport. With the exception of the *Astoria*, all of the following are with-

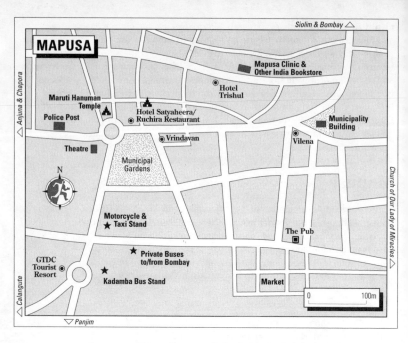

in easy walking distance of the bus stand. Advance reservation is strongly recommended, particularly for anyone planning to pull in during the night, as most rooms are booked out to business travellers by late afternoon.

Astoria, Assagao; ☎0832/262186. Located 2km west of Mapusa, this large roadside motel is a bit on the shabby side, but still a cut above most places in the centre. All the rooms are en suite and set well back from the road, with verandahs. ⑤.

GTDC Tourist Hotel, on the roundabout below the main square, opposite the *Kadamba* bus stand; ☎0832/262794 or 262694. Nothing special, but the en-suite rooms are large and clean enough, and there's a helpful tourist information counter in the lobby. Some a/c. ④.

Hotel Trishul, near Mapusa Clinic; ☎0832/262700. A large, no-frills lodge tucked away in the back streets above the main square, and the best fall-back if the *Vilena* is full. To find it, head along the lane up the hill past the Maruti (Hanuman) temple, and take the second turning on the right towards the Mapusa Clinic. ②–④.

Hotel Satyaheera, opposite Municipal Gardens at the top of the main square; ☎0832/262849 or 262949. Much the most comfortable option, and very good value, with well-appointed en-suite rooms, 24hr hot water, and some a/c. Ask for a room overlooking the square. ⑤.

Vilena, near the Municipality building, Mapusa Rd; ☎0832/263115. Run-of-the-mill mid-range hotel, offering the least expensive a/c rooms in town, in addition to good-value economy options, with or without attached bathrooms. There's also a dimly lit a/c bar and small rooftop restaurant. ②–⑤.

The Town

A dusty collection of dilapidated modern buildings scattered around the west-facing slope of a low hill, Mapusa is of little more than passing interest in itself, although on Friday mornings it hosts a lively **market** (whence the town's name, which derives from the Konkani words for "measure", *map*, and "fill up", *sa*). Calangute and Anjuna may be better stocked with souvenirs, but this vibrant bazaar is much more authentic. Visitors who have flown straight to Goa, and have yet to experience the rest of India, wander in from the coast to enjoy the pungent aromas of fish, incense, spices and exotic fruit, stacked in colourful heaps on the sidewalks. The majority of stall-holders are women from the surrounding villages, squatting in the shade of torn umbrellas. Local specialities to look out for include strings of spicy Goan sausages (*chouriço*), bottles of *toddi* spirit and the large green plantains grown in the nearby village of Moira. In the patch of open ground east of the main market area, you'll also find souvenir sellers from other parts of India, including the rainbow-clad Lamani women from Karnataka, South Indian stone carvers and the ubiquitous Kashmiri hawkers. Wandering among them are sundry freak shows, from run-of-the-mill snake charmers and kids dressed as itinerant religious ascetics (some with skewers stuck through their cheeks), to wide-eyed flagellants, blood oozing out of slashes on their backs.

Mapusa's market takes place each Fri 9am–2pm.

Finally, the covered arcades around the market are good places to stock up on cheap T-shirts and beachwear, and innumerable places to **change money** – official or otherwise – line the streets surrounding the main square, known as the **Municipal Gardens**.

Mapusa's one and only touristic sight is situated 2km east of the bazaar. Founded at the end of the sixteenth century, the church of **Our Lady of Miracles** boasts a fine gabled facade, but had to be completely rebuilt during 1961 after it was destroyed by fire. The blaze was apparently sparked off when the Portuguese army tried to blow up the nearby bridge in a vain attempt to stall the advance of Nehru's troops during the Liberation struggle.

Eating and drinking

Mapusa's most relaxing **restaurant** is the *Ruchira*, on the top floor of the *Hotel Satyaheera*, which serves a standard Indian menu with Goan and Chinese alternatives, and cold beer. Apart from the excellent fresh fruit and juice bars dotted around the market, the only other commendable place to eat and drink is the *Hotel Vrindavan*, on the east side of the main square, which dishes up Mapusa's best inexpensive South Indian-style snacks – *masala dosas*, *wadas*, *pakoras* and the like – along with an impressive range of ice creams, sundaes and shakes. Any number of cheaper but less salubrious Goan *thali* joints can be found in the streets east of the main square; the *Tourist Resort*'s drab *Have More* dining hall also does passable main meals, including some Chinese options. However, for a breather between bouts of shopping, you won't do better than *The Pub*, on the main road directly opposite the north side of the market complex (see map). From the terrace, you can survey the lively comings and goings in the market over an ice cream or ice-cold beer, and they serve main meals and a range of tourist-oriented snacks.

Naroa

The one monument in Bicholim *taluka* worth going out of your way to see – at least if you are interested in Goan Hindu architecture – is the secluded **Shri Saptakoteshwar temple** at NAROA, 5km south of the district headquarters. Ensconced in a thickly wooded valley amid well-watered areca plantations and *toddi* groves, this remote shrine

Divar Island is detailed on p.96.

is most easily reached from the south via Divar Island, from whose north shore a **ferry** chugs across the Mandovi River.

The temple **deity** here, a ferocious aspect of the god Shiva in the form of a stone *lingam*, or phallic-shaped cult object, has a long and turbulent history. Patronized during the fourteenth century by the Kadamba royal family, it was originally enshrined at Narve on Divar

Piedade and its church feature on p.96.

Island. When this temple was demolished in 1560 by the Portuguese – its masonry plundered to build the church in Piedade – the *lingam* was used as a well shaft until a party of Hindu marauders managed to rescue it. The idol was then smuggled across the river to Bicholim, where it was installed in a brand-new temple and revamped in 1668 by the Maharatha rebel leader, Shivaji.

With its shallow Moghul dome mounted on an octagonal drum, sloping tiled roofs, European-style *mandapa*, or assembly hall, and tall lamp tower, the present structure is regarded by art historians as the prototype of the modern Goan temple. Its **interior** is plain by Indian standards. Vaulted arches line the marble-floored hall, entered beneath an equestrian mural of Shivaji, and although the wood-walled shrine lacks the conventional embossed silver surround, its glaring-eyed golden *devta* is very fine.

Betim and Reis Magos

The concrete road bridge across the Mandovi River linking Panjim with the north bank collapsed on July 5, 1986, killing several people and sparking off a heated row about corruption in the government and the construction industry. The disaster was doubly embarrassing for those responsible, as the bridge had been in use for a lot less time than it had taken to build. Its replacement fared even worse, falling apart before it was even finished. The present structure, completed in 1992, looks sturdy enough, but if you are not convinced, jump on the ferry that shuttles between Panjim's old steamer jetty and the fishing and boat-building settlement of **BETIM**, 1km west of the bridge. Straddling the busy back road to Candolim and Calangute, the village is inundated with traffic during the day; the only incentive to stop here is a small Sikh temple, or **Gurudwara**, whose gleaming white Moghul domes and saffron pennant are visible from the opposite shore.

After winding through a string of ribbon developments, the coast road veers inland to a small market crossroads. A polychrome Hindu tree shrine, 20m before this, marks the turning to **REIS MAGOS**, 3km west of Betim bazaar. It's not on a bus route, but you can get there easily enough by motorcycle taxi from the main road if you're not up to walking. Its whitewashed gabled facade dominating the waterfront and visible from across the river in Panjim, Reis Magos **church** was built in 1555 and taken over soon after by Franciscan friars, charged with missionary responsibility for the colony at the time, who founded a small seminary here. Historians believe the original church was constructed on the ruins of an old Hindu temple, and the two bas-relief lion figures flanking the steps at the ends of the balustrades lend credence to this theory, being a typical feature of Vijayanagar temple architecture in the fourteenth and fifteenth centuries. A further indication of the site's former prominence is the Portuguese royal family's coat of arms, featured below the crucifix at the top of the gable. Two viceroys are also buried inside the church: one at the west entrance, the other to the north of the nave. The best preserved of the tombstones, both still in crisp condition with their Portuguese and Latin inscriptions clearly legible, is that of **Dom Luis de Ataide**, renowned as the hero of the 1570 siege of Old Goa, in which a force of 7000 defenders managed to keep an army of 100,000 Muslims (with 2000 elephants) at bay for ten months. The centrepiece of the church's elaborately carved and painted **reredos**, behind the high altar, is a multicoloured wood relief showing the Three Wise Men – or *Reis Magos*, after whom the town is named – bearing gifts to the baby Jesus. Each year, this scene is re-enacted by three local lads in the **Festa dos Reis Magos**, held in the first week of January, during Epiphany.

*Reis Magos
church is open
Mon–Sat
9am–noon &
4.30–5.30pm.*

Crowning the sheer-sided headland immediately above the church, Reis Magos **fort** was erected in 1551 to protect the narrowest point at the mouth of the Mandovi estuary. Like the 'Adil Shah's palace on the opposite bank, converted by the Portuguese after Albuquerque's defeat of the Muslims, it formerly accommodated viceroys and other dignitaries newly arrived from, or en route to, Lisbon, and in the early eighteenth century proved a linchpin in the wars against the Hindu Maharathas, who were never able to take it. These days, the bastion, surrounded by sturdy laterite walls studded with typically Portuguese turrets, is used as a prison and not open to the public, but you can clamber up the stoney slope to the ramparts for the views over the river.

*For a historical perspective
of the siege of
Old Goa, see
p.235.*

Fort Aguada

*There's a map
of Fort Aguada
and Candolim
on p. 122.*

West of Reis Magos, a long laterite peninsula extends into the sea, bringing the seven-kilometre-long Calangute beach to an abrupt end. **FORT AGUADA**, which crowns the rocky flattened top of the headland, is the largest and best-preserved Portuguese bastion in Goa. Built in 1612 to guard the northern shores of the Mandovi estuary from attacks by Dutch and Maharatha raiders, its name derives from the presence inside of several freshwater springs – the first source of drinking water available to ships arriving in Goa after the long sea

---

Forts

Crowning river mouths and hilltops along the whole length of the state, Goa's crumbling red-black **forts** stand as evocative reminders of the region's colonial past, dating from an era when this was a remote European trading post on the margins of a vast maritime empire. Laterite, the hard, heavily-pitted stone used to built them, was quarried locally and proved an efficient foil for the heavy weapons being developed in the sixteenth and seventeenth centuries, at the high watermark of Portuguese power in Asia.

The castles of medieval Europe were no match for improved gunpowder and cast-iron cannonballs, so the Portuguese, under the guidance of an Italian architect, Filipo Terzi, strengthened Goa's defences by erecting forts with low, thick walls, filled with cushions of earth and built at an angle to deflect shot. The large, V-shaped bastions, added to the battlements, were designed both to deflect incoming fire and to give greater range for the huge Portuguese revolving cannons.

Inside, buildings were chiselled out of solid rock, and the level of the ground around them was lowered to give extra defensive height. Underneath, store rooms and arsenals were excavated, inter-connected with a network of narrow tunnels and corridors, such as those still visible in Fort Aguada. These often led to concealed safe moorings at sea level – essential supply lines in times of siege. The whole was then encircled by deep dry moats and ditches to waylay foot soldiers and cavalry, though the Portuguese most feared attack from the sea by their trade rivals, the British and Dutch. The latter did penetrate the Mandovi estuary in 1604, but it was from the land that the most decisive invasion of the territory came, sixty years later, when the army of the Hindu Maratha leader, Shivaji (see p.237), poured virtually unopposed through a poorly defended interior border.

As the threat of attack diminished through the eighteenth and nineteenth centuries, the Portuguese forts gradually fell into disrepair, and today most of them, like the one at **Rachol** in Salcete (see p.172), have been completely reclaimed by vegetation, or their masonry plundered for building material. Only a handful of bastions remain intact, their walls, ditches and discarded cannons choked with weeds. Of these, **Fort Aguada**, above Sinquerim and Candolim beaches, is by far the most impressive, with **Chapora**, also in north Goa, a close second. Other forts worth visiting include **Terekol**, in the far north of the state (see p.154), and windswept **Cabo da Rama** (see p.197), in the south.

---

voyage from Lisbon. On the north side of the fort, a rampart of red-brown laterite juts into the bay to form a jetty between two small sandy coves; the gigantic cannon that once stood on it covered a blind spot in the fortification's defences. In the late 1970s, this picturesque spot, known as **Sinquerim beach**, was among the first places in Goa to be singled out for upmarket tourism. The *Fort Aguada Beach Resort* lords over the beach from the lower slopes of the promontory and is among the most expensive hotels in India: a swanky arrangement of chalets, swimming pools and overwatered lawns.

The Fort Aguada Beach Resort is reviewed on p.124.

The extensive ruins of the **fort**, formerly encircled at sea level by battlements of which only fragments now remain, can be reached by road: head south past the *Taj* village towards Nerul, and turn right after about 1km when you see a lane striking uphill through the woods. The surfaced road runs the length of the peninsula's high ridge to an impressive square-shaped **citadel**, joined to an anchorage, jetty and storehouses on the south side of the headland (now the site of Goa's largest prison) by a walled passage. Ringed by thick battlements, the heart of the fort was protected by two hundred cannon and a deep dry moat, which you still have to cross to get inside. Steps lead down from the middle of courtyard within to an enormous vaulted **cistern** capable of storing ten million litres of fresh water.

The other unusual feature of the fort is a four-storey Portuguese **lighthouse**, erected in 1864 and the oldest of its kind in Asia. Scaled via a spiral staircase, the oddly stumpy structure surveys the vast expanse of sea, sand and palm trees of Calangute beach on one side, and the mouth of the Mandovi to Cabo Raj Bhavan and the tip of the Mormugao peninsula on the other. Superseded by a modern lighthouse only in 1976, it used to house the colossal bell salvaged from the ruins of the monastery of St Augustus in Old Goa, which now hangs in Panjim's Our Lady of the Immaculate Conception (see p.69).

Aguada's church of **Saint Lawrence**, which you pass on your left before reaching the citadel on the road, is dedicated to the patron saint of sailors, whose statue presides over the high altar's reredos, clutching a model ship. Normally, the Portuguese erected churches outside their forts' battlements so as not to give the enemy a potential stronghold within firing distance of the inner defences, but Aguada was so sprawling it was deemed safe to site the shrine here. The overall design proved eminently successful: this was the only Portuguese fort in Goa never conquered during more than four hundred and fifty years of colonial rule.

Candolim

Compared with Calangute, 3km north along the beach, **CANDOLIM** is a surprisingly sedate resort, appealing in the main to

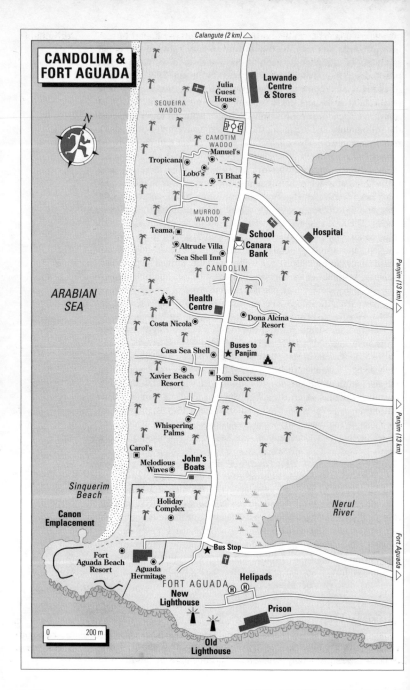

CANDOLIM &
FORT AGUADA

Calangute (2 km) △

Julia
Guest
House

Lawande
Centre
& Stores

SEQUEIRA
WADDO

N

CAMOTIM
WADDO'S

Manuel's

Tropicana

Lobo's

Ti Bhat

MURROD
WADDO

Teama

Altrude Villa
Sea Shell Inn

School

Canara
Bank

Hospital

CANDOLIM

*ARABIAN
SEA*

Health
Centre

Dona Alcina
Resort

Costa Nicola

Casa Sea Shell

Buses to
Panjim

Xavier Beach
Resort

Bom Successo

Whispering
Palms

Carol's

Melodious
Waves

John's
Boats

*Sinquerim
Beach*

Taj
Holiday
Complex

*Nerul
River*

Canon
Emplacement

Bus Stop

Fort
Aguada Beach
Resort

Aguada
Hermitage

FORT AGUADA

Helipads

New
Lighthouse

Prison

0   200 m

Old
Lighthouse

△ Panjim (13 km)

△ Panjim (13 km)

△ Fort Aguada

middle-aged package tourists from Scandanavia and the UK. That said, over the past five years its ribbon development of hotels and restaurants has sprouted a string of large holiday complexes, and during peak season the few vestiges of authentically Goan culture that remain here are drowned under a deluge of Kashmiri handicraft stalls, luridly lit terrace cafés and shops crammed with postcards and beachwear. Long gone is the time when this was a tranquil bolt hole for burgundy-clad *sanyasins* from the Rajneesh *ashram* at Pune. These days, the beach where they used to pull yoga poses on empty sands are lined with sun beds, parasols and shack cafés, and the surf is full of jet-skis, paragliders and huge inflatable banana rafts: tourist Goa at its most gruesome. On the plus side, Candolim has plenty of pleasant places to stay, many of them tucked away down quiet sandy lanes and better value than comparable guest houses in nearby Calangute, making this a good first stop if you've just arrived in Goa and are planning to head further north after finding your feet.

Practicalities

Buses to and from Panjim stop every twenty minutes or so at the stand opposite the *Casa Sea Shell*, in the middle of Candolim. A few also continue south to the *Fort Aguada Beach Resort* terminus, from where services depart every thirty minutes for the capital via Nerul village. **Taxis** can be located outside any of the major resort hotels listed below, or flagged down on the main road.

Accommodation

The best place to hunt for **accommodation** in Candolim is at the end of the lane that leads to the sea opposite the *Canara Bank*, at the north side of the village. The purpose-built concrete hotels in this ward, known as **Murrod Waddo**, are the preserve of predominantly young package tourists, but accept "walk-ins" if they have vacancies – though this is a rarity in high season. If you're having trouble finding somewhere, head for the *Teama* restaurant (see map) and ask for "Terence" (aka "Del Boy"), a local Mr Fix-It who'll know which places in the area have vacancies.

Inexpensive

Altrude Villa, Murrod Waddo; ☎0832/277703. Airy rooms with attached tiled bathrooms and verandahs. The larger ones on the first floor have sea views. ⑤.

Julia, Escrivao Vaddo; ☎0832/277219. At the north end of the village. Comfortable en-suite rooms, tiled floors, balconies, a relaxing, sociable garden, and easy access to the beach. ⑤.

Lobo's, Camotim Vaddo; no phone. In a peaceful corner of the village, this is a notch up from *Manuel's*, opposite, with larger rooms and a long common verandah on the ground floor. ④.

Candolim

Manuel Guest House, Camotim Waddo; ☎0832/277729. Small, well established, clean and cheap. All rooms have fans and attached shower toilets. ④.

Sea Shell Inn, Fort Aguada Rd, opposite the *Canara Bank*; ☎0832/276131. Homely, comfortable hotel on the roadside with large, immaculately clean rooms, safety lockers, laundry facility and a popular terrace restaurant. The tariff includes use of a nearby pool. A very good deal. ⑤.

Ti Bhat, Murrod Waddo; no phone. Simple but clean attached rooms with fans in one of Candolim's few remaining small, family-run guesthouses. Their rates are low for the area, and they do single occupancy. ③.

Moderate to expensive

Casa Sea Shell, Fort Aguada Rd, near *Bom Successo*; ☎0832/277879. A new block with its own pool, picturesquely situated beside a small chapel. The rooms are large, with spacious tiled bathrooms, and the staff and management welcoming and courteous. Arguably the best choice in this class. ⑥.

Costa Nicola, Vaddi; ☎0832/276343, fax 277343. Beautifully maintained Portuguese-style villa set in a relaxing garden. All rooms with verandahs; a model small-scale, low-impact resort, though frequently block-booked by Scandanavian tour companies. ⑥.

Fort Aguada Beach Resort, including *Aguada Hermitage* and *Taj Holiday Village*, Sinquerim beach; ☎0832/277501, fax 277733. Five-star opulence in hermetically sealed, manicured vacation campus. Pools, but no private beach. Accused of infringing environmental laws. ⑨.

Melodious Waves, Dando Vaddo; ☎0832/277711. A dozen recently built rooms with balconies in a quiet location, well back from the main road and two minutes through the dunes from a relatively peaceful stretch of beach. Tariffs reflect its proximity to the *Taj*, though. ⑥.

Tropicana Beach Resort, 835/b Camotim Vaddo; ☎0832/277732. Modern but tastefully designed chalets made of local stone and with traditional oyster-shell windows, grouped around a leafy lawn. Very pleasant. ⑥.

Xavier Beach Resort, Vaddy, off Fort Aguada Rd; ☎0832/277691, fax 276911. Peaceful, with luxurious rooms, large verandahs and views from sea-facing windows. They also have a popular rooftop cocktail bar upstairs, and terrace restaurant on the ground floor. ⑥.

Eating and drinking

Candolim's numerous beach **cafés** are a cut above your average seafood shacks, with pot plants, state-of-the-art sound systems and prices to match. Basically, the further from the *Taj* complex you venture, the more realistic the prices become. The main road is also dotted with restaurants serving the usual selection of fresh-fish dishes, with a handful of Continental options thrown in. Contrary to the advice dished out by the charter hotels, these are sanitary and considerably cheaper than their upmarket detractors claim.

Bom Successo, Fort Aguada Rd. An eclectic menu, occasional live jazz and classical Indian dance every Thursday.

Carol's, Dando Vaddo. Small and virtually indistinguishable from its neighbours, but this is arguably the best shack hereabouts, serving the usual range of fresh fish and prawns, and lobster to order for around Rs450.

Casa Sea Shell, in hotel of the same name. This is the place to head for topnotch *tandoori* and North-Indian dishes, although they also do a good choice of Chinese and European food, and the service is excellent. Moderate.

Sea Shell, Fort Aguada Rd. A congenial terrace restaurant that cooks seafood and sizzling meat meals to order – also good for vegetarians and anyone fed up with spicy Indian food. Try one of their delicious cocktails. Moderate.

Teama, Murrod Vaddo, opposite *Holiday Beach Resort*. One of the best places in the area to sample authentic Goan food. Try their prawn curry and rice house speciality, or milder fish *caldin*. Most main meals cost around Rs80, and they have a good breakfast menu. Occasional live music during the season.

Xavier's, Vaddy, off Fort Aguada Rd. A perennially popular hotel restaurant that welcomes non-residents. The a la carte menu (main dishes around Rs100) features mostly seafood, but they do regular barbeques, lots of *Mughlai*-style Indian dishes, baltis (ask for a *'karai'*) and even slap-up roast beef Sunday lunches. In addition, the rooftop terrace houses a lively cocktail bar with jazzy lights and a sound system. Happy hour 6–7pm.

Listings

Dance Performances of *Bharata Natyam* (India's most popular classical dance form) are given every Thursday evening at the *Bom Successo Bar and Restaurant*, on Fort Aguada Rd (☎0832/276132).

Dolphin-spotting Riding high on a recent BBC TV plug, *John's Boat Cruises* have cornered Candolim's lucrative dolphin-spotting market with their "No Dolphins, No Pay" policy, and British-safety-standard lifejackets. The trips start at 9am from "John's HQ" in Dando ward (see map), and cost Rs395 per head.

Foreign exchange If you need to **change money** and are not staying in a hotel with a foreign exchange facility, try the Lawande Centre, in the north of the village on the main road, which cashes travellers' cheques and bills, and is open on Sundays and bank holidays. They'll also cash money against your credit card in an emergency.

Photography The *Lindalifa Film Centre*, behind the government primary school, stocks and develops Konica and Kodak colour print film.

Travel agents Reputable travel agents in Candolim include *Davidair*, five minutes' walk north of the Lawande Centre (☎0832/276308 or 277626), and *United Air Travels*, 1239G-2 Maria Apartments, next to the Lawande Centre (☎0832/276722, fax 232144). Both reconfirm flights and book air, train, bus and catamaran tickets.

Zen and yoga Three-day, three-week or three-month meditation and yoga courses, one-to-one therapy sessions, and stress-release workshops are held in Candolim from September to May. Contact Jerome Vaney, A3/3 *Dona Alcina Resort*, Candolim (visiting hours 4–5pm).

Calangute

A 45-minute bus ride up the coast from the capital, **CALANGUTE** is Goa's busiest and most commercialized resort, and the flagship of the state government's bid for a bigger slice of India's package-tourist pie. In the 1970s and early 1980s, this once-peaceful fishing village epitomized Goa's reputation as a safe haven for hedonistic hippies. Indian visitors flocked by the busload from Bombay and Bangalore to giggle at the tribes of dreadlocked Westerners lying naked on the vast white sandy beach, stoned out of their brains on local *feni* and cheap *charas*. The odd party of prurient day-trippers still arrives from time to time, but invariably leaves disappointed; Calangute has cleaned up its act. Apart from the handful of stalwart budget travellers' bars and guesthouses on the edges of town, the "scene" has been almost entirely squeezed out by more mainstream holiday culture. Hoteliers today joke about the old days, when they used to rent out makeshift shacks on the beach to backpackers. Now many of them manage tailor-made tourist settlements, complete with air-conditioned rooms, swimming pools and plush lawns for groups of suitcase-carrying fortnighters.

Though heavily developed by Goan standards, Calangute is not yet the high-rise hell that many Asian resorts have become in recent years. Away from the narrow congested main road that runs from the bustling market square to nearby Baga, most hotels are small, two-storey buildings, hidden among the dunes behind a noise-proof curtain of coconut trees. However, as the rash of construction sites around the outskirts blossom into larger resort complexes, what little charm Calangute retains looks set to disappear. Without adequate provision for sewage treatment or increased water consumption, it's only a matter of time before the town starts to stew in its own juices, putting off the very tourists the developers are trying to attract.

Arrival and getting around

Buses from Mapusa and Panjim pull in at the small bus stand in the market square at the centre of Calangute. Some continue to Baga, stopping at the crossroads behind the beach en route. Get off here if you can (as the main road veers sharply to the right) – it's closer to most of the hotels. **Motorcycle taxis** hang around the little sandy square behind GTDC's *Tourist Resort*, next to the steps that drop down to the beachfront itself. Also ask around here if you want to rent a **motorcycle**. Rates are standard (Rs150–200 per day for a 100cc Yamaha); the nearest **service station** ("petrol pump") is five minutes' walk from the beach, back towards the market on the right-hand side of the main road. **Bicycles** are widely available from around Rs40 to Rs50 per day.

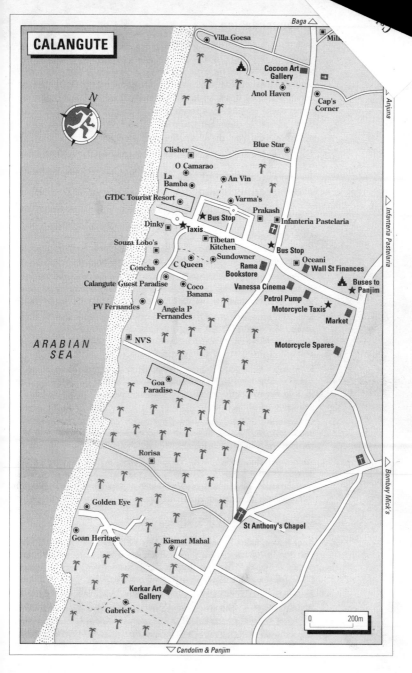

CALANGUTE

Villa Goesa

Mil...

Cocoon Art Gallery

Anol Haven

Cap's Corner

Blue Star

Clisher

O Camarao

La Bamba

An Vin

GTDC Tourist Resort

Varma's

Prakash

Bus Stop

Infanteria Pastelaria

Dinky

Taxis

Tibetan Kitchen

Souza Lobo's

Sundowner

Bus Stop

Oceani

Wall St Finances

Concha

C Queen

Rama Bookstore

Calangute Guest Paradise

Coco Banana

Vanessa Cinema

Buses to Panjim

Petrol Pump

PV Fernandes

Angela P Fernandes

Motorcycle Taxis

Market

NV'S

Motorcycle Spares

ARABIAN SEA

Goa Paradise

Rorisa

Golden Eye

Goan Heritage

Kismat Mahal

St Anthony's Chapel

Kerkar Art Gallery

Gabriel's

N

Baga △

▷ Anjuna

▷ Infanteria Pastelaria

▷ Bombay Mick's

▽ Candolim & Panjim

0   200m

Accommodation

Calangute is chock-full of **places to stay**, and demand only outstrips supply in the Christmas–New Year high season; at other times, it pays to haggle a little over the tariff, especially if the place looks empty. Most of the inexpensive accommodation is in concrete annexes tacked onto the backs of family houses. Though bare and basic, these usually have running water and fans. For a little extra, you can get a verandah or balcony, and an attached bathroom; nowhere is far from the shore, but sea views are more of a rarity. The top hotels are nearly all gleaming white, exclusive villa complexes with pools and direct beach access. High-season rates in such places are staggeringly steep (if you can get a room), as they cater almost solely for package tourists.

Inexpensive

Angela P. Fernandes, Umta Vaddo, south of beachfront. Calangute's most popular budget travellers' hang-out. Basic but fairly clean, with reliable water supply, fans and psychedelic murals. Cheaper rooms around the back. ①–②.

An Vin, 5/193 Umta Vaddo, behind the bus park. Six neat, clean rooms (some attached) in a hospitable family guesthouse. Good home cooking on request from a garrulous landlady, too. ②.

Gabriel's, just south of *Golden Eye* near the ice factory, Gaura Vaddo; no phone, fax 0832/277484. A congenial, quiet, family-run guesthouse mid-way between Calangute and Candolim. Shady garden, pleasant views from rear side across the *toddi* dunes, and close to the beach.

NV's, south Calangute. Homely, traditional Goan guesthouse right on the beach, run by fisher family and holding its own despite proximity to a large package resort. eleven rooms, four with breezy common balcony. A good budget option. ③–④.

O Camarao, 5/201 Umta Vaddo, just north of *GTDC Tourist Resort*; ☎0832/276229. Spruce, blue- and white-painted bungalow with immaculate rooms, verandahs and a restaurant. Very good value. ③.

Sundowner Holiday Home, 5/128 Umta Vaddo, behind *Tibetan Kitchen*; ☎0832/277267. Large, good-value rooms, some with windows on two walls, fans and attached bathrooms in a fairly modern building. The best rooms (with balconies) are on the upper storey. ④.

Moderate

Anol Haven, 6/85A Cobra Vaddo, opposite *Cap's Corner*; ☎0832/276532, fax 022/611 7034. Seven spanking new, airy rooms with balconies and en-suite bathrooms, just off the main drag in a quiet district. An improbably named place, but among the best deals in this category. ⑤.

La Bamba, next to GTDC *Tourist Resort*; ☎0832/276108. Small, cosy and well-maintained guesthouse close to the beach. Some sea-facing rooms. Breakfast available on request. ⑤.

Cap's Corner, Baga Rd, Cobra Vaddo; ☎0832/276587, fax 276583. Dull concrete building, but the rooms are very clean and comfortable, if a little overpriced. They also have one self-catering apartment with kitchen and fridge (⑦), and a relaxing terrace restaurant. ⑨.

CoCo Banana, 1/195 Umta Vaddo, down the lane past *Meena Lobo's* restaurant; ☎0832/276478, fax 279068. Very comfortable, spacious chalets, all with bathrooms, Swiss mosquito nets, extra-long mattresses and balconies, grouped around central garden. Good value. ⑨.

Golden Eye, A-1/189 Gaura Vaddo; ☎ & fax 0832/276187. Large rooms, balconies, sea views and a terrace restaurant, all smack on the beach. One of the first purpose-built hotels in Calangute. ⑥.

GTDC Tourist Resort, overlooking the steps to the beach; ☎0832/276024. The last resort: a grim concrete block with marginally less hideous cottages adjacent. The rates aren't bad, though. ④–⑤.

Kismat Mahal, E-1/221 Gaura Vaddo, near St Anthony's chapel; ☎0832/276067. Fourteen large and modern rooms, just behind the dunes. Good value. ④.

Expensive

Concha, Umta Vaddo; ☎0832/276056, fax 277555. Stylish old-colonial house, with banana plants in the garden, mosquito nets, verandahs and well-furnished rooms. Balconies cost extra. ⑦–⑧.

Goan Heritage, Gaura Vaddo; ☎0832/276027, fax 276120. A swanky two-star 3km south of the market; 68 rooms, lawns and a pool. ⑧.

Varma's Beach Resort, two minutes' east of GTDC *Tourist Resort*; ☎0832/276077, fax 276022. Attractive a/c rooms, with balconies overlooking a leafy garden. Secluded but close to the centre of the village. ⑧.

Villa Bomfim, Baga Rd; ☎0832/276105. Long-established resort hotel, now given over to package tourists, with a pleasant open-air restaurant, beauty parlour, safe deposit, money-changing and so on. ⑦.

Villa Goesa, Cobravaddo; ☎0832/277535, fax 276182. A stone's throw from the beach and very swish, set around a lush garden of young palms and lawns. Occasional live music and a cocktail bar. All rooms have balconies. ⑧.

The town and beach

The road from the **town** to the beach is lined with Kashmiri-run handicraft boutiques and Tibetan stalls selling Himalayan curios and jewellery. The quality of the goods on offer – mainly Rajasthani, Gujarati and Karnatakan textiles – is generally high, but so are the prices. Haggle hard and don't be afraid to walk away from a heavy sales pitch – the same stuff crops up every Wednesday at Anjuna's flea market. The **beach** itself is nothing special – its sand steeply shelves but is more than large enough to accommodate the huge numbers of high-season visitors. Most of the action centres on the scruffy beachfront below GTDC's unsightly *Tourist Resort*, where crowds of Indian women in saris and straw hats stand around watching their sons and husbands frolic in the surf. Nearby, stray cows nose through the rubbish left by the previous bus party, while an end-

Anjuna's flea market features on p.139.

less stream of ice cream and fruit sellers, *lunghi wallahs*, ear cleaners and masseurs, work their way through the ranks of Western sun-worshippers.

To escape the mêlée, head fifteen minutes or so south of the main beachfront area, towards the rows of old wooden boats moored below the dunes. In this virtually hawker-free zone, you'll only come across teams of villagers hauling in hand-nets at high tide or fishermen fixing their tack under bamboo sunshades. Wherever you hang out, though, remember that Calangute's "**no nudism**" rule is for real and enforced by special police patrols; this includes topless bathing. In addition, several incidents of **sexual harassment** and attempted rape have occurred here in recent years.

Eating and drinking

Calangute's **bars** and **restaurants** are mainly grouped around the entrance to the beach and along the Baga road. As with most Goan resorts, the accent is firmly on seafood, though many places tack a few token veggie dishes onto their menus. Western budget travellers' breakfasts (pancakes, porridge, muesli, eggs, etc) also feature prominently on most menus.

Blue Star, on the main Baga road, near *Stay Longer* guest house. Chocolate cake, tiramisu and sundry other German Bakery delights, including superb espresso and delicious milk *chai* with cardamom, ginger and frothy milk, served in a cosy café by the roadside.

Mr Cater's, GTDC *Tourist Resort*. Bustling terrace restaurant overlooking the beach and serving moderately priced *tandoori* seafood, meat sizzlers, *xacuti*, *cafreal* and a range of Indian veg dishes.

Clisher, north of GTDC *Tourist Resort*, behind the beach. Among the best of the beachside bar-restaurants, with the usual fresh seafood, good breakfasts, cold beer and sea views. Inexpensive to moderate.

Dinky, beside the steps to the beach. Standard seafood and beer bar, with a pleasant verandah for crowd watching. Popular with budget travellers.

Infantaria Pastelaria, near St John's Chapel, Baga Rd. Small roadside terrace that gets packed out for breakfast – piping hot croissants or freshly baked apple pie. Recommended.

NV's, south Calangute. A ten-minute trek down the beach, but well worth it for no-nonsense platefuls of grilled fish, calamari and crab, all fresh from the family boat.

Oceanic, on the market road, near roundabout. Rated for its great sharkfish kebabs and other seafood specialities, although portions are small and the traffic noise a distraction. Moderate.

Rorisa, up the lane west of St Anthony's chapel. Quiet café serving tasty Goan and western food, including great Bombay *alloo* and green fish curry; their banana pancakes are a must for breakfast.

Souza Lobo, on the beachfront. One of Goa's oldest restaurants and deservedly famous for its superb seafood; try their blow-out fish sizzlers or mouthwatering tiger prawns. Get there early, and avoid weekends. Moderate.

Tibetan Kitchen, off the beach road. Filling, inexpensive Tibetan food, including tasty cheese-fried *momo* and home-made cakes, with Western and Chinese options, full breakfasts, New Age music and chess sets.

Nightlife

Thanks to a concerted crackdown by the Goan police on beach parties and loud music, Calangute's **nightlife** is surprisingly tame. All but a handful of the **bars** wind up by 10pm, leaving punters to prolong the short evenings back at their hotels. One notable exception is *Tito's*, at the Baga end of the beach, which stays open until 11pm off season and into the small hours in late December and January. Calangute's trendiest (and priciest) night spot, it boasts a large sandy terrace overlooking the beach, a small dance floor and a techno-house DJ. When *Tito's* closes, the die-hards head across town to recently opened *Bombay Mick's*, where there's a good-sized circular dance space surrounded by tables, with jazzy lights and the area's most powerful sound system, complete with British DJs; entrance is Rs50, or free if you turn up before 11pm for a meal (they serve tasty steaks, prepared by an English chef). The only catch is that it's a fair way out of Calangute; most people take a taxi there and back, if only to avoid the police, who regularly bust tourists for riding rented motorcycles without international licences or insurance papers.

The only other places that consistently open late are a couple of dull hippy hangouts in the woods to the south of the beach road: *Pete's Bar*, a perennial favourite next door to *Angela P. Fernandes*, is generally the most lively, offering cheap drinks, backgammon sets and relentless reggae.

Further afield, *Bob's Inn*, between Calangute and Candolim, is another popular bar, famed less for its tasty Western food and extrovert owner than the group of ageing "heads" that holds court around a large table in the front bar. Also worth checking out while you're down that way is the *Golden Eye*, on the north side of Candolim beach, which draws crowds of young, well-heeled punters from the nearby package tour hotels.

Finally, don't miss the chance to sample some *pukka* Indian culture while you are in Calangute. The *Kerkar Art Gallery*, in Gaurwaddo, at the south end of town (☎0832/276017), hosts evenings of **classical music and dance** every Tuesday and Saturday from 6.30 to 8pm, held in the back garden on a sumptuously decorated stage, complete with incense and evocative candlelight. The recitals, performed by students and teachers from Panjim's Kala Academy, are kept comfortably short for the benefit of Western visitors, and are preceded by a short introductory talk. Tickets, available in advance or at the door, cost Rs200.

Listings

Art galleries The excellent *Kerkar Art Gallery* (Mon–Sat 10am–7pm) exhibits and sells paintings, sculpture and crafts by local Goan artists, and has two outlets: one down in Gaura Vaddo, and the other around the corner from *Shyam Books* on the main beach road. Also worth a browse is the European-run *Cocoon Art Gallery*, Baga Rd.

Banks If you need to change money, head for *Wall Street Finances* (Mon–Sat 9.30am–6pm), opposite the petrol pump and in the shopping complex on the beachfront, who exchange cash and travellers' cheques at bank rates. If they are closed, try the fast and friendly *ENEM Financial Services*, opposite the *Hotel Beiramar* in Baga (daily 8am–9pm). This is a good place to go if you've lost your passport or money and need help. The very friendly couple who run it also offer a free incoming fax service for customers.

Books The *Shyam* (aka *Rama*) secondhand bookshop, where the main Baga road bends north, stocks a vast range of paperbacks in several languages, including English, French, German, Dutch, Swedish and Japanese, but is a real rip-off. The *Friends Circulating Library*, opposite the temple in the market area operates an equally extortionate lending scheme.

Laundry *Ligia Dry Cleaners*, who have stalls next to the *Vanessa* cinema (near the petrol pump) and opposite the temple, wash and iron at fixed rates. There's also a tiny hole-in-the-wall laundry next to the taxi stand at the main entrance to the beach.

Travel agents For flight reconfirmation, and air, train and bus ticketing, try *MGM Travels* (☎0832/276073), on the roundabout opposite *Rama Books*; *Royal Tours and Travels* (☎0832/276109), opposite the GTDC *Tourist Resort*; or *Sea Breeze Travels* (☎0832/276234) around the corner from *Royal Tours and Travels* on the main road. Another reputable place is *Alfran Travels*, at 8 Romana Chambers (opposite the petrol pump), and *ENEM*, recommended above for their money-changing services (see "Banks"), also run a small travel desk offering standard agency services.

Baga

BAGA, 10km west of Mapusa, is basically an extension of Calangute; not even the locals agree where one ends and the other begins. Lying in the lee of a rocky, wooded headland, the only real difference between the two is that the scenery here is marginally more varied and picturesque. A small river flows into the sea at the top of the village, below a broad spur of soft white sand scattered with outriggers, from where a dirt track strikes across an open expanse of rice paddy towards Anjuna. A couple of years ago, few buildings stood at this far northern end of the beach other than a handful of old red-tiled fishers' houses nestling in the dunes. Since the package boom, however, Baga has developed more rapidly than anywhere else in the state, and now the main road running through the village is lined with hotels and restaurants, while the few remaining patches of virgin paddy inland are scarred with construction sites and holiday complexes. So if you're looking for a quiet stretch of beach, forget it and

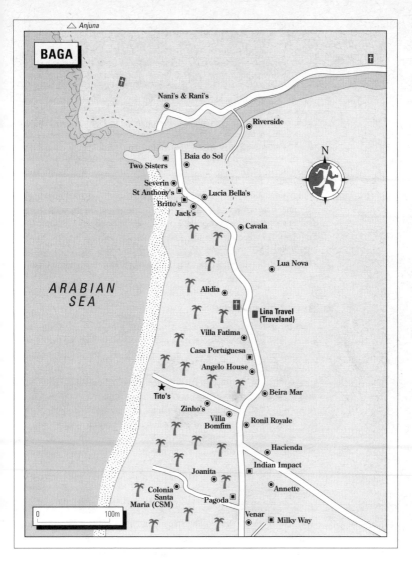

head further north. Once over the river, crossed by a hideous concrete box bridge, you enter a more tranquil hinterland of coconut plantations peppered with Hindu farming hamlets. This area has also recently acquired a couple of huge hotels, but at least you don't feel quite so boxed in as you do in the village proper.

Most of the action in Baga revolves around the sandy square and bus park close to the river mouth, where the main metalled road from

Boats to the Anjuna flea market

Every Wednesday, **boats** leave Baga beach for the flea market at Anjuna
(see p.139), from around 9am until just before sunset. How much you pay
for the twenty-minute trip depends on how many passengers the fishermen
manage to cram on board, but it usually works out the same as a motorcycle taxi. If you go, pack your cameras and any valuables in a plastic bag.
Accidents occasionally happen when the fishermen load their vessels to
the gunwales and then try to save time and fuel by cutting through a narrow channel between two rocks – straightforward enough on calm days,
but a hair-raising stunt when the sea is choppy.

Calangute peters out and the buses roll in from Mapusa and Panjim,
18km southeast. The restaurants nearby do a brisk trade during the
day and stay open late in the evening, when they fill up with punters
from the nearby resort hotels. Further south, a row of lookalike bamboo beach bars compete for custom with uniformly raucous techno
music systems. For some reason, *Vicky's* draws a bigger crowd than
the others, but they all charge the same for a beer and swing well into
the night during the season.

Accommodation

Accommodation is harder to arrange on spec in Baga than
Calangute, as most of the hotels have been carved up by the charter
companies; even rooms in smaller guesthouses tend to be booked
out well before the season gets under way. If you're keen to stay, you
may well have to hole up further down the beach for a night while
you hunt around for a vacancy. The rough-and-ready places dotted
around the fishing village usually have space; look for signs outside
restaurants on the main square. Cheap houses and rooms for rent are
also available on the quieter north side of the river, favoured by long-
staying travellers, although these are like gold dust in December and
January.

Inexpensive

Jack's, in the village; no phone. Fourteen small and basic rooms, all with
attached bathrooms and fans, behind the restaurant of the same name. ②.

Joanita, Baga Rd; no phone. Clean, airy rooms with attached baths and some
double beds, ranged around a quiet garden. ③.

Lucia Bella's, 7/173A Baga Rd; no phone. Cramped and not really pleasant
enough for a lengthy stay, but fine as a stopover until you find your feet. ②.

Martin's, 1928 Cobra Vaddo; no phone. Eight simple rooms, some with balconies, in a small two-storey family house. Good value. ②.

Meliss, 620 Anjuna Rd; no phone. Eight recently-built rooms in a clean, quiet
block on the north side of the river, all with attached shower toilets. Good off-
season discounts, too. ④.

Nani's and Rani's, north of the river; ☎0832/276313 or 277014. A handful of red-tiled, whitewashed cottages in a secluded back garden, popular with long-staying guests. Fans, common toilets, well-water and an outdoor shower. Recommended. ②.

Venar, 1963 Cobra Vaddo; ☎0832/276867. Large, immaculately neat rooms (some attached) in an old Portuguese-style house. Discount for singles. One of the best budget deals in town. ③.

Zinho's, 7/3 Saunta Vaddo; ☎0832/277383. Tucked away off the main road, close to *Tito's*. Half-a-dozen modest size, clean rooms near to the beach. Good value. ④.

Moderate to expensive

Alidia (Alirio & Lidia), Baga Rd, Saunta Vaddo; ☎0832/276835 or 279014, fax 276285. Attractive modern chalet rooms with good-sized verandahs looking on to the dunes, and a breezy rooftop terrace that's ideal for hammock swinging and yoga. Double or twin beds. Quiet and friendly. Recommended. ⑤–⑥.

Annette, north of Baga Rd opposite *CSM*; ☎0832/224485, fax 225042. Seven large ugly pink apartment blocks around a pool. ⑦–⑧.

Baia do Sol, on the square; ☎0832/276085. Baga's best (two-star) hotel is modern, immaculate and surrounded by a well-kept garden. No single occupancy in high season. Some a/c. ⑧.

Cavala, on the main road; ☎0832/277587. Modern building in tastefully traditional mould; simple rooms, bathrooms en suite and separate balconies. ⑥.

Colonia Santa Maria, down the lane from *Pagoda Restaurant*; ☎0832/272571. Two restaurants, a pool and shops in the heart of an exclusive package tour enclave. Popular with 18–30s. ⑧.

Hacienda, Baga Rd; ☎0832/277348. Nothing special but with big, airy rooms, balconies and a garden. ⑤.

Lua Nova, north of the main road, near the *Cavala Hotel*; ☎0832/277173. Peaceful and cosy; pool, sun beds on the lawn and individual balconies, though somewhat boxed in by its multi-storey neighbour. ⑦.

Riverside, on the river bank; ☎0832/276062. Newish, tasteful hotel with large comfy rooms, a good restaurant and river views. Moving into the package bracket, but the best value at this price. ⑦.

Ronil Royale, Baga Rd; ☎0832/276101, fax 276068. Baga's most upmarket hotel has ersatz Portuguese apartments overlooking two small pools, with a swish restaurant. A ten-minute walk from the beach. ⑨.

Villa Fatima, Baga Rd; ☎0832/277418. Thirty-two attached rooms in a three-storey building around a sociable garden terrace. Rates vary according to room size. ⑤.

Eating and drinking

Food options in Baga are confined to the **restaurants** clustered around the square at the top end of the village and the lookalike shack **cafés** behind the beach, with a string of popular terrace bars lining the main road. For a splurge, splash out on a candle-lit

Baja

Worth a look if you're staying in Baga are the Calangute listings on pp.130–132.

dinner in the *Casa Portuguesa*, around the corner from Calangute's most popular nightclub, *Tito's* (see p.131). Also in Calangute is the area's best breakfast venue, *Infantaria Pastelaria* (reviewed on p.130), fifteen minutes' walk towards town.

Britto's, on the square. Perennially the most popular restaurant in the village, with a predictable menu of reasonably priced seafood and Western dishes, and some Goan specialities.

Casa Portuguesa, Baga Rd. Traditional Portuguese and Goan food served by candlelight inside this romantic colonial villa or *alfresco* on a leafy lawn. The gregarious owner serenades diners with Amelia Rodrigues *fados* most evenings. Overpriced, but worth it for the atmosphere.

Indian Impact, Baga Rd. Quality *tandoori* fish and meat dishes prepared and served on a dimly lit terrace. Moderate to expensive.

Jack's, in the village. No-nonsense, inexpensive seafood joint also serving Goan-fried spicy vegetables and less than inspiring Chinese food.

Little Italy, 300m east along the Anjuna Rd, on the north side of the river. Tasty fresh pasta, pizza and other Italian specialities, served on a shady terrace overlooking the river.

Milky Way, midway between Calangute and Baga. Indian filter coffee, filled rolls (including delicious garlic cottage cheese) and other moderately priced snacks dished up in a shady garden.

Nani's and Rani's, on the north side of the river. Friendly family-run restaurant serving unremarkable but inexpensive food on a sociable verandah overlooking the river. Popular with budget travellers.

St Anthony's, off the square. The place to watch the sunset accompanied by an icy beer and Indian classical music on a better-than-average sound system. The main meals are a touch pricey, though.

Two Sisters, at the north end of Baga beach. This shack's muesli-curd-and-honey breakfasts are the healthiest and most delicious on offer in the village, and they serve the usual seafood and fries during the rest of the day.

Valerio's, next door to *Hotel Baia do Sol*. Sophisticated bar-restaurant with good sea and river views from a pleasant first-floor terrace. Live reggae music on Wednesdays after the flea market. Moderate to expensive.

Listings

Foreign exchange *ENEM Financial Services*, on the main road opposite *Hotel Beira Mar* (daily 8am–9pm), change travellers' cheques and cash at 1.5 percent below current bank rates.

Football Well worth checking out on Sunday afternoons is the regular football match between visiting British tourists and resident Kenyan students. Kick off is around 3pm. Bring your kit if you want a game.

Travel agent Well-established *Lina Travels*, 3/22 Villa Nova, on the main road near the *Casa Portuguesa* (☎0832/276196, fax 276124), specialize in bus and air ticketing, and are also agents for the *Damania* catamaran service.

Anjuna

ANJUNA, 8km west of Mapusa, is scattered over a wide area of paddy fields and coconut plantations, from the woods behind the southern end of its long, sandy beach, to the sun-baked sides of Vagator hill in the north. With its fluorescent-painted palm trees and infamous full-moon parties, the village is Goa at its most "alternative". Designer leather and lycra may have superseded cotton kaftans, but most people's reasons for coming are the same as they were

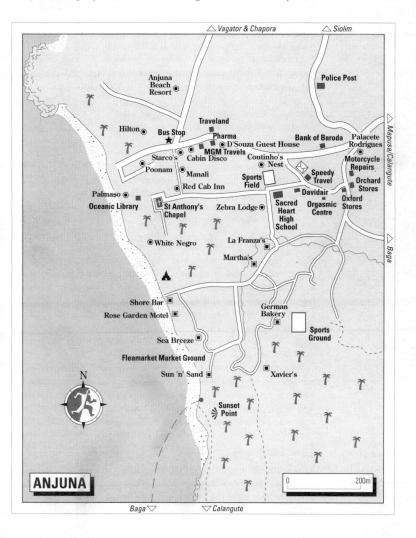

Anjuna's flea market takes place every Wednesday.

in the 1970s: drugs, dancing and lying on the beach slurping tropical fruit. Depending on your point of view, you'll find the headlong hedonism a total turn-off or heaven-on-sea. Either way, the scene looks here to stay, despite government attempts to stamp it out, so you might as well get a taste of it while you're in the area, if only from the wings, with a day-trip to the famous **flea market**.

One of the main sources of Anjuna's enduring popularity as a hippy hangout is its superb **beach**. Fringed by groves of swaying coconut palms, the stretch of soft white sand conforms more closely to the archetypal vision of paradise than any other beach on the north coast. Bathing is generally safer than at most of the nearby resorts, too, especially at the more peaceful southern end, where a rocky headland keeps the sea calm and the undertow to a minimum. North of the market ground, the beach broadens, running in an uninterrupted kilometre-long stretch of steeply shelving sand to a low red cliff. The village bus park lies on top of this high ground, near a crop of small cafés, bars and Kashmiri handicraft stalls. Every lunchtime, tour parties from Panjim pull in here for a beer, before heading home again, leaving the ragged army of sun-weary Westerners to enjoy the sunset.

The season in Anjuna starts in early November, when most of the long-staying regulars show up, and it peters out in late March, when they drift off again. During the Christmas and New Year rush, the village is inundated with a mixed crowd of round-the-world backpackers, refugees from the English club scene, Israeli ravers, and revellers from all over India, lured by the promise of the big beach parties. The rest of the time, though, Anjuna has a surprisingly simple, unhurried atmosphere – due, in no small part, to the shortage of places to stay. Most visitors who come here on market day, or for the raves, travel in from other resorts. That said, a couple of large package tour hotels have appeared over the past couple of years, which could radically alter the mix of visitors here. Only one-and-a-half hours' drive from the airport, Anjuna lies well within reach of the charter transfer buses and if, or when, the government get around to upgrading the road from the capital, the village could well go the same way as Baga.

Whenever you come, keep a close eye on your valuables. **Theft**, particularly from the beach, is a big problem. Party nights are the worst; if you stay out late, keep your money and papers on you, or lock them somewhere secure (see below). Thieves have even been known to break into local houses by lifting tiles off the roof.

Practicalities

Buses from Mapusa and Panjim drop passengers at various points along the tarmac road across the top of the village, which turns right towards Chapora at the main crossroads by *Starco's*. If you're looking for a room, get off here as it's close to most of the guesthouses.

The crossroads has a couple of small **stores**, a **motorcycle taxi** rank, and functions as a *de facto* village square and **bus stand**.

Accommodation

Most of Anjuna's very limited **accommodation** consists of small unfurnished houses, although finding one is a problem at the best of times – in peak season it's virtually impossible. By then, all but a handful have been let to long-staying regulars who book by post several months in advance. If you arrive hoping to sort something out on spec, you'll probably have to make do with a room in a guesthouse at

---

The Anjuna flea market

Anjuna's Wednesday **flea market** is the hub of Goa's alternative scene, and *the* place to indulge in a spot of souvenir shopping. A few years back, the weekly event was the exclusive preserve of backpackers and the area's semi-permanent population, who gathered here to smoke *chillums*, and to buy and sell clothes and jewellery they probably wouldn't have the nerve to wear anywhere else: something like a small pop festival without the stage. These days, however, everything is more organized and mainstream. Pitches are rented out by the metre, drugs are banned and the approach roads to the village are choked solid all day with air-conditioned buses and Ambassador cars ferrying in tourists from resorts further down the coast. Even the lepers and other beggars have to pay *baksheesh* to be here.

The range of goods on sale has broadened, too, thanks to the high profile of migrant hawkers and stall-holders from other parts of India. Each region or culture tends to stick to its own corner. At one end, Westerners congregate around racks of New Age rave gear, Balinese batiks and designer beachwear. Nearby, hawk-eyed Kashmiris sit cross-legged beside trays of silver jewellery and papier-mâché boxes, while Tibetans, wearing jeans and T-shirts, preside over orderly rows of prayer wheels, turquoise bracelets and sundry Himalayan curios. Most distinctive of all are the Lamani women from Karnataka, decked from head to toe in traditional tribal garb, selling elaborately woven multicoloured cloth, which they fashion into everything from jackets to money belts, and which makes even the Westerners' party gear look positively funereal. Elsewhere, you'll come across dazzling Rajasthani mirrorwork and block-printed bedspreads, Keralan woodcarvings and a scattering of Gujarati appliqué. One old man even sells anklets and armbands made from peacock feathers.

What you end up paying for this exotic merchandise largely depends on your ability to **haggle**. Lately, prices have been inflated as tourists not used to dealing in rupees will part with almost anything. Be persistent, though, and cautious, and you can usually pick things up for a reasonable rate.

Even if you're not spending, the flea market is a great place just to sit and watch the world go by. Mingling with the sun-tanned masses are bands of strolling musicians, itinerant beggars, performing monkey acts and snake charmers, as well as the inevitable hippy jugglers, clad in regulation waistcoats and billowing pyjama trousers. You wonder what the Indian day-trippers must make of it all.

Boats

Fishing boats shuttle between Anjuna and Baga beach every Wednesday from just below the market ground. You can also catch a boat back to Arambol from here in the evening; see p.152.

first, although most owners are reluctant to rent out rooms for only one or two days at a time. Basically, unless you mean to stay for at least a couple of months, you'll be better off looking for a room in Calangute, Baga or nearby Vagator or Chapora.

Inexpensive

Coutinho's Nest, Soronto Vaddo; ☎0832/274386. Small, very respectable family guesthouse on the main road, in the centre of Anjuna. Their immaculately clean rooms, with bamboo beds, are among the village's best budget deals. ③.

D'Souza, c/o *Michael's Pharmacy*; ☎0832/274347 or 274439. Six very basic rooms, with en-suite showers but common toilets in an unappealing location by the roadside. OK for a night or two, though. ①.

Hilton, on the main road near the bus park; ☎0832/274432. Rooms in a characterless outbuilding, 500m behind the beach. Some attached shower-toilets. ④.

Manali, south of *Starco's*; ☎0832/274421. Anjuna's best all-round budget guesthouse has simple rooms opening on to a yard, fans, safe deposit, money-changing, a sociable terrace-restaurant and shared bathrooms. Very good value, so book in advance. ②.

Martha's, 907 Montero Vaddo; ☎0832/273365. Five well-kept rooms, including one pleasant house, run by a warm family. Basic amenities include kitchen space and running water. ③–⑤.

Red Cab Inn, De Mello Vaddo; ☎0832/273312. Run-of-the-mill rooms ranged around a courtyard and busy restaurant. Check out their ludicrously overpriced "Executive Chalet" – a lurid confection of red-painted concrete with blue lights and Day-Glo mobiles.

Starco's, on the crossroads; no phone. Dark, cramped rooms around a yard but with a good restaurant and an owner with the longest fingernails in India. ③.

Zebra Lodge and Camping, near Sacred Heart High School; no phone. Five neat rock-bottom rooms with common toilets, separate verandahs and a garden. Camping space costs Rs10 per night. ①.

Moderate to expensive

Anjuna Beach Resort, De Mello Vaddo; ☎0832/274433. Fifteen spacious, comfortable rooms with balconies and attached bathrooms, in a new concrete building at the north edge of the village. Those on the upper floor are best. Good value. ⑤.

Bougainvillea (Grandpa's Inn), Gaunwadi, at the east side of village on the main Mapusa road; ☎0832/274370 or 2743271, fax 252624. A bastion of

---

Water shortages

Anjuna has, thanks to the extra inhabitants it attracts over the winter, become particularly prone to **water shortages**. These tend not to affect many visitors, as the drought only begins to bite towards the end of March when the majority have already left. For the villagers, however, the problem causes genuine hardship. Use well water very sparingly and avoid water toilets if possible – traditional "dry" ones are far more ecologically sound.

Anjuna-style alternative chic, under new management, though still pitched at well-heeled party lovers, with ten tasteful rooms, terrace restaurant, wet-bar, billiards room, karate and yoga lessons, and poolside jam sessions. ⑧.

Don Joao Resort, Sorranto Vaddo; ☎0832/274325. An unsightly multi-storey hotel, slap in the middle of the village, and pitched squarely at charter tourists, with a poolside restaurant, fridges in the rooms and inflated rates: precisely the kind of place Anjuna could do without. ⑦–⑧.

Poonam, east of the bus park; ☎0832/273247. Double-storey purpose-built guesthouse with a leafy garden and a café. The rooms are clean, but rudimentary and overpriced. Their larger suites are better value. ⑤.

Palacete Rodrigues, near *Oxford Stores*; ☎0832/273358. Old Portuguese-style residence converted into an upmarket guesthouse. Carved wood furniture, and a relaxed, traditional Goan feel. Single occupancy available. ⑤–⑥.

Palmasol Guest House, Praia de St Anthony, behind the middle of the beach; ☎0832/273258. Large, comfortable rooms very near the beach, with running water, verandahs and a relaxing garden. ⑤.

White Negro, 719 Praia de St Anthony, south of the village; ☎0832/273326. Pleasant chalets catching sea breezes, all with attached bathrooms and 24hr running water. Also a lively restaurant and friendly management. ⑤.

Eating and drinking

Both the beachfront and village at Anjuna are awash with good **places to eat and drink**. Most are simple semi-open-air, thatched palm-leaf affairs, specializing in fish and Western food. All serve cold beer, invariably with thumping techno music in the background. On the beach, you'll also be approached every ten minutes by women selling fresh **fruit**, including watermelons, pineapples and locally grown coconuts.

German Bakery, east of the market ground (look for the sign on the main road). Pricey but mouthwatering main meals and wholefood snacks, with real cream cheese, peanut butter, houmous, honey slices, sophisticated sounds and relaxing wicker chairs.

Lafranza's, south end of village on the road to the market ground. The budget travellers' choice: big portions of tasty fresh fish and fries, with plenty of veg options.

Martha's Breakfast Home, near *Lafranza's*, off the road to the market. Secluded breakfast garden serving fresh Indian coffee, crepes and American waffles, in addition to regular menu.

Anjuna

Rose Garden Motel, on the beach south of the *Shore Bar*. Not to be confused with the *Rose Garden Restaurant* in the village. The exhaustive menu here features superb, reasonably priced seafood sizzlers and tasty Indian-vegetarian dishes.

Sea Breeze, market ground. Does a roaring trade in cold beer and snacks on Wednesdays. At other times the vast *tandoori* fish is tasty and good value, especially for groups; order in advance.

Shore Bar, in the middle of the beach. Draws a dope-smoking crowd for sunset after the flea market and most Saturdays, with the best sound system in Anjuna. Light and main meals served as well as drinks.

Starco's, on the crossroads. Somewhat sophisticated bar-restaurant serving tasty *tandoori* seafood and Western dishes, inside or on the roadside terrace.

Sun 'n' Sand, market ground. Renowned for its whopping fresh-fruit salads served with crumbled coconut and curd. Great for inexpensive, healthy breakfasts.

Xavier's, east of market ground. Difficult to find, but worth it for its classy seafood and Chinese menu. Deservedly among Anjuna's most popular restaurants; the place for a splurge.

Nightlife

Anjuna has become a popular rave venue in recent years, attracting partygoers from all over the world. Most of the big events take place around the Christmas–New Year full-moon period, although smaller parties happen whenever their organizers manage to muster the increasingly large pay-offs demanded by local police (you'll know if they haven't got the cash together when the lanes become clogged by Israelis roaring around on *Enfields* in search of some action). At other times, nightlife centres on the *Shore Bar*, in the middle of the beach, which has a pounding sound system. The biggest crowds show up on Wednesdays after the market to watch the sunset from the steps in front of the bar, accompanied by the latest ambient trance mixes from London. The music gains pace as the evening wears on, winding up around 11pm, when there's an exodus over to the *Guru Bar*, further up the beach, or to the *Primrose Café* in Vagator, both of which stay open until after midnight. When it eventually gets its act together, the *Alcove*, overlooking Ozran Vagator beach, will be another worthwhile night spot, although its owners are still seeking "permission" from the local police to install a serious sound system. More mainstream musical entertainment is on offer at *Temptations*, in the *Red Cab Inn* just below *Starco's* crossroads, where Indian classical recitals and guitar-based cover bands feature with fire dancers on Mondays, starting at 7pm.

Listings

Foreign exchange The *Manali Guest House*, *Oxford Stores* and nearby *Orchard Stores* all change money, although they slap on a hefty commission. Note that the *Bank of Baroda* on the Mapusa road doesn't do foreign exchange, nor is it a good place to leave valuables, as a few years back thieves climbed through an open window and stole a number of "safe custody" envelopes.

Library The *Oceanic Circulating Library* (Mon–Sat 9am–2pm & 5–7pm; ☎0832/273286), near the *White Negro Bar*, stocks a good selection of quality fiction and non-fiction. A labour of love run by a retired local woman, this place is a worthy recipient of any novels you might want to ditch before leaving.

Motorcycle repairs Anjuna's two motorcycle repair workshops are both up the road from the *Oxford Stores*. The smaller one, further back from the roadside, is more helpful. Fuel and some spares, such as inner tubes and spark plugs, can be bought from the store on the *Starco's* crossroads.

Pharmacy *St Michael's Pharmacy*, Soronto Vaddo, near the *Starco's* crossroads, is open 24hr.

Photography *Oxford Stores* stock and process colour print film.

Post office The post office is on the Mapusa road, 1km inland, with an efficient poste restante counter.

Travel agents *MGM* (☎0832/274317), *Traveland* (☎0832/2773207) and *Connexions* (☎ & fax 0832/2774347) are east of *Starco's* on the main Mapusa road; *Speedy* (☎0832/273266) lies between the post office and *Rose Garden Restaurant*. All are reliable and efficient.

Yoga Classes are held daily at the *Orgasmic* New Age health centre, near the *Palacete Rodrigues* hotel, where you can also study acupuncture, osteopathy and martial arts, as well as browse their book and wholefood shelves.

Vagator

Barely a couple of kilometres of cliff tops and parched grassland separate Anjuna from the southern fringes of its nearest neighbour, **VAGATOR**. A desultory collection of ramshackle farmhouses and picturesque old Portuguese bungalows scattered around a network of leafy lanes, the village is entered in the east via a branch off the Mapusa road, which passes a few small guesthouses and restaurants before running gently down to the sea. Dominated by the red ramparts of Chapora fort, Vagator's broad white sandy beach – known as **Big Vagator beach** – is undeniably beautiful, spoiled only by the daily deluge of whisky-swilling, snap-happy tour parties that spill across it at lunchtimes.

For details of Chapora fort, see p.149.

Far better to head down to the next cove south. Backed by a steep wall of crumbling palm-fringed laterite, **Ozran** (or **Little Vagator**) **beach** is more secluded and much less accessible than either of its neighbours. To get there, walk ten minutes from Big Vagator, or drive to the end of the lane off the main Chapora–Anjuna road, from where a footpath drops sharply down to a wide stretch of level white sand (look for the mopeds and bikes parked at the top of the cliff). At this southern end of the beach, a row of makeshift cafés provides shade and sustenance for the predominantly young crowd that hangs out here during the day. Nearby, a sculpted Shiva face stares con-

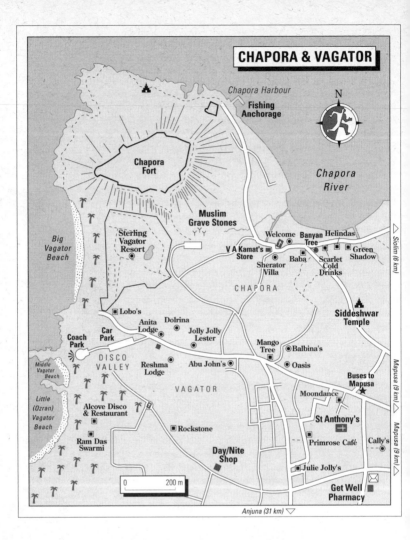

Chapora Harbour

Fishing Anchorage

N

Chapora Fort

Chapora River

Muslim Grave Stones

Big Vagator Beach

Sterling Vagator Resort

Welcome   Banyan Helindas
              Tree

V A Kamat's
Store   Baba   Scarlet   Green
                              Cold   Shadow
Sherator   Drinks
Villa

CHAPORA

Siddeshwar Temple

Lobo's

Anita   Dolrina
Lodge
**Coach
Park**   Jolly Jolly
              Lester
**Car
Park**

Mango   Balbina's
Tree

DISCO
VALLEY   Reshma   Abu John's   Oasis
          Lodge
*Middle
Vagator
Beach*

VAGATOR

**Buses to
Mapusa**

Moondance

*Little
(Ozran)
Vagator
Beach*

Alcove Disco
& Restaurant

Rockstone

St Anthony's

Ram Das
Swarmi

**Day/Nite
Shop**

Primrose Café   Cally's

Julie Jolly's

0   200 m

**Get Well
Pharmacy**

Siolim (6 km) ▷

Mapusa (9 km) ▷   *Mapusa (9 km)* ▷

Anjuna (31 km) ▽

templatively out of a rock, and a freshwater spring trickles through a lush tangle of vegetation into a shady pool at the foot of the cliff – ideal for washing off the salt after swimming. In spite of the Goan nudism laws, topless bathing is very much the norm here; not that the locals, nor the odd groups of inebriated men that file past around mid-afternoon, seem in the least bit perturbed.

Like Anjuna, Vagator is a relaxed, comparatively undeveloped resort that appeals, in the main, to travellers on tight budgets with time on their hands. Accommodation is limited, however, and visitors for whom Ozran beach and the village's lively **café scene** hold a particularly strong appeal frequently find themselves travelling to and from Baga every day until a vacancy turns up in one of the guesthouses.

Practicalities

Buses from Panjim and Mapusa, 9km east, pull in every fifteen minutes or so at the crossroads on the far northeastern edge of Vagator, near where the main road peels away towards Chapora. From here, it's a one-kilometre walk over the hill and down the other side to the beach, where you'll find most of the village's accommodation, restaurants and cafés. The only official place in Vagator to **change money** – cash and travellers' cheques – is the *Primrose Café*, on the south side of the village, which charges at bank rates and hands out free encashment certificates. If you want to rent a **motorcycle**, *Prakash Auto Service*, near the *Sea Green Chinese Restaurant*, has the usual gamut of Yamahas, Honda Kinetics, Enfields and clapped-out Rajdoots.

Accommodation

Accommodation in Vagator is generally more relaxed and pleasant than in neighbouring Chapora, revolving around a few family-run budget guesthouses, a pricey resort hotel and dozens of small private properties rented out for long periods. The usual charge for a house is between Rs2000 and Rs4500 per month; ask around the cafés and back lanes south of the main road. **Water** is also very short here, and should be used frugally at all times.

Abu John's, halfway between the crossroads and the beach; no phone. Self-contained chalets in quiet garden; all with bathrooms and running water. No off-season discounts. A comfortable mid-range option. ⑤.

Anita Lodge, north of the road near the beach; ☎0832/274348. Five basic concrete rooms with Western water toilets and small balconies, in a modern roadside bungalow. See the manager of *Anita Wine Shop* opposite for bookings, money-changing and STD telephone. ②.

Balbina's, Menndonca Vaddo; no phone. Cosy little place below the main road, with views of the fort across the valley and a terrace café for guests. Quiet, and the rooms (all attached) are well maintained. ③.

Cally's, near St Andrew's Church, behind *Bella Bakery*; ☎0832/273382. A spanking new block owned by the same family as *Dolrina's*, 20min back from the beach, with clean tiled bathrooms and views from relaxing verandahs across the fields. Good value. ⑤.

Dolrina, north of the road near the beach; ☎0832/274347. Nestled under a lush canopy of trees, Vagator's largest and most popular budget guesthouse is run by a friendly Goan couple; attached or shared bathrooms, a sociable common verandah, individual safe deposits and roof space. Single occupancy rates, and breakfasts available. ③–④.

Green Peace, 1639 Deul Vaddo; no phone. A medium-size, recently built guesthouse tucked away east of the village centre, offering comfortable en-suite accommodation. New beds and neatly tiled bathrooms. ④.

Vagator

Jolly Jolly Lester, halfway between the crossroads and Big Vagator beach; no phone. Four pleasant doubles with tiled bathrooms, plus a small restaurant, all in attractive woodland. Single occupancy possible. ③.

Oasis Guest House, 100m west of the crossroads, near *Jerry's*; no phone. A concrete house surrounded by trees, with largish rooms (the one upstairs has its own terrace), bamboo furniture, shared bathrooms and running water. ④.

Palm Grove, Deul Vaddo; ☎0832/2274388. Fourteen en-suite rooms (the pricier ones are larger and newer) behind a roadside budget travellers' café, east of the village centre on the Mapusa road. The courtyard features of brightly-painted *tulsi vrindavan*. ④–⑤.

Reshma (Mrs Bandobkhar's), next to the *Anita Wine Shop*; no phone. Inexpensive rooms in a newish building with running water, owned and managed by friendly local lady. ④.

Parties

Hedonism has been a feature of the expatriate Westerners' social scene in Goa since the mid-sixteenth century, when mariners and merchants returned to Lisbon with tales of unbridled drunkenness and debauchery among the colonists. The French traveller, François Pyrard, was the first to chronicle this moral decline in a journal that is peppered with accounts of wild parties and sleaze scandals (it was Pyrard who originally spilled the beans on Portuguese noblewomen's predeliction for poisoning their husbands with datura to render them unconscious while they entertained army officers in their boudoirs).

Following the rigours of the Inquisition, a semblance of morality was restored, which prevailed through the Portuguese era. But the traditional Catholic life of Goa's coastal villages sustained a rude shock in the 1960s with the first influx of "hippies" to Calangute and Baga beaches. Much to the amazement of the locals, the preferred pastime of these would-be *sadhus* was to cavort naked on the sands together on full-moon nights, amid a haze of *chillum* smoke and loud rock music blaring from makeshift PAs. The villagers took little notice of these bizarre gatherings at first, but with each season the scene became better established, and by the late 1970s the **Christmas and New Year** parties, in particular, had become huge events, attracting thousands of foreign travellers from all over Asia.

It was around that time that DJs such as **Goa Gill** made a name for themselves, playing the kind of dismal Pink Floyd and Grateful Dead discs you still occasionally hear in the sadder cafés of south Calangute. By the mid-1980s, however, acid rock had given way to the driving rhythms and electronically generated sounds of acid house and techno, and the party scene received a dramatic face lift. Mirroring the shift from LSD to Ecstasy as the preferred dance drug, tight lycra and fluoro fractal prints supplanted floppy cotton, and the drifty dope-and-dub-reggae scene succumbed to rave culture, with ever greater numbers of young clubbers pouring in for the season on cheap charter flights.

Goa's now legendary party scene has even spawned its own distinctive brand of psychedelic dance music, known as **"Goa Trance"**. Distinguished by its wild, multi-layered synth lines and sub-bass rhythms, this off-shoot of techno encompasses both the punchy ("dark", "hard" or "intense") tracks played at the height of the night and the more ambient offerings designed

Sterling Vagator Beach Resort, behind Big Vagator beach; ☎0832/273276, fax 273314. Upmarket resort hotel pitched at wealthy Bombayites by new management. A/c "cottages" (with TVs, fridges and attached bathrooms) grouped around a large pool at the top of the hill, or behind the beach at sea level; two multi-cuisine restaurants, safe deposit, and money changing. ⑨.

Eating, drinking and nightlife

Vagator's many cafés and restaurants are scattered along the main road and the back lanes that lead to Ozran beach. There are also several seafood joints behind Big Vagator beach, one or two of which serve Indian dishes in addition to the usual fish-rich Goan specialities. **Nightlife** focuses on the *Primrose Café*, out towards Anjuna, which boasts a beefier-than-average sound system and a late bar. A

---

to ease dancers gently through the dawn (aptly dubbed "hands in the air morning music"). Artists such Juno Reactor and Hallucinogen added the fine touches that coined the new sound, but when household-name DJs Danny Rampling and Paul Oakenfold started playing Goa Trance in clubs and on national radio stations back in the UK, they generated a huge following among music lovers who would otherwise never have even heard of the Indian state. Articles on trance, meanwhile, appeared in serious music magazines such as *i-D* and *Mixmag*, and Goa Gill and a host of other DJs now have their own **websites** on the internet, many of them including clips of the latest tracks, as well as examples of the iconographic, psychedelic art that has become synonymous with the Goa scene in recent years.

In spite of the growing interest in Goa Trance, the plug was effectively pulled on the state's party scene by the police in 1994–5. For years, drug busts and bribes provided the notoriously corrupt local cops with a lucrative source of *baksheesh*. But after a couple of drug-related deaths, a spate of sensational newspaper articles in the regional press, and a decision by Goa Tourism to promote upmarket tourism over backpackers, the police began to demand impossibly large bribes to allow the parties to go ahead – sums that the organizers could not hope to recoup. Although the big New Year and Christmas events continued unabated, smaller parties, hitherto held in off-track venues such as "Disco Valley" behind Middle Vagator beach, started to peter out, much to the annoyance of local people, many of whom had become financially dependent on the raves and the punters they pulled in to the villages. This is particularly true of the "*chai* ladies", local women who sell cakes, snacks, and hot tea through the small hours, sitting on palm-leaf mats in the glow of gas lamps.

The winter of 1996–7 saw something of a revival in the party scene, as police and government officals acquiesced to local complaints. Even so, Goa is still a far cry from Ibiza and the island of Ko Pha Ngan in southern Thailand, and if you're expecting full-on raves every night, you'll be disappointed. Parties are only certain to take place at Christmas and New Year, when the hilltop above Vagator and an expanse of paddy behind Anjuna host big events. At other times, keep your ear to ground for the tell-tale roar of massed Enfields, as hard-core Israeli ravers ride off to secret locations in the countryside. Wherever you go, though, **steer clear of drugs**: a half-gram of *charas* is enough to put you behind bars for a lengthy spell; get busted with an Ecstasy tablet, and you're looking at seven to ten years in Fort Aguada prison.

great place for a sundowner is the *Alcove Bar & Restaurant*, which overlooks Ozran beach next to *Ram Das Swami's*. The go-ahead owner, a local village headman who has been one of the driving forces behind local parties in recent years, plans to turn it into a night spot, with an expensive sound system and foreign DJs to rival the *Primrose Café*.

Abu John's, between the crossroads and the beach. Relaxing terrace restaurant specializing in seafood and meat barbecues. Moderate.

Alcove, next to *Ram Das Swami's*, above Ozran beach. This unsightly new clifftop complex enjoys the best location for miles, with spellbinding sea views through the palms. The food is also a cut above the competition, and the service slick. Try their fish dish of the day, washed down with a cocktail.

Jolly Jolly Lester, halfway between the village crossroads and Big Vagator beach. Not to be confused with *Julie Jolly's*, near the *Primrose*. This one's smaller, offering a better selection of inexpensive seasonal seafood, salads and tasty Western-style veg dishes.

Lobo's, behind the beach. Best of the beach places. Mostly Goan-style seafood, with some unadventurous Western and vegetarian alternatives. Inexpensive.

Mango Tree, near the crossroads and bus stop. Moderately-priced sizzlers, seafood and deliciously spicy stir-fries prepared in front of you. Not the cheapest place around, but the food is consistently good.

Moondance, near St Anthony's church. A large shack restaurant set back off the main road, and offering Vagator's most eclectic menu: Mexican, Italian and Chinese main meals starting at around Rs80 per head.

Primrose Café and Restaurant, on the southern edge of the village. Goa's posiest café-bar livens up around 8pm and serves tasty German wholefood snacks, light meals and cakes, as well as drinks.

Ram Das Swami, above Ozran beach. Terrible service, but the portions are generous, the food tasty, and the sea views superb. Inexpensive.

Rockstone, east of *Ram Das Swami*. A cosy, pint-sized café that dishes up budget travellers' grub. *Bluebird* nearby offers more of the same.

Chapora

Crouched in the shadow of a Portuguese fort on the opposite, northern side of the headland from Vagator, **CHAPORA**, 10km from Mapusa, is busier than most north coast villages. Dependent on fishing and boat-building, it has, to a great extent, retained a life of its own, independent of tourism. The workaday indifference to the annual invasion of Westerners is most evident on the main street, lined with as many regular stores as travellers' cafés and restaurants. It's highly unlikely that Chapora will ever develop into a major resort, either. Tucked away under a dense canopy of trees on the muddy southern shore of a river estuary, it lacks both the space and the white sand that have pulled crowds to Calangute and Colva.

If you have your own transport, however, Chapora is a good base from which to explore the region: Vagator is on the doorstep, Anjuna is a short ride to the south, and the ferry crossing at Siolim – gateway to the remote north of the state – is barely fifteen minutes away by road. The village is also well connected by bus to Mapusa, and there are plenty of sociable bars and cafés to hang out in during the evenings, when the main street is clogged with what looks like the contents of half-a-dozen Amsterdam coffee shops. The only drawback is that accommodation tends, again, to be thin on the ground. Apart from the guesthouses along the main road, most of the places to stay are little houses in the woods – invariably rented out for the whole winter to long-stayers.

The only real sight to speak of is the **fort**, most easily reached from the Vagator side of the hill. At low tide, you can also walk around the bottom of the headland, via the anchorage, and the secluded coves beyond it, to Big Vagator, then head up the hill from there. The red-laterite bastion, crowning the rocky bluff, was built by the Portuguese in 1617 on the site of an earlier Muslim structure (whence the village's name – from *Shahpura*, "town of the Shah"). Intended as a border watch post, it fell to various Hindu raiders during the seventeenth century, before finally being deserted by the Portuguese in 1892, after the territory's frontiers had been forced further north into the *Novas Conquistas* region. Today, the fortress lies in ruins, although you can still see the heads of two **tunnels** that formerly provided supply routes for besieged defenders, as well as a scattering of Muslim **tombstones** on the southern slopes of the hill, believed to be relics of pre-colonial days. However, the main incentive to climb up here are the superb **views** from the bastion's weed-infested ramparts, which look north to Morgim and Mandarem beaches, and south towards Anjuna.

Practicalities

Direct **buses** arrive at Chapora three times daily from Panjim, and every fifteen minutes from Mapusa, with departures until 7pm. **Motorcycle taxis** hang around the old banyan tree at the far end of the main street, near where the buses pull in. Air, train, bus and catamaran **tickets** may be booked or reconfirmed at *Soniya Tours and Travels*, next to the bus stand.

Chapora also boasts a better-than-average general **store**: in addition to basic provisions such as food and kerosene, *V.A. Kamat's*, at the west end of the main street, stocks sun cream, colour film, postcards and other tourist essentials.

Finally, anyone running short of reading material should head for the tiny *Narayan Books*, next door to *Baba Restaurant* on the main street, which rents out, sells and part-exchanges **secondhand books** in a range of languages.

Accommodation
If you want to check into a cheap guesthouse while you sort out more permanent **accommodation**, try the popular *Shertor Villa*

(☎0832/424335; ③), off the west side of the main street. Nearly all its rooms, ranged around a sheltered back yard, come with fans and running water. If this place is full, try the *Helinda* (①–③), at the opposite end of the village, which has rock-bottom options and a couple of more comfortable rooms with attached shower-toilets, as well as a good restaurant. As a last resort, the dilapidated *Amora* (①), between the *Helinda* and the chapel down the lane, has grotty rooms in an extension to the local fishing tackle shop.

Eating and drinking

Finding somewhere to **eat** in Chapora is easy: just take your pick from the crop of inexpensive little cafés and restaurants on the main street. The popular *Welcome*, halfway down, offers a reasonable selection of cheap and filling seafood, Western and veg dishes, plus relentless reggae and techno music, and backgammon sets. The *Preyanka*, nearby, is in much the same mould, but has a few more Indian and Chinese options. Alternatively, try the more secluded *Green Shadow*, next door to the *Helinda*, which specializes in *tandoori* fish and chicken. If you're suffering from chilli-burn afterwards, *Scarlet Cold Drinks* and the *Sai Ganesh Café*, both a short way east of the main street, knock up deliciously cool fresh-fruit milkshakes.

Pernem and the far north

Sandwiched between the Chapora and Arondem rivers, the predominantly Hindu *taluka* of **Pernem** – in the *Novas Conquistas* area – is Goa's northernmost district and one of its least explored regions. Apart from the fishing village of **Arambol**, which attracts a sizeable influx of backpackers seeking a rustic alternative to the resorts south of the River Chapora, the beautiful Pernem coastline of long sandy beaches, lagoons and coconut plantations is punctuated with few settlements equipped to cope with visitors. However, the picturesque journey north from Arambol to **Terekol fort**, on the Maharashtran border, provides ample incentive to spend a day away from the beach.

Car ferries across the river run 6.30am–9.30pm and take ten minutes.

Heading to Pernem from Anjuna, Vagator, or Chapora, you have to travel a few kilometres inland to pick up the main Calangute road, as it runs north, over a low ridge of laterite hills, to the river crossing at **Siolim**. Boatmen sometimes paddle tourists over the estuary from Chapora, too, although their dug-outs are unstable when laden with passengers and they can't carry motorbikes. The two **car ferries** that chug back and forth across the river from the ramp at Siolim charge a couple of rupees for the ten-minute trip, one of the high points of the journey north. Fisherwomen, their gaily-coloured cotton saris tied tightly around their legs, board the boats carrying baskets full of mackerel on their heads, while nearby canoes stacked with fruit and vegetables bob about at the water-borne fresh-produce **market** that is held here most mornings. Sadly, a major roadbridge is nearing completion (the ferries currently have to squeeze through its unfinished ferro-concrete supports), which will put the boats out of business, so enjoy this memorable crossing while you can.

Once across the river, bear right until you reach a fork in the road, where a sign to "Harmal/Terekol" (right) marks the quick route to Arambol. Alternatively, head left from the ferry dock and follow the scenic back road along the north bank of the Chapora River, past a crumbling old Catholic church, as far as a deserted beach called **Morgim** (or Morji). A seemingly endless expanse of soft white sand stretches north from here, rounding a rocky headland where the local fishing fleet is beached, after which it widens and empties completely. If you really want to get away from everything, **Mandarem**, 3km further north, with its palm-fringed dunes and acres of space, is perfect. Apart from the odd fisherman or tourist buzzing along the hard sand at low tide, the only signs of life are a couple of makeshift **cafés** serving tea, soft drinks, fish, *dal* and rice. The easiest way to get to Mandarem is to follow the road that cuts north along the coast from Morgim towards Davanvado; park your bike when you see a café on the left.

Pernem

For the majority of bleary-eyed bus travellers who roll through it on the long haul from Bombay, **PERNEM**, the district headquarters, is another of those nameless, lacklustre settlements you pull into at some unearthly hour of the night and only stay in long enough for the bus driver to grab a packet of *bedees* and a glass of *chai*. Heaped around a crossroads on the NH17, it functions as a service station and as a market for the dozens of small farming villages scattered across the surrounding rice terraces and *toddi* groves.

The town, 2km south of the Maharashtran border, is also renowned as the site of Goa's grandest Hindu mansion, **Deshprabhu House**, set amid shady woodland 1km northeast of the bazaar – the home of a wealthy land-owning family that sided with India during the Independence struggle with Portugal, and were thus allowed to keep their property after 1961. The present incumbent, Jitendra Deshprabhu and his family, still live in their grand ancestral seat, which presides over a huge estate encompassing some two-dozen or so villages. It can be reached by following the main road east from Pernem bazaar, and turning left when you see a grand mock-Moghul archway at the end of a long drive.

Although Deshprabhu House may be visited without prior appointment, it is a good idea to phone ahead through any GTDC tourist office to check that a member of the family will be at home when you call, otherwise the *chowkidar* will not show you around. Built in the nineteenth century, the pink-painted mansion comprises sixteen courtyards and a dozen or so different wings; it also houses a **temple** and a small **museum** where you can study portraits and photographs of Deshprabhu's past, along with other family heirlooms such as a pair of silver palanquins.

*Deshprabhu
House has no
entrance
charge or set
opening times;
call through
any GTDC
tourist office
first.*

Passing through Pernem bazaar, you cannot fail to notice the town's other well-known monument. The entrance to the turquoise-painted **Shri Bhagwati temple**, which stands on a raised square of dusty red dirt just above the crossroads, is flanked by a pair of colossal multicoloured elephants. Its deity, a ferocious form of Shiva's consort Parvati hewn from jet-black rock, presides over a modern shrine; the fragments of pedestals and pillars scattered over the forecourt date from a much older Kadamba structure.

Arambol

Of the fishing settlements dotted along the north coast, only **ARAM-BOL** (also known as **Harmal**), 32km northwest of Mapusa, is remotely geared for tourism – albeit in a very low-key, low-impact fashion. If you're happy with basic amenities, this is the most appealing village in the area, offering two very fine **beaches** and a healthy dose of peace and quiet. Parties are occasionally held here, drawing revellers across the river from Anjuna and Vagator, but these are rare intrusions into an otherwise tranquil, out-of-the-way corner of the state. However, all this could well change if local landowner Jitendra Deshprabhu (see above), and his cronies push through proposals to site a sprawling five-star resort here. The complex, which the planners hope to build atop the headland at the north end of the village, will, in addition to the usual water-guzzling swimming pools and lawns, comprise an eighteen-hole golf course, intended to pull in rich Japanese punters. Advocates of the project claim it will bring greater prosperity to Arambol; the locals, marshalled by the village priest, seem unanimously unconvinced, claiming the development will further deplete already scarce water supplies and drive out the budget tourists who provide a livelihood for many low-income families in the village.

Modern Arambol is scattered around an area of high ground west of the main coast road, where most of the buses pull in. From here, a bumpy lane runs downhill, past a large secondary school and the village church, to the more traditional end of the village, clustered under a canopy of widely spaced palm trees. The main **beach** lies 200m further along the lane. Strewn with dozens of old wooden fishing boats and a line of tourist café-bars, the gently curving bay is good for bathing, but much less picturesque than its neighbour around the corner.

The smaller and less frequented of Arambol's two beaches can only be reached on foot by following the stoney track over the sun-bleached headland to the north. Beyond an idyllic, rocky-bottomed cove, the trail emerges to "**Paradise beach**", a broad strip of soft white sand hemmed in on both sides by steep cliffs. Behind it, a small freshwater lake extends along the bottom of the valley into a thick jungle. Hang around the banks of this murky green pond for long enough, and you'll probably see a fluorescent-yellow human figure or two appear from the bushes at its far end. Fed by boiling hot springs, the lake is lined with sulphurous mud, which, when smeared over the body, dries to form a surreal, butter-coloured shell. The resident hippies swear it's good for you and spend much of the day tiptoeing naked around the shallows like refugees from some obscure tribal initiation ceremony – much to the amusement of Arambol's Indian visitors. Nearby, in the woods immediately behind the lake, other members of the lunatic fringe have taken to living in the branches of an old banyan tree. The scene resembles nothing so much as a cross between *Lord of the Flies* and *Apocalypse Now*.

Anyone pining for a coastal walk will enjoy the trail that scales the headland at the northern edge of the beach. Keep walking along this path for long enough and you'll eventually drop down to **Querim** (pronounced "Keri") **beach** – another spectacular stretch of white sand, fringed with fir trees, which you'll have virtually to yourself.

It is possible to reach Querim beach by road: turn left 8km north of Arambol where you see white writing on the asphalt.

Practicalities

Buses to and from Panjim (via Mapusa) pull into Arambol every half-hour until noon, and every ninety minutes thereafter, at the small bus stop on the main road. A faster private **minibus** service from Panjim arrives daily opposite the *chai* stalls at the beach end of the village. **Boats** leave here every Wednesday morning for the ninety-minute trip to the flea market at Anjuna. Tickets should be booked in advance from the *Welcome Restaurant* by the beach (Tues–Sun 8–9am & 8–9pm; Rs120), which also rents out motorcycles (Enfields and 100cc Yamahas). The **post office**, next to the church, has a poste restante box. A couple of places in the village **change money**: *Delight*, on the east side of the main road, and *Tara Travel*, directly opposite, where you can also reconfirm and book air and catamaran tickets.

Anjuna flea-market is covered on p.139.

Apart from a couple of purpose-built chalets on the edge of the village, most of Arambol's **accommodation** consists of simple houses in the woods behind the beach. Some of the more expensive places have fully equipped kitchens and showers, but the vast majority are standard-issue bare huts, with "pig" toilets and a well in the back garden. Long-stay visitors either bring their own bedding and cooking stuff, or kit themselves out at Mapusa market. The best place to stay if you only have a couple of days, however, is the *Ganesh Bar* (②–③), in the cove between the two main beaches. Scattered over the hillside directly above the café, it consists of a handful of small, new chalets with clean outhouses and superb sea views from their verandahs. The bar is also the best place in Arambol to enjoy the sunset over a chilled beer.

Finding **food** is, as ever, less problematic than finding a bed. The *Welcome Restaurant*, next to the main entrance to the beach, is a popular and sociable café serving a good range of locally caught seafood, with *toddi* to order. The palm-leaf bar-restaurants on the beach itself are slightly pricier, but still good value. Best of the bunch, on the south side of the main beach, is *Jah Kingdom*. Run by a couple of Senegalese Rastas, it serves copious salads, seafood and fruit cocktails with an African accent, and is a popular place to congregate at sunset. For simple, filling Indian food, though, you can't beat the no-nonsense *chai* stalls at the bottom of the village. *Sheila's* and *Siddi's* cheap and tasty *thalis* both come with *puris*, and they have a good travellers' breakfast menu of pancakes, eggs and curd. *Dominic's*, also at the bottom of the village (near where the road makes a sharp ninety-degree bend), is renowned for its fruit juices and milkshakes, while *Sai Deep*, a little further up the road, does generous fruit salads with yoghurt. Over towards "Paradise" beach, *Lakes Paradise* is the best pit stop, serving good espresso coffee and convincing Dutch apple pie.

Terekol

North of Arambol, the sinuous coast road climbs to the top of a rocky, undulating plateau, then winds down through a swathe of thick woodland to join the River Arondem, which it then follows for 4km through a landscape of vivid paddy fields and coconut plantations dotted with scruffy red-brick villages. The tiny enclave of **TEREKOL**, the northernmost tip of Goa, is reached via a clapped-out car ferry (every 30min from 6.30am–9.30pm; 5min) from the hamlet of Querim, 45km from Panjim. Before you reach the jetty, however, keep your eyes peeled for a turning on the left (marked with white painting on the road surface), which leads across the fields to a gorgeous beach, backed by firs.

*For more on
Querim beach,
see p.153.*

After the long and scenic drive, the old **fort** that dominates the estuary from the north bank of the Arondem is a bit of an anti-climax. Hyped as one of the state's most atmospheric historic monuments, it turns out to be little more than a country house marooned on a lonely, sun-parched hillside, with the red-dusty smoke stacks of the giant *USHA* iron-ore complex smouldering in the background. The fort was built by the Maharathas at the start of the eighteenth century, but taken soon after by the Portuguese, who held on to it more or less continuously until they were ousted by Nehru in 1961. Nothing much of any importance ever happened here, except in 1825, when the liberal Goan governor general, Dr Bernardo Peres da Silva, used it as a base for an armed insurrection against the Portuguese – the first of several such rebellions. The governor's own troops mutinied at the

eleventh hour, however, and were massacred by their colonial overlords. Thereafter, Terekol disappeared into obscurity until 1954,
when a band of Goan Gandhi-ites (*satyagrahas*) hoisted an Indian
tricolour over the ramparts in defiance of Portuguese rule.

If your visit coincides with the arrival of a guided tour, you may
well get a chance to look around the gloomy interior of the **Chapel
of St Anthony**, in the fort's claustrophobic cobbled square; at other
times it's kept firmly locked.

Practicalities

The few visitors that venture up to Terekol tend to do so by motorbike, heading back at the end of the day to the relative comfort of
Calangute or Baga. If you run out of fuel, it's useful to know that the
nearest **service station** is at Arambol, though be warned that it frequently runs out of gas and closes. One of GTDC's daily tours from
Panjim (see p.65) comes up here, as does one daily *Kadamba* **bus**
from the capital; alternatively, the 7am bus from Siolim, on the
Chapora, pulls in at the Querim ferry an hour later.

Accommodation is limited to the recently revamped *Hotel Tiracol
Fort Heritage* (☎0834/720705 or 02366/68248, fax 0834/283326;
⑦–⑨), which you should book at least four days in advance. Boasting
superb views down the coast over Querim beach, its rooms are pleasant
and comfortable, but way overpriced at Rs950 for the economy options,
to around Rs2000 (plus taxes) for a luxury suite. The **restaurant** downstairs, kept busy in the daytime by bus parties, offers the usual seafood,
Indian and Chinese dishes, as well as beer and soft drinks.

Travel details

For details of services on the new Konkan Railway, which runs through
northeastern Goa, see p.76.

By bus

Arambol to: Panjim (12 daily; 1 hr 45min).

Baga to: Panjim (every 15min; 45min).

Calangute to: Panjim (every 30min; 40min).

Candolim to: Panjim (every 15min; 30min).

Mapusa to: Anjuna (hourly; 30min); Arambol (12 daily; 1hr 45min); Baga
(hourly; 30min); Bicholim (hourly; 1hr); Bombay (24 daily; 14–18hr);
Calangute (hourly; 45min); Chapora (every 30min; 30–40min); Panjim
(every 15min; 25min); Pernem (6 daily; 1hr 45min); Vagator (every
30min; 25–35min).

By ferry

Betim to: Panjim (every 15min; 5min).

Querim to: Terkol (every 30mins; 5min).

Siolim to: Chopdem (every 15min; 10min).

Chapter 3

South Goa

S outh Goa can claim both some of the state's least savoury and most stunning sights, from the chimney stacks, iron-ore mounds and slums of the Mormugao peninsula to deserted beaches and tropical forests bordering Karnataka. In the minds of most visitors, however, the region means only one thing: **Colva beach**. Backed for most of its length by tall green *toddi* trees, the 25 kilometres of pure white sand ranks among South Asia's most spectacular beaches. On the whole, its resorts are attractive, too, catering for long-stay budget travellers as well as two-week sun seekers; nevertheless, the hitherto tranquil extremities of the beach have spawned ultra-luxurious holiday complexes, whose swimming pools and lawns creep close to ramshackle fishing settlements. **Colva**, the area's most developed centre, has been carved up by the charter industry, but **Benaulim**, 2km south, remains relatively unspoilt, with small family guesthouses far outnumbering package hotels.

Travellers flying into Goa land at Dabolim airport, 4km southeast of unappealing **Vasco da Gama**, the south's first city and largest port. The jumping-off point for Colva, however, is **Margao** – district headquarters of Salcete *taluka* and the region's principal market and transport hub – from where metalled roads fan west to the coast and east across fertile farmland to the Zuari River. Scattered over the plain around Margao are dozens of picturesque villages, many harbouring stately colonial **country houses**. These, together with Margao market and a couple of Hindu temples, provide the focus for most day-trips inland.

Accommodation price codes

All **accommodation prices** in this book are coded using the symbols below. In principle, the prices given are for the **least expensive double rooms in high season** (mid-Dec to mid-Jan). Local taxes have been included in each case, unless specifically stated otherwise.

① Up to Rs100	④ Rs225–350	⑦ Rs750–1200
② Rs100–150	⑤ Rs350–500	⑧ Rs1200–2200
③ Rs150–225	⑥ Rs500–750	⑨ Over Rs2200

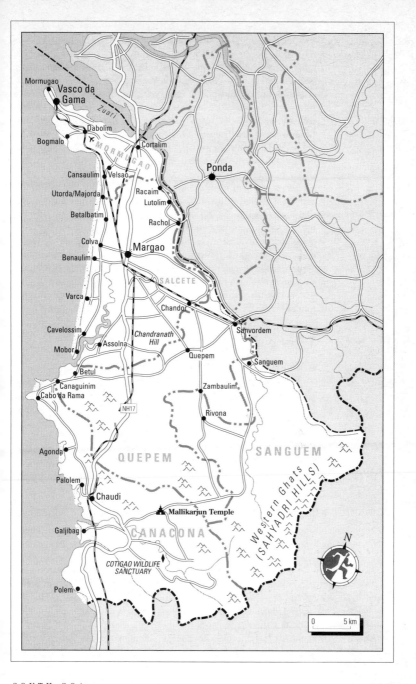

If you've time on your hands and an urge to venture off-track, rent a car or motorcycle, or jump on a long-distance bus bound for Goa's far south. Two routes lead to this remote corner of the state. The more scenic coast road cuts through the palm groves behind Colva beach to cross the Sal River at **Cavelossim**, then scales a stepped laterite plateau to atmospheric **Cabo da Rama** (Cape Rama), where a ruined Portuguese fort perches atop a narrow headland. Further east, the busy NH14 Panjim–Mangalore highway scythes south past **Chandreshwar Hill**, site of a hilltop Hindu temple, to **Quepem** *taluka*, eventually winding over the Ghat mountains to **Canacona** *taluka* along an impressive stretch of road. Only two hours from Margao, Goa's southernmost district sees few visitors. Yet its rocky coast shelters a string of beautiful beaches, set against a backdrop of forest-cloaked hills. Of these, **Palolem**, 2km west of the district's only real town, **Chaudi**, is the only one geared up for tourists. Beyond here, a couple of sand-filled bays lie all but silent save for the occasional chop of a *toddi* tapper's machete and the thud of falling coconuts. The clock, however, is ticking on this area's tranquillity. Thanks to the recently completed Konkan Railway, south Goa is now accessible by direct express train from Bombay and the densely populated coastal plain of southwest India, which can only increase tourist traffic into this ecologically fragile region.

Vasco da Gama

VASCO DA GAMA (commonly referred to as "Vasco"), 29km by road southwest of Panjim, sits on the narrow western tip of the Mormugao peninsula, overlooking the mouth of the Zuari River. This strategically important site was first acquired by the Portuguese in 1543, and by the end of the century was one of the busiest ports on India's west coast. When the city of Old Goa was threatened by the Maharathas in 1685, its women, children and non-combatant men were moved here and interned for safe-keeping in **Mormugao fort**, erected on the top of the headland to control the movement of ships in the estuary. Today, the bastion lies deserted and in ruins, but the modern town that spills around the bay to its east continues to prosper. A large proportion of Vasco's 150,000-strong population are immigrants from neighbouring states. Drawn here by the prospect of employment in the town's iron-ore and barge-building yards, many end up living in the slum encampments that have grown over the past decade on the outskirts.

Dominated by the unsightly storage tanks of *Hindustan Petroleum*'s oil refinery, Vasco is unremittingly drab and industrial, and no place to spend time if you can help it. Many visitors, however, find themselves having to pass through here at some point, either to book a ticket and catch a train from the station (Goa's principal railhead), or en route to nearby Dabolim airport. Apart from a browse around the small **bazaar**, crammed into the narrow streets

northwest of the main square, there's absolutely nothing to see or do
in the town. If you've time to kill, jump in a taxi or auto-rickshaw, or
rent a bicycle from the stall on the square, and head off to Bogmalo
beach, 8km southeast.

Practicalities

Vasco is laid out in a grid, bordered by Mormugao Bay to the north,
and by the train line on its southern side. Apart from the cluster of oil
storage tanks, the town's most prominent landmark is the **train station** at the south end of the main Dr Rajendra Prasad Avenue. Tickets
may be booked at the hatches inside the station, the only place in
Goa where you can make reservations using *Indrail* passes.

Arriving in Vasco by **bus** from Panjim or Margao, you'll be
dropped in the inconveniently situated interstate *Kadamba* terminus, 3km east of the town centre. Local **minibuses** are on hand to
ferry passengers from here to the more central market bus stand,

---

Dabolim airport

Dabolim, Goa's only airport, lies on top of a rocky plateau, 4km southeast of Vasco da Gama. Although it has recently acquired a new terminal building, this run-down navy aerodrome is a far cry from the sophistication of Western airports, with the shells of old Russian military aircraft rotting outside camouflaged hangars, and construction workers and civilian ground traffic moving freely across the runway between flights. Less interesting are the immigration formalities, which generally take upwards of one hour as ranks of khaki-clad officials scrutinize, stamp and recheck passports and disembarkation slips.

After changing money in the **arrivals hall** at the *State Bank of India*'s equally slow **foreign-exchange desk** (open for flights), charter tourists are whisked off by their reps to air-conditioned buses, while other travellers head for the handy pre-paid **taxi counter** next to the exit. Fixed fares to virtually everywhere in the state are displayed behind the desk; pay here and give the slip to the driver when you arrive at your destination. *Hertz* is also represented in the arrivals concourse, offering both **self-drive** and **chauffeur-driven car rental**.

Kadamba **buses** (Rs30) meet domestic *Indian Airlines* flights, dropping passengers at the main bus stand in Panjim, and outside the *Indian Airlines* office on Dr D. Bandodkar Road, in the northwest of town. However, the least expensive way to get from the airport is to walk to the nearby main road (left out of the terminal building), and pick up a **local bus** to Vasco or Panjim – though this is more hassle than it's worth if you're weighed down with luggage. Some travellers talk their way onto a charter bus to one of the coastal resorts by slipping the rep in charge a tip.

Facilities in Dabolim's first floor **departures hall** include another pint-size *State Bank of India* (Mon, Tues, Thurs & Fri 10.30am–1.30pm, Sat 10.30am–noon), a sub-post office and branches of several domestic airlines: *Indian Airlines* (daily 7.15am–2pm; ☎0834/512788), *Skyline NEPC* (daily 9.30am–5pm; ☎0834/513987) and *Jet* (daily 9.30am–5pm; ☎0834/511005). There's a very ordinary and overpriced cafeteria, too, but it doesn't open in time for early morning domestic departures, so if you're looking for a filling breakfast, head across the road from the front of the terminal building to the staff canteen, where you can grab piping hot *pao bhajis* for a few rupees. Finally, don't forget the Rs300 **airport tax**, which must be paid at the *State Bank* counter before you check in.

---

located at the top of the square. **Auto-rickshaws**, and Ambassador and motorcycle **taxis**, hang around on the corner of Swatantra Path and Dr Rajendra Prasad Avenue, near the train station and the small **cycle rental** stall. If you need to **change money**, call at the *State Bank of India* (Mon–Fri 10am–2pm, Sat 10am–noon) on the north end of FL Gomes Road. For **tourist information**, try GTDC's helpful counter in the lobby of the *Tourist Hostel* (daily 9.30am–5pm).

Accommodation

Thanks to its business city status, Vasco boasts a better-than-average batch of **hotels**. Most are plush mid-range places, although several no-frills lodges near the train station cater for budget travellers. The prices listed below apply to peak season; at other times, discounts can usually be negotiated.

Inexpensive

Annapurna, Dattatreya Deshpande Rd; ☎0834/513655. The best of the budget bunch. Neat, clean and close to the train station, with a good restaurant downstairs. Advance booking recommended. ④.

Gangotri, opposite the MPT Institute, Swatantra Path; ☎0834/512577. Plain but clean en-suite rooms (some a/c) with fans, and a bar-restaurant on the ground floor. Recently revamped. ④–⑤.

GTDC Tourist Hostel, off Swatantra Path; ☎0834/510829 or 513119. Large rooms with fans and attached shower-toilets, plus an information counter, photography shop, laundry and travel agent in the lobby. Very good value. Some a/c. ③–④.

Monalisa Ashiyana, Third Floor, Adarsh Building, Swatantra Path; ☎0834/513347. Bog-standard government-approved lodge around the corner from the station. ④. The slightly cheaper *Adarsh* downstairs (③) is a good fallback.

Urvashi, FL Gomes Rd; ☎0834/511625. A comfortable budget hotel, east of the square, that would be more pleasant without the fishy fumes wafting from the nearby docks. Some a/c. Good value. ②–④.

Moderate to expensive

Citadel, Pe Jose Vaz Rd; ☎0834/512097, fax 513036. Currently the best value among Vasco's many modern mid-range hotels: comfortable en-suite rooms, *Star* satellite TV, some a/c and off-season discounts. ⑤.

La Paz, Swatantra Path; ☎0834/513302, fax 513503. The town's top hotel has 72 central air-conditioned rooms, plush bars and restaurants, a gym and courtesy buses to the beach and airport. Good value at this price. ⑦.

Maharaja, opposite *Hindustan Petroleum*; ☎0834/513075, fax 512559. Swanky marble reception and spacious, spotless rooms, but dismal views over the refinery. Some a/c. ④–⑤.

Nagina, Dattatreya Deshpande Rd; ☎0834/513674. Bland but central, secure and comfortable enough. Its cheapest rooms are a good deal. Some a/c. ③–⑤.

Rukmini, near MPT Hall, Dattatreya Deshpande Rd; ☎0834/512350. Much the same as the *Nagina*, only further from the centre. ③–⑤.

Eating and drinking

In general, the best places to eat are the restaurants attached to Vasco's classier hotels.

Annapurna, Ground Floor, *Hotel Annapurna*, Dattatreya Deshpande Rd. Inexpensive pure-veg South Indian and Punjabi-style *thalis*, and traditional milk sweets, served on tin trays in a plain but clean canteen.

Goodyland, Swatantra Path. Spanking new and self-consciously Western fast-food joint, with glacial a/c. Good for moderately priced pizzas, veg patties, Bengali sweets and milkshakes.

Gulzar, *Hotel Nagina*, Dattatreya Deshpande Rd. Goan and non-veg specialities, including reasonably priced chicken *cafreal*, mutton *xacuti*, and fresh-
fish *balchâo*. Delicious vegetable *makhanwalla*, too.

Nanking, off Swatantra Path, five minutes' walk east of train station. Minimal
decor but mountainous portions of cheap and tasty Chinese food.

Regency, *Hotel La Paz*, Swatantra Path. Top-notch air-conditioned restaurant
with a mixed international menu, pot plants, and piped muzak. Expensive.

Tradition, GTDC *Tourist Hostel*, off Swatantra Path. Inexpensive snacks and
main meals, mostly meaty Punjabi dishes with a few Chinese alternatives,
served in a drab dining hall – or on a balcony if the barrage of Hindi videos gets
too much.

Around Vasco da Gama

The rocky terrain **around Vasco da Gama** harbours too few places of
interest to warrant a special excursion, but many travellers spend
time here before catching a flight from **Dabolim airport**. In this case,

---

The sinking of the Ehrenfels

Mormugao Bay, the natural harbour at the mouth of the Zuari estuary, was
the scene of one of the most bizarre and audacious episodes of World War
II, immortalized in the Hollywood film *Sea Wolves*, starring Roger Moore
and Gregory Peck, and by James Leasor's rip-roaring account, *The
Boarding Party* (see "Books" in Contexts, p.261).

  Following the outbreak of hostilities in 1939, one Italian and four
German ships made a dash for Goa – at that time the nearest neutral port
in the Arabian Sea. The vessels anchored in Mormugao harbour, safe in the
knowledge that the Allies would not dare jeopardize their cosy relationship
with Portugal by an armed attack. While most of the Axis crews sat out the
last years of the war on board ship, the radio operator of the 7752-ton
Ehrenfels was kept busy using a transmitter hidden in the engine room,
broadcasting details of Allied shipping movements to U-boats prowling the
coast. This information, gleaned from an extensive network of agents all
over India, was causing catastrophic losses for the Allies: 46 ships were
sunk in the Arabian Sea less than six weeks.

  Eventually, the British traced the transmissions to the *Ehrenfels*, but
were unable to intervene because of a potential political backlash. The
solution to this dilemma, devised by the top-secret Special Operations
Executive (SOE), reads like a script from an old Ealing comedy. The five
Italian and German ships were to be stolen or sunk by a team of veteran
civilians recruited from the ranks of the Calcutta Light Horse, a gentle-
men's regiment that was more a social club than a fighting unit. If captured, these men – a motley crew of middle-aged company directors,
accountants, tea planters and jute merchants – could feasibly claim the
raid was a drunken prank conceived while on leave in the Portuguese territory.

  After a crash course in basic commando skills, the fourteen men were
dispatched by train to Cochin, on the southwest coast of India. There they

---

secluded **Bogmalo beach**, a short ride by taxi from the town centre, is the most congenial spot to while away a few idle hours. Alternatively, head west to **Mormugao**, Vasco's busy port, and hop on a ferry to **Dona Paula** – a return trip of around ninety minutes. From the middle of the estuary, you can see the tiny **Sao Jacinto island** nestled on the Zuari River's south bank, its old Portuguese lighthouse poking above the canopy of coconut palms. Joined to the mainland by a narrow causeway, this tranquil spot, reached by bus from Vasco or Panjim, offers a short woodland walk with sea views as an alternative to lazing on the beach.

Around
Vasco da
Gama

Mormugao Bay

After emerging from the scruffy western fringes of Vasco da Gama, NH17 crosses the train tracks to begin its steady climb up the steep north flank of the peninsula towards **MORMUGAO BAY**. Out in the estuary, container vessels wait to load up with iron ore, shipped down from the hills of the Goan interior and piled in huge red heaps

For more back-ground on Goa's iron ore industry, see p.247.

met up with an SOE officer and a plastic-explosives expert who, together with a hastily assembled Bengali crew, had sailed from Calcutta in an old mud dredger called *Little Phoebe* – the only seaworthy tub not already requisitioned by the British navy. Meanwhile, another member of the Calcutta Light Horse was covertly organizing diversions that would lure the German crews ashore on the night of the attack. These included a glitzy reception at the Portuguese Governor's residence for the officers, and, for the rest of the crews, a week of complimentary hospitality in Mormugao's brothels, paid for by the British secret service.

The raid went off smoothly. As *Little Phoebe* chugged into Mormugao Bay during the small hours of March 9, 1943, her crew, clutching sten guns and with faces blackened, could hear music and raucous laughter drifting across the water. Using long bamboo ladders, they crept aboard the *Ehrenfels* and began to dismantle her anchor chains. However, the Germans, who had been half-expecting an assault, set off incendiary devices and kerosene bombs. During the ensuing commotion, valves in the ship's sides were opened and its holds flooded, though not before the raiders had destroyed the radio room. Keeping close to the shore to avoid the Portuguese search lights, *Little Phoebe* slipped out of the harbour, as the five Axis ships burned in her wake, having been scuppered by their crews.

Newspaper reports the next day claimed that German and Italian sailors had set fire to their own ships in desperation at their internment in Goa. No one knew the true cause of the sinkings until years later. Yet the Calcutta Light Horse's greatest hour is nowadays regarded as a major turning point in the war. Deprived of their eyes and ears on land, the German U-boats were unable to pick up merchant ships with such ease in the Arabian Sea, and left for Singapore and Africa, thus allowing the Allied military build-up that ultimately blocked the Japanese eastward advance through Burma.

at the quayside. Unless you're seriously into barge spotting, the only reason to venture here is to pick up the **ferry** across the Zuari to Dona Paula (see p.77), which leaves five times each day (the last one at 5.15pm) from the concrete jetty beyond the police/customs check post. This is also a good spot from which to view the tumbledown seventeenth-century Portuguese **fort**, **chapel** and colonial **villas** perched atop the promontory, now shrouded with vegetation and in an advanced state of decay.

Bogmalo

Immediately south of the airport, the Mormugao peninsula's sun-parched central plateau tumbles to a flat-bottomed valley lined with coconut trees and red-brick huts. The sandy **beach** at the end of the cove, looking across the water to Sao Jorge island, would be even more picturesque if not for the monstrous multi-storey edifice perched above it. Until *Oberoi* dumped a huge five-star hotel here a decade ago, **BOGMALO** was just another small fishing village, hemmed in by a pair of palm-fringed headlands at the northern end of Colva Bay. The village is still here, complete with tiny white-washed chapel and gangs of hogs nosing through the trash, but its environs have been transformed. Pricey café-bars blaring Western music have crept up the beach, while the clearing below the hotel is prowled by assiduous Kashmiri handicraft vendors.

Even so, compared with Calangute or Colva, Bogmalo is still a small-scale resort. If you're staying here, and haven't come to Goa to get away from it all or party, then you'll find it congenial enough. The beach is clean and not too crowded, the water reasonably safe for swimming, and there are plenty of places to eat, drink and shop. Lying a stone's throw from Dabolim airport, it's also a convenient place to overnight if you're catching an early morning flight.

Practicalities

Bogmalo can be reached by **bus** or **taxi** from Vasco da Gama, 8km northwest. It's also near enough to the airport (see p.160) for a last-minute dip before catching a plane. If you're thinking of staying, note that **accommodation** is very limited and best booked ahead. The *Sarovar Park Plaza* overlooking the beach (☎0834/513291 or 513311, fax 512510; ⑨) offers formula five-star luxury, with all the trimmings, including a pool, central air conditioning and a sun ter-race. The *El Mar Beach Resort* (☎0834/555030; ③), on the oppo-site side of the village, is altogether more humble, with plain, newly renovated rooms, attached bathrooms and a small covered verandah with a restaurant. It's slap on the beach, friendly and good value. More upmarket is nearby *Joet's* (☎0834/555036; ⑤), which boasts thirteen comfortable rooms with balconies; most are booked during the season by British charter companies, but they generally have a couple of vacancies. The two remaining places to stay lie just outside

Bogmalo, next to the naval base on the top of the hill. Oldest-established of the pair is *Vinny's* (☎0834/555170; ⑤–⑦), a comfortable, efficient and friendly hotel that's popular with package tourists and a good place to overnight before catching a plane from Dabolim. If it's full, try the newly opened *Raj Resort* next door (☎0834/555177, fax 518854; ⑤–⑦), which has a Mughlai-style restaurant with carved wood furniture, brass hookah pipes, curios and comfy cushions.

What Bogmalo lacks in places to stay it makes up for in **bars** and **restaurants**. Most of the places dotted along the beach depend on a steady trickle of refugees from the *Oberoi*, and have whacked up their prices accordingly. The *Full Moon Kneipe*, outside the main hotel entrance, takes the lion's share of the overspill. Its menu of mainly seafood and chicken dishes, including locally caught tiger prawns and lobster, is predictably expensive, and the portions are not overly generous, but no one seems to mind. The *Sea Cuisine* opposite offers identical dishes and prices, but tends to be less crowded at lunchtimes. Further up the beach, all the café-bars are in much the same mould; only the music changes.

Sao Jacinto island

The wooded oval-shaped islet of **SAO JACINTO**, 7km east of Vasco da Gama, is among the more photogenic landmarks punctuating the journey to Panjim from Dabolim airport on NH17. Connected to the rocky southern shore of the Zuari River by a narrow causeway, its landward side cradles a whitewashed **chapel**, whose stone steps double up as a landing stage for the island's tiny population of *toddi* tappers and *feni* brewers. Nearby, a cluster of crumbling colonial-style houses clings to the hill, smothered in lush foliage.

Apart from a near-derelict Portuguese **lighthouse**, Sao Jacinto harbours little of real note, although the rough woodland trail that encircles the island may tempt those not too pushed for time to pull off the highway for half an hour or so. Beginning at the hamlet just beyond the chapel, the path picks its way through the trees to a clearing at the top of the hill, presided over by the small **church** whose gable, nosing above the trees, is visible from the main road. The old lighthouse stands at the opposite end of the clearing from where the track drops down to Sao Jacinto village: an easy walk of around fifteen to twenty minutes.

Margao (Madgaon)

MARGAO, the capital of prosperous Salcete *taluka*, is regarded as Goa's second city, even though it's marginally smaller than Vasco da Gama, 30km northwest. Surrounded by fertile farmland, the town has always been an important agricultural market, and was once a major religious centre, boasting a university with a library of ten-

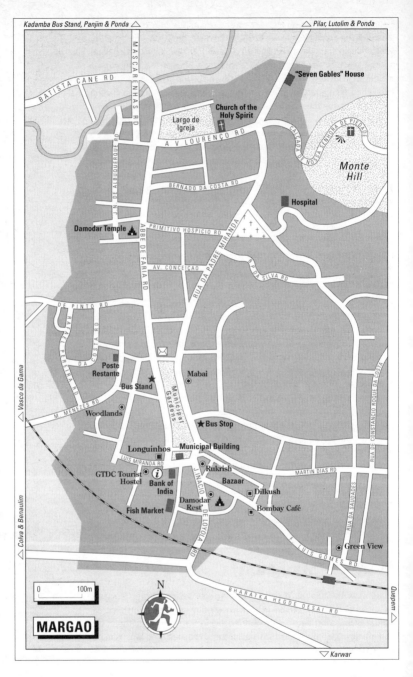

"Seven Gables" House

Church of the Holy Spirit

Largo de Igreja

BATISTA CANE RD

MASCARNHAS RD

AV. LOURENÇO RD

CALÇADA DE NOSSA SENHORA DE PIEDAR

Monte Hill

BERNADO DA COSTA RD

Hospital

J.N. DE ALBUQUERQUE RD

Damodar Temple

PRIMITIVO HOSPICIO RD

ABBE DE FARIA RD

RUA DA PADRE MIRANDA

BP DA SILVA RD

AV. CONCEIÇÃO

DE PINTO RD

RAFAEL PEREIRA RD

DA COSTA RD

Poste Restante

Mabai

Bus Stand

Municipal Gardens

Woodlands

M. MENEZES RD

Vasco da Gama ◁

★ Bus Stop

Longuinhos — Municipal Building

LUIS MIRANDA RD

GTDC Tourist Hostel

Bank of India

Rukrish

J. INACIO DE LOYOLA RD

Bazaar

MARTIN DIAS RD

RUA DE CONSTANCIO ROQUE DA COSTA

Dilkush

Damodar Rest.

Bombay Café

Fish Market

Colva & Benaulim ◁

RUA DA SAUDADES

F. LUIS GOMES RD

Green View

0   100m

N

BHARATKA HEGDE DESAI RD

Quepem △

MARGAO

▽ Karwar

thousand books, and dozens of wealthy temples and *dharamsalas* – however, most of these were destroyed when the Portuguese absorbed the area into their *Novas Conquistas* during the seventeenth century. Today, Catholic churches still outnumber Hindu shrines, but Margao has retained a markedly cosmopolitan feel, largely due to a huge influx of migrant labour from neighbouring Karnataka and Maharashtra.

If you are only in Goa for a couple of weeks and keen for a taste of urban India, a morning here should suffice. Clogged solid with slow-moving streams of auto-rickshaws, clapped-out buses, Ambassador cars, bicycles and handcarts, the town centre – a hotch-potch of 1950s municipal buildings and modern concrete blocks – simmers under a haze of petrol fumes and dust. The main reason most foreign visitors brave this mêlée is to shop in Margao's excellent **market**, a rich source of authentic souvenirs and a fascinating place to browse. While you're here, a short rickshaw ride north to visit the stately **Church of the Holy Spirit**, in the heart of a run-down but picturesque colonial enclave, is also worthwhile.

Arrival and information

For travellers arriving in Goa at the **train station**, 1km southeast of the town centre, Margao makes a much more congenial place to disembark than Vasco, one hour further down the line. **Auto-rickshaws** queue outside the station to ferry passengers to the **city** (or "market") **bus stand**, on the chaotic Praça Jorge Barreto, from where local buses leave for a variety of destinations in south Goa (note that the stop for Colva and Benaulim is in front of the *Kamat Hotel*, on the east side of the square). Buses from north Goa and out of state pull into the **Kadamba bus stand**, 2km north, on the outskirts. You can pick up connections to Panjim, Mapusa, Chaudi (Canacona), Karwar (hourly) and Gokarna (direct at 1pm) here, or else head into town on one of the mini-van taxis or auto-rickshaws that line up near the exit on the main road.

GTDC's **information office** (Mon–Fri 9.30am–5.30pm; ☎0834/222513), which sells tourist maps and keeps useful lists of train and bus timings, is inside the lobby of the *Tourist Hostel*, on the southwest corner of the square.

Accommodation

It's hard to think of a reason why anyone should choose to **stay** in Margao with Colva and Benaulim a mere twenty-minute bus ride away, but there are plenty of hotels within walking distance of the train station and Praça Jorge Barreto, and these can be handy if you have an early morning train to catch, or arrive here too late at night to get anywhere else.

Green View, Station Rd; ☎0834/720151. Among the few cheerless cheapos outside the train station licensed to take tourists. This one has attached rooms and a popular veg *thali* joint on the ground floor. ②.

GTDC Tourist Hostel, behind the Municipal Building; ☎0834/720470 or 721966. Standard good-value government block, with 69 simple en-suite rooms and a restaurant. A safe budget option. Some a/c. ③–④.

Mabai, 108 Praça Jorge Barreto; ☎0834/721658. The *Woodlands'* only real competitor is frayed around the edges, but clean and central. Some a/c. ⑤.

Milan, Station Rd; ☎0834/721715. Standard budget lodge that's a good fall-back if the *Green View* is full, but otherwise best avoided. ②.

Railway retiring rooms, train station. Three large but grungy double rooms and a six-bed dorm: the cheapest place in town. Contact the ticket collector's office on platform 1. ①.

Rukrish, opposite the *State Bank of India*; ☎0834/721709. Best of the rock-bottom lodges in the town centre, with passably clean rooms – some over-looking the main road and market. ③.

Woodlands, Miguel Loyola Furtado Rd; ☎0834/721121. Margao's most popular mid-range hotel stands around the corner from the *Tourist Hostel*. Its budget ("non-deluxe") rooms are a bargain but often booked up. Advance reservation recommended. Some a/c. ③–⑥.

The Town

For many travellers, what appeal Margao may have is frequently eclipsed by the lure of magnificent Colva beach, 6km west, or by the elegant stately homes and sleepy villages scattered across Salcete *taluka*. But the town can be a pleasant place to wander around, at least once you've escaped the mayhem of the main square, the **Praça Jorge Barreto**. The town's heart and transport hub, this shady public park is frequented mainly by office workers and street vendors who crash out here to beat the afternoon heat. On its south side stands the stalwart **Municipal Building**, a red-washed colonial edifice erected in 1905 that now houses the town library.

The congested streets south of the square form the heart of Margao's famous **bazaar**, which stretches to within a stone's throw of the train station. Most of the action revolves around a labyrinthine covered market, where you'll find everything from betel leaves and sacks of lime paste, to baby clothes, incense, spices and cheap Taiwanese toys heaped on tiny stalls. When the syrupy thick air in here gets too stifling, head for the nearest exit and explore the streets around the market. Among the most popular is the lane given over to cloth merchants and tailors, where, after a little haggling – invariably done over a glass of milky sweet *chai* – you can have shirts, suits and dresses made to measure at knock-down rates.

The dusty square south of the covered market is the site of a small Shiva **temple**, and an atmospheric place to hang out at evening *puja* time, when local Hindus file past rows of flower *wallis* and beggars, sitting cross-legged on the floor, to leave offerings of coconuts and garlands at the shrine. If you're lucky, you may also catch an itinerant snake charmer putting his fangless cobras through their paces, watched by crowds of rapt onlookers.

An equally engaging spectacle is Margao's **fish market**, a short way down the lane running south opposite the Municipal Building. The best time to come is early in the morning (8–10am), when most of the serious shopping takes place. Catches from the length of coastal Salcete are brought here in head baskets by fisherwomen, to be piled in glistening heaps and sold to Margao's housewives and restaurateurs from the nearby resorts. Dressed in their bright cotton *sarees* (many of the older ones with home-rolled cigars jammed in the corner of their mouths), the women are as fascinating a spectacle as the exotic seafood lying at their feet, so be sure to bring a camera and plenty of film. For the market's most extraordinary photo opportunity, though, you'll have to hang around until 1pm, when the off-cuts from the day's commerce are throw away in a dump behind the market, attracting a huge flock of Brahmini **kites** and **eagles**. From the walkway behind the GTDC *Tourist Hostel*'s first floor restaurant, you have a great view of the feast – a seething mass of feathers, beaks and talons which, for any Westerner unaccustomed to seeing birds of prey en masse like this, is an unforgettable sight.

The Largo de Igreja

A five-minute rickshaw ride north of Praça Jorge Barreto up busy **Rua Abbé de Faria** (named after the Goan founder of modern hypnotism) lie the dishevelled remnants of Margao's **colonial quarter**. Once, this leafy suburb of colour-washed houses and tree-lined avenues must have been a peaceful enclave; nowadays, however, raucous traffic pours through on the main Panjim and Ponda roads, shattering the serenity of its central square, the **Largo de Igreja**.

For a potted biography of Abbé de Faria, see p.71.

Surrounded on three sides by some of the city's oldest houses, the square is dominated by the majestic **Church of the Holy Spirit (Espirito Santo)**, built in 1565 on the site of an ancient Hindu temple. This act of desecration, perpetrated by the infamous temple buster, Diogo Rodrigues, Captain of Rachol Fort, must have enraged the local gods, for the first chapel erected here had to be rebuilt on several occasions after it was burned to the ground by marauding Muslims. The present structure, one of the finest examples of late-Baroque architecture in Goa, dates from 1675, by which time the Jesuit seminary founded next door had been moved to a safer spot at Rachol. Forming a striking contrast with the brilliant red exposed brickwork of its side and rear walls, the church's pristine white facade is flanked by a pair of square towers, crowned by domes. The **interior**, entered via a door on the north side, is equally impressive, with an elaborately carved reredos dedicated to the Virgin Mary, a gilded pulpit, and an ornate stucco ceiling. As you leave, look out for the peacock motif moulded onto the wall of the north transept. Art

The Church of the Holy Spirit is open daily 6.30am–noon & 4–9pm.

The seminary at Rachol is described on p.173.

historians claim this auspicious Hindu symbol, vehicle of Saraswati, the goddess of purification and fertility, was deployed to inspire awe among new converts as they filed into church.

The monumental **cross** in the middle of the square, standing in the shade of a giant mango tree, also dates from the late seventeenth century. Mounted on a wedding-cake-confection pedestal, it is carved with images from the Easter story, among them Judas' bag of blood money, a cockerel and a crown of thorns.

"Seven Gables" (Sat Banzam Gor)

Tours of "Seven Gables" can sometimes be arranged through Margao tourist office (see p.167).

Five minutes' walk northeast of Largo de Igreja, on the main Ponda road, stands one of Goa's grandest houses, **"Seven Gables"**. Originally the house sported a row of seven typically Goan high-pitched gables (whence its Konkani name, *Sat Banzam Gor*, which means "seven shoulders"). Now, only three of these remain, but the mansion – commissioned in 1790 by Sebastiao da Silva, emissary and private secretary of the Portuguese Viceroy – is still an impressive sight. Casual visits are not encouraged, but no one will mind you photographing the exterior from the roadside.

The house's Rococo-style facade is beautiful, with oyster-shell windows, wrought-iron balconies and decorative scrollwork highlighted in limewash. If you're lucky enough to gain entry, you'll see Seven Gables' sweeping staircase, halfway up which stands a private chapel dedicated to Saint Anna. The da Silvas were among the first families in Goa permitted to celebrate Mass in their own home, so this oratory, whose rear projects over a leafy inner courtyard, is a historical monument in its own right. Look out, too, for the painted terracotta portraits framed by pediments lining the stairwell. Upstairs, airy salons are crammed with antique rosewood furniture, glass chandeliers, silverware and Chinese porcelain. One particularly opulent room also features some fine red-and-gold brocaded damask wall hangings, set off by a black-and-white marble floor.

Monte Hill

If you feel like stretching your legs, head up the Calçada de Nossa Senhora de Piedade (Our Lady of Mercy), which winds from the hectic crossroads east of Largo de Igreja to the top of **Monte Hill**. The small chapel overlooking the clearing at the end of the lane is always locked, but the fine views over Margao and Salcete's sand-fringed coastal plain – a solid swathe of palm forest broken by open patches of green paddy – make this ten- to fifteen-minute walk worthwhile. Blot out the modern concrete apartment blocks on the northern edge of town, and you can easily imagine what the old quarter, whose shaggy gardens and red-tiled rooftops spread from the foot of the hill, must have looked like two or three hundred years ago.

Eating and drinking

After a browse around the bazaar, most visitors make a beeline for *Longuinhos*, the long-established hangout of Margao's English-speaking middle classes, and arguably the best place in town to **eat**. If you are on a tight budget, try one of the cramped pure-veg cafés along Francisco Luis Gomes Road, which do a brisk trade in *masala dosas* and other inexpensive South Indian snacks. A couple of these, notably the *Bombay Café*, open early for breakfast.

Bombay Café, Francisco Luis Gomes Rd. Popular with office workers and shoppers for its inexpensive vegetarian snacks, served on tin trays by young lads in grubby cotton uniforms. A mostly male clientele.

Dilkush, Francisco Luis Gomes Rd. Another good stand-up South Indian-style snack joint close to the market, offering plenty of cheap and filling veg dishes.

Kamat Hotel, east side of Municipal Gardens. Far and away the town's best Udipi restaurant. In additional to excellent *thalis* and *masala dosas*, they serve giant *puris*, and deliciously spicy *samosas*. If the ground floor is too crowded, head upstairs.

Longuinhos, opposite the *Tourist Hostel*, Rua Luis Miranda. Relaxing, old-fashioned bar-restaurant serving a reasonable selection of moderately priced meat, fish, and veggie main meals, freshly baked savoury snacks (including more-ish veg or prawn patties), cakes and drinks.

Shri Damodar, opposite Gandhi Market, Francisco Luis Gomes Rd. One of several inexpensive café and ice cream parlours ranged around the temple square. This one is the cleanest, and has an air-cooled "family" (read "women's") room upstairs.

Listings

Banks Money-changing facilities are available at the *State Bank of India* (Mon–Fri 10am–2pm, Sat 10am–noon), on the west side of the square, and the *Bank of Baroda*, behind Grace Church on the lane that leads east from the market, where you can also draw money on *Visa* cards. However, transactions in both of these can be time consuming, and it is invariably quicker to change money at *Paramount Travels*, Antonio Dias Building (opposite the GTDC *Tourist Hostel*, next door to *Longuinhos*), although the rates are not always as good.

Left luggage Luggage can be deposited at the cloakroom on platform 1 of the train station (daily 7am–2pm & 3–9.30pm), provided it is securely locked, rucksacks included.

Music shops *Trevor Electronic Supplies*, 5 Luis Miranda Rd (around the corner from the *Tourist Hostel*), stocks a good range of Western, Indian and Goan audio cassettes. An even better selection is on offer at *VP Sinari's*, although this place is harder to find; look for a lane leading between the blocks of offices and shops on the north side of Luis Miranda Road, and head to the far end of the courtyard inside. For cheap Konkani and Hindi pop compilations, check out the stalls in the market.

Post office The **GPO is** at the top of the Municipal Gardens, although its **poste restante** is in a different building, 200m west on the Rua Diogo da Costa.

Margao

Train reservations The *Indian Railways* reservation and enquiry counter at Margao train station (daily 8.30am–12.30pm & 2–5pm) is to the right of the main entrance. Note that reservations on *Indrail* passes can only be made at Vasco da Gama station. When this book was researched, the station was closed pending the completion of conversion work on the line, but should be open again by November 1997.

Travel agents Bookings for the Panjim–Bombay catamaran service can be made at the *Damania Shipping* office in the lobby of the GTDC *Tourist Hostel*. For other air and bus tickets, try government-approved *Paramount Travels*, at the Antonio Dias Building, next door to *Longuinhos* on Luis Miranda Rd (☎0834/731150 or 720112, fax 732572), or *Pinto International*, in the basement of the *Mabai Hotel*, 108 Praça Jorge Barreto (Mon–Sat 9am–1pm & 2–5.30pm; ☎0834/733200, fax 732530).

Around Margao

The picturesque farming villages strewn across the verdant country-side around Margao host a scattering of evocative colonial monuments and a handful of Hindu temples – in Marmagao, Ponda, Quepem, Salcete and Sanguem *talukas* – that can be visited on day-trips from the coast. Stately-home hunters should head straight for **Lutolim**, in the northeast of Salcete *taluka*, where some of Goa's most elegant old-family houses languish behind well-tended gardens. A short detour east on the way takes you to **Rachol**, site of a sixteenth-century Jesuit seminary and a newly inaugurated museum dedicated to Christian art. **Ponda**, the state's main temple town, also lies just across the Zuari River from Lutolim, and is a worthwhile extension to this short foray north.

Ponda is covered in Chapter One on p.97.

The area's remaining attractions are scattered east of the Margao. Foremost among them is the famous Perreira-Braganza/Menezes-Braganza house at **Chandor**, renowned as Goa's most splendid mansion, whose subsiding walls harbour a horde of eighteenth-century antiques. If you have your own transport, it's possible to head east from here towards the hilly interior, taking in the Hindu temple at **Zambaulim** en route to **Rivona**'s ancient rock-cut Buddhist hermitage, both in eastern Sanguem *taluka*. Alternatively, loop south from Chandor and round off the day watching the sunset from the top of **Chandreshwar Hill**, near Parvath, with its sixteenth-century Shiva temple and superb panoramic views over the coast.

Rachol

The Catholic **seminary** at the small scattered farming village of **RACHOL**, 7km northeast of Margao, rises proudly from the crest of a laterite hillock, surrounded by the dried-up moat of an old Muslim **fort** and rice fields that extend east to the banks of the nearby Zuari River. During the early days of the Portuguese conquests, this was a border bastion of the Christian faith, perennially under threat from Muslim and Hindu marauders. Today, its painstakingly restored sixteenth-century church and cloistered theological college, one wing of which has recently been converted into a museum, lie in the midst of the Catholic heartland, presiding over a parish of whitewashed chapels and wayside crosses. The seminary itself harbours nothing you can't see on a grander scale in Old Goa, but is definitely worth a quick trip from the main road if you are heading to Lutolim, 4km further north. Blue-painted *Holy Family* **buses** run here every hour or so from Margao's city bus stand, dropping passengers immediately below the church.

Rachol seminary

Rachol seminary was founded in 1580 by the Jesuits after its predecessor at Margao had been ransacked by the Muslims. The institution originally comprised a hospital and school for the poor, as well as the theological college; it also boasted India's third-ever printing press, installed by Father Thomas Stephens, the first Englishman to set foot in the subcontinent. During its 58 years of service, the press published sixteen books, including the *Christian Purana* (1616), the first translation of the Gospels into an Indian language (Maharathi).

Built in 1576 – and renovated several times since – the seminary's splendid **church**, dedicated to Saint Ignatius Loyola, is in excellent condition. Its richly carved and gilded main altarpiece, enlivened with touches of turquoise, cream and brown, features a uniformed figure of **Saint Constantine**, the first Roman emperor to convert to Christianity, and now revered as the protector of women against widowhood. Fragments of his bones, sent here from Rome in 1782, are enshrined near the main doorway, along with a small glass vial that originally contained a sample of the saint's blood. One reredos behind the altar holds a beautifully carved statue of the infant Jesus, found on the coast of Africa and brought to Goa by a Jesuit priest, who installed it in his church in Colva, where it reputedly performed miracles until being moved to Rachol.

No visit to Rachol seminary is complete without a tour of the college proper. Knock at the doorway to the right of the church, and a guide will show you up a flight of stairs – lined with fragments of Hindu sculpture unearthed during the construction of the seminary – to a first-floor corridor. Punctuated by huge oyster-shell windows, this looks down onto a spacious courtyard whose paving stones conceal an ancient **water tank** – a remnant of the Shiva temple that formerly stood on the spot. You'll also be shown the seminarians' living quarters and wood-panelled studies, a library full of dusty leather-bound tomes in Latin and Portuguese, portraits of Goan bishops past and present, and old class photographs of Indian seminarians and their European teachers. Whereas the college used to open its doors to young men not intending to take up Holy Orders, today it prepares its pupils exclusively for the priesthood with a demanding seven-year course in philosophy and theology.

For background on Colva's "Menino" Jesus, see p.184.

*Rachol's
Museum of
Christian Art
is open
Tues–Sun
9.30am–
12.30pm &
2.30–5pm;
Rs5.*

Rachol's **Museum of Christian Art** was established in 1991 by the Indian National Trust of Architecture and Cultural Heritage and the Gulbenkian Foundation of Portugal, who financed extensive restoration work to the building. Assembled in its light and airy ground floor hall is a sizeable collection of antique Roman Catholic art objects, ranging from large silver processional crosses to pocket-size ivory ornaments, damask silk clerical robes and some fine wooden icons, mostly dating from the seventeenth and eighteenth centuries. Among the quirkier exhibits is a mobile Mass kit, designed for Goa's missionaries and peripatetic Jesuit priests.

Rachol fort

Before the evangelization of Goa during the sixteenth century, Rachol hill was encircled by an imposing **fort**, built by the Muslim Bahmani dynasty that founded the city of Ela (Old Goa). Taken from the Sultan of Bijapur by the Hindu Vijayanagars in the fifteenth century, it was ceded to the Portuguese in 1520 in exchange for military help against the Muslims. One hundred cannons once nosed over the battlements, but when, during the late eighteenth century, the borders of the territory were pushed back further east into the *Novas Conquistas* area, these were redeployed and the fort eventually

---

The stately homes of Goa

The palatial **country houses of Goa** are sprinkled throughout the state's rural heartland and mostly date from the early eighteenth century, when the Portuguese were raking off handsome profits from their African colonies and the gold and gemstone trade with Brazil. However, their owners were not generally Europeans, but native Goans: wealthy merchants and high-ranking officials who were granted land as golden handshakes. Kept afloat by rent from their estates, these families weathered the decline of the Empire to emerge as a powerful aristocracy, frequently intermarrying to preserve their fortunes. Many, however, had their estates confiscated and parcelled out to former tenants after Independence in 1961. Deprived of their chief source of income, some now struggle to maintain their rambling properties, living in one wing and selling off heirlooms to make ends meet. In such cases, donations from visitors for the upkeep of the buildings are gratefully received.

The architecture of Goa's eighteenth-century stately homes was heavily influenced by European tastes, while remaining firmly rooted in a strong vernacular tradition. The materials and construction techniques mostly originated in India: red laterite for the walls and pillars, and local wood, overlaid with curved terracotta roof tiles from Mangalore (Karnataka). Many of the sumptuous furnishings, luxurious to the point of decadence, were imported: fine porcelain and silk came from China, Macau and Korea, cut glass and mirrors from Venice, chandeliers from Belgium, and tapestries from Spain or Portugal. Some furniture was also shipped here, but most was fashioned by Goan craftsmen out of rare rosewood brought

---

abandoned. Today, the red-, yellow- and white-stone archway that spans the road below the seminary is the only fragment left standing. You can, however, follow the course of the old **moat** around the base of the hill, along with the resident herd of water buffalo.

Lutolim

Peppered around the leafy tree-lined lanes of **LUTOLIM**, 10km north-east of Margao, are several of Goa's most beautiful colonial mansions, dating from the heyday of the Portuguese empire, when this was the country seat of the territory's top brass. Lying just off the main road, the village is served by eight daily buses from Margao, which drop passengers on the square in front of a lopsided-looking church. The cream of Lutolim's country houses all lie within walking distance of here, nestled in the woods, or along the road leading south. However, you shouldn't turn up at any of them unannounced; visits have to be arranged in advance (see box below for details). If you are pushed for time, the pick of the crop is Miranda house, two minutes from the square; Salvador Costa house, 1km out of the village, comes a close second.

Also worth a visit while you're in the area is Lutolim's model village, "**Ancestral Goa**", which showcases life in the region a century ago using miniature mock-ups of village scenes.

---

from Ceylon or Africa. Among the finest examples of the furniture-maker's craft – and a feature of most Goan mansions still – are the chapels used to celebrate Mass and important religious festivals. Looking more like giant cupboards than shrines, these elaborately carved oratories often contain gilded altars and ivory statues of saints.

The exterior of the houses, too, incorporates several peculiarly Goan features. Most distinctive of these is the pillared porch, or *balcão*. Surmounted by a pyramidal roof and flanked by a pair of cool stone benches, this is where Goan families traditionally while away sultry summer evenings. In larger houses, the *balcão* opens onto a covered verandah that extends along the length of a colour-washed classical facade, whose Rococo mouldings and pilasters are picked out in white. Another typical Goan trait, noted by the traveller François Pyrard in the early seventeenth century, is the use of oyster shells instead of glass for windows. The wafer-thin inside layer of the shells was cut into rectangular strips and fitted into wood frames to filter the glare of the Goan sun. Sadly, most have long been replaced by glass, but you'll still come across them from time to time in more traditional villages, where the art of oyster-shell window-making survives.

Goa's most famous stately homes are situated in Salcete *taluka*, but you'll also find villas in other areas, especially Santa Cruz (near Panjim), Piedade (Divar Island), Anjuna and the north end of Colva village. While some (such as the grand Perreira-Braganza house) welcome walk-in visitors, others (notably the Miranda and Costa family homes in Chandor, and "Seven Gables" in Margao) can only be seen by appointment, arranged through your hotel or the local GTDC tourist office.

Miranda house

A dirt track peels left off the road running west from Lutolim's church square to the **Miranda house**, hemmed in by high walls and a tangle of tropical foliage. One of Goa's oldest stately homes, it was built in the early 1700s but renovated at the end of the nineteenth century, when cast-iron balconies, mosaic floors and a cool inner verandah were added. The mansion's present owner, a direct descendant of its original occupants, is the famous Goan cartoonist Mario Miranda, who lives here with his wife and son. Formerly the Mirandas made their money through cultivating areca, the palm from which betel nut derives, and several spindly specimens still stand outside the house, silhouetted against its plain classical facade; the front door is crowned with the Miranda coat of arms (presented by the King Dom Lu í s of Portugal in 1871). Unusually for a double-storey Goan house, the salons, chapel, living rooms and bedrooms all lie on the ground floor, fronted by a deep verandah.

The rooms upstairs include a grand dining hall and library, and another of the wings is reached via a steep staircase, at the head of which you'll be shown a hole bored through the wall; just wide enough for a musket barrel, this guarded the approach to apartments where the family hid during the Rane revolts of the late nineteenth century. The rebel Rajput clan, forced south from Rajasthan in the 1700s, played an important part in the Independence movement, but dabbled in a bit of banditry on the side, terrorizing this wealthy corner of Salcete, and the Mirandas in particular.

Salvador Costa house

The elegant **Salvador Costa house**, ten minutes' walk west of the church square, dates from the late eighteenth century, and, fronted by a beautiful pastel-painted verandah, has retained a distinctly *fin-de-siècle* feel, with stained-glass windows and fading sepia photographs of family members hanging on the walls. Its most famous feature, however, is an opulent **chapel**, gilded from floor to ceiling and crammed with ivory statues and candles, which the resident Senhora Costa Dias opens for prayers at noon. Also worth a close look as you are shown around are the delicate mosaic floors, the finely carved four-poster in the master bedroom, and some exquisite pieces of Cantonese porcelain on polished table tops and rosewood chests of drawers.

Roque Caetan Miranda house

The **Roque Caetan Miranda house**, which stands on the roadside two minutes' walk south of the main square (back towards Margao), was built in 1846, at the height of the family's feud with the Ranes. The grandparents of the present owners had to flee for their lives at one stage, but the house and its contents came through intact. These days, it is maintained by two middle-aged sisters and a brother from

Bangalore, who are currently renovating the property to attract groups of charter tourists from the coast. This involves slapping lots of gloss paint on to the walls and, regrettably, over hitherto polished antique furniture. The finest pieces are to be found in the splendid first-floor salon, which also contains a couple of cut-glass chandeliers and family portraits.

"Ancestral Goa"

Rather pompously billed as "a centre for the preservation of art, culture and environment", Lutolim's "**Ancestral Goa**" exhibition, near the *Big Foot Dance Floor*, a short way east of the village on the Ponda road, turns out to be a refreshingly old-fashioned model village, of the kind that kids, in particular, will find fascinating. The aim is to show a cross-section of Goan village life as it was a hundred years ago, with different miniature houses representing the different occupations and social classes, from fisher folk and fruit-*wallis* in the market to the grand Portuguese colonial homes of the land owners. An additional attraction is a giant fourteen-metre sculpture of **Sant Mirabai**, which the site's creators, proudly quoting the *Limca Book of Records*, claim is the "longest laterite sculpture in India". You can also wander among spice and fruit gardens, watch rubber tappers in action, and enjoy the shade of adjacent teak plantations.

*Ancestral Goa
(☎0834/
777034) is
open daily
9am–6pm.*

Chandor

Thirteen kilometres east of Margao, across the fertile rice fields of Salcete, lies sleepy **CHANDOR** village: a scattering of tumbledown villas and farmhouses ranged along shady tree-lined lanes. Between the late sixth and mid-eleventh centuries, this was the site of ancient *Chandrapura*, capital of the Kadamba dynasty, which ruled Goa until its conquest by the Vijayanagars in 1367. Known to medieval Arab cartographers as Zindabar, the city declined when the royal court decamped to Govapuri on the Zuari River in 1017, and crumbled completely after a sound sacking by the ruthless Muslim warlord Ghiyas-ud-din Tughluq three hundred years later.

Excavations carried out in Chandor in 1921 revealed traces of a pre-Kadamba settlement. Tucked away in the north of the village (1km east of the square), the foundations of an ancient Shiva temple, marked by a blue sign, are believed to date from the third or fourth century AD. Among the finds yielded by the dig here were a copper donatory plaque, contemporary with the temple and the oldest written words ever discovered in Goa, and numerous fragments of two-thousand-year-old pottery. These have been removed to the state archeological museum in Old Goa, but a solitary headless Nandi bull, garlanded and smudged with vermilion powder by local Hindus, still stands *in situ*.

Perreira-Braganza/Menezes-Braganza house

In addition to its uninspiring ancient remains, Chandor is famous in Goa for the huge stately home that sprawls across the south side of its church square. Fronted by a spectacular Portuguese-style facade, the **Perreira-Braganza/Menezes-Braganza house** is stuffed with old furniture, paintings and porcelain, and makes one of the most rewarding day-trips in South Goa. Visitors generally travel here by taxi, but you can also get to Chandor by bus from Margao (8 daily; 45min), or by train via Chandragoa station, 1km northwest. Visitors can turn up without an appointment, but it is still a good idea to telephone the tourist office before leaving. Alternatively, contact the family business, *Agua de Fonte*, opposite the *Blue Fountain Cinema* in Margao (☎0834/223754).

Although parts of the house date from the 1500s when its owners were Hindus, most were built after the Braganza family had converted to Catholicism in the eighteenth century. Two separate wings were originally commissioned to accommodate the two sons and their wives. When no male heirs issued from either marriage, sons-in-law were drafted in for the daughters and granted inheritance rights on condition they adopt the Braganza title (hence the double-barrelled names). Descendants of both branches of the family still occupy their respective sides of the house; the most frequently visited of these is the left (east) wing.

The east wing

When he lived here as a boy, Senhor Alvaro de Perreira-Braganza, the owner of the mansion's **east wing**, was pampered by twenty servants. Nowadays, however, he can barely afford to shore up the gaping cracks to the rear of the building that widen after each monsoon. The long double-storeyed facade at the front, by contrast, is still in fine shape. Twenty-eight windows, each with its own wooden balustrades (made with weather-resistant shipbuilding timber specially imported from Holland), flank the main entrance. These were reputedly designed to catch the balmy Zephyr breezes, but now allow clouds of red dust to blow in from the road and settle on the polished floors and furniture inside. Reached via a grand staircase, the top floor comprises a series of plush interconnecting salons, reception rooms, dining halls and the family's private chambers, ranged around a central courtyard; the ground floor, now empty, used to accommodate the kitchen and servants' quarters.

The grandest room in the house, if not in all of Goa, is the **Great Salon**, or ballroom. Sumptuous crystal chandeliers hang from its ceiling, decorated with floral motifs overlaid with a crisscross pattern of painted zinc netting. The walls are beautifully marbled to match the floor and upholstery. Prominent among the pieces of furniture here is a pair of stately high-backed chairs, bearing the family crest, which were presented to the Perreira-Braganzas by King Dom Luís of Portugal.

The remaining rooms contain eighteenth-century furniture, much of it made from local *seeso* (martel wood), lacquered by craftsmen from the nearby village of Cuncolim, or inlaid with mother-of-pearl. The airy corridor at the back of the house is also crammed with curiosities, including several dead bats, birds' nests, boomerangs and a sedan chair. Express an interest and you may also be shown the Perreira-Braganza's private chapel, among whose treasure number relics of the Cuncolim Martyrs, and, more precious still, Saint Francis Xavier's gold-and-diamond-encrusted fingernail. Recently retrieved from a local bank vault, this now occupies pride of place on the main altar.

*For more on
the Cuncolim
Martyrs, see
p.88. The life
story of Saint
Francis Xavier
is featured on
p.92.*

The west wing

The design of the mansion's **west wing**, belonging to the Menezes-Braganza family and also open to visitors, mirrors that of its neighbour, but has a less cluttered feel. Lovers of antiques, in particular, will drool over its superb collection of Chinese porcelain. Other highlights include several seventeenth- and eighteenth-century portraits of family members on glass, a pair of large ceramic elephants and a set of four matching conversation chairs, housed in the library. The five thousand or so leather-bound (and worm-eaten) tomes shelved here were mostly collected by Luis de Menezes-Braganza (1878–1938), a famous journalist and freedom fighter, whose offspring also became involved in the independence struggle (the Menezes-Braganzas were one of the few wealthy Christian families in Goa to actively oppose Portuguese rule). Forced into exile in 1950, they returned twelve years later and were astonished to find their home untouched, although the property had lapsed into a state of disrepair from which it is only now begining to recover.

Zambaulim and Rivona

Two historically significant religious sites, one Hindu the other Buddhist, lie in the district of Sanguem, hidden in the foothills of the Western Ghats. Neither are of more than passing interest, but the road that leads to **Zambaulim** and **Rivona**, winding through the picturesque Pareda valley, makes a pleasant detour from Chandor, 10km northwest.

Zambaulim

If you're travelling from Chandor, head east from the church square until you reach a right turn in the main road. After approximately 4km, this brings you out at Tilamola crossroads; go straight on here for 3km to **ZAMBAULIM**, site of the **Shri Damodar temple**, which stands to the right of the road below a dusty square. The precinct, an important Hindu pilgrimage centre, was rebuilt in the 1950s and 1960s, supplanting a typically Goan-style *devul*, or temple, with a polychrome concrete eyesore loosely inspired by the architecture of medieval Orissa in northeast India. The building may be modern, but

Around
Margao

*The Church of
the Holy Spirit
in Margao is
covered on
p.169.*

its presiding deity, a manifestation of Shiva, is centuries old. It is also associated with a well-known legend in which the son of a wealthy local landowner and his bride were murdered on their wedding day by a gang of thugs hired by a jealous suitor. A temple was erected in Margao to mark the tragedy, but this was pulled down by the Portuguese to make way for their Church of the Holy Spirit. The *lingam*, however, was smuggled to this out-of-the-way spot, where it is still enshrined beside an image of Lakshminarayan.

Rivona

Backed by densely wooded hills, the ramshackle hamlet of **RIVONA**, 2km southeast along the road from Zambaulim, lies in the middle of nowhere, which is presumably why a small community of Buddhist monks holed up here sometime in the seventh century. Their cells, a pair of tiny rock-cut sanctuaries nicknamed the **Pandava caves**, are buried in the forest outside the village, carved out of a slab of overhanging laterite. To find them, follow the road through Rivona until it sweeps into a sharp bend; a signpost marked "Shri Sansthan Gokarn" points left up a motor-cyclable dirt track to the caves, which nestle in the shade of an old tamarind tree hung with strips of auspicious red cloth as votive offerings.

The main opening to the caves is at the bottom of the rock, next to a small stepped well and ablutions tank. Flanked by a sixteenth-century bas-relief of the Hindu monkey god Hanuman, this leads, via a low-roofed tunnel, to the cell on the upper level, although you're better off peering in from the opposite side as the excavations are pitch-black and infested with snakes.

Also worth a look while you're in Rivona is the **Shri Yimleshwar temple**, located on the edge of the village near the turn-off for the caves. The shrine, which houses an old *Shivalingam*, is architecturally undistinguished, but enjoys a picturesque situation, its olive-green and terracotta-red sanctuary tower rising from swathes of fastidiously terraced rice paddy.

Parvath

In the far southeastern corner of Salcete *taluka*, a semicircular ridge of hills blisters out of the coastal plain, cloaked with deep green forest and crowned by a solitary temple spire. The cream- and red-painted **Shri Chandeshwar temple** at **PARVATH**, 12km southeast of Margao on the main Quepem road, sits on a hilltop with spellbinding views from its 370-metre summit. A metalled road winds up the north flank of the hill through a series of tortuous switchbacks. Along the way, increasingly grandiose glimpses of the Goan hinterland are revealed through the cashew trees, while the boulder-strewn clearing at the top affords a sweeping vista of sand-fringed *toddi* forest, sprinkled with small villages. This panorama is at its most serene around dusk, when the sun sinks into the sea behind a haze of wood-smoke, produced by the evening cooking fires burning below on the plain.

According to an ancient Sanskrit inscription, a temple has stood on this magical spot for nearly 2500 years. However, the present building, dedicated to Shiva, is comparatively modern, dating from the late 1600s. The only part of the shrine that is definitely a vestige of the Vedic age is its cavernous inner sanctum, hollowed from a huge black boulder, around which the site's seventeenth-century custodians erected a typically Goan-style structure, capped with a red-tile roof and domed sanctuary tower.

The road up Chandreshwar Hill peters out at a small car park just below Parvath, from where a long flight of steps (fashioned from discarded slabs of twelfth-century buildings) leads steeply up to the temple. Having paid the requisite penance in sweat, pilgrims arrive puffing and panting at the main entrance for *darshan*, or the ritual viewing of the god. Inside, a wild-eyed golden Chandreshwar deity, Shiva as "Lord of the Moon", stares out from an ornately decorated sanctum, wrapped in brocaded silk. His accessory deities, or *pariwar devtas* – medieval images of Shiva's consort and son, Parvati (west) and elephant-headed Ganesh (east), sculpted in stone – are housed in small niches to the rear of the shrine. This circumambulatory passage, which you should walk around in a clockwise direction, hugs the base of the boulder that forms the temple's heart.

Similar-sized chunks of rock are scattered around the dusty clearing outside, along with fragments of masonry from previous temples sited here, including a small **Nandi bull** that lies discarded among the rubble opposite the main entrance. The graffiti-splattered boulder to the south of the clearing can be climbed, and is a good place from which to admire the views west out to sea and south across the Assolna estuary to the Cabo da Rama headland.

Practicalities

You'll need your own **transport** to get to Parvath, as there are no buses up the hill and too little traffic for hitching to be viable. Travelling from Margao, look for a right turn across the fields about a kilometre beyond the main Chandor junction (marked by a yellow sign in Hindi). It's also possible to approach Chandreshwar Hill from the south via the village of Bamanbhat, 3km southwest of Quepem. Finally, there are no *chai* or cold-drink stalls at Parvath – let alone cafés or restaurants – so bring **food supplies** with you. The nearest **accommodation** is at Margao.

Colva beach

Spectacular **COLVA BEACH**, 6km west of Margao, constitutes the longest unbroken stretch of white sand in the state, spanning 25km from the Mormugao peninsula in the north to Cabo da Rama (Cape Rama) in the south. Lined by a broad band of deep green coconut plantations, the beach sweeps south to the horizon, seemingly empty save for an occasional rank of wooden outriggers or a fleet of trawlers bobbing in the middle of the bay. However, appearances from this distance are deceptive. Nestling under the lush tree cover is a string of fishing settlements and *toddi* tappers' hamlets, interconnected by a network of sandy tracks and metalled lanes that feed onto a busy north–south highway. Over the past decade or so, several of these settlements have been developed for tourism, and now dozens of concrete hotels have displaced traditional mud-walled dwellings amid the dunes and open patches of rice paddy.

Colva, at the middle of the beach, is the area's main tourist trap, sucking in the lion's share of southern Goa's package tour trade, in addition to a steady stream of independent travellers. Its rash of hotels and beach bars peters out further north, but erupts again at **Majorda**, where several swanky five-star holiday complexes rise from the surrounding fields. Lying in the shadow of the ugly (and potentially lethal) *Zuari Agro Chemical* plant (see p.247), this top end of the beach is the least appealing.

If you can do without crowds but not your creature comforts, head south from Colva to the less commercialized village of **Benaulim**, whose plentiful budget accommodation and quiet sands make it a big hit with independent travellers. Further south still, the largely empty beach features a series of jarring cultural juxtapositions, as fishing settlements stand cheek-by-jowl with a string of mega-luxurious resorts. The most intrusive of these occurs around **Cavelossim** and **Mobor**, where a long spit of soft white sand noses into the Assolna estuary, forming a natural border between Salcete and Quepem *talukas*.

Although a couple of **buses** each day run from Vasco da Gama along the coast road to Colva village (via Dabolim airport), the most straightforward way to approach Colva beach is through **Margao**, from where regular buses, and a busy fleet of auto-rickshaws and taxis, service most of the coastal settlements. Having found your feet, the best way to get around the area is by rented **bicycle**. The hard sand exposed at low tide supports heavy Hero cycles, allowing you to make the most of the hawker-free stretches between resorts.

Colva

A hot-season retreat for Margao's moneyed middle classes since long before Independence, **COLVA** is the oldest and largest – but least appealing – of south Goa's resorts. Its leafy outlying *vaddos*, or wards, are pleasant enough, dotted with colonial-style villas and ramshackle fishing huts, but the beachfront is dismal: a lacklustre collection of concrete hotels, souvenir stalls and fly-blown snack bars strewn around a bleak central roundabout. Each afternoon, busloads of visitors from out of state mill around here after a paddle on the crowded foreshore, pestered by postcard *wallahs* and the little urchins whose families camp on the outskirts. The ambience is not improved by heaps of rubbish dumped in a rank-smelling ditch that runs behind the beach, nor by the stench of drying fish wafting from

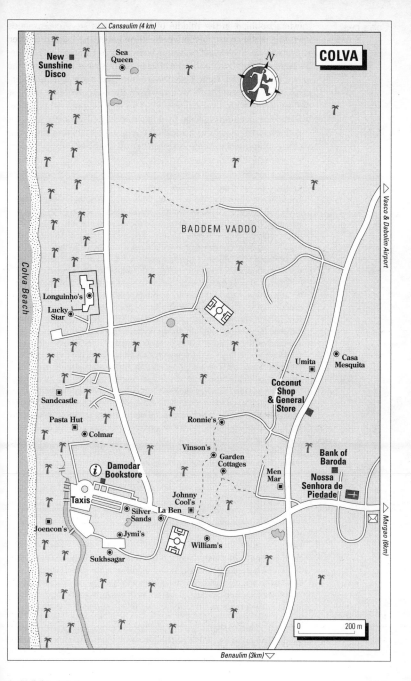

COLVA

Colva Beach

BADDEM VADDO

New Sunshine Disco

Sea Queen

Longuinho's

Lucky Star

Sandcastle

Pasta Hut

Colmar

Damodar Bookstore

Taxis

Joencon's

Silver Sands

Jymi's

Sukhsagar

La Ben

Johnny Cool's

William's

Garden Cottages

Vinson's

Ronnie's

Men Mar

Umita

Casa Mesquita

Coconut Shop & General Store

Bank of Baroda

Nossa Senhora de Piedade

0   200 m

the nearby palm-thatch village. If, however, you steer clear of this central market area, and stick to the cleaner, greener outskirts, Colva can be a pleasant and convenient place to stay for a while. Swimming is relatively safe (the local lifeguards, strutting around the sands in shorts and tight T-shirts, are more for show than anything else), while the sand, at least away from the beachfront, is spotless and scattered with beautiful shells. As for the fishy fumes, these are evidence of an enduring local fishing industry, and, as such, are a far healthier smell than the aroma of cut grass emanating from the water-guzzling resort complexes further up the coast.

Colva's miraculous "Menino" Jesus

Local legend has it that the statue of "Menino" (or "Baby") Jesus in the church of Igreja de Nossa Senhora de Piedade was discovered by a Jesuit missionary, Rev Father Bento Ferreira, in the mid-seventeenth century. The priest and his party had been shipwrecked off the coast of Mozambique and, having swum to safety, spotted a flock of vultures circling a stack of rocks ahead. The object of their attention was a statue of the baby Jesus, washed ashore after being dumped into the sea by Muslim pirates.

When Father Ferreira was posted to Colva in 1648, he took the statue, by now a minor miracle worker, with him. Installed on an appropriately grand altar, it quickly acquired cult status, drawing large crowds of devotees for the annual *Fama* ("fame") festival when the image was ritually exposed for public veneration. However, disaster struck following the suppression of the religious orders in 1836. Forced to flee, the Jesuits took the Menino with them to the seminary at Rachol (see p.173), along with a considerable hoard of jewellery and cash. Naturally, the villagers were furious, and petitioned the head of the Jesuit Order in Rome for its return. When he pleaded "finders, keepers", they took their grievance to the Viceroy, and, when that failed, to the King of Portugal, Dom João V, who promptly wrote to the governor general of Goa insisting the statue be sent back. It wasn't, however, so the disgruntled villagers gave up and commissioned a copy, which they adorned with a gold and diamond ring that had dropped off the original while it was being moved to Rachol. The old statue, meanwhile, mysteriously lost its powers, much to the chagrin of the Jesuits, and the evident satisfaction of the inhabitants of Colva, who claimed its healing abilites had been concentrated in the ring and transferred to their replica.

Today, the mark-two Menino still cures the sick, who flock here every year on the second Monday in October for the *Fama* festival – the only time the image is removed from the church's triple-locked vaults. After being paraded in a solemn procession around the building, it is stripped of its finery and dipped in the nearby river, while pilgrims eagerly scoop cupfuls of the water for good luck. They then file past the statue, installed for the day on the high altar, leaving behind wax limbs, eyes, stomachs and other disembodied bits and pieces as petitions (these are later melted down by the priests and resold). Among other religious souvenirs you'll come across if you're in Colva for the event are *medidas*, lengths of string the same height as the magical statue, which devotees believe contain a sample of its miraculous properties.

Colva is nowadays better known for its beach than its parish church, yet the whitewashed **Igreja de Nossa Senhora de Piedade** ("Our Lady of Mercy"), founded in 1630 and rebuilt in the eighteenth century on the village square, houses one of Goa's most venerated cult objects: the miraculous statue of **"Menino" Jesus** (see box).

Arrival

Buses leave Margao every thirty minutes for Colva (from outside the *Kamat Hotel* on Praça Jorge Barreto), dropping passengers at the main beachfront, and at various points along the main road. The thirty- to forty-minute trip costs virtually nothing, but can be a real endurance test towards the end of the day when the conductors pack on punters like sardines. Far better to jump in an **auto-rickshaw** for Rs40, or squeeze into a shared **taxi**. Heading in the opposite direction, from Colva to Margao, these pick up passengers at the entrance to the beach, along the main road leading to the village, and from the crossroads 200m west of the church. The fare costs between Rs7–10, depending on the number of people the driver manages to cram in. Regular mini-van and Ambassador taxis line up on the north side of the beachfront, next to the public toilets, and outside several of the upmarket resort hotels, including the *Silver Sands* and *Penthouse*.

Accommodation

Mirroring the village's rapid rise as a package tour resort, Colva's plentiful **accommodation** encompasses both bare cockroach-infested cells and swish campuses of chalets and swimming pools, with a fair selection of good-value guesthouses in between. Most of the mid- and top-of-the-range places are strung out along the main beach road or just behind it. Budget rooms are easier to come by amid the more peaceful palm groves and paddy fields north of here: the quarter known as "Ward 4", which is accessible via the path that winds north from *Johnny Cool's* restaurant, or from the other side via a lane leading west off the main Colva–Vasco road. Tariffs in this district remain under Rs100 even during peak season, though elsewhere they generally double. From mid-December to mid-January advance booking is nearly always essential.

Inexpensive

Casa Mesquita, 194 Vasco Rd, Ward 3; no phone. Large rooms, with rickety four-poster beds but no fans or attached shower-toilets, in fading old colonial-style house. Relaxing mosaic-floored verandahs, Western water toilet, and some cheap dorm beds available on request. Good value. ①.

Garden Cottages, Ward 4; no phone. Immaculately maintained, attractive budget guesthouse in Colva's most tranquil quarter. Spacious twin-bedded en-suite rooms with fans, and a garden. Very popular and excellent value, so book ahead. ②.

Colva beach

Jymi's, opposite *Sukhsagar*; ☎0834/737752. Large, old-established budget travellers' hotel, with passable en-suite rooms. A good place to hole up until you find somewhere nicer, as it usually has vacancies. ④.

Lucky Star, near the fishing *bastee*, north of the beachfront; no phone. One of several small rock-bottom guesthouses at the northwest end of the village. This one boasts a sizeable terrace, sea views and a restaurant next door. ①.

~~**Ronnie's**, Ward 4; no phone. Standard cell-block rooms, all with attached~~ shower-toilets and idyllic views west over the paddy fields from verandahs. ②.

Vinson's, Ward 4. The newest of this ward's good-value cheapos. Quiet and secluded. ①.

Moderate to expensive

Colmar, on the beachfront; ☎0834/721253. Colva's oldest purpose-built hotel overlooks the beach and comprises 45 comfortable chalets, and some cheaper non-attached rooms, grouped around a central lawn. No advance bookings, but good off-season discounts. Some a/c. ④–⑤.

La Ben, on the beach road; ☎0834/722009. Neat, clean, and good value at this price, though better known for its rooftop restaurant. ⑥.

Longuinho's, north of the beach front; ☎0834/722918, fax 722919. Swish campus hotel with lawns opening on to the beach. Most rooms have a/c and sea views, and there's an in-house travel agent and foreign exchange desk. Good-value half-board deals. ⑧.

Tours

GTDC operate a **sightseeing tour** out of Colva, more popular with domestic tourists than foreigners, but cheaper than those run by the charter companies. Its main drawback is the number of places crammed into a long day, which means you rush around the sights at an uncomfortable pace. Starting with a visit to Pilar seminary, the "North Goa Darshan" tour (daily; depart 10am, return 6pm; Rs80) takes in Chorao Island, the Saptakoteswar temple at Naroa, Mayem Lake, Mapusa, Vagator, Anjuna and Calangute beaches, and Aguada fort. Tickets should be booked in advance through GTDC's information counter in the lobby of the GTDC's *Tourist Cottages* complex on the beachfront.

A few private buses also leave Colva at 9am on Wednesday mornings for the **Anjuna flea market**, taking around 1hr 45min each way. The trips cost a hefty Rs100, but this works out cheaper than a taxi, and saves you a lot of hassle: getting to Anjuna by bus involves three separate changes and lots of waiting around – hardly worth it if you're only staying for the day. Tickets for buses to the flea market are sold at various outlets along the main beach road.

Finally, day-long **boat trips** to deserted Sao Jorge island, off the Mormugao peninsula, are touted at many of Colva's cafés and by boys handing out fliers on the beach. Often billed as "Dolphin-Spotting Cruises", these generally leave on Fridays, cost approximately Rs300, including food and a "welcome drink". If you decide to go, take a hat and plenty of sun cream as neither the boats, nor the island, have much shade.

Sea Queen, 1km north of beachfront; ☎0834/720499 or 7342576, fax 734256. The village's poshest resort complex is 200m from the beach, with large a/c rooms, a pool and most other mod cons. Ridiculously expensive for walk-in customers, though. ⑨.

Silver Sands, on the beach road; ☎0834/737744–8. Sixty-six average rooms ranged around a pool, with à la carte restaurant and health club. Facilities include car rental, money-changing and courtesy bus to airport. Popular with package companies, but shabbier than the others at this price. Some a/c. ⑤.

Sukhsagar, opposite the *Penthouse*; ☎0834/721888. Nothing special from the outside, but its en-suite rooms are clean, light and airy, and the best deal in this price range. There's also a pleasant palm-shaded garden to relax in. Some a/c. ⑤.

William's, on the beach road; ☎0834/721077 or 733964, fax 732852. Flashy package tour complex, 400m from the beach, that accepts walk-in customers. Good all-round facilities include a tennis court, plus a pool with wet bar. Some a/c. ⑦.

Eating and drinking

When the season is in full swing, Colva's beachfront sprouts a row of large seafood **restaurants** on stilts, some of them very ritzy indeed, with tablecloths, candles and smooth music. The prices in these places are top-whack, but the portions are correspondingly vast, and standards generally high. Travellers on tight budgets are equally well catered for, however, with a sprinkling of **shack-cafés** at the less frequented ends of the beach, and along the Vasco Road.

Joencon's, second restaurant south from beachfront. The classiest of Colva's beach restaurants. Agonizingly slow service and pricey, but the food is superb: try their flamboyant fish sizzlers, mouthwatering tandoori sharkfish or Chinese and Indian vegetarian specialities.

Johnny Cool's, opposite *William's Resort*, on the beach road. Roadside café-bar with views across the fields behind. Serves dozens of different beers and spirits, and arguably the best pizza in Goa. Inexpensive.

La Ben's, on the beach road. Pleasant rooftop restaurant with a predictable menu and sea views. A good sunset spot. Moderate.

Men Mar, Vasco Rd. Indifferent food, but their *lassis*, prepared with fresh fruit and home-made curd, are delicious. Open for breakfast.

Pasta Hut, *Colmar Hotel*. Western food, mostly pasta and some veg dishes, served up on covered terrace. A hit with 18–30 package tourists, but an uninspiring location.

Sandcastle, north of the beachfront. Hippy beach hangout bar-restaurant famed for its pizza, pasta and apple pies. Inexpensive.

Silver Sands, on the beach road. Swish indoor à la carte restaurant with an impressive selection of pricey Goan, Indian and Continental dishes. Good place for a splurge.

Umita, Vasco Rd. Down-to-earth Goan and Indian veg cooking served up by a friendly Hindu family. Try their blow-out "special" *thalis* or whopping fresh-fruit-and-curd breakfasts. Opens early.

Nightlife

Although never an established rave venue, Colva's **nightlife** is livelier than anywhere else in south Goa, thanks to its ever-growing contingent of young package tourists. Most of the action centres on the bars just beyond the big stilt restaurants, south of the main beachfront. Also worth checking out if you're staying in north Colva is the *New Sunshine*'s garden disco, which draws its custom from the *Sea Queen* package tour complex opposite. All of these places make their money on drinks, and are thus beyond the pocket of most Indians and long-staying visitors. If you'd prefer to get plastered somewhere cheaper and less pretentious, try *Johnny Cool's*, midway between the beach and Colva crossroads. *Men Mar*, on the Vasco Road, also serves beers, snacks and *lassis* until around 10.30pm, as does nearby *La Village*'s small terrace café.

Listings

Books *Damodar Book Store*, shop No. 4 on the beachfront, stocks a good selection of reasonably priced secondhand paperbacks in English. They will also part-exchange any books you've finished with, and have the best range of postcards in Colva. In addition, *Men Mar*, on the Vasco road, keeps a cabinet of well-thumbed paperbacks in a variety of languages, which they rent to travellers at fixed rates that cover a refundable deposit.

Car rental *Hotel Skylark* does car rental for around Rs1000 per day, or you can organize a taxi yourself for considerably less at the beachfront rank.

Foreign exchange *Thomas Cook's* handy mobile bank calls at Colva every weekday from 3–4.30pm, and changes cash and travellers' cheques at competitive rates. You'll find it just north of the beachfront on the way to the *Colmar Hotel*. Otherwise, try *Sanatan Air Travel Agency* (Mon–Sat 9.30am–7pm; ☎ & fax 0834/225876), 200m east of Colva church, where you can make withdrawls on *Visa* and *Mastercard*, and arrange bank drafts and international money orders.

Fuel Sold by the *Bisleri* bottle from a little house behind the Menino Jesus College, just east of *William's Resort* – the only fuel stop in Colva.

Motorcycle rental Ask around the taxi rank, or in front of *Vincy's Hotel*, where 100cc Yamahas are on offer at the usual rates. Their owners will advise you to avoid Margao if you haven't got a valid international drivers' licence, as the approach road passes the police post.

Post office Colva's sub-post office, opposite the church in the village, has a small but reliable poste restante box.

Swimming pool The *Silver Sands Hotel*, on the beach road, charges non-residents around Rs40 per hour to use their pool.

Travel agents *Sanatan*, S-15 Sanzgiri Arcade, near Colva church (Mon–Sat 9.30am–7pm; ☎ & fax 0834/225876), books and reconfirms domestic and international flights, and arranges deluxe bus, catamaran and train tickets to other parts of India.

Majorda and Utorda

North of Colva, the sand stretches for 12km to meet the Mormugao peninsula, marred by the metallic chimneys and pressurized storage

Dhiri: the Goan bullfight

In 1996, a home-grown animal rights group made history in Goa when, after a protracted campaign, it successfully brought about a ban on **bullfighting**, until then the state's most popular spectator sport after cricket and football. Known in Konkani as **dhiri**, Goan bullfights were certainly less cruel than their Spanish counterparts, as rather than facing teams of strutting, sequined matadors armed with swords, the bulls fought each other. That said, the encounters were unquestionably violent, and a miserable experience for the animals involved, whose necks would be badly scratched by their opponents' horns, causing bloodshed and occasional fatalities – the essence of the anti-bloodsports lobby's legal argument against *dhiri*. Because of the ban, you're unlikely to come across a staged bullfight these days, but the Goan High Court's ruling may be overturned in the future, in which case the following account, while not condoning what was undoubtedly an ordeal for the bulls, will shed light on an essential, centuries-old part of Goan culture.

Dhiri (literally "tight lock") is thought to have originally been devised by cowherds as a means to relieve the tedium of cattle-watching. Encouraged by the Portuguese, it became incorporated into village church feast days (*festas*) during the colonial era and, prior to the ban, packed out large stadia in Panjim and Margao. More commonly, however, bullfights were held on dusty patches of waste ground on the edges of small towns and villages, fenced off with walls of cotton sheeting.

Bouts were fought by (but never between) two main breeds: sleek grey-black water buffalo and lumpy-necked cream-coloured brahmins, with bizarre action-hero names like "Tyson", "Rambo" and "Hanuman". The animals were thoroughbreds, selected for their colour, weight, the length and strength of their horns, and, most importantly, for their readiness to fight. The rewards of successful breeding were great, with champions drawing huge crowds and commanding high ticket prices, not to mention substantial cash prizes.

Before the fight, spectators placed bets, or *apostas*, with bookies, or warmed up their gambling glands with a game of dice at a side stall; others dangled precariously from the branches of trees to get a better view, or pitched stones at people in front of them who were in the way as the bulls were brought on. In the centre of the ring, a moustachioed master of ceremonies swaggered to and fro, brandishing a long stick, while a rapid-fire Konkan commentary crackled over the PA. With noses raised, the animals then pawed the dirt with their hooves. This was the crucial moment when a yellow-bellied bull would catch a whiff of imminent defeat, turn tail and crash out of the *dhiri* ground in a cloud of dust. The least sign of reluctance, however, was met by the bulls' determined trainers with a firm yank of the testicles, designed to force the animal into a closing charge. When the heads finally clashed, a thud like a heavy coconut landing on hard sand would ellicit a roar from the crowd. Their horns firmly locked, the bulls then struggled to force each other backwards. Sometimes, the bout was over in seconds. Other fights lasted for an hour or more as the exhausted beasts, blood oozing from gashes on their necks, struggled for supremacy. Eventually, however, one of them threw in the towel and made a desperate dash for the nearest exit, sending the excited crowd scurrying for safety.

tanks of *Zuari Agro*'s giant fertilizer plant. Seepages from this complex, recently dubbed by a Goan green group as "an industrial time bomb", caused ground water pollution and the death of tonnes of fish here during the mid-1970s; its presence overlooking one of the world's most beautiful beaches is a continued source of controversy.

Another debate rages over the two luxury hotels that loom above the dunes and well-irrigated paddy fields of **MAJORDA** and **UTORDA** villages, 4km north of Colva. Local environmentalists assert these were erected without adequate consultation and that the immense amounts of water needed to maintain their lawns and swimming pools (supplied, the greens allege, by illegally drilled bore holes), causes dry-season shortages for villagers. While the litigation cases against the hotels' owners crawl through Goan courts, package tourists from the UK and mainland Europe continue to flock here, lured by glossy brochure images of this otherwise idyllic strip of palm-fringed shore. However, if you're not staying in either of the resorts, there's little reason to venture up here: the beach south of Benaulim is more peaceful and picturesque.

Practicalities

Transfer **buses** whisk newly arrived charter tourists from Dabolim airport to Majorda and Utorda's resorts, but a couple of buses each day also run between Colva and Cansaulim, a busy village on the train line at the far north end of the beach, if you want to get here independently; taxis also hang around outside both big **hotels**. With 120 air-conditioned rooms and cottages dotted around its lawns, the four-star *Majorda Beach* (☎0834/730204, fax 730212; ⑨) is the largest of the two resorts, boasting indoor and outdoor pools, tennis and squash courts, a sauna, health club, large sun terrace and billiards room. Its competitor, the five-star *Goa Penta* (☎0834/738342, fax 733978; ⑧) is slightly smaller but equally luxurious, with air-conditioned rooms and chalets around a large clover-shaped pool. In-house entertainment includes occasional live music in the buffet-restaurant, and limbo dancers, believe it or not.

The only budget **place to stay** in the area is the modest *Goodfaith Lodge* in Majorda village (☎0834/734322, fax 734252; ③), which offers simple en-suite rooms, with fans and small balconies, in a modern double-storey concrete annexe, ten minutes from the beach. The *Shangri-La* (☎0834/733937, fax 730404; ⑦), directly opposite, is a pleasant mid-range place, with two bar-restaurants and comfortable rooms, but its peak-season tariffs are extortionate.

Benaulim

According to Hindu mythology, Goa was created when the sage Shri Parasurama, Vishnu's sixth incarnation, fired an arrow into the sea from the top of the Western Ghats and ordered the waters to recede. The spot where the shaft fell to earth, known in Sanskrit as Banali ("place where the arrow landed") and later corrupted by the

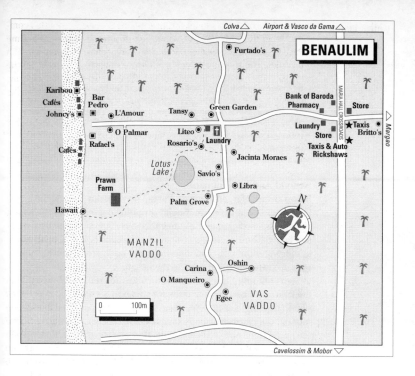

BENAULIM

Furtado's

Karibou
Cafés   Bar
              Pedro
Johncy's   L'Amour   Tansy   Green Garden

O Palmar   Liteo
Rafael's   Rosario's   Laundry
Cafés

Bank of Baroda
Pharmacy   Store

Laundry   ★Taxis
Store   Britto's

Jacinta Moraes   Taxis & Auto
                  Rickshaws

MARIA HALL CROSSROADS

Margao ▷

*Lotus
Lake*   Savio's

Prawn
Farm   Libra

Hawaii   Palm Grove

N

MANZIL
VADDO

                 Carina   Oshin
              O Manqueiro
                    Egee   VAS
0   100m   VADDO

Portuguese to **BENAULIM**, lies in the dead centre of Colva Beach, 7km west of Margao. Only a decade ago, this fishing and rice farming village, scattered around the coconut groves and paddy fields between the main Colva–Mobor road and the dunes, had barely made it onto the backpackers' map. Now, the shady lane leading through it is studded with small guesthouses and souvenir stalls, while in the past two or three seasons, several enormous package resorts have mushroomed on the outskirts. If these attract the number of tourists they are designed for, the essentially *sossegarde* character of Benaulim will be radically transformed in the coming years. For the time being, though, rice cultivation and fishing, along with remittance receipts from relatives working overseas, remain as central to the local economy as tourism, and the beach is gloriously unspoilt.

Either side of Benaulim's scruffy esplanade, gently shelving sands shimmer away almost to the horizon, littered with photogenic wooden outriggers that provide welcome shade if the walk from the palm trees to the sea gets too much. Hawkers, itinerant masseurs and fruit *wallahs* appear from time to time, but you can easily escape them by heading south towards neighbouring Varca (see below), where tourism has thus far made little impact. Moreover, the sea is safe for swimming, being generally jellyfish-free.

Muggings in Benaulim

Reports have been reaching the *Rough Guides* office of **muggings** in Benaulim. This is not an entirely new phenomenon but the attacks have clearly become more frequent and more violent over the past few seasons, with dozens of tourists robbed or assaulted on the road from the village to the beach: one had chilli pepper thrown in his eyes, and another's arm was broken in a scuffle during the winter of 1995–6. The presence of *lathi*-wielding policemen has improved the situation, but if you walk the road between the beachfront and Benaulim after dark, do so in a group rather than alone.

Arrival and information

Buses from Margao, Colva, Varca, Cavelossim and Mobor roll through Benaulim every half-hour, dropping passengers at the Maria Hall crossroads. Ranged around this busy junction are two well-stocked **general stores**, a couple of **café-bars**, a **bank**, **pharmacy**, **laundry** and the taxi- and auto-rickshaw rank, from where you can pick up **transport 2km west** to the beach.

Signs offering **bicycles** and **motorbikes** for rent are dotted along the lane leading to the sea: rates are standard, descending in proportion to the length of time you keep the vehicle. If you need to **change money**, the nearest place is the *Sanatan Travel Agency* in Colva (see p.188), or one of the banks in Margao (see p.171). Benaulim's own *Bank of Baroda* (Mon–Fri 9am–1pm, Sat 9am–noon) only handles *Visa* card encashments; the *L'Amour Beach Resort* also has a foreign-exchange counter for residents. Finally, international and domestic **flights** can be booked or reconfirmed at *Sarken Tour Operators*, and *L'Amour*, which also does de-luxe bus, train and catamaran ticketing for cities elsewhere in India.

Accommodation

Benaulim's **accommodation** largely consists of small budget guesthouses, scattered around the leafy lanes 1km or so back from the beach. Most are featureless annexes of spartan tiled rooms, with fans and, usually, attached shower-toilets; the only significant difference between them is their location. As few places have telephones, the only way to find a vacancy is to hunt around on foot, although if you wait at the Maria Hall crossroads or the beachfront with a rucksack, someone is bound to ask if you need a room. During peak season, the village's few mid-range hotels tend to be fully booked, so reserve in advance if you want to stay in one of these.

L'Amour, on the beachfront; ☎0834/723720. Benaulim's longest established hotel is a comfortable 30-room/cottage complex, with terrace restaurant, travel agent, money-changing and some a/c. No single occupancy. ⑤–⑥.

Carina, Tamdi-Mati, Vas Vaddo; ☎0834/734166. This good-value upmarket hotel, recently enlarged with a spacious roadside annexe, lies in a tranquil location with a pool, bar-restaurant, foreign exchange and room service. Some a/c. ⑦.

Egee, Vas Vaddo; no phone. Half-a-dozen nicer-than-average budget rooms on first floor above a family house. ②.

Jacinta Moraes, 1608/A Vas Vaddo; ☎0834/722706. Half-a-dozen largish clean rooms with fans, attached shower-toilets and sound plumbing. Some Western toilets. Very good value. ②.

Libra Cottages, Vas Vaddo; ☎0834/731740. In much the same mould as Jacinta Moraes, only with a couple more rooms, including two economy options around the back. ②.

Liteo Cottages, opposite tailor's shop, on the beach road; ☎0834/721173. Very large, clean rooms (all en-suite and with balconies) in the centre of the village. Hardly the most inspiring location, but good value if tariffs are maintained. ③.

O Manqueiro, Vas Vaddo; ☎0834/734164. Very basic budget accommodation in the secluded south of the village, run by a family with a predilection for plastic fruit. Mostly shared toilets. The rooms on the top floor are best. ②.

O Palmar, opposite *L'Amour*; no phone. A row of slightly shabby sea-facing chalets, virtually on the beach, and with their own verandahs. Those at the rear are the most apealing, as they're not plagued by wind-blown rubbish from the beachfront. ④.

Oshin, Mazil Vaddo; ☎0834/722707. Large, triple-storey complex set well back from the road, with views from balconies over the tree tops from top floor rooms. Spacious and clean, with en-suite bathrooms. A notch above most places in this area, and good value. ④.

Palm Grove, Tamdi-Mati, 149 Vas Vaddo; ☎0834/722533. Secluded hotel surrounded by beautiful gardens, with a luxurious new block around the back, some a/c, pleasant terrace restaurant and friendly management. A bike ride back from the beachfront, but by far the most pleasant place in its class. Recommended. ④–⑦.

Rosario's, Vas Vaddo, off the second (west) crossroads; ☎0834/734167. The village's most popular budget guesthouse, with common or attached bathrooms and small balconies, but no views. ①–②.

Eating and drinking

By far the most popular **places** to **eat** are the shack cafés in the beachfront area, where *Johncy's* catches most of the passing custom. However, you'll find better food at lower prices in the smaller terrace restaurants further along the beach and scattered around the village. Arguably the best of bunch is the *Palm Grove*'s congenial garden restaurant, and there is a string of lookalike café-bars which dot the lane leading to it. For fresh seafood, though, the *Hawaii* shack is hard to beat.

Cacy Rose, 100m west of Maria Hall. Good-sized portions of inexpensive food (pancakes and porridge), with a fair choice of Goan, Indian and veg dishes, as well as breakfasts, served on roadside terrace.

Hawaii, south of the village behind the beach. Among the best shack restaurants for miles, run by a warm local family. Their seafood, grilled or flash-fried in tasty Worcester sauce, is straight off the boats, the portions huge and the prices fair, and they serve stiff pegs of the village's finest *feni*. To find it, head south down the beach, or walk down the lane leading south off the beach road to the government prawn farm and head across the dunes from there.

Karibou, the last shack in the row running north from *Johncy's* at the beachfront. Easily the best seafood in this area, served by a friendly American-Israeli/Goan couple. Try one of their fish steaks steeped in rich garlic butter sauce. A good venue for a sundowner, too.

Pedro's, on the beachfront. Long waits, but the food – mostly fish steaks served with home-made sauces – is freshly cooked and tasty. Inexpensive.

Rafael's, on the beachfront. Rough-and-ready beach café serving all the usual stuff, plus fried rice, salads and deliciously stodgy oven-hot coconut pudding.

Palm Grove, Tamdi-Mati, Vas Vaddo. Mostly Goan seafood, with some Indian and Continental options, dished up alfresco in cosy garden café-restaurant. Worth the trip out here.

Tona, *L'Amour* hotel, on the beachfront. Their Chinese dishes are definitely worth a splurge, but the rest of the menu is overpriced, and the service poor.

South of Benaulim

South of Benaulim, the main road, running parallel with Colva beach, passes through a string of small settlements dominated by outsize whitewashed churches. Bumpy back lanes peel west at regular intervals, winding across the rice fields to the fishing hamlets huddled in the dunes, and to the secluded luxury resort hotels that punctuate the beach. By the time you reach **Cavelossim**, gateway to the package enclave and trawler anchorage of **Mobor**, the palm cover has all but petered out, while the pale green profile of the **Sahyadri Hills** beckons to the southeast.

Unless you're booked into one of the big resorts or are following this more tranquil coast road south in preference to the hectic Margao–Chaudi highway (NH17), there's little reason to venture into the far southwest corner of Salcete *taluka*. Away from the beach, the scenery is flat and monotonous, and, with the notable exception of **Varca**, none of the villages make provision for travellers.

Varca

If you're staying in Benaulim, you're bound at some point visit **VARCA**: the row of beached wooden fishing boats 2km south of Benaulim belong to its community of Christian fishers, whose palm-thatch long houses line the foot of the grassy dunes. Of the tourists that pedal past, few stay longer than a few hours crashed in the shade of an outrigger. However, it is possible to find **rooms to rent** in family houses by asking around the village. Facilities are ultra-basic, with well water and pig toilets the norm, but if you're looking to stay somewhere authentically Goan, yet not too far off-track, Varca is worth considering. Bear in mind that a bicycle and cooking equipment are essential for long spells, as you'll probably have to shop for and cook your own food.

The only blots on the otherwise unspoilt landscape around Varca are the *Resorte de Goa* (☎0834/745066, fax 745310; ⑨) – a recently built three-star resort, whose 56 rooms and bright-painted chalets cluster around a pool and sun terrace, with two bars, two restaurants and sea views – and the large and very swish *Ramada Renaissance* (☎0834/245200, fax 245335; ⑧–⑨), which boasts waterfalls in reception, a nine-hole golf course, Polynesian restaurant, poolside disco and casino.

Cavelossim and around

Sleepy **CAVELOSSIM**, 11km south of Colva, straddles the coast road and is the last major settlement in southwest Salcete: its only claim to fame. A short way beyond the village's picturesque church **square**, a narrow lane veers left (east) across an open expanse of paddy fields to the Cavelossim–Assolna **ferry crossing** (last departures: 8.30pm from Cavelossim, 8.45pm from Assolna; Rs2), near the mouth of the Sal River. If you're heading south to Canacona, turn left off the ferry – not right as indicated on local maps – and carry on as far as Assolna bazaar, clustered around a junction on the main road, from where regular buses leave for Margao, 12km north. A right turn at this crossroads takes you southwest into Quepem, and on towards windswept Cabo da Rama (Cape Rama).

A congenial **place to stay** in Cavelossim is the *Hotel Dona Samaria* in Tamborim Waddo (☎0834/745672, fax 745673; ⑤), a short way west of the main road. It's a quiet place with helpful staff and a family atmosphere, but has the drawbacks of an eco-unfriendly swimming pool, and the fact that a huge concrete arrow sited in the dunes between it and the beach is periodically used as a practice target by the Indian navy's squadron of ageing fighter jets. This only happens a couple of days each month, though, and at these times the hotel owner or villagers will warn you.

Mobor

The main road from Cavelossim continues south across a two-kilometre-long tract of exposed rolling dunes, coming to an abrupt end at **MOBOR**, terminus for buses arriving from Colva, Benaulim and Margao. Tapering into the Sal estuary, this remote spit of sand at the southern tip of Colva beach supported, until less than a decade ago, nothing more than a tiny *toddi*-tapping and fishing settlement. Since then, however, no less than seven ritzy resort complexes have appeared amid the coconut plantations, bringing with them planeloads of package tourists, a crop of beach cafés, Kashmiri handicraft shops – and considerable controversy. Whatever the rights or wrongs of individual cases (currently being thrashed out in court), few would deny that these sprawling concrete campuses – complete with swimming pools, golf courses, and, in one case, a monumentally kitsch mock sailing ship – do nothing to enhance the area's natur-

For more on the controversial new beach developments, see p.246.

al beauty. So if you've come here hoping to find an unspoilt stretch of beach, forget it and press on further south.

Accommodation

Averina, near the the *Leela Beach*, Mobor; ☎0834/746303. Four-star place with 144 rooms, a coffee shop, tennis court, gym and horseshoe-shaped pool. Very near the beach. ⑨.

Dona Sylvia, Mobor; ☎0834/746321, fax 746320. A huge charter hotel with 240 rooms, including some two-storey cottages, grouped around a pool. Accused of destroying sand dunes to improve the view. ⑨.

Gaffino's, Mobor; ☎0834/723439. The smallest of Mobor's hotels has 16 rooms with river views, and a small restaurant. Family-run. ⑥.

Leela Beach, Mobor; ☎0834/746363, fax 746352. A swanky arrangement of spacious villas set amid 45 acres of lawns, boasting seven multi-cuisine restaurants, a disco, huge pool and superb sports facilities. It's also the environmentalists' big green meany, accused of felling *toddi* trees, displacing locals, dumping sewage into the river and polluting ground water. ⑨.

Old Anchor, Mobor; ☎0834/723005. A hot contender for the ugliest hotel in Goa, thanks to its hideous replica galleon. Inside are 238 double-bedded studio rooms, with mod cons that include a pool, sauna and work-out room. Alleged to have levelled dunes and built within 200-metre exclusion zone (see p.246). ⑧.

Canacona *taluka*

Ceded to the Portuguese by the Rajah of Sund in the Treaty of 1791, Goa's far south – **Canacona** *taluka* – was among the last parts of the territory to be absorbed into the the *Novas Conquistas*, and has thus retained a distinctly Hindu feel: multicoloured *tulsi* plant pots stand outside its dishevelled red-tiled village houses, while stray cows wander freely across the potholed roads. The area also boasts some of the state's most outstanding scenery. Set against a backdrop of the jungle-covered Sahyadri Hills (an extension of the Western Ghat range), a string of pearl-white coves and sweeping beaches scoop its indented coastline, enfolded by laterite headlands and colossal piles of black boulders that tumble into the sea.

So far, tourism has made little impression on this beautiful landscape. With the exception of **Palolem**, whose near-perfect beach attracts a steady flow of day-trippers and longer-staying travellers during high season, the area's coastal settlements remain firmly rooted in a traditional fishing and *toddi*-tapping economy. However, the red gash of the Konkan Railway threatens to bring Canacona's days as a tranquil rural backwater to an end. When it's fully operational (by late 1997), the line will connect the district by direct "super-fast" express train to Bombay, Panjim and Mangalore: the developers' bulldozers and concrete mixers are sure to follow.

The Konkan Railway controversy is featured on p.249.

In the meantime, several pristine beaches and a large tract of tropical forest await anyone pining for peace and quiet. The region's
main transport artery is the NH17, which crawls across the Sahyadri
and Karmali Ghats towards Karnataka via the district headquarters,
Chaudi. Bus services between here and Margao are frequent; off the
highway, however, bullock carts and bicycles far outnumber motor
vehicles. The only way to do the area justice, therefore, is by motorcycle, although you'll have to rent one further north and drive it
down here as few are available in situ. Accommodation is also thin on
the ground, confined to Palolem, Agonda, and one small beach on
the state borders.

Chaudi

CHAUDI (aka Chauri, or Canacona), 33km south of Margao, is the
Canacona district's bustling headquarters. Packed around a junction
on the main Panjim–Mangalore highway, it is primarily a transport
hub, of interest to visitors mainly because of its proximity to
Palolem, 2km west. Buses to and from Panjim, Margao, and Karwar
in Karnataka *taluka* trundle in and out of a scruffy square on the
main street, where taxis and auto-rickshaws wait to ferry passengers
to the villages scattered across the surrounding fields.

If you spend much time in Palolem, you're sure to nip into Chaudi
to shop for provisions, or simply soak up its gritty Indian atmosphere, which comes as a refreshing contrast to the dreamy beaches
nearby. The small covered **market** is an essential source of fresh fruit
and vegetables; several stalls sell stoves, cooking equipment and
other hardware, while the excellent *Udipi* restaurant, a short way
south of the main crossroads, is one of the few places for miles you
can eat *pukka* South Indian food: try their filling Rs15 *thalis*, or
spicy fried *pakora* and *samosas* – all freshly prepared, and piping
hot if you come around 5pm. They also do delicious *lassis*, sweetened with traditional syrups.

Cabo da Rama (Cape Rama)

Cabo da Rama (Cape Rama), the long boney finger of land that juts
into the sea at the south end of Colva Bay, takes its name from the
hero of the Hindu epic, the *Ramayana*, who, along with his wife
Sita, holed up here during his exile from Ayodhya – one of several
such sacred sites in central and southern India. This one, however, is
more grandiose than most, commanding spectacular views north
over the length of Colva Beach, and down the sand-splashed coast of
Canacona. The easily defensible promontory was crowned by a **fort**
centuries before the Portuguese cruised in and wrested it from the
local Hindu rulers in 1763. They erected their own citadel soon after,
but this now lies in ruins, lending to the laterite headland a forlorn
end-of-the-world feel.

The road to Cabo da Rama, leading past Canaguinim's huge wind turbine, ends abruptly in front of the fort's **gatehouse**. Once inside, either turn right and scale the battlements, where a crumbling turret still houses a couple of rusty old Portuguese cannons, or else head straight on past the chapel, swathed in colourful bougainvillea bushes, towards the west end of the peninsula. Until 1955, the bastion housed a prison; now its only habitable building is a lonely government **observation post**, occupied from time to time by a couple of young scientists from Dona Paula's Institute of Oceanography, who are marooned here for weeks on end until a chopper swoops in to rescue them.

From the bungalow, a steep path passes through a gap in the boundary walls to a narrow ridge, eventually emerging from the wooded bluff beyond at the windswept tip of the cape. The sea views from this serene spot are superb, but be careful while clambering over the boulders stacked above the shoreline – a few years ago, a lad from the nearby village fell to his death here while hunting pigeons.

Practicalities

A small fuel station stands at the unmarked turning for Cabo da Rama on the coast road, 7km east of the village. Regular **buses** also run here from Margao (4–5 daily; 1hr 30min), pulling into the car park in front of the fort. If you should miss the last one back at 4pm, a **café** 400m east along the road has a couple of rooms for rent (①). The village's only other **bar** is situated 200m from the fort; its friendly owner, Augustino Fernandes, can usually rustle up a plate or two of spicy fish curry or rice if you need **food**.

Agonda

Heading south from Cabo da Rama, the coast road climbs through fragrant cashew forest to the pass over **Karmali Ghat**, from which it descends against a stunning vista of wooded spurs and plains that sweep into the sea. If you fancy a swim, turn west off the main road shortly after it reaches level ground (14km southeast of Cabo da Rama, or 7km northwest of Chaudi), and make for **AGONDA**, where a three-kilometre spread of white sand beckons. Backed by three tree-covered hills, the beach ranks among the most spectacular in Canacona *taluka*, although unusually large waves make it less than ideal for kids and weak swimmers. Finding a patch of shade can be a problem, too, unless you head for the cluster of smooth brown boulders at the bottom end, beyond which the village's fishing fleet shelters in a sandy cove.

Agonda has not always been as tranquil as it appears today. In 1982, a dozen absentee landlords sold the palm groves behind the beach to a Delhi-based hotel chain, backed, according to rumours at the time, by Rajiv and Sonia Gandhi. Construction work began soon after on a luxury resort complex and eighteen-hole golf course, but soon floundered when local *toddi* tappers refused to vacate the plot, claiming the hotel would ruin their traditional livelihoods. The tenants even threatened to defend their land rights by force, and daubed a rock in the middle of the bay with the slogan: "Your tourists will never be safe here". The project, however, was never completed. Embroiled in costly court cases, the developers eventually backed down and left a huge unfinished concrete hulk languishing in the woods, to be claimed by a troupe of monkeys.

This acrimonious episode may in part explain the relative scarcity in Agonda of facilities for visitors. At present, there are only two **places to stay** in the village, both situated at the far (south) end of the beach. The better of the pair is the *Dunhill Bar & Restaurant* (☎0834/647328; ①), which has a handful of basic rooms with breezy verandahs, and pig toilets around the back. It's a clean and peaceful place, and the family who run it serve spicy Goan-fried mackerel, rice and curry to order on their small terrace. If they're full, *Caferns* (☎0834/647235; ①) down the road is a good fall-back.

Palolem

PALOLEM, 2km west of Chaudi, pops up more often in glossy holiday brochures than any other beach in Goa; not because the village is a major package tour destination, but because its crescent-shaped bay, lined with a swaying curtain of coconut palms, is irresistibly photogenic. Hemmed in by a pair of wooded headlands, a perfect curve of white sand arcs north from a pile of gargantuan boulders to the spur of **Sahyadri Ghat**, which here tapers into the sea, draped in vegetation and studded with large rocks. In addition, the water recedes from the top end of the bay at low tide to expose a narrow causeway, connecting the beach with a small island inhabited by black-faced langur monkeys.

Until recently, Palolem was south Goa's best kept secret. Over the past three or four years, however, it's become a popular target for day-trippers from the package resorts further north, who travel down in mini-bus taxis or pleasure boats, and disappear home around sunset, leaving the village to the increasing numbers of backpackers who hole up here for the winter. Inevitably, this influx has spawned a rash of beach shacks, cafés, parasols and Karnatakan hawkers (there's even an unsightly satellite dish on the beach these days), but Palolem has remained an essentially traditional village, where the easy pace of life is still dictated more by the three daily rounds of *toddi* tapping than the exigencies of tourism. Every afternoon, family groups gather on the beach to haul in hand-nets cast from canoes out in the bay, with the young men tugging on the ropes, and their mothers and sisters piling the catch into palm-leaf baskets. *Feni* aficionados will find plenty to rave about here, too. The telltale roar of stills emanates from little shacks once each week in quieter corners of the village. Head down to the beach the next morning, and

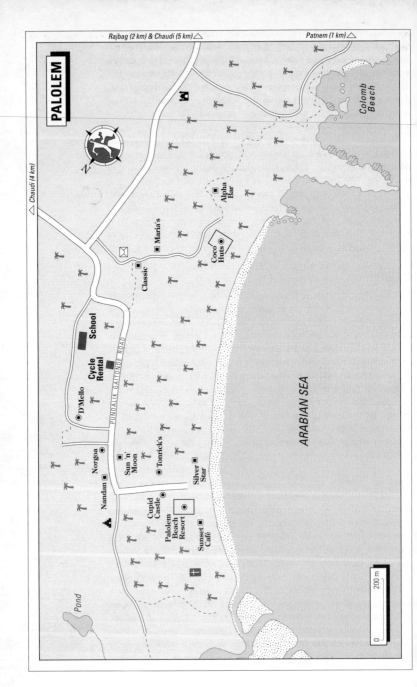

PALOLEM

Rajbag (2 km) & Chaudi (5 km) △   Patnem (1 km) △

Chaudi (4 km) △

N

Colomb
Beach

ARABIAN SEA

Alpha
Bar

Maria's

Coco
Huts

Classic

School

Cycle
Rental

PUNDALIK GAITONDE ROAD

D'Mello

Norgoa

Sun 'n
Moon

Tonrick's

Silver
Star

Nandan

Cupid
Castle

Palolem
Beach
Resort

Sunset
Café

Pond

200 m

0

you'll see the fruits of this labour being loaded on to boats for "export" to Karnataka. The locals keep plenty of the best stuff for themselves, though, both for consumption at home, and in the little bars dotted around the groves behind the beach.

When you grow tired of lazing on the beach, a number of tempting **walks** beckon. South of Palolem, a string of beautiful and easily accessible beaches make perfect seaside ambles (see "Colom, Patnem and Rajbag" on p.204), while to the north it is possible to explore the forest-cloaked spur of Sahyadri Ghat on foot. Head along the main street, but instead of turning left towards the main beachfront area, carry on through the Hindu quarter, past the new prawn farm, until you reach a footbridge. From here, a well-trodden path winds into the woods on the far side of the estuary, dividing into a tangle of narrow trails as it penetrates the lush forest. One leads steeply uphill to a pass, where you can strike off through dense undergrowth in search of a rock from which to admire the spellbinding views over the tree canopy and down the coast. If you attempt this, though, bear in mind how easy it is to get lost in such thick woods; mark your trail regularly, and carry as much water as possible.

Practicalities

Frequent **buses** run between Margao and Karwar (in Karnataka) via Chaudi (every 30min; 2hr), where you can pick up an **auto-rickshaw** (Rs30) or **taxi** (Rs50) 2km west to Palolem. Alternatively, get off at the Char Rostay ("Four-Way") crossroads, 1.5km before Chaudi, and walk the remaining kilometre or so to the village. A couple of buses each day also go all the way to Palolem from Margao; these stop at the end of the lane leading from the main street to the beachfront.

Jellyfish

Palolem, and several other sheltered beaches in the far south of Goa, suffers from a jellyfish problem, as evidenced by the blobs of viscous aquatic matter festering on its sands. These have been dumped here by fishermen, but you can be sure their mates are alive and lurking in the shallows, waiting to nobble unwary bathers.

Goa has roughly two kinds of jellyfish: a large transluscent variety with long dangling tentacles that will give you a nasty sting but nothing worse; and a much smaller yellow type whose venom can be fatal. Thankfully, the latter is extremely rare, and only hangs out in deep water. The former beast, by contrast, is all too common. If it stings you, ignore the locals' advice to smear the welts with fresh cow dung, and pop a couple of antihistamine tablets (available in any pharmacy); calamine lotion will also suppress the symptoms. Failing that, a douse with *toddi* vinegar is better than nothing. The pain peaks after around forty-five minutes, and disappears altogether in three to four hours, although it often leaves a nasty-looking scar that can last for a few weeks.

The last bus from Palolem to Chaudi/Margao leaves at around 4.30pm; check with the locals for the precise times, as these change seasonally.

Cycles may be rented from a stall halfway along the main street for the princely sum of Rs3 per hour (with discounts for longer periods). The village has several **public telephones**: avoid the one in the *Beach Resort*, which charges more than double the going rate for international calls, and head for the much cheaper ISD/STD booth 100m down the lane (next to the bus stop). At present, there is nowhere in either Palolem or Chaudi to change money; the nearest bank with a foreign-exchange facility is in Margao (see p.171).

Accommodation

With the exception of the *Beach Resort*'s tent camp and a handful of recently built budget guesthouses, most of Palolem's **accommodation** consists of simple rooms in family homes, with basic washing and toilet facilities shared by visitors and members of the household. The easiest way to find a place is to walk around the palm groves behind the beach with a rucksack on; sooner or later someone will approach you. Rates vary from Rs40–80, depending on the size of the room, and time of year. The cheapest places, however, are to be found in Colom, around the headland south of Palolem village, where Hindu fishing families rent rooms, and occasionally small houses, to long-staying foreigners. Further south still, behind Patnem beach, you can hole up in palm-leaf shelters for around Rs20 per night; ask for these at the shack cafés.

Coco Huts, south end of Palelom beach; ☎0834/643104. Thai-style bamboo and palm-thatch huts on stilts, lashed to *toddi* trees around a sandy clearing, slap on the beach. The "rooms" have fans, electric light and safe lockers, but toilets are shared, and the leaf walls offer little privacy. ④.

Cupid Castle, on the road to the beachfront; no phone. An original name, but these newly-built rooms are characterless, and a little too close to the beachfront for comfort. Nonetheless, they're clean, spacious, and have attached bathrooms. ④.

D'Mello, Pundalik Gaitondi Rd; ☎0834/643057. A mix of attached and non-attached rooms, some in a concrete annexe set back from the main road. A bit on the grubby side, but OK for a night or two. ②–④.

Maria's, south of the village, near the *Classic* restaurant; no phone. Five simple rooms opening on to an orchard of banana, fruit and spice trees. All attached shower-toilets, and very friendly management. A good deal. ②.

Norgoa, Gaitondi Rd; no phone. Half-a-dozen basic rooms of varying size, with shared shower-toilets, on the main road through the village. They also have six, budget-priced bamboo "huts" (①) in the front garden. ③.

Palolem Beach Resort, on the beachfront; ☎0834/643054. Twin-bedded canvas tents, each with their own locker, lights and fans, grouped under a shady *toddi* grove in a walled compound. In addition, there's a handful of small en-suite rooms. The big drawback here is noise from the busy terrace restaurant. ③–④.

Tonrick's, on the road to the beachfront; ☎0834/643239. The village's most comfortable mid-range rooms, with en-suite toilets, running water, fans and verandahs. Clean and central. ④.

Eating and drinking

With the beach now lined along its entire length by brightly lit shack cafés, finding somewhere to **eat** in Palolem is not a problem, although the locals have to buy in most of their fish from Margao and Karwar (they only catch mackerel in their hand nets). The one outstanding place hereabouts is the *Classic* restaurant, where you can tuck into delicious, freshly baked Western wholefood and cakes. More popular among budget travellers, though, is *Sun 'n' Moon*, in the middle of the village; when it closes, the die-hard drinkers head through the palm trees to *Dylan's* bar on the beach, which stays open until the last customer has staggered home. For optimum sunset views of the bay, head for the obscurely named *Found Things* bar and restaurant, at the far southern end of Palolem beach, which faces due west. Travellers on tight budgets should also note the row of tiny **bhaji stalls** outside the *Beach Resort*, where you can order tasty and filling breakfasts of *pao bhaji*, fluffy bread rolls, omlettes and *chai* for next to nothing.

Beach Resort, Palolem beach front. The one place to definitely avoid: indifferent, overpriced food and grating background music.

Classic (aka "German Bakery"), south of the centre. Tucked away in a quiet corner of Palolem village, this is the most sophisticated café in the area, with tablecloths, smooth fusion sounds and attentive staff. The food – freshly baked cakes (including tiramisu to die for), Indian main meals and mouthwatering desserts – is equally appealing, though at way above average prices.

Maria's, south side of the village, near *Classic* restaurant. Authentic Goan food, such as chicken *vindaloo*, fried calamari (*ambot tik*) and spicy vegetable side dishes, prepared entirely with local produce and served alfresco on

---

Dolphin-spotting

Dolphin-spotting has become a major growth industry in Palolem over the past few years. From as early as 7am, boats loaded with tourists buzz around the island to the north and into the next bay, where a school can usually be located (though sometimes only with the help of a good set of binoculars). Don't expect any aerobatics, though; Goan dolphins prefer to laze along at a leisurely pace than to pull Sea World-style stunts for the cameras.

Organized **excursions**, arranged either through the staff of the *Palolem Beach Resort* or the *Blue Star* café (second on the left down the beach), last from one-and-a-half to three hours, and cost anywhere between Rs100 and Rs400, depending on how large a group the boatman has managed to get together, and how well you haggle. If this seems excessive, you can see dolphins for free most evenings around sunset time from the end of the headland on the south side of the bay.

a terrace. Maria's garrulous husband, Joseph, makes a mean *feni*, too, flavoured with cummin, ginger or lemongrass.

Sun 'n' Moon, Gaitondi Rd. This small restaurant's terrace gets packed out in the evenings, thanks to the consistently good, inexpensive food, served by friendly staff. Mountainous seafood sizzlers are the house speciality, but they also do tasty *tandoori* meat, fish and vegetarian dishes. There have been rumours that the restaurant may have to move in 1997–8, though it will certainly keep the same name.

Colom, Patnem and Rajbag

A stoney path threads its way through the boulders and *toddi* groves at the south end of Palolem beach to the Hindu hamlet of **COLOM**, clustered around the rocky shore of two palm-shaded coves. Several families here rent out huts and **rooms** to travellers (see "Accommodation", above), and there are a handful of small cafés where you can buy drinks and snacks, but these are the only discernible trickle-down from Palolem's recent tourist boom.

The long white beach beyond Colom, known as **PATNEM**, is equally peaceful, although the fir trees behind it nowadays shade a string of ramshackle cafés, some of which rent out palm shelters to backpackers. This is a good place to spend the Hindu festival of Shivratri (Feb/March), when the village deity, accompanied by an exuberant crowd, is carried to the sea for its annual dip. Afterwards, bunches of bananas are thrown into the surf for boys to retrieve; the lad who collects the most receives a cash prize from the local priest.

For almost total isolation, you'll have continue south and scale the headland dividing Patnem from beautiful **RAJBAG** beach, which stretches is an unbroken sweep to the mouth of the Talpona River. Sadly, a large chunk of land here was recently acquired by a major hotel chain, and Gurkha security guards now patrol a plot that will almost certainly sprout a five-star holiday complex within the next couple of years – so enjoy the tranquillity while you still can.

The next beach beyond Talpona is Galjibag, covered on p.206.

It's possible to press on even further **south from Rajbag**, by crossing the Talpona via a hand-paddled passenger ferry, which usually has to be summoned from the far bank. Once across, a short walk brings you to **Talpona beach**, backed by low dunes and a line of straggly palms, where you'd be unlucky to come across another tourist.

The Mallikarjun temple

Few non-Hindu visitors make it to the **Mallikarjun temple**, 7km northeast of Chaudi (look for the signpost on the NH14). Yet this small Shiva shrine is one of Goa's oldest – not that you'd know it from the outside, which is awash with concrete and coloured paint. Its interior, however, has largely escaped heavy-handed renovation, thanks to a ban imposed by the Department of Archeology. Some of the finest surviving art is to be found in the assembly hall or *man-*

dapa, whose stocky pillars writhe with sculpted musicians, dancers and floral motifs. At the far end, an elaborately embossed door jamb opens on to the inner sanctum, where a *Shivalingam* with a metallic mask is enshrined.

The Mallikarjun temple is also the venue for Canacona's largest Hindu festivals, including the five-day **Ratasaptami** (Feb), when the deity is paraded around the precinct in a large wooden chariot, or *rath*, and religious plays are performed at night. During **Shivratri** (March), the *lingam* goes for a dip in the sea at Rajbag beach, born by devotees in a silver palladin. However, the biggest crowds show up here for **Shigmotsava** (Feb/March), to participate in a mass procession involving brightly coloured umbrellas.

Cotigao Wildlife Sanctuary

The **COTIGAO WILDLIFE SANCTUARY**, 10km southeast of Chaudi, was established in 1969 to protect a remote and vulnerable area of forest lining the Goa-Karnataka border. Encompassing 86 square kilometres of mixed deciduous woodland, the reserve is certain to inspire tree lovers, but less likely to yield many wildlife sightings: its tigers and leopards were long ago hunted out, while the gazelles, slothbears, porcupines, panthers and hyenas that allegedly lurk in the woods rarely appear. You do, however, stand a good chance of spotting at least two species of monkey, a couple of wild boar and the odd gaur (the primeval-looking Indian bison).

The Cotigao Wildlife Sanctuary is open daily except Thurs 9.30am–5.30pm; admission costs Rs3, with small additional charges for cameras.

The main reason for the scarcity of fauna here – and throughout Goa – is **deforestation**. Cotigao was set up to combat this problem, but its existence has generated other calamities for local people. Accused by the authorities of poaching and stripping the forest for firewood and building materials, the Kunbi and Velip subsistence farmers, whose settlements lie inside the sanctuary, live under the constant threat of eviction. The villagers claim such accusations are merely a smoke screen for more nefarious logging and hunting scams perpetrated by wealthy city-ites, and for the government's dubious practice of planting money-making eucalyptus and rubber trees in the reserve instead of indigenous species.

Political problems aside, Cotigao, best visited between October and March, is a peaceful and scenic park that makes a pleasant daytrip from Palolem, 12km west. Any of the buses running south on NH14 to Karwar via Chaudi will drop you within 2km of the gates. However, to explore the inner reaches of the sanctuary, you really need your own transport. **Guides**, available free from the Forest Warden's office – next door to the reserve's small **Interpretative Centre** – can show you to a 25-metre-high treetop watchtower, overlooking a **waterhole** that attracts a handful of animals around dawn and dusk. Written permission for an overnight **stay**, either in the watchtower or the Forest Department's small *Rest House* (①), must be obtained from the Deputy Conservator of Forests, 3rd Floor,

Junta House, Panjim (☎0832/225926), as far in advance of your visit as possible. If you get stuck, however, the wardens can arrange a tent, blanket and basic food.

Galjibag

One of Goa's most remote beaches, **GALJIBAG**, 16km south of Chaudi, is reached by turning left off NH14 after a large double-river bridge. The approach to the beach, fringed by wispy fir trees, hugs the south bank of the Talpona River, passing a string of Hindu hamlets and a massive new railway bridge. You'll need your own transport to get there, and the village, sandwiched between two estuaries, is devoid of tourist facilities, but its tranquil beach is refreshingly unspoilt and well worth a foray from Palolem if you feel like a change of scenery. Cold drinks, alcoholic and otherwise, are available at Galjibag's only **café**, tucked away in the *toddi* groves 50m north of the village church.

Polem

Nestled within a stone's throw of the state border, **POLEM**, 30km south of Chaudi, is Goa's southernmost beach, and sufficiently secluded to have been overlooked even by the sand-hopping hippies heading between Goa and Gokarna, in Karnataka. The hundred-metre strip of smooth white sand, enfolded by a pair of rocky headlands, is thus far immaculately clean and unspoilt, and visited regularly by dolphins and fish eagles. A word of warning: this is a conservative village whose inhabitants are unused to Western sunbathing habits, so be discreet if you strip off on the beach.

It is possible to get to within striking distance of Polem by **bus** from Panjim, Margao or Chaudi: catch any service heading south down NH14 to Karwar (every 30min), and get off 2km before the

---

Crossing the Goa-Karnataka border

If you're heading south from Goa towards Jog Falls or the Hindu pilgrimage town of Gokarn (covered in Chapter Four, p.225), you'll have to cross the state border at a road barrier a short way before the river bridge, near the town of Karwar. For travellers on buses, or in cars, this is a straightforward procedure; you probably won't even have to fill in the requisite form. Anyone who is crossing into Karnataka on a rented motorbicycle, however, can expect some **hassle from the police**. The standard scam is to take your passport, scrutinize it with a very stern face, and then inform you that you can't continue south because of some directive from Panjim. Of course, this is all a ploy to extract *baksheesh*, and like it or not, you'll probably have to shell out at least Rs100 to continue. Curiously enough, the cops are honest when it comes to recognizing you on the return trip, and will politely wave you through the barrier after signing the ledger in their office.

---

border at the *Milan Bar* (you'll know you've overshot the turning if you see a service station on the left). The owner of this roadside café will show you the path leading across the paddy fields to Polem, a pleasant fifteen-minute walk.

Travel details

By bus

Benaulim to: Cavelossim (hourly; 20min); Colva (every 30min; 10min); Margao (every 30min; 15min); Mobor (hourly; 25min).

Chaudi to: Gokarna (1 daily; 3hr); Karwar (every 30min; 1hr); Palolem (2 daily; 15min).

Margao to: Belgaum (3 daily; 3hr 30min); Bombay (2 daily; 16–18hr); Chaudi (every 30min; 1hr 40min); Cabo da Rama (4 daily; 1hr 40min); Cavelossim (8 daily; 30min); Chandor (hourly; 45min); Colva (hourly; 20–30min); Gokarna (1 daily; 4hr 30min); Hubli (2 daily; 6hr); Karwar (every 30min; 2hr); Lutolim (8 daily; 30min); Mobor (8 daily; 35min); Mangalore (2 daily; 7hr); Mapusa (10 daily; 3hr); Panjim (every 30min; 1hr 30min); Pune (1 daily; 12hr); Rachol (every 2hr; 30min).

Vasco da Gama to: Bangalore (1 daily; 16hr); Belgaum (6 daily; 6hr); Bogmalo (hourly; 20min); Colva (2 daily; 30min); Mangalore (2 daily; 11hr); Margao (every 15min; 1hr); Panjim, via Sao Jacinto (every 15min; 45min–1hr); Pilar (every 15min; 30min).

By plane

Dabolim airport (Vasco da Gama) to: Bangalore (6 weekly; 1hr); Bombay (4–5 daily; 1hr); Delhi (2 daily; 2hr 30min); Hyderabad (4 weekly; 2hr 55min); Cochin (daily; 1hr 10min); Madras (3 weekly; 2hr 30min); Thiruvananthapuram (1 daily; 2hr 15min).
In addition, there are daily charter flights from Europe during peak season.

By train

When this book was researched, all train services to and from Goa were cancelled pending the completion of track conversion work on the branch line into Karnataka. This work, however, should be completed by late 1997, when it will once again be possible to travel inland to Hospet (for Hampi), and the Karnatakan capital, Bangalore, as well as north to Bombay, central India and Delhi. For more information on services to Bombay via the recently completed Konkan railway, see p.76.

Chapter 4

Around Goa

Relaxing though Goa's towns and coastal resorts may be, they are far from representative of the rest of the country, and many visitors are tempted across the state border into neighbouring **Karnataka**, beyond the limits of Portuguese colonial influence, for a taste of the "real" India. Even if you're only here two weeks, it's perfectly feasible to do this. Indeed, a foray over the Western Ghats to the **Deccan plateau** – with its open vistas of semi-arid rolling plains – or south down the lush **Konkan coast**, may well provide some of the most vivid experiences of your trip. And don't let the prospect of long overland journeys deter you. A number of southwest India's most exotic and rewarding sights lie a mere day's drive from Goa, set amid landscapes that differ wildly from the palm groves and paddy fields of the coast. Moreover, travelling to them can be fascinating and fun, yielding glimpses of everyday life in both remote, rural villages and the sprawling cities just beyond Goa's eastern border.

The single greatest incentive to venture away from the beaches has to be the extraordinary ruined city of **Vijayanagar**, better known as **Hampi**. Situated ten hours by road east of the coast, this vast archeological site harbours the evocative remains of palaces, temples and bazaars dating from the fifteenth and sixteenth centuries, when this was the capital of a huge Hindu empire – in its heyday among the largest and most powerful in Asia. The city was destroyed by Muslim armies in 1565, but enough finely carved stone buildings survive to occupy interested visitors for days. Hampi's setting is impressive too: an otherworldly jumble of smooth boulders, piled in colossal heaps around the banks of the Tungabhadra River, with banana plantations and rice paddy cutting vibrant swathes of green through the rocky terrain. People travel the length of India to see Hampi, and few visitors from Goa return disappointed.

The other obvious target for a trip out of state, the Hindu pilgrimage town of **Gokarn**, four-and-a-half hours south of Panjim, is a less well-established stop on the tourist trail. This might well change when the Konkan Railway is running all the way to Mangalore, but

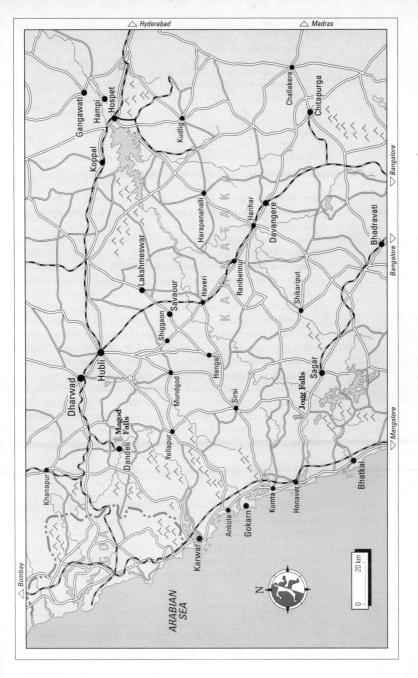

Accommodation price codes

All **accommodation prices** in this book are coded using the symbols below. In principle, the prices given are for the **least expensive double rooms in high season** (mid-Dec to mid-Jan). Local taxes have been included in each case, unless specifically stated otherwise.

① Up to Rs100	④ Rs225–350	⑦ Rs750–1200
② Rs100–150	⑤ Rs350–500	⑧ Rs1200–2200
③ Rs150–225	⑥ Rs500–750	⑨ Over Rs2200

for the time being, the majority of Gokarn's foreign visitors are backpackers taking time out from long tours of India. They come both for the heady religious atmosphere of the town, which harbours a couple of major temples and plenty of attractive vernacular architecture, and to laze on the exquisite beaches to the south, as yet only accessible on foot.

En route to Gokarn, a worthwhile sidetrip is the journey through the hills and forests of the Ghats to **Jog Falls**, the highest waterfalls in India. Tourist facilities and public transport services in the adjacent village are minimal (most Indians visit only for the day), but the scenery is dramatic, and the road trip across the mountains an adventure.

When the Konkan Railway is fully functional, travelling along the coast between Goa and Ankola, jumping-off place for Gokarn, should be straightforward, with fast and frequent services on modern trains. Running in tandem with the rail route, the recently revamped coastal highway is also well served by buses from Panjim, Margao and Chaudi. The same is true of the main eastbound road artery crossing the Western Ghats to **Hospet**, the nearest sizeable town to Hampi, which will also be accessible by train from Goa by the end of 1997. You'll find a full rundown of transport services to the destinations covered in this chapter at the beginning of the relevant accounts, and there's a summary in "Travel details" on p.229.

Hospet

Charmless **HOSPET**, ten hours by bus east of Goa, is of little interest except as a springboard for the ruined city of Vijayanagar (Hampi), 13km northeast. If you arrive late and want somewhere fairly comfortable to sleep, it makes sense to stay here and catch a bus or taxi out to the ruins the following morning. Otherwise, hole up in Hampi itself, where the setting more than compensates for the basic facilities.

Getting there

Two or three clapped out government **buses** leave Panjim's *Kadamba* stand (platform 9) each morning for Hospet, the last one

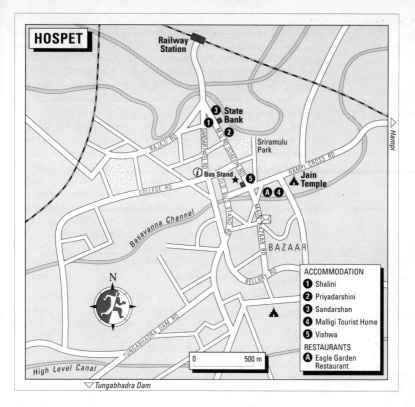

at 10.30am. The journey takes you across the Western Ghats and the rolling, dark-soiled plains of the Karnatakan Deccan, via the major industrial cities of Hubli and Gadag. Brace yourself for a long, hard slog; all being well, it should take nine or ten hours, but delays and breakdowns are frustratingly frequent. Travellers unaccustomed to long-distance bus journeys in India may also find the experience somewhat nerve-racking, as the drivers often attempt seemingly suicidal manoeuvres, swinging on to the rough margins of the road to overtake or avoid oncoming vehicles. This is particularly true of the faster private services, which you'll see advertised on boards around Panjim's main bus stand; they may get you there an hour or two sooner, but you're less likely to enjoy the trip because of the breakneck speeds. **Tickets** for *Kadamba* and KSRTC (Karnatakan State Road Transport Corporation) services should be booked at least one day in advance at the hatches in the bus stand.

For the past few years, **trains** heading east from Goa into Karnataka have been suspended due to conversion work on the line across the Ghats. Schedules for the new services were not available when this book was researched, but by the time the upgraded route is completed in late 1997, you should be able to obtain accurate timings from the Indian Railways counter in the *Kadamba* bus stand (see p.64), and Vasco and Margao stations. The latter will serve as the chief departure point for eastbound trains and from here you'll be able to catch direct express services to Hospet – a much more comfortable and relaxing option than the bus. As on most Indian trains, tickets should be booked as far in advance as possible. For a small fee, this can be done through travel agents in the resorts, which will save you the hassle of travelling into town and standing in long queues yourself.

The most comfortable way of getting to Hospet/Hampi, of course, is to take a **taxi**. Rates vary wildly, but you should count on paying around Rs1000 per day, which includes the driver's meals, overnight charges and fuel. Most taxi-*wallahs* will offer you a "fixed rate" for the trip, but in reality these are always negotiable; after Bombay, Hampi is their most lucrative run, and competition for punters stiff, so haggle hard over the price, and do this yourself rather than relying on your hotel or guesthouse owner.

Arrival and information

Hospet's **railway station** is 1500m north of the centre. Auto-rickshaws are thin on the ground, and often the only way to get into town is by cycle rickshaw (Rs20). The long-distance **bus stand** is nearer the centre, 250m down MG (Station) Rd, which runs south from the railway station. Services from Goa pull in here from 6pm to 8pm, depending on departure times. Bookings for the return trip can be made at the ticket office on the bus stand concourse (daily 8am–noon & 3–6pm), where there's also left luggage.

For details on transport to Hampi, see p.210.

You can **change currency** at the *State Bank of India* (Mon–Fri 10.30am–2.30pm, Sat 10.30am–12.30pm). *The State Bank of Mysore* (same hours) on MG Rd changes travellers' cheques; or, better still, try the reception desk at the *Malligi* hotel.

Accommodation and eating

Accommodation in Hospet, concentrated around MG Rd, ranges from budget to mid-price. By far the most popular place to stay is the *Malligi Tourist Home*, but the *Priyadarshini* is equally good value, and nearer the bus and railway stations.

There's little to do in Hospet, so you'll probably pass a fair amount of time **eating and drinking**. Many of the hotels have good dining rooms, but in the evening, the upscale (though affordable) *Eagle Garden*, behind the *Malligi*, is the most congenial place to hang out, serving tandoori and chilled beer from 7pm to 11pm (bring lots of mosquito repellent). *Shanbhog*, an excellent little Udipi restaurant next to the bus station, is a perfect pit stop before heading to Hampi, and opens early for breakfast.

Malligi Tourist Home, 6/143 Jambunatha Rd, 2min walk east of MG Rd (look for the signs) and the bus stand; ☎08394/58101, fax 57038. Friendly, Western-style hotel with 116 clean, comfortable rooms (some a/c). They sell the otherwise hard-to-find journal "Homage to Hampi", and offer foreign exchange. In addition, their alfresco *Madhu Paradise* restaurant/bar serves great veg food. ③–⑤.

Priyadarshini, MG Rd, over the road from the bus stand, towards the railway station; ☎08394/58838. Rooms from rock-bottom singles to doubles with TV and a/c (some balconies). Large and bland, but spotless and very good value. Two good restaurants: the veg *Chalukya* and, in the garden, non-veg *Manasa*, which has a bar. ②–⑤.

Sandarshan, MG Rd, between the railway station and bus stand; ☎08394/58574. Budget rooms, some with bath. ②–③.

Shalini, MG Rd, across the canal on the right-hand side as you approach from the railway station; ☎08394/58910. Very basic, small lodge; some rooms with bath. ①.

Vishwa, MG Rd, right opposite the bus stand; ☎08394/57171. No-frills lodge, with mostly en-suite rooms. The *Shanthi* canteen serves breakfast, South Indian snacks, and unlimited veg "meals". ②.

Hampi (Vijayanagar)

> *The city of Bidjanagar [Vijayanagar] is such that the pupil of the eye has never seen a place like it, and the ear of intelligence has never been informed that there existed anything to equal it in the world. . . . The bazaars are extremely long and broad. . . . Roses are sold everywhere. These people could not live without roses, and they look upon them as quite as necessary as food. . . . Each class of men belonging to each profession has shops contiguous the one to the other; the jewellers sell publicly in the bazaars pearls, rubies, emeralds and diamonds. In this agreeable locality, as well as in the king's palace, one sees numerous running streams and canals formed of chiselled stone, polished and smooth. . . . This empire contains so great a population that it would be impossible to give an idea of it without entering into extensive details.*
>
> Abdu'r-Razzaq, the Persian ambassador,
> who visited Vijayanagar in 1443.

The ruined city of **VIJAYANAGAR**, "the City of Victory" (also known as **HAMPI**, the village at the heart of the site), spills from the south bank of the Tungabhadra River, littered among a surreal landscape of golden-brown granite boulders and leafy banana fields. According to Hindu mythology, the settlement began its days as Kishkinda, the monkey kingdom of the Ramayana, ruled by the monkey kings, Vali and Sugriva, and their ambassador, Hanuman; the weird rocks – some balanced in perilous arches, others heaped in colossal, hill-sized piles – are said to have been flung down by their armies in a show of strength.

Between the fourteenth and sixteenth centuries, this was the most powerful Hindu capital in the Deccan. Travellers such as the

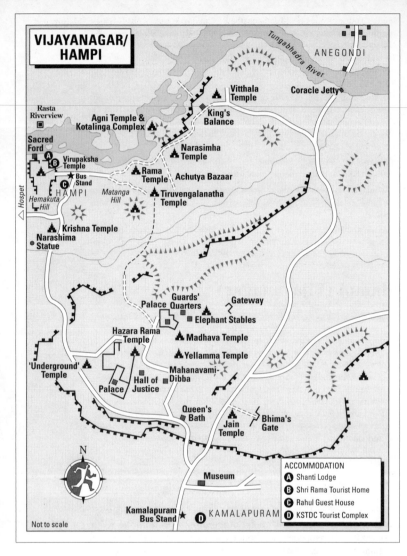

VIJAYANAGAR/HAMPI

Tungabhadra River

ANEGONDI

Vitthala Temple

Coracle Jetty

Rasta Riverview

Agni Temple & Kotalinga Complex

King's Balance

Sacred Ford

Narasimha Temple

Virupaksha Temple

Rama Temple

Achutya Bazaar

Bus Stand

HAMPI

Matanga Hill

Tiruvengalanatha Temple

Hemakuta Hill

△ Hospet

Krishna Temple

Narashima Statue

Guards' Palace Quarters

Gateway

Elephant Stables

Hazara Rama Temple

Madhava Temple

Yellamma Temple

'Underground' Temple

Mahanavami-Dibba

Palace

Hall of Justice

Queen's Bath

Jain Temple

Bhima's Gate

N

Museum

ACCOMMODATION

- **A** Shanti Lodge
- **B** Shri Rama Tourist Home
- **C** Rahul Guest House
- **D** KSTDC Tourist Complex

Not to scale

Kamalapuram Bus Stand

D KAMALAPURAM

Portuguese chronicler Domingo Paez, who stayed for two years from 1520, were astonished by its size and wealth, telling tales of markets full of silk and precious gems, beautiful, bejewelled courtesans, ornate palaces and joyous festivities. However, in the second half of the sixteenth century, the dazzling city was devastated by a six-month Muslim siege. Only stone, brick and stucco structures survived the ensuing sack – monolithic deities, crumbling houses and abandoned temples dominated by towering *gopuras* – as well as the sophisticated irrigation system that channelled water to huge tanks and temples.

Thanks to the Muslim onslaught, most of Hampi's monuments are in disappointingly poor shape, seemingly a lot older than their four or five hundred years. Yet the serene riverine setting and air of magic that lingers over the site, sacred for centuries before a city was founded here, make it one of India's most extraordinary locations. Even so, mainstream tourism has thus far made little impact: along with streams of Hindu pilgrims and tatty-haired sadhus, who hole up in the more isolated rock crevices and shrines, most visitors are budget travellers straight from Goa. Many find it difficult to leave, and spend weeks chilling out in cafés, wandering to whitewashed hilltop temples and gazing at the spectacular sunsets.

The best months to come to Hampi are from October to March, when daytime temperatures are low enough to allow long forays on foot through the ruins. From Christmas through early January, however, the site is swamped by an exodus of travellers from Goa that has been increasing dramatically over the past few years; there have even been Anjuna-style full-moon parties, complete with techno sound systems and bus-loads of Israeli ravers. The influx also attracts its share of dodgy characters, and **crime** has become a problem in the village at this time; so if you want to enjoy Hampi at its best, come outside peak season.

A brief history

This was an area of minor political importance under the Chalukyas; the rise of the Vijayanagar empire seems to have been a direct response, in the first half of the fourteenth century, to the expansionist aims of Muslims from the north, most notably Malik Kafur and Muhammad-bin-Tughluq. Two Hindu brothers from Andhra Pradesh, Harihara and Bukka, who had been employed as treasury officers in Kampila, 19km east of Hampi, were captured by the Tughluqs and taken to Delhi, where they supposedly converted to Islam. Assuming them to be suitably tamed, the Delhi Sultan despatched them to quell civil disorder in Kampila, which they duly did, only to abandon both Islam and allegiance to Delhi shortly afterwards, preferring to establish their own independent Hindu kingdom. Within a few years they controlled vast tracts of land from coast to coast. In 1343 their new capital, Vijayanagar, was founded on the southern banks of the River Tungabhadra, a location long considered sacred by Hindus. The city's most glorious period was under the reign of Krishna Deva Raya (1509–29), when it enjoyed a near monopoly on the lucrative trade in Arabian horses and Indian spices passing through the coastal ports.

Thanks to its location and massive fortifications, Vijayanagar was virtually impregnable. In 1565, however, following his interference in the affairs of local Muslim Sultanates, the regent Rama Raya was drawn into a battle with a confederacy of Muslim forces, 100km away to the north, which left the city undefended. At first, fortune appeared to be on the side of the Hindu forces, but there were as many as 10,000 Muslims among them, and loyalties may well have been divided. When two Vijayanagar Muslim generals suddenly deserted, the army fell into disarray. Defeat came swiftly; although members of his family fled with untold hoards of gold and jewels, Rama Raya was captured and suffered a grisly death at the hands of the Sultan of Ahmadnagar. Vijayanagar then fell victim to a series of destructive raids, and its days of splendour were brought to an abrupt end.

Getting to Hampi from Hospet

Karnataka Tourism's daily guided **tour** only stops at three of the sites in Hampi and spends an inordinate amount of time at the far less interesting Tungabhadra Dam. Even so, it can be worth it if you're short of time; tours leave from their office at Rotary Circle (Taluk Office Circle), east of Hospet bus station (9.30am–5.30pm; Rs70 including lunch).

Frequent local **buses** run from Hospet to Hampi between 6.30am and 7.30pm; the journey takes thirty minutes. If you arrive late, you can either stay in Hospet, or take a taxi or one of the rickshaws that gather outside the railway station. It is also possible to catch a bus to Kamalpura, at the south side of the site, and explore the ruins from there, catching a bus back to Hospet from Hampi *Bazaar* at the end of the day. **Bicycles** are available for rent at several stalls along Hospet's street, but the trip to, around, and back from the site is a long one in the heat; you'd have to be made of sturdy stuff to do it on foot. Finally, some hotels in Hospet can organize for you to hook up with trained **guides** in Hampi; ask at the *Malligi* or *Priyardarshini*.

Arrival and information

Buses from Hospet terminate halfway along the main street in Hampi bazaar, a little east of the Virupaksha temple. On the opposite side of the street, the **tourist information** counter might be able to put you in touch with a guide, but not much else; if you're coming from Hospet, you'd do best to organize a guide from there (see above). **Rented bikes**, available in the bazaar for Rs5 per hour, are only really of use if you're planning to explore Anegondi across the river; most paths around Vijayanagar are too rough to cycle. The only place in Hampi with a licence to **change money** (including travellers' cheques) is the *Swambhu Restaurant* opposite *Shanti Lodge*. However, their rates are poor, and most visitors use the *Mallingi*'s facility in Hospet.

Police, thieves and mosquitoes

Hampi is generally a safe site to wander around, but a spate of armed attacks on tourists over the past three or four years means that you ought to think twice before venturing on your own to a number of known **trouble spots**. Foremost among these is Matanga Hill, to the right of Hampi bazaar as you face away from the Virupaksha temple, dubbed "sunrise point" by local guides because it looks east. Here muggers have been jumping Westerners on their way to the temple before dawn, escaping into the rocks with their cameras and money. If this has happened recently, the police will prevent you from walking the path up to the temple, but even at other times it's advisable to go in a group, and to leave valuables behind.

The other hassle to watch out for in Hampi is the **police** themselves, who are not averse to squeezing the odd backhander from tourists. You'll see *chillums* smoked in the cafés, but possession of hashish (*charas*) is a serious offence in Karnataka, liable to result in a huge bribe, or worse. There have also been reports of local cops arresting, and extracting *baksheesh* from, Western men who walk around shirtless. Another reason to stay fully dressed in Hampi, particularly in the evenings, is that it is a prime **malaria zone**. Sleep under a mosquito net if you have one, and smother yourself in insect repellent well before sunset.

Accommodation

If you're happy to make do with basic amenities, Hampi is a far more enjoyable place to stay than Hospet, with a couple of congenial **guesthouses** and plenty of cafés to hang out in after a long day in the heat. Staying in the village also means you can be up and out early enough to catch the sunrise over the ruins – a mesmerizing spectacle.

Deservedly the most popular place to stay is *Shanti Lodge* (☎08394/51368; ①), just north of the Virupaksha temple (follow the lane around the side of the temple enclosure; the lodge is 30m further on the right). Run by atheist yoga-teacher Mr Shivanand and his two sons, it comprises a dozen or so twin-bedded cells ranged on two storeys around a leafy inner courtyard. It's basic (showers and toilets are shared), but spotless, and all rooms have windows and fans. Roof space is also available if the lodge is fully booked. After *Shanti*, the next best is the spartan *Rahul Guest House* (no phone; ①), with rudimentary washing and toilet facilites, on the opposite side of the bazaar. The *Shri Rama Tourist Home*, next to the Virupaksha temple, offers rock-bottom accommodation mainly for Hindu pilgrims, and there are several more lookalike guesthouses lining the north side of the bazaar, most of them with rooftop restaurants. The only remotely upscale place to stay within reach of the ruins is KSTDC's *Hotel Mayura Bhavaneshwari* (☎08394/5374) at Kamalapuram. It's pleasant enough, with clean en-suite rooms and a restaurant, but the village lacks the charm of Hampi.

Travellers on low budgets and with time on their hands tend these days to stay on the north side of the river, where accommodation –

most of it in private houses or complexes of shacks – is cheap and primitive, but the atmosphere more relaxed than around the bazaar. The most popular place is the *Rasta Riverview* (no phone; ①), just up from the coracle jetty, but you'll find plenty more in a similar mould further up the road.

The site of Vijayanagar

Although spread over 26 square kilometres, the ruins of Vijayanagar are mostly concentrated in two distinct groups: the first lies in and around **Hampi bazaar** and the nearby riverside area, encompassing the city's most sacred enclave of temples and ghats; the second centres on the **royal enclosure** – 3km south of the river, just northwest of Kamalpuram village – which holds the remains of palaces, pavilions, elephant stables, guard houses and temples. Between the two stretches is a long boulder-choked hill and swathe of banana plantations, fed by ancient irrigation canals.

Frequent **buses** run from Hospet to Hampi bazaar and Kamalpuram, and you can start your tour from either; most visitors prefer to set out on foot or bicycle from the former. After a look around the soaring **Virupaksha temple**, work your way east along the main street and river bank to the beautiful **Vitthala temple**, and then back via the **Achyutaraya complex** at the foot of Matanga Hill. From here, a dirt path leads south to the royal enclosure, but it's easier to return to the bazaar and pick up the tarred road, calling in at **Hemakuta Hill**, a group of pre-Vijayanagar temples, en route.

On KSTDC's whistlestop guided **tour**, it's possible to see most of the highlights in a day. If you can, however, set aside at least two or three days to explore the site and its environs, crossing the river by coracle to **Anegondi** village, with a couple of side hikes to hilltop view points: the west side of Hemakuta Hill, overlooking Hampi bazaar, is best for sunsets, while **Matanga Hill**, though plagued by thieves in recent years, offers what has to be one of the world's most exotic sunrise vistas.

Hampi bazaar, the Virupaksha temple and riverside path

Lining Hampi's long, straight main street, **Hampi bazaar**, which runs east from the eastern entrance of the Virupaksha temple, you can

---

Festivals at Vijayanagar

Vijayanagar's main **festivals** include, at the Virupaksha temple, a **Car Festival** with street processions each February, and in December the marriage ceremony of the deities, which is accompanied by drummers and dances. An annual **music festival**, *Purandaradas Aradhana* (Jan/Feb), takes place in the Vitthala temple to celebrate the birth anniversary of the poet-composer Purandaradasa; concerts of Carnatic (south Indian) classical music take place over three days in the temple's atmospheric *mandapa*.

---

still make out the remains of Vijayanagar's ruined, columned bazaar, partly inhabited by today's lively market. Landless labourers live in many of the crumbling 500-year-old buildings.

Dedicated to a local form of Shiva known as Virupaksha or Pampapati, the functioning **Virupaksha temple** (daily 8am–12.30pm & 3–6.30pm) dominates the village, drawing a steady flow of pilgrims from all over southern India. The complex consists of two courts, each entered through a towered *gopura*. The larger gateway, on the east, is approximately 56m high, each storey with pilastered walls and sculptures flanking an open window. It is topped by a single wagon-vault and *kalasha*, a pot-shaped finial. In the southwest corner a water channel runs along a large columned *mandapa*.

A colonnade surrounds the inner court, usually filled with pilgrims dozing and singing religious songs; in the middle the principal temple is approached through a *mandapa* hallway whose carved columns feature rearing animals. Rare Vijayanagar-era paintings on the *mandapa* ceiling include aspects of Shiva, a procession with the sage Vidyaranya, the ten incarnations of Vishnu, and scenes from the Mahabharata; the style of the figures is reminiscent of local shadow puppets. Faced by a brass image of Nandi, a *Shivalingam* is housed in the small sanctuary, its entrance decorated with painted *makaras*, semi-aquatic mythical animals whose bodies end with foliage instead of a tail. Blue water spouts from their mouths, while above them flicker yellow flames. Just outside the main temple's wall, immediately to the north, is a small earlier temple, thought to have been the "ancestor" of the Virupaksha.

The **sacred ford** in the river is reached from the Virupaksha's north *gopura*; you can also get there by following the lane around the temple past *Shanti Lodge*. A *mandapa* overlooks the steps that originally led to the river, now some distance away. **Coracles**, known in Kannad as *putti*, ply from this part of the bank, just as they did five centuries ago, ferrying villagers to the fields and tourists to the popular *Uma-Shankar Café* on the other side. The path through the village also winds to an impressive ruined bridge and on to the hilltop Hanuman shrine – a recommended round walk described on p.223.

To reach the Vitthala temple, walk east from the Virupaksha, the length of Hampi bazaar. At the end, a path on the left, staffed at regular intervals by conch-blowing sadhus and an assortment of other ragged mendicants, follows the river past a café and numerous shrines, including a Rama temple – home to hordes of fearless monkeys. Beyond at least four Vishnu shrines, the paved and colonnaded **Achutya Bazaar** leads due south to the **Tiruvengalanatha temple**, whose beautiful stone carvings – among them some of Hampi's famed erotica – are being restored by the ASI. Back on the main path again, make a short detour across the rocks leading to the river to see the little-visited waterside **Agni temple** – next to it, the Kotalinga complex consists of 108 (an auspicious number) tiny *linga*, carved on a flat rock. As you approach the Vitthala temple, to the south is an archway known as the **King's Balance**, where the rajas were weighed against gold, silver and jewels to be distributed to the city's priests.

Vitthala temple

Although the area of the **Vitthala temple** does not show the same evidence of early cult worship as Virupaksha, the ruined bridge to the west probably dates from before Vijayanagar times. The bathing ghat may be from the Chalukya or Ganga period, but as the temple has fallen into disuse it seems that the river crossing (*tirtha*) here has not had the same sacred significance as the Virupaksha site. Now designated a World Heritage Monument by UNESCO, the Vitthala temple was built for Vishnu, who according to legend was too embarrassed by its ostentation to live there. The tower of the principal Vishnu shrine is made of brick – unusual for south India – capped with a hemispherical roof; in front is an enclosed *mandapa* with carved columns, the ceiling of which has partly collapsed. Two doorways lead to a dark passageway surrounding the sanctuary.

For an account of Anegondi, on the opposite bank of the river to Vitthala, see p.223.

The open *mandapa* features slender monolithic granite pillars. As in so many Indian temples, guides gleefully make them "sing" different notes in a scale by tapping them. Outer columns sport characteristic Vijayanagar rearing horses, while friezes of lions, elephants and horses on the moulded basement display sculptural trickery – you can transform one beast into another simply by masking one portion of the image.

In front of the temple, to the east, a stone representation of a wooden processional *rath*, or chariot, houses an image of Garuda, Vishnu's bird vehicle. Now cemented, at one time the chariot's wheels revolved. The three *gopura* entrances, made of granite at the base with brick and stucco multi-storey towers, are now badly damaged.

Hemakuta Hill and around

Directly above Hampi bazaar, **Hemakuta Hill** is dotted with pre-Vijayanagar temples that probably date from between the ninth and eleventh centuries (late Chalukya or Ganga). Three are of the *trikutachala*, "three-peaked hills" type, with three shrines facing into a common centre. Aside from the architecture, the main reason to clamber up here is to admire the views of the ruins and surrounding countryside. Looking across miles of boulder-covered terrain and banana plantations, the sheer western edge of the hill is Hampi's number-one sunset spot, attracting a crowd of blissed-out tourists most evenings, along with a couple of entrepreneurial *chai*-wallahs.

A couple of interesting monuments lie on the road leading south towards the main, southern group of ruins. The first of these, a walled **Krishna temple** complex to the west of the road, dates from 1513. Although dilapidated in parts, it features some fine carving and shrines. On the opposite side of the road, a fifty-metre-wide processional path leading east through what's now a ploughed field, with stray remnants of colonnades straggling along each side, is all that remains of an old market place.

Hampi's most-photographed monument stands just south of the Krishna temple in its own enclosure. Depicting Vishnu in his incarnation (*avatar*) as the Man-Lion, the monolithic **Narashima statue**, with its bulging eyes and crossed legs strapped into meditation pose, is one of Vijayanagar's greatest treasures.

The southern and royal monuments

The most impressive remains of Viyayanagar, the city's **royal monuments**, lie some 3km south of Hampi bazaar, spead over a large expanse of open ground. Before tackling the ruins proper, it's a good idea to get your bearings with a visit to the small **Archeological Museum** (daily except Fri 10am–5pm) at Kamalapuram, which can be reached by bus from Hospet or Hampi. Turn right out of the Kamalapuram bus stand, take the first turning on the right, and the museum is on the left – two minutes' walk. Among the sculpture, weapons, palm-leaf manuscripts and paintings from Vijayanagar and Anegondi, the highlight is a superb scale-model of the city, giving an excellent bird's-eye view of the entire site.

To walk into the city from the museum, go back to the main road and take the nearby turning marked "Hampi 4km". After 200m or so you reach the partly ruined massive inner city wall, made from granite slabs, which runs 32km around the city, in places as high as 10m. The outer wall was almost twice as long. At one time, there were said to have been seven city walls; coupled with areas of impenetrable forest and the river to the north, they made the city virtually impregnable.

Just beyond the wall, the **citadel area** was once enclosed by another wall and gates of which only traces remain. To the east, the small **ganigitti** ("oil-woman's") fourteenth-century **Jain temple** features a simple stepped pyramidal tower of undecorated horizontal slabs. Beyond it is **Bhima's Gate**, once one of the principal entrances to the city, named after the Titan-like Pandava, prince and hero of the Mahabharata. Like many of the gates, it is "bent", a form of defence that meant anyone trying to get in had to make two 90-degree turns. Bas-reliefs depict such episodes as Bhima avenging the attempted rape of his wife, Draupadi, by killing the general Kichaka. Draupadi vowed she would not dress her hair until Kichaka was dead; one panel shows her tying up her locks, the vow fulfilled.

Back on the path, to the west, the plain facade of the fifteen-metre-square **Queen's Bath** belies its glorious interior, open to the sky and surrounded by corridors with 24 different domes. Eight projecting balconies overlook where the water would have been; traces of Islamic-influenced stucco decoration survive. Women from the royal household would bathe here and umbrellas were placed in shafts in the tank floor to protect them from the sun. The water supply channel can be seen outside.

Continuing northwest brings you to **Mahanavami-Dibba**, or "House of Victory", built to commemorate a successful campaign in Orissa. A twelve-metre pyramidal structure with a square base, it is said to have been where the king gave and received honours and gifts. From here he watched the magnificent parades, music and dance performances, martial art displays, elephant fights and animal sacrifices that made celebration of the ten-day Dusshhera festival famed throughout the land. Carved reliefs of dancers, elephant fights, animals and figures decorate the sides of the platform. Two huge monolithic doors on the ground nearby may have once been part of a building atop the platform, of which no other signs remain. To the west, another platform – the largest at Vijayanagar – is thought to be the basement of the **King's Audience Hall**. Stone bases of a hundred pillars remain, in an arrangement that has caused speculation as to how the building could have been used; there are no passageways or open areas.

The two-storey **Lotus Mahal**, a little further north and part of the "zenana enclosure", or women's quarters, was designed for the pleasure of Krishna Deva Raya's queen: a place where she could relax, particularly in summer. Displaying a strong Indo-Islamic influence, the pavilion is open on the ground floor, whereas the upper level (no longer accessible by stairs) contains windows and balcony seats. A moat surrounding the building is thought to have provided water-cooled air via tubes.

Beyond the Lotus Mahal, the **Elephant Stables**, a series of high-ceilinged, domed chambers, entered through arches, are the most substantial surviving secular buildings at Vijayanagar – a reflection of the high status accorded to elephants, both ceremonial and in battle. An upper level, with a pillared hall, capped with a tower at the centre, may have been used by the musicians who accompanied the royal elephant processions. Tender coconuts are usually for sale under the shade of a nearby tree. East of here, recent archeological excavations have revealed what are thought to have been the foundations of a series of Vijayanagar administration offices, which until 1990 had been buried under earth deposited by the wind.

Walking west of the Lotus Mahal, you pass two temples before reaching the road to Hemakuta Hill. The rectangular enclosure wall of the small **Hazara Rama** ("One thousand Ramas") **temple**, thought to have been the private palace temple, features a series of medallion figures and bands of detailed friezes showing scenes from the Ramayana. The inner of two *mandapas* contains four finely carved, polished, black columns. Many of the ruins here are said to have been part of the Hazara Rama Bazaar, which ran northeast from the temple. Much of the so-called **Underground Temple**, or Prasanna Virupaksha, lies below ground level and spends part of the year filled with rainwater. Turning north (right) onto the road that runs west of the Underground Temple will take you back to Hampi bazaar, via Hemakuta Hill.

Anegondi and beyond

With more time, and a sense of adventure, you can head across the Tungabhadra to **Anegondi**, a fortress town predating Vijayanagar and the city's fourteenth-century headquarters. The most pleasant way to go is to take a *putti*, a circular rush-basket coracle, from the ford 1500m east of the Vitthala temple; they also carry bicycles.

Forgotten temples and fortifications litter Anegondi village and its quiet surroundings. The ruined **Huchchappa-matha temple**, near the river gateway, is worth a look for its black stone lathe-turned pillars and fine panels of dancers. **Aramani**, a ruined palace in the centre, stands opposite the home of the descendants of the royal family; also in the centre, the **Ranganatha temple** is still active. A huge wooden temple chariot stands in the village square.

To complete a five-kilometre loop back to Hampi from here (best attempted by bicycle), head left (west) along the road, winding through sugar cane fields towards the sacred **Pampla Sarovar**, signposted down a dirt lane to the left. The small temple above this square bathing tank, tended by a swami who will proudly show you photos of his pilgrimage to Mount Kailash, holds a cave containing a footprint of Vishnu.

Another worthwhile detour from the road is the hike up to the tiny whitewashed **Hanuman temple**, perched on a rocky hilltop north of the river, from where you gain superb views over Hampi. The steep climb takes around half an hour. Keep following the road west for another 3km and you'll eventually arrive at an impressive old stone bridge dating from Vijayanagar times. The track from the opposite bank crosses a large island in the Tungabhadra, emerging after twenty minutes at the sacred ford and coracle jetty below the Virupaksha temple. This rewarding round walk can, of course, be completed in reverse, beginning at the sacred ford. With a bike, it takes around three hours, including the side trips outlined above; allow most of the day if you attempt it on foot, and take plenty of water.

Eating and drinking

During the season, Hampi spawns a rash of travellers' **cafés** and temporary tiffin joints, as well as a number of laid-back shack bars tucked away in more secluded corners. Among the many **restaurants** in the bazaar, *Welcome* and *Krishna* are firm favourites with Western tourists, serving a predictable selection of pancakes, porridge, omelettes and veggie food. *Swambhu*, opposite *Shanti Lodge*, is another typical travellers' joint, renowned for its fresh pasta and soft cheese (steer clear of the latter if there have been lots of power cuts). A relative newcomer to Hampi's café scene is *Suresh*, behind the *Shri Rama Tourist Home*, whose delicious "shak-sheeka" (made with eggs, cheese and spinach) is served on banana leaves; it's also a good place for breakfast.

Manmasa, at the top of the bazaar past the Hospet turning, serves up a better than average selection of Indian food, prepared by an experienced Rajasthani chef (his korma is superb). You can also get filling thalis and a range of freshly cooked snacks in the *Rahul Guest House*. However, the prize for Hampi's best all-round café has to go to the *Mango Tree*, hidden away in the banana plantations beyond the coracle jetty. The food is fairly run-of-the-mill, but the relaxing riverside location is hard to beat.

You can get authentic Western-style bread and cakes through *Shanti Lodge*; place your order by early evening and the cakes are delivered the following day.

Jog Falls

Hidden in a remote, thickly forested corner of the Western Ghat mountains, **Jog Falls**, 154km southeast of Panjim, are the highest waterfalls in India, more impressive even than Dudhsagar.

For a description of Dudhsagar Falls, near Goa's eastern border, see p.110.

These days, they are rarely as spectacular as they were before the construction of a large dam upriver, which impedes the flow of the **River Sharavati** over the sheer red-brown sandstone cliffs. However, the surrounding scenery is spectacular at any time, with dense scrub and jungle carpeting the sparsely populated, mountainous terrain. The views of the falls from the scruffy collection of *chai* stalls on the opposite side of the gorge is also impressive, unless, that is, you travel up here during the monsoons, when mist and rain clouds envelop the cascades. Another reason not to visit during the wet season is that the extra water, and abundance of leeches at this time, make the excellent hike to the floor valley dangerous. If you can, head up here between November and January, and bring stout footwear. The trail starts just below the bus park and winds steeply down to the water; confident hikers also venture further downriver, clambering over boulders to other pools and hidden viewpoints, but you should keep a close eye on the water level and take along a local guide to point out the safest path.

Practicalities

Getting to **Jog Falls** by public transport from Goa is not easy. First, you have to reach **Karwar**, just across the border, and change there on to the single daily **bus** that leaves around mid-morning, arriving at Jog Falls some eight hours later, after dark, and returning early the next day. With a car or motorbike, the falls are best approached from the coast along one of several scenic routes through the Ghats. The easiest and best maintained of these heads inland from **Bhatkal**, but for a truly unforgettable experience, risk the tortuous, bumpy back route from **Kumta**, which takes you through some breathtaking landscape. There are very few villages, and no fuel stops, along the way, so stock up beforehand, and make sure your vehicle is in good shape.

Accommodation is limited, to say the least. The *PWD Inspection Bungalow* (①), on the north side of the gorge, has great views from its spacious, comfortable rooms, but is invariably full and has to be booked in advance from the nearest major town, **Shimoga**. The small youth hostel, ten minutes' walk down the Shimoga road, is filthy and unfriendly. Most travellers make do with a raffia mat on the floor of one of the houses behind the *chai* stalls ranged around the square. One local family offers a room with bathroom and freshly cooked meals for Rs50 per person – the owner meets incoming buses. The only food available in Jog Falls are the uninspiring (eggy) snacks served up at the *chai* stalls.

Gokarn

Set behind a broad white-sand beach, with the forest-covered foothills of the Western Ghats forming a blue-green backdrop, **GOKARN** (also spelled Gokarna), 154km south of Margao, is among India's most scenically situated sacred sites. Yet this compact little coastal town – a Shaivite centre for more than two millennia – remained largely "undiscovered" by Western tourists until a little under a decade ago, when it began to attract dreadlocked and didgeridoo-toting travellers fleeing the commercialization of Goa. Now it's firmly on the tourist map, although the Hindu pilgrims pouring through still far outnumber the foreigners that flock here in winter.

Even if you've had your fill of beaches, Gokarn definitely deserves a trip down the coastal highway. An old-established pilgrimage place with a markedly traditional feel, it will give you a stronger taste of Hindu India than anywhere else in the region: shaven-headed brahmins sit crosslegged on their verandahs murmuring Sanskrit verses, while pilgrims file through a bazaar crammed with religious paraphernalia to the sea for a holy dip. An added incentive is the superb scenery punctuating the journey here. Winding up thicky wooded spurs and headlands, the road regularly yields tantalizing glimpses of cobalt-blue bays, lined by unfeasibly white beaches where you'd be unlucky to run into another tourist all day.

Getting there

Direct **buses** leave Margao's interstate *Kadamba* stand every day for Gokarn at 1pm, pulling in around four-and-a-half hours later. You can also get there by catching any of the services that run between Goa and Mangalore, and jumping off either at **Ankola**, or at the Gokarn junction on the main highway, from where frequent private mini-buses and *tempos* run the rest of the way. The route is straightforward by **motorcycle**, with a better-than-average road surface, and frequent fuel stops along the way. Travelling on a rented bike also gives you the option of heading down sandy side lanes to explore some of the gorgeous beaches glimpsed from the road. The only drawback is **crossing the border**, which can involve a *baksheesh* transaction (see "Crossing the Goa–Karnataka border" box in Chapter 3, p.206).

Arrival and information

KSRTC (Karnataka State Road Transport Corporation), Goan *Kadamba* and private service **buses** terminate halfway down Gokarn's main bazaar, within easy walking distance of the town's limited accommodation.

The nearest place to **change money** is the *State Bank of India* in the market town of **Karwar**, ninety minutes north on the main highway, so make sure you bring enough cash with you as the trip up there can take most of a day. If you do run short and need to go to the bank, the best bus to catch is the 8.15am service to Panjim.

Accommodation

Gokarn has a small, but not bad, choice of **guesthouses**. After staying in the village for a couple of days, however, many visitors strike out for the beaches, where apart from the handful of picturesque brick-and-mortar **huts** on the north side of Kootlee beach (invariably booked out to long-staying tourists from late-Sept through March), accommodation consists of primitive **palm-leaf shacks** with beaten-earth floors, scattered in the trees. If you're lucky, you might find one with a lockable wooden door and a well nearby, but don't bank on it. Many people end up sleeping rough on the sand, but the nights can be chilly, and robberies are common, so come prepared. Leave your luggage and valuables behind in Gokarn (most guesthouses will store your stuff for a fee), and if you plan to spend any time on the beaches, consider investing in a cheap mattress from the bazaar – you can always sell it on when you leave.

As a last resort, you can nearly always find a bed in one of the **pilgrims' hostels**, or *dharamshalas*, dotted around town. With dormitories or bare, cell-size rooms and basic washing facilities, these are intended mainly for Hindus, but Western tourists are welcome if there are vacancies: try the *Prasad Nilaya*, just down the lane from *Om Hotel*.

KSTDC Tourist Home, high on a hill above Gokarn (look for the sign on the left as you arrive). Large rooms, each with tiled bathroom, sit-out and garden overlooking the coast and out to sea. The staff are helpful and serve meals to order. Good option if you have your own transport. ②.

Nimmu House (no phone), a minute's walk from the temples. Gokarn's best budget guesthouse, with six clean rooms (shared showers). Roof space for Rs15, and a reliable left-luggage facility. ①.

Om Hotel, 5min down the lane leading north off Car St; ☎08386/46440. Conventional economy hotel pitched at middle-class Indian pilgrims, with plain, good-sized en-suite rooms and a dingy bar that serves cold beer – a rarity in Gokarn. The next best option after the *Nimmu*. ③.

Shastri's, Car St; ☎08386/46220. The best of the uniformly drab and run-down guesthouses lining the main street: rooms both with and without bath, and rock-bottom single occupancy rates. ①.

Vaibhav Nivas, off the main road, 5min across town from the bus stop; ☎08386/46289. Friendly, popular place, with very cramped rooms, mostly without bathrooms, but clean enough. You can eat here, too, and leave luggage if you're heading off to Om beach. ①.

The Town

Gokarn **town**, a hotch-potch of wood-fronted houses and red terra-cotta roofs, is clustered around a long L-shaped bazaar, its broad main road – known as Car Street – running west to the town beach, a sacred site in its own right. Hindu mythology identifies it as the place where Rudra (another name for Shiva) was reborn from the underworld, through the ear of Mother Earth, after a period of penance. Gokarn is also the home of one of India's most powerful *Shivalinga* – the **Pranalingam**, which came to rest here after being carried off by Ravana, the evil king of Lanka, from Shiva's home on Mount Kailash in the Himalaya. Sent by the gods to reclaim the sacred object, Ganesh, with the help of Vishnu, tricked Ravana into letting him look after the *lingam* while he prayed, knowing that if it touched the ground it would take root and never be moved. When Ravana returned from his meditation, he tried to pick the *lingam* up, but couldn't, because the gods had filled it with "the weight of three worlds".

The *Pranalingam* resides in Gokarn to this day, enshrined in the medieval **Shri Mahabaleshwar temple**, at the far west end of the bazaar. It is regarded as so auspicious that a mere glimpse of it will absolve a hundred sins, even murder of a brahmin. Local Hindu lore also asserts that you can maximize the *lingam*'s purifying power by shaving your head, fasting, and taking a holy dip in the sea before *darshan*, or ritual viewing of the deity. For this reason, pilgrims traditionally begin their tour of Gokarn with a walk to the beach. They are aided and instructed by their personal *pujari* – one of the bare-chested priests you see around town, wearing sacred caste threads, and with single tufts of hair sprouting from their shaven heads – whose job it is to guide the pilgrims. Next, they visit the **Shri**

Mahaganpati temple, a stone's throw east of Shri Mahabaleshwar, to propitiate the elephant-headed god Ganesh; non-Hindus are welcome to visit both shrines. En route, check out the splendid *rath*, or chariot, that stands at the end of the bazaar next to the Mahaganpati temple. During important festivals, notably Shiva's "birthday", Shivratri (Feb/March), deities are installed inside this colossal carved-wood cart and hauled by hand along the main street, accompanied by drum bands and watched by huge crowds.

The beaches

Notwithstanding Gokarn's numerous temples, shrines and tanks, most Western tourists come here for the beautiful **beaches** situated to the south, beyond the lumpy laterite headland that overlooks the town. The hike to them takes in some superb coastal scenery, but be sure to carry plenty of water and wear a hat.

To pick up the trail, head along the narrow alley opposite the south entrance to the Mahaganpati temple, and follow the path uphill through the woods. After twenty minutes, you drop down from a sunbaked rocky plateau to **Kootlee beach** – a wonderful kilometre-long sweep of pure white sand, sheltered by a pair of steep-sided promontories. Drinks and simple food can be ordered from the palm-leaf *chai* stalls and seasonal cafés that spring up here during the winter, and some of the villagers offer very basic accommodation in huts. However, well-water is in short supply, toilets are nonexistent, and you have to bring your own bedding.

It takes around forty minutes to hike from Kootlee to the next beach, scaling the headland to the south and following the steep gravel path as it zigzags down the other side to the sea. The views along the way are stunning, especially when you first glimpse exquisite **Om beach**, so-named because its distinctive twin cresent-shaped bays resemble the auspicious Om symbol. For the past decade or so, this has been the all but exclusive preserve of a hard-core hippy fringe, many of whom spend months here wallowing in a *charas*-induced torpor. However, the arrival of a dirt road from Gokarn, and the recent acquisition of the land by developers, may well squeeze the scene out. If the concrete mixers ever do descend, though, it's unlikely they'll ever reach Gokarn's two most remote beaches, which lie another forty- to sixty-minute walk over the hill. Tantalizingly inaccessible and virtually devoid of fresh water, **Half-Moon** and **Paradise** beaches, reached via difficult dirt paths across a sheer hillside, are only for intrepid sun lovers happy to bring in their own supplies. If you're looking for near-total isolation, this is your best bet.

Eating and drinking

Gokarn town offers a good choice of **places to eat**, with a crop of busy "meals" joints along Car Street and the main road. Most popular, with both locals and tourists, is the brightly lit *Pai Restaurant*, which dishes up fresh and tasty vegetarian *thalis*, *masala dosas*, crisp *wadas*, teas and coffees until late. The other commendable "meals" canteen, around the corner on Car Street, is also called the *Pai Hotel*; it's much smaller, but their snacks are excellent, and the milk coffee delicious. *Shree Shakti Cold Drinks*, also on Car Street, serves mouthwatering fresh cheese, hygienically made to an American recipe and served with rolls, garlic and tomato; the owner also makes his own peanut butter, and sells filling toasties and *lassis*.

At the west end of town, near the beach, the excellent *Vishwar Café*, specializing in seafood and travellers' staples, is pick of the crop. They have an even better branch at Kootlee beach, with a Tibetan chef who knocks up delicious fresh prawn dishes, American chop suey and *momos* (Tibetan steamed dumplings). It's a popular place to eat but the service is very slow, so arrive soon after sunset to avoid a long wait. The *Spanish Restaurant*, near the Vishwar, is best at midday, when you can lounge on mats and eat pitta and houmous (only available when the elelctricity supply is running).

Finally, the best place to eat on **Om beach**, where a string of cafés compete for custom by blaring loud techno music, is the *Namaste*, at the north end. Try their delicious cinnamon rolls; the *thalis* are best avoided. The other joints are indifferent, at best.

Travel details

More detailed travel information features in the "Getting there" sections preceding the accounts in this chapter. For a rundown of current train services, disrupted due to conversion work on the line when this book went to print, contact any train station, tourist office, travel agent, or the Indian Railways counter in Panjim's Kadamba bus stand.

By bus

Hospet to: Gokarn (1 daily; 10hr); Hampi (every 30min; 20min); Panjim (2–3 daily; 10hr).

Jog Falls to: Panjim (daily; 7hr).

Gokarn to: Ankola (every 30min; 30min); Chaudi (1 daily; 2hr 30min); Karwar (4 daily; 1hr 30min); Margao (1 daily; 4hr); Panjim (1 daily; 5hr)

Contexts

A brief history

References to **prehistoric settlement** in Goa are limited to a handful of oblique mentions in ancient Sanskrit texts. However, it seems likely that the region, like others in southern India, experienced major upheavals around 1500 BC as Aryan invaders pushed south across the Indian peninsula from the northwest. The peoples they displaced migrated ahead of them, intermingling with the aboriginal inhabitants of central India, so when the Aryan tribes eventually arrived in Goa some time before 600 BC, the local population was of mixed race, comprising forest-dwelling hunter-gatherers and small groups of shifting cultivators.

Settled agriculture was first introduced to the region by the fair-skinned Aryan invaders, who drained areas of the coastal plains and cleared tracts of forest to farm. This early land-reclamation project is believed to have provided the historical basis of Goa's **origin myth**, recorded in the Vedas (sacred Hindu scriptures) more than three thousand years ago. According to the myth, Goa was created when Vishnu, in his sixth incarnation as the sage **Parasurama**, fired an arrow from the top of the Western Ghats into the Arabian Sea. He commanded the waves to withdraw and claimed the land up to the spot where the arrow fell as his kingdom (see p.190).

The ancient Greeks knew of the existence of Goa, which they referred to as *Melinda*, but the first solid historical record of the region dates

from the third century BC, when it formed a distant southwest province of the mighty **Mauryan empire**, based at Magadha in the Ganges Valley. Having filled the power vacuum that ensued from the break-up of Alexander the Great's empire in northwest India, the Mauryans expanded south to annex the Konkan coast, which Ashok, the second and greatest of the Mauryan emperors, renamed **Aparanta**, or "Beyond the End". He also dispatched Buddhist missionaries to evangelize the locals, but met with little success: when the empire collapsed after Ashok's death in 232 BC, Hinduism reasserted itself as the region's predominant religion.

The Hindu Golden Age

A succession of powerful **Hindu dynasties** held sway over Goa for the next seven hundred years from their capitals elsewhere in India, installing puppet governors and exacting tribute from them in exchange for military protection. However, while the Pallavas, Chalukyas and Rashtrakutas wrestled for control of southern India and the Deccan plateau, a home-grown dynasty emerged in Goa itself. Having declared independence from the Pallavas in 420 AD, the **Kadambas** gradually came to dominate the region, forging marital alliances with their powerful neighbours and founding a royal family that would endure well into the next millennium.

In 973, when the Kadambas' old allies and overlords, the Chalukyas, finally defeated their arch rivals, the Rashtrakutas, the Goan kings took this as their cue to oust the latter's governors from the capital, **Chandrapura** (see p.177). Shortly afterwards, they shifted northwest to another site on the banks of the Zuari River. Blessed with a deep harbour, the new Kadamba capital, known as **Govapuri** (or Gopakkapattana, today's Goa Velha), was perfectly placed to profit from the thriving maritime trade between the Malabar coast, Arabia and the Hindu colonies in Southeast Asia.

The move soon paid off. Within a decade, the Kadambas had amassed a fortune from the shipments of spices and horses that passed through their port, ploughing huge sums into civic building and the construction of exquisite stone temples throughout the kingdom. Muslim merchants from East Africa and Arabia were also encouraged to settle, and they added to the splendour by erecting mosques and villas in the capital. It was only a matter of time before such opulence attracted the attention of Muslim raiders who, during the eleventh and twelfth centuries, were pouring in ever greater numbers across India from the northwest. The old alliance with the Chalukyas had thus far protected Goa from Muslim incursions, but when the last ruler of the dynasty died in 1198, the kingdom lay exposed and vulnerable to attack from the Deccan.

Muslim invasions

The first **Muslim raids** on Goa took place late in the **tenth century**, orchestrated by the warlord Mahmud of Ghazni from Delhi. Directed mainly at the Kadambas' temples, which housed most of the region's treasure, the incursions grew more frequent and destructive as the twelfth and thirteenth centuries progressed, culminating with the iconoclastic excesses of **Ala ud-din Khalji**, the Sultan of Delhi, and Muhammed Tughluq. Successive sackings of Govapuri reduced it to ruins, and the beleagured Kadambas were forced to flee to their former capital at Chandrapura. This, too, was eventually destroyed, although not before Govapuri had been rebuilt.

The spirit of religious tolerance that prevailed between Goa's Arab merchants and their Kadamba hosts (even during the Muslim raids of the medieval era) vanished almost overnight in 1350 with the arrival of the **Bahmanis**. Driven by a new religious fanaticism, the invaders instigated a systematic persecution of the Hindus, smashing up temples and murdering priests. Many of the most sacred deities were smuggled to the safety of the interior, but nearly all of the ornately carved shrines were destroyed: only one – the tiny **Mahadeva Mandir** at **Tambdi Surla** in central Goa (see p.109), hidden in the forests at the foot of the Western Ghats – has survived.

The rise of Ela

This first period of Bahmani rule was short-lived, for in 1378, the Hindu **Vijayanagar** kings swept into the region across the Ghats from their capital at Hampi on the Deccan plateau. Exacting revenge for the earlier slaughter of their co-religionists by the Bahmanis, they massacred the Muslim inhabitants of the Goan capital, which the invaders occupied until it was counterattacked nearly a century later in 1470. This time the Bahmanis made sure of victory by launching a massive two-pronged invasion, with a vast army from the east, and a navy of 120 warships from the sea.

The city they conquered, however, had already lapsed into decline. Blocked by silt, its once thriving harbour had been left high and dry, forcing the Bahmanis to move to a more convenient location further north on the banks of the Mandovi River. Known as **Ela**, this new capital, erected on the site of Hindu religious centre founded by the Vijayanagars, would soon become the wealthiest city on India's southwest coast.

The transformation of Ela from sleepy sacred site to prosperous port was masterminded by the **Sultans of Bijapur**, who succeeded the Bahmanis in 1490. The rapidly expanding horse trade with Arabia enabled their first leader, **Yusuf Adil Shah**, to embark on a major building spree. During his short twenty-year rule, the Sultan erected a huge mosque and a grand fort-palace overlooking the Mandovi, as well as a double-storey summer palace for his harem further upriver at a village called Pahanji (see p.61).

The Portuguese discoveries

With the Moors ousted from the Iberian peninsula and Christendom established in the North African port of Ceuta in 1415, the crusading European superpowers were seeking fresh pastures. The recently discovered Americas provided the Spanish with potentially rich pickings, while the rival Portuguese turned their sights towards the African Gold Coast and beyond. The **Portuguese discoveries** gained momentum as the fifteenth century progressed, their initial goal to spread Christianity and locate the mythical Christian ruler Prester John, whom the Portuguese hoped would aid them in their quest against Islam in Africa. Later, however, the lure of cheap silk, pearls and spices overshadowed other motives, particularly after Dias rounded the Cape of Good Hope in 1488. If a route across the Indian Ocean could be opened up, it would bypass the much slower trans-Asian caravan trail, threatening the old Venetian-Muslim monopoly on Indian luxury goods, and providing direct access to the spice islands of the Philippines.

Aided by maps drawn up by previous Portuguese overland explorers, **Vasco da Gama** took 23 days to sail from East Africa to India, reaching the Malabar Coast for the first time in 1498. He mounted another expedition two years later to establish a trading post and base for Portuguese operations at Cochin, and then a third in 1502.

Albuquerque and the conquest of Goa

On da Gama's 1502 expedition, a small fleet was left behind to patrol the coast, one of whose detachments was commanded by the man credited with the "discovery" of Goa, **Alfonso de Albuquerque**. It was purely by chance that Bijapuri-controlled Goa ever made it onto the colonial map: a Muslim fleet, assembled by the ruler of Calicut to counter the Portuguese threat to his trade monopoly in the area, had been destroyed off the Malabar coast, and withdrew to the Bijapuri safe port of Goa. Informed of the fleet's whereabouts by a Vijayanagar captain, Albuquerque set sail to finish it off. The small garrison at Panaji fort was unprepared for the attack by the better-armed Europeans and capitulated without a fight. However, by the time Albuquerque had mopped up what was left of the Muslim fleet, he had seen for himself the strategic potential of the territory's capital, Ela, and decided to attack, forcing its Muslim defenders into the hinterland.

While the Portuguese were wondering what to do with their new acquisition, the chief minister and regent of the newly enthroned thirteen-year-old Sultan of Bijapur, **Ismail 'Adil Shah**, ordered a massive counteroffensive. Albuquerque and his soldiers held out for a couple of weeks, but were eventually pushed back to the mouth of the Mandovi River, where, with supplies of food and water dwindling and hemmed in by cannon-fire from Panaji fort, they remained for three months, their only escape route blocked by heavy monsoon seas. The storms eventually subsided and the Portuguese were able to limp back to base. Seeing this as a chance to slip back to Bijapur, the sultan and his ministers also withdrew, but left Goa inadequately defended. Albuquerque soon seized the opportunity to mount a ferocious second attack on the city on November 25, 1510, St Catherine's Day, which, this time, resulted in a decisive victory. The Portuguese swarmed through Ela, routing the Muslims and strengthening its defences against the inevitable Bijapuri backlash.

Work on fortifying the city progressed at an extraordinary pace and was completed by the time Albuquerque left Goa in 1511. The 'Adil Shah launched a counterattack soon after Albuquerque's death four years later, but to no avail. Ela was by then securely under Portuguese control and would remain so for another 450 years.

Conversion to Christianity

The zeal with which the Portuguese had seized Ela from the Muslims did not subside after the conquest. Rather, it was channelled in another direction: the **dissemination of Christianity**, which both justified the colonial enterprise, and endowed it with the air of a religious crusade.

Ela's Muslims fled from the city in 1510, but a large contingent of Hindus remained (Portugal's alliance with the Bijapuris' enemies, the Vijayanagars, had ensured their safety), and it was towards them that the first Christian **missionaries**, representatives of the Franciscan Order invited by the king of Portugal, directed their attention when they arrived. Under Albuquerque's administration, the Church was relatively tolerant, relying on persuasion rather than force to claim converts. The Governor also encouraged his soldiers to marry local women in the knowledge that the children of such alliances would be raised as Christians.

Such tactics proved effective but were deemed too liberal by Goa's first vicar general, whose arrival in 1532 signalled the start of a markedly more oppressive regime. Supported by the newly arrived zealous **Jesuits**, he passed a law in 1541 ordering the closure of all Hindu temples. This was followed four years later by the outlawing of collective worship of idols and the exiling of all Brahmin priests. The proclamation also sparked off an orgy of iconoclasm, with more than 350 shrines plundered and razed across the territory.

Worse was to follow. In 1559, idols were banned from private houses, and soon after, the Tribunal of the Holy Office, better known as the **Inquisition**, descended on Goa to weed out anyone who dared deviate from the dogmas of the Roman Catholic Church. Imprisoned in the dungeons of the Inquisition's headquarters in 'Adil Shah's former palace, suspects were subjected to appalling torture that, according to one contemporary chronicler "combined all that the ferocity of savages and the ingenuity of civilized man had till then invented". Tools of the Goan torturers' trade include "stretching racks, thumbscrews, leg crushers, holy water, burning sulphur, candles, quicklime and spiked wheels over which the victims were drawn with weights on their feet". Once every two to three years, these gruesome props would also be used for mass **autos da fé**, literally "acts of faith", in which suspected heretics would be tortured into "confessing" their sins. Anyone who cracked during these public trials (a *fait accompli* given the brutal nature of the tortures inflicted on them) was then executed in front of assembled dignitaries and clergy, usually by being burnt alive. The number of those who died in this way is thought to have run into thousands.

Even two hundred years of the Inquisition, however, failed to eradicate Hinduism altogether. A large number of deities were smuggled into the Portuguese-free zone in the middle of the state, where they were enshrined in secret temples, tended by priests in exile and worshipped by devotees under cover of darkness, who risked their lives to pray. Many of these temples still exist in Goa, hidden in the woods and valleys of Pernem, Satari, Sanguem and Canacona *talukas*.

"Goa Dourada"

By the time the Inquisition arrived in Goa in 1560, the territory's golden age was already in full swing. Situated at the nexus of Asia's most prosperous trade routes, the city of Old Goa raked in vast profits from the shipment of spices to Europe and Arabian horses into the subcontinent, earning for it the nickname **"Goa Dourada"**, or "Golden Goa". Taxes levied on the movement of goods through its port financed a prolific **building boom**, as dozens of splendid churches and cathedrals were erected in the capital – monuments worthy of Goa's role as the linchpin of Christianity in Asia.

Lured by the seemingly inexhaustible supply of heathen souls to save, representatives of various **religious orders** began to pour in to staff these lavish buildings, accompanied by an even greater deluge of **immigrants**. During the colony's heyday, an estimated 2500 people left Portugal each year, causing a chronic shortage of workers in the mother country and precipitating a recession

there that would contribute in no small part to Goa's eventual decline. Many Portuguese emigrants perished during the sea voyage, but enough survived to swell the city's population to around 300,000 – bigger than either London or Lisbon at that time, in spite of the appalling **epidemics** that regularly decimated the city. The permanent population was further boosted by a transient contingent of soldiers, sailors and traders who came to seek their fortune.

Littered around the more salubrious suburbs of Asia's largest metropolis were the elegant villas and grand colonial residences of the **hidalgos**, or Portuguese nobility. The lifestyle led by this wealthy elite was, in spite of the Church's high profile, famously decadent. Accounts by contemporary travellers – notably the Frenchman François Pyrard, who visited Goa after being shipwrecked in the Maldives in 1608 – describe the rounds of unbridled debauchery that prevailed among Goa's aristocracy. Sexual mores were notoriously lax, with prostitution and adultery rife among both the upper and lower classes. Pyrard even claimed that wealthy women of the colony regularly used to drug their husbands with extract from the hallucinogenic *datura* plant to facilitate their adulterous liaisons: in small quantities, the substance induced sleep and memory loss, allowing lovers to steal into their mistresses' boudoirs undetected.

When reports of this decadence finally filtered back to Lisbon, King Dom João III dispatched a party of young Jesuit priests to remedy the situation. Among them was **Francis Xavier** (see p.92), the most successful missionary of his day, who, after a brief sojourn as a seminary teacher in 1545, used the city as a base for his evangelical missions to the Malabar coast and the Moluccas in Southeast Asia. The saint's body, which for centuries remained miraculously free from signs of decomposition, is today enshrined in Old Goa's Basilica of Bom Jesus, the most magnificent of Goa's churches and spiritual nerve centre of Roman Catholicism in India. However, neither the Jesuits nor the Inquisition's subsequent crackdowns on Goa's licentious behaviour were to make much impact.

Decline

The writing was on the wall for Goa long before the source of its wealth – from total control of Asia's booming maritime trade – ran dry in the seventeenth century. The roots of the colony's **decline** lay in its ill-chosen location. Situated amid low-lying swampland, the city swarmed with malaria-carrying mosquitoes. In addition, outbreaks of cholera and typhoid were common, spread by the sewage that piled up and swilled through the streets during the rains. **Epidemics** plagued the city from the start, and by the late 1600s, its population had plummeted to less than a tenth of its previous peak. The Mandovi River had also begun to silt up, and ships were finding it increasingly difficult to dock at the quayside.

Ultimately, though, politics and not disease were to bring about the colony's eventual demise. The first blow was struck by the sultans of Bijapur. After 'Adil Shah's death in 1557, his son, Ali, negotiated an alliance between the region's five main Muslim nations against the Hindu Vijayanagars. This bore fruit eight years later when the Muslim coalition defeated their arch adversaries at the **Battle of Talikota**. The sack of the Hindu capital lasted for sixth months and furnished the attackers with enough booty to erect some of India's finest Islamic monuments in Bijapur. However, squabbles over the loot divided the Muslim league, although the Ahmednagar and Bijapuri dynasties stuck together to launch a combined attack on the Portuguese shortly after.

Following successful offensives against several trading posts and colonies further north, Goa was besieged by the Muslims in 1570: a fleet blockaded the port, while a massive army encircled the city itself, defended by a force of less than one hundred Portuguese soldiers and black slaves. The attack, however, failed. Bogged down in Goa's swamps, the invaders eventually succumbed to cholera and were forced to retreat after a year-long siege.

Further threats to Goa's survival followed as the struggle between European powers for trade supremacy in the region intensified. Foremost among the challengers to Portuguese maritime hegemony were **the Dutch**, whose lighter and more manoeuvrable ships easily outsailed the old-fashioned, ungainly Portuguese galleons. Mercantile rivalries were given an added edge by religious differences: determined not to allow Asia to be carved up by the proselytizing Roman Catholics, the Protestant Dutch systematically whittled away at Portugal's Oriental colonies, claiming the Moluccas in 1641, Ceylon in 1663,

and Macau and several strongholds on the Malabar coast soon after. A futher blow was dealt by the Persians when they captured Hormuz, at the entrance to the Gulf, to control the most direct route to Europe, while pepper-smuggling **privateers** found it increasingly easy to slip through the net cast by the Portuguese navy in the Indian Ocean.

With its trade monopoly broken, its port blocked by silt, its administration in tatters and its population decimated by disease, Goa was well and truly on its last legs by the end of the seventeenth century.

The Maharatha Wars 1664–1739

Meanwhile in the Deccan, a formidable new challenge to European ambitions in India was taking shape. From their homeland in the Northwestern Ghats, the Hindu **Maharathas**, led by the indomitable and militaristic **Shivaji**, were proving a thorn in the side of the mighty Moghul emperors, who ruled most of northern India at this time. For years, the Portuguese watched the skirmishes between these two native powers from the wings, but when Shivaji sacked the Moghul stronghold of Surat in 1664, both sides petitioned the Portuguese for support, and the viceroy found himself on the brink of involvement in the conflict.

He avoided commitment on this occasion, but was outmanoeuvred a couple of years later when a Moghul army massed on the Goan border and demanded safe passage through the territory, which it was reluctantly granted. This provided the ambitious new Maharatha chief **Sambhaji**, Shivaji's son, with precisely the excuse he needed to attack the Portuguese trading post of Chaul, a short way south of British Bombay. The Portuguese responded by attacking Ponda, recently seized by the Maharathas from the neighbouring *rajah*, but the offensive failed, with disastrous consequences for the Portuguese. No sooner had they retreated towards the Goan capital than the opposing Hindu army surged forward in an attack to annex chunks of Bardez and Salcete.

Outflanked and with no hope of reinforcements, the viceroy decided to appeal to God for help. Hurrying to the Basilica of Bom Jesus (see p.90), he opened up the tomb of Saint Francis Xavier and placed inside it his viceregal regalia, putting the fate of the colony in the miracle-working hands of its patron saint. His faith proved well founded. Within days, the Moghuls appeared on the border, forcing the Maharathas to beat a hasty retreat.

War between the Hindu rebels and their Muslim overlords kept the two sides busy for the next couple of decades, but Goa found itself in the firing line again in 1737. The Maharathas, led this time by Sambhaji's son, **Shapu**, were beseiging **Bassein**, a major Portuguese fort and coastal settlement north of Bombay. In order to waylay any potential Portuguese reinforcements, he also mounted a diversionary raid on Goa, seizing Margao and encircling the bastion at Rachol. Had Shapu realized just how weak the Goans had become since the last war, he would no doubt have pressed on to take the capital. However, fierce resistance at Bassein led him to overestimate the defensive capacity of his Portuguese adversaries, and the Maharatha leader opted for a truce. The **Treaty of May 1739** ceded control of Portugal's northern provinces (including Bassein but not Daman) to the Hindus, in exchange for the complete withdrawal of Maharatha forces from Goa. In addition, the Portuguese agreed to pay a hefty sum in **compensation**. This, coming in the wake of other territorial losses and financial setbacks inflicted by its European rivals, totally impoverished the territory, whose capital now lay virtually deserted and in ruins.

The Novas Conquistas

The Maharatha surrender let the Portuguese off the hook, but they found the humiliation hard to stomach and tried to regain the provinces lost in the treaty of 1739. However, both the Maharathas and British, who had gained a number of important footholds on India's west coast (among them a couple of former Portuguese possessions), proved too powerful. Instead, Portugal sought to enlarge Goa as a way of boosting morale and compensating for their recent defeats. Bicholim and Satari, two rural districts to the west of Mapusa, were assimilated in 1780–81, and Pernem in the far north later that decade. Finally, in 1791, the Rajah of Sunda handed over Ponda, along with Sanguem, Quepem and Canacona in the south. These acquisitions, known as the **Novas Conquistas** (New Conquests), were quickly integrated with the older established districts of Tiswadi, Bardez

and Salcete – the **Velhas Conquistas** (Old Conquests) that formed a buffer zone around the capital – and the frontiers of modern Goa were finally fixed, maintained even after the colony was absorbed into India more than a century and a half later.

The British and French, meanwhile, were embroiled in the **Napoleonic Wars**, which spilled over into minor skirmishes along the coast of India. The Portuguese managed to remain neutral, but in 1798, the British thought it prudent to dispatch a small fleet to protect Goa against attack by the French and their South Indian ally, **Tipu Sultan of Mysore**. However, the Goan Viceroy objected to this violation of Portuguese sovereignty and insisted the British withdraw. They did, but returned the following year, occupying the forts at Aguada and Cabo Raj Bhavan (where a small British military cemetery still lies; see p.78). This **British occupation** lasted a decade without ever escalating into a major conflict. For by now the British had tightened their grip on the rest of India, and the Portuguese, fearing that any provocation might result in the seizure of the Goan capital, chose to acquiesce.

The rise of Panjim

The **nineteenth century** was a period of great flux in Goa. Money was still trickling in from the gold and ivory trade with East Africa, but the capital had lapsed into irreversible decay, eclipsed by the Portuguese's more recently established colony of Brazil. When the Frenchman Abbé Cottineau visited Goa in 1822, he found only churches marooned in rubble and jungle, while Richard Burton, in his 1850 travelogue *Old Goa and the Blue Mountains*, remarked that the city was a scene of "utter destitution", its population " . . . as sepulchral-looking as the spectacle around them".

Disease and the decline of the empire had taken their toll, but the demise of the once proud metropolis was hastened by the departure of its few remaining inhabitants to a more salubrious site further west along the Mandovi. In a bid to escape the mosquitoes and ongoing cycles of pestilence that had afflicted Goa since its foundation three hundred years earlier, Viceroy **Conde de Alvor** proposed a move to Mormugao – the tip of a rocky peninsula west of the modern city of Vasco da Gama. Accordingly, civic buildings and houses in the old capital were demolished to provide masonry for the new location, and the colonial government prepared to decamp. However, the scheme was shelved in 1707 after de Alvor was posted back to Lisbon, leaving Old Goa in a shambolic state from which it would never recover.

At the start of the nineteenth century, **Panjim** was a small fishing settlement of around two hundred houses, with a decrepit Muslim fort, a handful of chapels and churches, and the 'Adil Shah's former summer palace presiding over its waterfront. However, its healthy position and proximity to both the open sea and the remains of Old Goa city made it an obvious candidate for the site of the colony's new capital. **Dom Manuel de Portugal e Castro**, viceroy between 1827 and 1835, is the man widely credited with Panjim's metamorphosis. He ordered the levelling of dunes and the draining of swamps around the town to create additional land for building, and oversaw the construction of the impressive administrative blocks that still stand in the city centre today. By the mid-nineteenth century, Panjim had become a bustling city of tree-lined avenues and leafy seaside suburbs.

The independence movement

As the size of Panjim increased, so too did disenchantment with direct rule from Lisbon. Calls for Goa to be made a republic or be absorbed into British India were echoed in Portugal, which at this time was divided by civil war. When the fighting ended in 1834, the government of Queen Maria II sought to placate dissenters in the colony by bestowing the governorship of Goa on a Goan, nationalist **Bernado Peres da Silva**, whose brief it was to implement a programme of sweeping reforms. These, however, floundered because of fears that da Silva, being a local man, would bend too easily to pressures from political factions in the territory.

The mounting distrust culminated in a **coup** attempt by the Goan military. It was unsuccessful but led to the appointment of a new governor, the former viceroy and founding father of Panjim, Dom Manuel de Portugal e Castro. But even he was unable to stave off the series of further mutinies by the army that resulted in the bloody **"massacre of Gaspar Dias"**, when, on May 4, 1835, the fort at Gaspar Dias was destroyed by rebel soldiers and the regiment posted inside it slain.

When the dust settled after the mutiny, the Portuguese remained in power, although drastic measures were now clearly required if the rising tide of disenchantment in Goa was to be stemmed. Frustration with Portuguese rule was felt most keenly by the Hindus, who were still treated as second-class citizens by the administration. Iniquitous colonial laws (some of which were introduced as late as 1910) denied them access to government jobs and positions of influence, even though many of the colony's most prosperous merchants and businessmen were Hindu.

Prominent politicians had successfully publicized Goa's plight in Europe, but it was through the local press that the fledgling **freedom movement** found its wings. In spite of stringent censorship laws, the newly created newspapers provided a platform for the separatists, whose ideas found favour both among the educated classes at home and influential Goan expatriates in Bombay.

However, after Portugal had itself been declared a republic in 1926, Goa's independence struggle sustained a major setback. For the next 46 years, Portuguese foreign policy was to be laid down by the right-wing dictator **Salazar**. Staunchly pro-colonial, he refused to relinquish control of Goa or Portugal's remaining possessions in Africa and Southeast Asia, even though the impoverished mother country could scarcely provide for itself, let alone prop up its flagging foreign territories. The end of colonial rule would, one way or another, have to be brought about by force.

Liberation

Pressure on Portugal to grant Goa its freedom intensified following the withdrawal of the British from India in 1947, but Salazar remained as resolute as ever, refusing even to negotiate with the newly independent Indian government. In the end, Prime Minister **Jawaharlal "Pandit" Nehru** ran out of patience and sent in the armed forces. Mounted in defiance of a United Nations resolution, **"Operation Vijay"** met with only token resistance from the Portuguese: the Indian army overran Goa, and Portugal's other two enclaves, Daman and Diu, in two days, with barely a shot fired on either side.

The offensive was heralded as an act of heroic **liberation** by India but met with a more ambivalent response in Goa. Many people feared assimilation would result in a loss of cultural identity and a drop in the high standard of living the territory enjoyed compared with neighbouring states. However, the Indian government ensured a relatively smooth transition by making Goa a **Union Territory** with semi-independent status and its own ruling body, or Legislative Assembly.

Recent history

Since independence, Goa has continued to prosper, bolstered by receipts from **iron-ore** exports and a booming **tourist industry**, but is struggling to hold its own against a tidal wave of **immigration** from elsewhere in India. Its inhabitants voted overwhelmingly to resist a proposed merger with neighbouring Maharashtra in the 1980s, and successfully lobbied for **Konkani**, the mother tongue of most Goans, to be granted official-language status in 1987.

The territory was declared a fully fledged state of the Indian Union in the same year, but has since been dogged by **political instability**. No fewer than seven chief ministers have been in power since 1986, which has somewhat impeded policy-making. Meanwhile, the State Legislative Assembly continues to be dominated by the Congress Party-I (formed out of Mahatma Gandhi's freedom movement), who fended off a strong challenge from the pro-Goan opposition, Maharashtrwadi Gomantak Poxx (MGP), in the 1994 elections. The extreme-right-wing Hindu fundamentalists, the BJP (Bharatiya Janata Party), have failed to make substantial gains in Goa, despite having a major impact in the national arena. Commentators claim this is due to the BJP's support for merger of the state with Maharashtra, a policy which has alienated their natural constituency, Goa's Hindu majority. Rather than side with the BJP and risk losing their semi-autonomous status, the Hindus have tended to support Congress, which in turn has stiffened the BJP's resolve to enforce the merger if, and when, it ever comes to power in the region.

In the meantime, environmental and development issues rather than communalism have dominated political life in the state, with the Konkan Railway controversy (see p.249) and tourism-related debates attracting considerable coverage in the state press. Reacting to a gradual decline in charter tourism over the past two or three years, the state Minister for Tourism, Willy D'Souza, put forward plans to attract more domestic visitors to the region by creating casinos in some resorts. Widespread opposition, however, provoked an abrupt U-turn, and calls for more culturally appropriate ways of reversing the decline.

The religions of Goa

Three great religions – Hinduism, Christianity and Islam – are represented in Goa, and they play a vital part in the everyday lives of the population. Indeed, some religious festivals, like Diwali and Easter, have become elevated to such a stature that they are among the region's main cultural events, while temples and churches provide a focus for social as well as devotional life.

Roughly speaking, **Christian** Goa encompasses the centre of the state: the coastal region of Tiswadi, Salcete and Bardez *talukas*. Known as the *Velhas Conquistas*, or Old Conquests, this area is still littered with whitewashed churches and wayside crosses, and its houses are very much in the Portuguese mould. The **Hindu** heartland lies in the hilly interior around the town of Ponda, and to the far north and south of the state, dubbed the *Novas Conquistas*, or New Conquests. These areas were acquired relatively late in the colonial era, and have retained a more obviously Indian feel. Islam has almost entirely died out in the state, with only a small remaining community.

However, even in outlying districts, it's not uncommon to find churches and temples side by side. For in spite of the systematic religious persecution of Portuguese times, the respective communities today live happily together, even, on occasions, participating in each others' reli-

gious festivals (Hindus and Christian neighbours, for example, commonly exchange sweets for Diwali). The two major faiths have also taken on many common traits: Goan temples incorporate features of Italian Renaissance architecture, while Christian worship frequently has the devotional air of Hindu rituals, with garlanded icons and prayers sung in Konkani.

Hinduism

The product of several millennia of evolution and assimilation, **Hinduism** was the predominant religion in Goa long before the arrival of Christianity, and is today practised by two thirds of the region's population. Although underpinned by a plethora of sacred scriptures, it has no single orthodoxy; prophet, creed nor doctrine, and thus encompasses a wide range of different beliefs. Its central tenet is the conviction that human life is an ongoing series of rebirths and reincarnations (*avatars*) that eventually leads to spiritual release (*moksha*). An individual's progress is determined by **karma**, very much a law of cause and effect, where negative decisions and actions impede the process of upward incarnations, and positive ones, such as worship and charitable acts, accelerate it. A whole range of deities are revered, which on the surface can make Hinduism seem mind-bogglingly complex, but with a loose understanding of the *Vedas* and *Puranas* – the religion's most influential holy texts – the characters and roles of the various gods and goddesses become apparent (see box below).

Every Hindu (from the Persian word for Indian) is born into a rigid social class, or **varna** (literally "colour"), each with its own specific rules and responsibilities. In descending hierarchical order, the four *varnas* are: *brahmins* (priests and teachers), *kshatriyas* (rulers and warriors), *vaishyas* (merchants and cultivators) and *shudras* (menials). The first three classes, known as "twice-born", are distinguished by a sacred thread worn from the time of initiation, and are granted full access to religious texts and rituals; members of the fourth *varna* are occasionally excluded from some of Indian's most sacred shrines, and are requested to avoid direct physi-

Hindu Gods and Goddesses

The Hindu pantheon is dominated by the primary gods **Shiva** and **Vishnu**, and to a lesser extent **Brahma**, the Creator, who collectively control the powers of destruction and preservation. Throughout India, Hinduism is organized around the two main sects – Vaishnavism and Shaivism – whose followers regard either Vishnu or Shiva as the pre-eminent deity. In Goa, however, you'll find images associated with both featuring in the same temple, although the central shrine and its accessory deities (*pariwar devtas*) will generally be from the same "family".

SHIVA

Most temples in Goa are dedicated to Shiva, even though the all-powerful God of Creation and Destruction has never been incarnate on earth. Known in Goa by a variety of names (most commonly Manguesh, Naguesh or Saptakoteswara), he is often depicted with four or five faces, holding a trident, draped with serpents, and bearing a third eye in his forehead. In temples he is identified with the **lingam**, or phallic symbol, resting on the yoni pedestal, a representation of female sexuality. Whether a statue or a *lingam*, though, Shiva is always guarded by his faithful bull-mount, **Nandi**, and often accompanied by a consort, who assumes various forms and is looked upon as the vital energy, or *shakti*, that empowers him.

VISHNU

The chief function of **Vishnu**, the Pervader, is to keep the world in order, preserving, restoring and protecting. With four arms holding a conch, discus, lotus and mace, Vishnu (sometimes referred to in Goa as Vitthala, Narcenha or Narayan) is blue-skinned, and often shaded by a serpent, or is shown resting on its coils afloat the Primordial Ocean.

Vaishnavites, generally distinguishable by the two vertical lines of sandalwood paste on their foreheads, recognize Vishnu as the supreme Lord, and hold that he has manifested himself on earth nine times. These **incarnations** (*avatars*) have been as a fish (Matsya), tortoise (Kurma), boar (Varaha), man-lion (Narsingh), dwarf (Vamana), axe-wielding *brahmin* (Parasuram), Rama, Krishna and Buddha. Vishnu's future descent to earth as Kalki, the saviour who will come to restore purity and destroy the wicked, is eagerly awaited.

Vishnu's most important incarnation, however, was as **Krishna**. In this guise, he assumes different faces, but is most popularly depicted as the playful cowherd who seduces and dances with cowgirls (*gopis*), giving each the illusion that she is his only lover. He is also pictured as a small, chubby, mischievous baby, known for his butter-stealing exploits, who inspires motherly love in women. Like Vishnu, Krishna is blue, and often shown dancing and playing the flute.

Rama, Vishnu's other main *avatar*, is the chief character in Hinduism's most popular epic, the *Ramayana*. Born a prince in Ayodhya, he was denied succession to the throne by one of his father's wives, and was exiled for fourteen years, together with his wife Sita. The *Ramayana* details his exploits during these years, and his defeat of the demon King of Lanka, Ravana. When Rama was reinstated as

cal contact with higher castes. Below all four categories, groups whose jobs involve contact with dirt or death (such as undertakers, sweepers or leather workers) were traditionally classified as **Untouchables** – later renamed, following the campaign of Mahatma Ghandi, as *Harijans*, or "Children of God". Discrimination against this lowest stratum of society is now a criminal offence, but Untouchability is by no means a thing of the past.

Within the four *varnas*, social status is further defined by *jati*, classifying each individual by family and occupation. A person's *jati* is synonymous with his or her **caste**, which places restrictions on all aspects of life from food consumption, religious obligations and contact with other castes, down to the choice of marriage partners.

Temples

Religious life for Hindus revolves around the **temple**. Known as *devuls* or *mandirs* ("Houses of God") in Konkani, these sacred structures house the focal point of communal worship: the deity, or **devta**. Ranging from simple stones to solid-

king in Ayodhya, he put Sita through a "trial by fire" to prove that she had remained pure while in the clutches of Ravana. Sita passed the test unharmed, and is thus revered as the paradigm of female purity, honesty and faithfulness.

DURGA

Durga, the fiercest of Hinduism's female deities, is an aspect of Shiva's more conservative consort, **Parvati** (the goddess of peace, known as Shantadurga in Goa), who is remarkable only for her beauty and fidelity. In whatever form, Shiva's consort is **shakti**, the primal energy that spurs him into action. Among Durga's many aspects (each one a terrifying goddess eager to slay demons), are Chamunda and Kali, but in all her forms she is Mahadevi, the "Great Goddess". Statues show her with ten arms, holding the head of a demon, a spear, and other weapons; she tramples demons underfoot, or dances over Shiva's body. A garland of skulls drapes her neck, and her tongue hangs from her mouth, dripping with blood.

GANESH

Chubby and smiling, elephant-headed **Ganesh**, the first son of Shiva and Parvati, is invoked by Goan Hindus before almost every major undertaking (except funerals), and is the focus of one of the region's major religious festivals, Ganesh Chathurti (see p.49). Seated on a throne or lotus, his image is often placed above temple gateways, in shops and houses; in his four arms he holds a conch, discus, bowl of sweets (or club) and a water lily, and he's nearly always attended by his vehicle, the rat. Credited with

writing the epic poem the *Mahabharata* as it was dictated by the sage Vyasa, Ganesh is regarded as the god of learning, lord of success, prosperity and peace.

LAKSHMI

The comely goddess **Lakshmi**, usually shown sitting or standing on a lotus flower, and known in Goa as Mahalsa or Mahalakshmi, is the goddess of wealth, and the embodiment of loveliness, grace and charm. As Vishnu's consort, she appears in different aspects alongside each of his *avatars*. The most important of these are Sita, wife of Rama, and Radha, Krishna's favourite *gopi*. In some temples, she is shown with Vishnu, in the form of Lakshmi-Narayan.

SARASWATI

The most beautiful Hindu goddess, **Saraswati**, the wife of Brahma, sits or stands on a water lily or peacock, playing the lute, *sitar* or *veena*. Associated with the sacred central Indian River Saraswati, she is seen as the goddess of purification and fertility, but equally revered as the inventor of writing, the queen of eloquence and goddess of music.

HANUMAN

India's great monkey god, **Hanuman**, features in the *Ramayana* as Rama's chief aide in his fight against the demon king of Lanka, Ravana. Depicted as a giant monkey wielding a mace, Hanuman is the deity of acrobats and wrestlers, but is also seen as Rama and Sita's greatest devotee, and an author of Sanskrit grammar.

gold statues, cult objects are venerated not as mere symbols of divine power, but as actual embodiments of a particular god or goddess. The buildings in which they are enshrined also vary in scale and splendour according to how important the *devta* is: some are modest concrete affairs, while others are soaring multicoloured piles crammed full of finery.

The culmination of worship, or **puja**, is always the moment of **darshan**, or ritual viewing of the deity. After ringing a bell in front of the shrine, the worshipper steps forward, salutes the god or

goddess (sometimes by prostrating him- or herself), and presents an offering of fruit, incense, flowers or money to the temple priest (*pujari*). They are then given a spoonful of holy water (*tirtha*) and *prasad* – food (usually a sugary bonbon) that has been blessed by the deity. Meanwhile, the bare-chested *brahmin* priests busy themselves with the daily round of readings and rituals: waking, bathing, dressing and garlanding the *devta*, chanting Sanskrit texts, and smearing vermillion paste (*tilak*) on the foreheads of worshippers.

Non-Hindus are welcome to **visit Goan temples**, but you're expected to observe a few simple conventions. The most important of these is to dress appropriately: women should keep their shoulders and legs covered, while men should wear long trousers or *lunghis*. Always remove your shoes at the entrance to the main hall (not the courtyard), and never step inside the doorway to the shrine, which is strictly off limits to everyone except the *pujaris*. **Photography** is nearly always prohibited inside the temple but allowed around the courtyard. Finally, if there is a passage (*pradakshena*) encircling the shrine, walk around it in a clockwise direction.

A more detailed account of Goan temples, including their historical background and a rundown of their chief architectural features, appears on p.92.

Christianity

Roman Catholicism was imposed on Goa by the Portuguese in the sixteenth century, spread by proselytizing missionaries, and zealously upheld by the dreaded Inquisition, which weeded out heretics and ruthlessly persecuted any converts deemed to have lapsed into "pagan" ways (see p.235). The Inquisition's chief weapons were the infamous *autos da fé*, or "acts of faith", in which individuals suspected of heresy were tortured and, if found guilty, burnt at the stake. In later years, Hindus and Muslims were allowed to practise their religions openly, but by this time Christianity had firmly taken root, albeit in a form that retained too many indigenous traits to meet with Portuguese approval. Among the more notable differences between Goan Christianity and that of the motherland was the persistence of the **caste** structure, with virtually all priests coming from the *brahmin* caste. To this day, a large number of priests wear the sacred thread and caste marks, while devotion to the Madonna, the linchpin of Goan Catholicism, bears a striking resemblance to the *devi*, or goddess worship of Hinduism. Today, a little under a third of the total population is Christian, and the state trains priests and nuns in its seminaries and convents for service throughout India.

The spiritual heart of Christianity in Goa is the Basilica of Bom Jesus in Old Goa (see p.90), whose crypt houses the sacred relics of **Saint Francis Xavier** – the region's patron saint. Every ten years, his corpse, which for centuries remained miraculously incorrupt, is exposed for public veneration: an event witnessed by tens of thousands of pilgrims. Francis Xavier was against Indians entering the clergy, but his opposition was ultimately ignored, and the region's church has long been staffed by native Goans, some of whom are even in line for canonization.

On Sundays families flock to Mass togged out in their best clothes. Saints' Days celebrating the patron saint of the village church also draw large congregations, as do the numerous religious festivals held around the state (see p.48). As you'll see if you come across one, these, and more routine church services, have a uniquely Goan atmosphere: violinists accompany the hymn singing, garlands adorn the Madonnas and high altars, and Mass is said in Konkani.

The most spectacular **Goan churches** are located in Old Goa (see p.81), whose grandiose four-hundred-year-old cathedrals have earned for the site UNESCO World Heritage status. However, several other equally impressive buildings lie in less frequented parts of the state. Most are left open and can be visited freely, but in more out-of-the-way villages you may have to ask the local priest to unlock the doors for you. It's also a good idea to dress respectably when visiting churches, and to leave a small donation for the upkeep of the building when you leave.

Islam

Islam was originally brought to Goa in the eleventh century by Arab merchants, who played a pivotal role in maritime trade along the Malabar Coast south of Goa. Encouraged by local Hindu rulers, wealthy Muslims erected mosques and put down roots in the region, practising their religion freely. However, this period of peaceful coexistence came to an abrupt end in the thirteenth century with the arrival from the northwest of marauders from Delhi and the Deccan. By the fourteenth century, an intolerant brand of Islam was in the ascendancy, as the raiders made permanent settlements, forcing out the Hindus, whom they regarded as heathen idol worshippers. The Bahmani conquests of the mid-1300s finally brought Goa under Muslim rule, with temples razed and their deities banished to the relatively inaccessible foothills of the Western Ghats.

While Hinduism weathered the religious persecution of the Portuguese era, Islam petered out

almost completely in Goa, and today only a ves-
tigal Muslim community remains. Distinguished
by their half-beards and skullcaps (the women
wear enveloping veils called *burqas*, or long
shirts and pyjama trousers known as *shalwa-
camises*), most live in and around Ponda, where
the state's main mosque, the Safa Masjid, is
located (see p.97).

Green issues in Goa

Goa's coastal resorts may have acquired the
trappings of Western consumerism, but a large
proportion of its inhabitants still lead traditional lifestyles, meeting their needs from the land
and trading surplus produce. Villagers draw
water from communal wells or streams; food
comes straight from the fields, sea or kitchen
garden; milk, meat and manure from domestic
animals; and raw materials for building and
crafts from the forest.

Green groups have achieved remarkable success in bringing environmental issues to the
attention of the public, both in Goa and abroad,
but the task they face is an uphill one. Impeded
for decades by a near-bankrupt colonial administration, the pace of development has increased
exponentially since independence. Dissenters,
however, are all too often dismissed as "back-
ward", or else fall foul of bureaucracy, an ineffi-
cient legal system and political expedience, not
to mention corruption, which is rife in many
areas of public life.

Water

The most contentious environmental issue in
Goa is the use and abuse of water. As the population continues to rise, augmented by immigrants from neighbouring states and an ever-
growing annual deluge of foreign visitors, water
is growing increasingly scarce: in many coastal
villages wells often run dry by late February. The
problem is compounded by pollution from industrial plants and mines, and by deforestation of
the interior, which interferes with the state's river
systems.

Goa receives around two and a half metres of
rain during the annual monsoon – more than
double the national average. Yet the dry season

is regularly accompanied by droughts affecting
thousands of villagers. The main reason the
wells and irrigation ducts dry up is that an estimated 80 percent of the annual rainfall flows
straight into the sea. The response to the problem by the Indian government in the 1970s was
to commission a series of dams at the foot of
the Western Ghats to regulate the flow of water
to the densely populated coastal plain. However,
as is often the case with such large-scale engi-
neering projects in India, the benefits reaped
from the schemes have thus far proved scant
reward for the huge sums of money invested in
them.

The Selaulim Dam, begun in south Goa in
1972 and now the *bête noire* of the Goan green
lobby, exemplifies the potential drawbacks of
dam-building as a response to the region's water
problem. Plagued by financial setbacks and political scandals, the project ended up costing ten
times its original estimate and fell more than five
years behind schedule. In addition, it necessitated the clearance of 706 hectares of virgin forest
– exacerbating water shortages by causing soil
erosion and an eventual drop in rainfall – and the
relocation of 643 families, many of whom now
endure substandard housing and soil that is too
poor to farm. Another criticism of the dam is that
its water was pumped to luxury resorts and a
chemical plant on the coast years before it
arrived in the towns of south Goa, while water
promised to local farmers has yet to materialize.

Among the few beneficiaries of water shortages in Goa are the "peddlars" – private hauliers
who tap communal wells and transport their contents in tankers to villages where the supply has
been exhausted. Writs have been served to prevent this trade, but few peddlars have so far been

brought to book: water transportation is so lucrative during the dry season that most can easily afford to pay off the local police.

The lowering of water tables on the coast, which has allowed many wells to become polluted with salt water, is frequently cited by the government as a reason to build more dams. Yet there has been little evidence that such projects actually alleviate the problem. In many cases, the promises of short-term financial gain for local companies or politicians turns out to be the real motive. For example, winter water shortages in the north Goan coastal village of Arambol are frequently used to justify the construction of a large dam upstream. Villagers, however, believe that the new supply may be diverted to the luxury hotel and golf course currently being planned by the local landlord (see p.152).

Tourism

Goa has been among India's leading **tourist destinations** since the early 1970s, when it first began to lure travellers off the trans-Asian "hippy trail". In those early days, the scene was decidedly low-key, with the majority of visitors staying in private family homes or makeshift huts on the beach. Luxury hotels were few and far between, concentrated on the north coast and a strip at the south end of Colva Beach.

Goa's era as a hippy haven came to an end in 1987 when the then state governor announced a relaxation in the laws forbidding the construction of large five-star resort complexes. Hot on the heels of this came the much-publicized "Master Plan for Tourism". Henceforth, the government declared, backpacking budget travellers, who had hitherto formed the mainstay of tourism in the area, would be discouraged in favour of wealthier, high-spending package visitors.

Luxury vs budget tourism

Goa has indeed become firmly established on the package tourist map, with five **charter flights** per day bringing fresh batches of fortnighters into the state direct from Europe, and dozens of newly opened luxury hotels doing a roaring trade in villages that were formerly the preserve of budget travellers. However, beneath the glossy brochure images lurk a number of **problems** that belie the government's attempts to represent tourism as a godsend for Goa.

At the centre of the **local opposition to tourism** are the five-star hotels. Located within a stone's throw of the beach, many of these purpose-built resorts have wilfully ignored, or deviously circumvented, laws prohibiting construction within five-hundred metres of the mean high water mark. They are also water-intensive, with lush lawns, swimming pools, Western toilets, bathtubs and fountains to feed. Some obtain water by illegally tapping ground sources (thereby lowering alluvial levels and increasing the risk of saline pollution); others enjoy piped supplies while local villagers have to carry water from wells.

The impact of **luxury resorts** on the environment can be considerable in other ways, too: rubbish and untreated sewage may be dumped beside them, *toddi* trees felled to make room for new buildings, and sand dunes cleared for gardens. In some cases, the developers have even forcibly relocated local villagers, who have retaliated by picketing the offending hotels and mounting demonstrations in nearby towns. Accusations of **harassment** and physical intimidation against the ringleaders of such campaigns have also been reported. Nor do the resorts tend to bring many economic benefits to local people: profits invariably end up in Bombay or Delhi, while their presence forces up the prices of food and housing.

Opposition to tourism from Goan pressure groups and the media is not directed solely at five-star resorts, either: budget travellers have also come in for flack. Critics complain about the threat to moral values posed by **nudity** on the beaches, and **drugs**, particularly heroin, have become a problem in some coastal villages. In addition, the presence of large numbers of budget travellers in out-of-the-way settlements may have a detrimental impact on the local environment: backpackers consume less water per day than the average package tourist, but they tend to stay for longer and thus place a protracted burden on scarce supplies. The price of **food** and other basic commodities has also risen dramatically in some budget tourist enclaves, where fish and fruit are beyond the means of low-income families during peak season.

The future

If mass tourism is allowed to develop unchecked in Goa, prospects are very bleak indeed. Unwilling to heed the hard-learned lessons of countries such as Spain, Thailand and Indonesia, local government and developers remain bent on making a fast buck, without investing adequately in the **future**. Such short-term vision could well have disastrous consequences.

Calangute, the state's most popular resort, typifies what happens when development runs out of control. Multi-storey hotel complexes have been thrown up along the entire length of the beach, yet the village lacks a sewage treatment plant, provision for waste disposal and decent roads. In addition, many of the ritzy new resorts have been so hastily erected that they are certain to deteriorate badly over the next three or four years. By then, though, the village will be so built-up and polluted that the tourist trade will have moved on to fresh pastures: to less developed villages further up the coast at first, and later out of the region altogether.

The state's anti-tourism lobby is trying hard to highlight such dangers, filing writs against developers that ignore environmental laws, organizing demonstrations and publicizing their grievances at home and abroad; yet their efforts have failed to stem the flow of visitors to the region, or halt the inexorable spread of concrete along the coast. Foreign tour operators also remain impervious to local concerns. While paying lip service to green ideas in their brochures, many of the larger companies continue to patronize resorts that have been singled out for criticism by environmental groups, thereby encouraging the developers to build new ones in hitherto unspoilt areas.

It would be far from desirable for tourists to stop coming to Goa as the livelihoods of too many local people already depend on the trade. In the long term, a small-scale and more environmentally friendly form of tourism is the only viable option. Village-style family guesthouses may not appeal to most package tourists, but at least they exact a lower cost on the environment; the income they generate also directly benefits the villagers, rather than property speculators and shareholders in distant cities. The trouble is that budget tourists are precisely the kind of visitors the government is seeking to discourage. What really stands in the way of a sustainable tourism in Goa is the reluctance of policy-makers and law-enforcers to sanction changes from which

they themselves will gain little, or nothing, in the short term.

Obviously, you can make a difference: try to use as little water as possible, and avoid hotels with lawns and swimming pools, or resort complexes that have chopped down trees or dispossessed villagers of land. Finally, if you book a package holiday and find yourself in a hotel that has infringed environmental legislation, complain to its owners, or, better still, write to your tour operator when you get home: only through punter pressure (ie from their charter company clients) will the developers be persuaded to act in a more ecologically responsible way.

If you want to find out more, contact *The Goa Foundation* (above the Mapusa Clinic, Mapusa, 403 507 Goa), or check out their informative book *Fish Curry and Rice* (available through the *Foundation*'s office or the bookshop at the *Mandovi Hotel*, Panjim), which gives a detailed account of the Goan environment and the organizations set up to protect it. The UK-based NGO *Tourism Concern* also publishes a regular bulletin on Goa, with updates on legal proceedings and addresses you can write to if you want to express your support for local campaigns, or wish to voice objection to particular developments.

Industry

Goa is a predominantly rural state, but a few isolated packets of heavy **industry** have sprung up over the past three decades, posing a serious threat to the environment and potential health risks for local people. The oldest-established and most controversial is the **Zuari Agro Chemical Fertilizer Plant** (*ZAC*) on the Dabolim plateau, near Vasco da Gama. Overlooking the north end of beautiful Colva Beach, the factory first made headlines in the mid-1970s when toxic chemicals from it found their way into the water table, decimating fish populations and raising fears about the plant's overall safety. *ZAC* has been modernized since, but its productive capacity has increased enormously and environmentalists remain concerned about the risk of ammonia and other toxic gasses escaping from its old-fashioned and poorly maintained storage tanks. In addition, **emissions** from the factory's chimney stacks are said to have affected the health of villagers nearby, while **tanker trucks** carrying loads of lethal chemicals routinely use local roads.

Another chemical plant to have sparked off controversy in Goa is the **Hindustan Ciba Energy** complex near Old Goa. Leakages of chlorine and other potentially dangerous compounds have been reported by villagers living nearby. A rerun of the *Union Carbide* gas tragedy in Bhopal may also have been narrowly averted here when a cylinder containing the lethal compound methyl chloride nearly ruptured.

Mining

Head into the hilly heart of Goa, and you're bound to encounter a couple of open-cast **ore mines**. Forming gigantic red gashes across the landscape, these colossal industrial eyesores generate more foreign currency than all of Goa's five-star resorts put together: around $170 million per annum, or 10 percent of the state's GDP. Unfortunately, they also inflict untold damage on the region's ecology, causing **soil erosion** on a massive scale, and destroying extensive tracts of forest- and farmland.

The roots of the environmental problems lie in the nature of open-cast mining itself. To extract one tonne of ore, you have to dig up between two and three times that amount of surplus dirt; the thirteen million tonnes of iron and manganese ore that Goa exports every year leave around forty million tonnes of rock and soil waste in their wake, most of which get dumped on massive heaps around the edges of the mines. With the onset of the monsoons, rain-water drains the **slag heaps** of their finer soil and flushes it into streams and rivers. These then clog up with **silt**, causing frequent floods in low-lying rice-cultivating areas: paddy fields ruined for decades by slicks of red mud are nowadays a common sight in and around mining areas.

Dust is another hazardous by-product of the mining industry. Travelling through the eastern Bicholim or Ponda *talukas*, you'll pass villages and stretches of forest completely covered in a pall of fine red dirt. This not only stifles vegetation; it also blows into houses, wells and people's food, and has caused a dramatic increase in **respiratory disorders** in towns such as Cuchorem-Sanvordem, whose train station is the hub of ore transportation in central Goa.

The response of the mine owners to such problems has been sluggish. However, they may soon be forced to clean up their act or face bankruptcy. Some Goan rivers have silted up to such an extent over the past few decades that the barges which transport the ore to Mormugao harbour, at the head of the Zuari estuary near Vasco da Gama, are only able to operate in the period after the rains, when water levels are highest. Several mines have to shut down towards the end of the dry season. Spurred on by the example of a few large operators, the industry is now madly planting its tips with trees in an attempt to forestall the rate of the erosion. However, whether or not their efforts prove to be "too little, too late" remains to be seen.

The Konkan Railway

Buffered in the east by jungle-covered hills, and to the north and south by hundreds of kilometres of water-logged coastal plain, Goa was for centuries among the most physically isolated parts of peninsular India, reached more easily by sea than by land. The arrival of the *South Central Railway*'s branch line and national highway network improved communications, but the state remained relatively inaccessible until the completion in 1997 of a superfast rail link along the coast between Bombay and Mangalore. In spite of the economic benefits its advocates claim it will bring to the region, the **Konkan Railway** (dubbed "the Chord of Dischord" by the Goan press) has been the hottest political and environmental controversy in Goa since independence.

Plans for a coastal train line were mooted in the early 1950s and a geological survey was carried out in 1974, but the scheme only got off the ground in 1990 with the formation of the *Konkan Railway Corporation (KRC)*. When the bulldozers moved in to begin work, the full implications of the project became apparent and a grass-roots anti-railway campaign quickly gathered momentum.

The environmentalists' main concern was that the **proposed route** of the Konkan Railway, between Pernem and Canacona *talukas*, would destroy large areas of ecologically fragile (and agriculturally important) *khazan* lands (see p.251), interfering with water levels and increasing the risk of an outbreak of **Japanese encephalitis** in the region. This deadly disease has recently resurfaced in Goa in areas that have been affected by road-construction work: if embankments and cuttings impede the flow of water across the *khazans*, human and animal waste builds up to create the perfect breeding ground for the *Culex vishnui* mosquito, which carries the disease. Furthermore, environmentalists argued, the railway would impinge apon key archeological sites (including Old Goa), and cause widespread **deforestation** and **soil erosion**. Finally, the proposed route would cost far more that one passing through Goa's less ecologically fragile midland region. Seeing that the project could not by this stage be stopped altogether, **realignment** of the route thus became the opposition's main objective.

By the summer of 1995, work on the original route had reached a point of no return, and the realignment lobby had given up hope of achieving anything more than minor modifications to it. Before long, huge bridge supports straddled rivers from Chapora in north Goa, to Talpona, near Palolem, in the south, while giant red earth workings gashed the lush coastal plain, excavat-

ed by teams of poor migrant labourers from Karnataka and Maharashtra, who lived in makeshift shanty encampments around the construction sites.

KRC, meanwhile, was plagued by a series of political **scandals** and **financial setbacks**. Controversy surrounding the scheme from its inception affected the sale of railway bonds, causing a chronic shortage of funds, while high-level fraud was also exposed. In the end, the Indian taxpayer had to make up the shortfall after the World Bank downscaled their support in response to press exposure of *KRC*'s incompetence and corruption. In spite of these setbacks, work proceeded and the first section of the line was opened to passengers in early 1997. By 1998, the problematic stretches (in Pernem and Canacona) will have been completed, and five high-speed trains per day will be running between Bombay and Mangalore. All being well, the backers should recoup their investment in a decade; the debt to the environment will doubtless take a lot longer to repay.

Natural history

A fast-growing population, industrialization and the spread of coastal tourist resorts have inflicted pressures on the rural landscape, but Goa is still a state of beautiful and varied scenery with its own distinct flora and fauna. Many species have been hunted out or squeezed eastwards over the past fifty years, but enough survive to make a trip into the countryside worthwhile. Walking on less frequented beaches or through the rice fields of the coastal plain, you'll encounter dozens of exotic birds, while the hill country of the interior supports an amazing variety of plants and trees. The majority of Goa's larger mammals keep to the dense woodland lining the Karnatakan border, where three nature sanctuaries afford them some protection from the hunters and loggers that have wrought such havoc in this fragile forest region over the past few decades.

Geography

Rarely in India do you find such a wide range of different landscapes packed so tightly, or wilderness areas situated so close to modern towns and resorts, as in Goa. Broadly speaking, the state may be divided into three major **habitats**: the low-lying coastal plain, the laterite plateau country of the midland region, and the lush, forest-cloaked hills of the Western Ghats. Crammed into a fifty-kilometre-wide strip, these different terrains form a closely integrated ecosystem that is sustained by a tangle of rivers

and tributaries meandering westwards into the Arabian Sea.

The **Western Ghats** (from the Sanskrit word for "sacred steps") are Goa's most important topographical feature. Running parallel to the coast at a mean elevation of between 900m and 1200m, the sheer mountains, which extend along the entire length of peninsular India, impede the path of the monsoon rain clouds as they sweep in from the southwest. The moist deciduous forest draped over their flanks thus act like a giant sponge, soaking up the rainwater on which the region depends, and channelling it down to the plains. **Deforestation** of this sparsely populated region – home to over 3500 different varieties of flowering plants (a third of India's total), and a rich assortment of mammals, birds, reptiles and insects – is a worsening problem: without the trees to modulate the flow of water, flooding and soil erosion are spoiling crops and destroying centuries-old irrigation systems.

From the foot of the Ghats, steep-sided **laterite plateaux** extend west, covered in scrub and savannah grasslands. Although the soil in this midland region is thin, the floors and sides of the many well-watered valleys are important agricultural zones, carpeted with fragrant cashew trees (the source of Goa's main cash crop) and areca groves. This is also the home of the state's largest **spice plantations**, as well as its lucrative iron- and manganese-ore **mines**, which form gigantic trenches of red against the green and yellow backdrop.

The majority of Goa's inhabitants live on the 105-kilometre-long **coastal strip**, whose fertile rice fields and coconut groves, together with a thriving fishing industry, provide the bulk of the region's food. The epicentre of the region's industry and tourism, this is also the most ecologically vulnerable area of Goa. Demand for new building space, and the shift away from traditional subsistence farming methods, have led to the drainage of wetlands and the destruction of many **mangrove swamps**, while the threat of pollution from chemical plants, power stations and sewage from the resorts looms ever larger (see "Green Issues", p.245).

Khazans

According to the *Skadna Purana*, an ancient Sanskrit scripture written sometime during the first half of the first millennium AD, the region now known as Goa was created when the sage Shri Parasurama, sixth incarnation of the god Vishnu, shot an arrow from the Western Ghats into the Arabian Sea, and then reclaimed the land where it fell. Scholars believe this myth derives from the colonization of the area by settled agriculturalists in the Vedic Age (around 1500 BC), and that Parasurama's arrow represents the process of land reclamation that ensued. Today, the saline flood plains lining Goa's tidal estuaries, known as **khazans**, have still not been submerged under sea water, and remain the focus of the region's lowland economy. This fertile patchwork of paddy fields and palm grove enables local farmers to cultivate rice, fruit and vegetables, and provide salt, fish and shells for the production of limewash.

Lying well below sea level, *khazans* are maintained by a complex man-made system that has altered little over the past few millennia. The first lines of defence are the impenetrable **mangrove swamps** growing along the edges of Goa's estuaries, backed where necessary by sturdy laterite walls. Behind these, a grid of **bunds** – embankments made from mud, straw and areca poles – protect the fields, while sluice gates operate like valves to regulate the flow of water onto and off the land. As salt water kills off most crops, retention of fresh monsoon flood waters is essential for cultivation. However, on very low-lying *khazans*, where villagers plant only a single crop of rice, the sluices are left open for most of the year and the flooded fields used for fish farming.

Stable for centuries, the fragile ecology of the *khazans*, which comprise 18,000 hectares of Goa's coastal plain, is now under **threat** from a variety of sources. Large tracts of wetland have been drained and built on as urbanization gathers pace in the state, bringing with it increased amounts of sewage. Other causes of **pollution** include chemicals swept down from the iron-ore mines by stream, and oil swilled out of ships' bilges in the estuaries. The Konkan Railway (see p.248) has also carved a great red scar down the coastal plain, causing flooding in parts of Bardez, Bicholim, Salcete, Mormugao and around Ponda. However, the greatest potential risk to the *khazans* is posed by **poor land management**. A gradual breakdown in the indigenous *communidades* system of land tenure (see below) has led to increasingly widespread neglect of the ditches and sluice gates, and even their wilful destruction. Landless peasants not engaged in rice production have been known to illegally dynamite dykes so that the fields behind them may be used for more lucrative (but ecologically unsustainable) fish or prawn farming, a practice dubbed as "**bund busting**".

The consequences of destroying the *khazans* are not only environmental. Flooded, polluted land is the perfect breeding ground for the *Culex vishnui* mosquito, carrier of the deadly disease **Japanese encephalitis**, which killed nearly one hundred people during the 1992 monsoons, and may well have been what wiped out the population of Old Goa two hundred years ago. Hard-liners in the environmental lobby prophesy that unless the *khazans* are protected, modern Goa could well go the same way.

Land settlement and usage

Settled agriculture has been practised in Goa for over four thousand years, introduced by Aryan invaders during the Vedic Age. Prior to this, the region was inhabited by small groups of **semi-nomadic cultivators**, who cleared tracts of forest for their crops. This form of land use is still practised by tribal peoples (*adivasis*) in the most remote areas of Goa, where it is known as **kumeri**. The government has been trying for years to weed out the *kumeri* cultivators, arguing that shifting cultivation farming promotes soil erosion. However, recent studies have shown shifting cultivation to be well suited to the otherwise uncultivable hill country. The government's opposition to *kumeri* seems more motivated by greed than concern for the environment: kicking the *kumeri* cultivators off their traditional land means it can be clear-felled, its hardwood sold off at a profit, and then replanted with fast-growing and lucrative eucalyptus trees – a policy pursued even in so-called protected forest areas such as Cotigao (p.205).

Shifting cultivation only accounts for a tiny percentage of land use in Goa. Most of the farmable land these days is given over to the production of **rice** or **coconuts**. The region's two main crops formerly met subsistence needs, but following the sudden surge in population caused by the arrival of the Portuguese, huge amounts of grain had to be imported from elsewhere in India. This forced the colonial administration to intensify production, which it did by introducing new farming methods (including high-yielding – but disease-prone – strains of rice) and a more strictly organized system of land tenure. The **communidades** system, originally devised by the Saraswat Brahmins during the fifth century AD but refined under the Portuguese, placed control of all land not owned privately into the hands of the local villagers, who collectively granted the rights to farm it to the highest bidders. Proceeds from these auctions were then used to pay government taxes and maintain community properties (such as temples), while anything left over was divided up evenly among the male villagers. The replacement after independence of the *communidades* with the *panchayat*, or *council* system – a brainchild of the British – is often cited as a cause of environmental degradation in rural areas. With former *communidades* land now owned by the state, local villagers lack the incentive to protect it from unscrupulous developers.

Crops

Goa's main staple, **rice**, is grown in paddy fields (*cantors*) right across the coastal strip, and on patches of flat ground between the laterite plateaux in the middle of the state known as *molloi*. Two different crops are planted: *sorondio* is sown during the monsoon in June and harvested in November, and *vangana* is cultivated during the dry season between October and February using irrigation water stored in reservoirs and ponds. Each stage of the process involves days sloshing around in thick mud, or being bent double under blazing sunshine. Without such toil, though, many thousands of Goans would go hungry: rice is the mainstay of the rural economy, providing a livelihood for the state's landless sharecroppers and subsistence farmers.

Coconut cultivation, along with fishing, is the main moneymaker in many coastal villages. The principal derivative of this ubiquitous plant is its sap, or *toddi* – used to distil the local liquor, *feni* – but other parts are put to good use, too. The *copra* oil squeezed from the young nuts is used for cooking, or sold to soap and cosmetic manufacturers; the coarse hair surrounding the shell produces fibre for rope, coir-matting and furniture upholstery; dried palm fronds make baskets, brooms and thatch; while the wood from fallen trees is used to make rafters for houses.

Further inland, you'll come across clusters of more spindly palm trees. More delicate than their coconut cousins, **areca** trees – the source of betel nuts that are ground and chewed by millions of Indians as *pan* – require constant irrigation and plenty of shade. Finally, alongside these are often planted fruit trees, most commonly mango (*ambo*), jackfruit (*ponos*), and cashews (*cazu*), whose fruit (which grows separately from the nut), produces a strong smelling juice that Goans use to make *feni*.

Flora

Goa supports more than 3500 species of flowering **plants** – 27 percent of India's total – as well as countless lower orders of grasses, ferns and brackens. The greatest floristic diversity occurs in the Western Ghats, where it is not uncommon to find one hundred or more different types of trees in an area of one hectare. Many were introduced by the Portuguese from Europe, South America, Southeast Asia and Australia, but there are also a vast number of indigenous varieties which thrive in the moist climate.

Along the coast, the **toddi palm** predominates, forming a near-continuous curtain of lush foliage. Spiky **spinifex** also helps bind the shifting sand dunes behind Colva and Calangute beaches together, while **causerina** bushes form striking splashes of pink and crimson during the winter months.

In the towns and villages of central Goa, you'll encounter dozens of beautiful **flowering trees** that are common in tropical parts of India but unfamiliar to most Europeans and North Americans. The **Indian laburnum**, or cassia, throws out masses of yellow flowers and long seed pods in late February before the monsoons. This is also the period when **mango** and **Indian coral** trees are in full bloom; both produce bundles of stunning red flowers.

Among the most distinctive trees that grow in both coastal and hill areas is the stately **banyan**, which propagates by sending out shoots frrom its lower branches. The largest-known specimen, recorded in neighbouring Maharashtra, grew over an area of two hundred metres with a staggering circumference of 577m. The banyan is also revered by Hindus and you'll often find small shrines at the foot of mature trees. Another tree regarded as sacred by Hindus (and by Buddhists, because Buddha is believed to have attained enlightenment beneath one), is the **peepal**, which has distinctive spatula-shaped leaves. Temple courtyards often enclose large *peepals*, usually with strips of auspicious red cloth hanging from their lower branches.

Tree lovers and botanists should not miss an opportunity to visit the **Western Ghats**, which harbour a bewildering wealth of flora, from flowering trees and plants, to ferns and fungi. These are among Asia's densest rainforests. Sheltered by a leafy canopy that may rise to a height of twenty metres or more, buttressed roots and giant trunks tower above a luxuriant undergrowth of brambles, creepers, and bracken, interspersed by brakes of bamboo. Common tree species include the **kadam**, **sisso** or martel, **kharanj** and **teak**, distinguished by its straight, bare trunk and broad leaves. There are dozens of representatives of the *Ficus*, or fig, family too, as well innumerable (and ecologically destructive) **eucalyptus** and **rubber** trees, planted as cash crops by the Forest Department.

Mammals

During a fact-finding expedition to Goa in the 1970s, the eminent Indian naturalist, Salim Ali, complained the only animal he saw was a lone leopard cat lying dead at the roadside. For although the state harbours more than fifty species of **mammals**, visitors to the coast are unlikely to spot anything more inspiring than a monkey or tree squirrel. Most of the exciting animals have been hunted to the point of extinction, or else have fled into neighbouring Karnataka. The few that remain roam the dense woodland lining the Western Ghats, in the sparsely populated far east, glimpsed only by forest-dwelling tribespeople, or enthusiasts prepared (and equipped) to spend several days and nights trekking through the jungle. Even so, it's nice to know they are still there, and if Goa's three

wildlife sanctuaries are adequately protected over the coming decade, populations stand a strong chance of recovering.

One animal you definitely won't come across is the tiger, which has been completely hunted out. However, several kinds of **big cat** survived the depredations of the colonial era. Among the most adaptive and beautiful is the **leopard** or **panther** (*panthera panthus*), known in Konkani as the *bibto vag*. Prowling the thick forests of Sanguem and Canacona *talukas*, these elusive cats prey on monkeys and deer, and occasionally take domestic cattle and dogs from the fringes of villages. Their distinctive black spots make them notoriously difficult to see amongst the tropical foliage, although their mating call (reminiscent of a saw on wood) regularly pierces the night air in remote areas. The **leopard cat** (*Felis bengalensis*), or *vagati* in Konkani, is a miniature version of its namesake, and more common. Sporting a bushy tail and round spots on soft buff or grey fur, it is about the same size as a domestic cat and lives around villages, picking off chickens, birds and small mammals. Another cat with a penchant for poultry, and one which Goan villagers occasionally keep as a pet if they can capture one, is the docile **Indian civet** (*Viverricual indica*), or *katanoor*. recognizable by its lithe body, striped tail, short legs and long pointed muzzle.

Wild cats share their territory with a range of other mammals unique to the subcontinent. One you've a reasonable chance of seeing is the **gaur**, or Indian bison (*Bos gaurus*), known in Goa as the *govo redo*. These primeval-looking beasts, with their distinctive sleak black skin and knee-length white "socks", forage around bamboo thickets and shady woods. The bulls are particularly impressive, growing to an awesome height of two metres, with heavy curved horns and prominent humps.

With its long fur and white V-shaped bib, the scruffy **sloth bear** (*melursus ursinas*), or *bhalu*, ranks among weirder-looking inhabitants of Goa's forests. Sadly, it's also very rare, thanks to its predilection for raiding sugar-cane plantations, which has brought it into direct conflict with man. Sloth bears can occasionally be seen shuffling along woodland trails, but you're more likely to come across evidence of their foraging activities: trashed termite mounds and chewed-up ants' nests. The same is true of both the portly **Indian porcupine** (*Hystix indica)*, or *sal*, which you see a lot less often than the mounds of earth it digs up to get at insects and cashew or teak seedlings, and the **pangolin** (*manis crassicaudata*), or *tiryo*: a kind of armour-plated anteater whose hard grey overlapping scales protect it from predators.

Full-moon nights and the twilight hours of dusk and dawn are the times to look out for **nocturnal animals** such as the **slender loris** (*Loris tardigradus*). This shy creature – a distant cousin of the lemur, with bulging round eyes, furry body and pencil-thin limbs – grows to around twenty centimetres in length. It moves as if in slow motion, except when an insect flits to within striking distance, and is a favourite pet of Goa's forest people. The **mongoose** (*Herpestes edwardsi*) is another animal sometimes kept as a pet. Rudyard Kipling's "Rikitikitavi", known in Konkani as the *mongus*, keeps dwellings free of scorpions, mice, rats and other vermin. It will also readily take on snakes, which is why you often see it writhing in a cloud of dust with king cobras during performances by snake charmers.

Late evening is also the best time for spotting **bats**. Goa boasts four species, including the **fulvous fruit bat** (*Rousettus leshenaulti*), or *vagul* – so-called because it gives off a scent resembling fermenting fruit juice – **Dormer's bat** (*Pipistrellus dormeri*), the very rare **rufous horse-shoe** bat, and the **Malay fox vampire** (*Magaderma spasma*), which feeds off the blood of live cattle. **Flying foxes** (*Pteropus gigantus*), the largest of India's bats, are also present in healthy numbers. With a wingspan of more than one metre, they fly in cacophonous groups to feed in fruit orchards, sometimes falling foul of electricity cables on the way: frazzled flying foxes dangling from live cables are a common sight in the interior of Goa.

Other species to look out for in forest areas are the **Indian giant squirrel** (*Ratufa indica*), or *shenkaro*, which has a coat of black fur and red-orange lower parts. Two and a half times larger than its European cousins, it lives in the canopy, leaping up to twenty metres between branches. The much smaller **three-striped squirrel** (*Funambulus palmarum*), or *khadi khar*, recognizable by the three black markings down its back, is also found in woodland. However, the **five-striped palm squirrel** (*Funambulus pennanti*) is a common sight all over the state, especially in municipal parks and villages.

Forest clearings and areas of open grassland around Molem (see p.108) and Cotigao (see p.205) are grazed by four species of **deer**. Widely regarded as the most beautiful is the **cheetal** (*axis axis*), or spotted axis deer, which congregates in large groups around water holes and salt licks, occasionally wandering within villages to seek shelter from its predators. The plainer buff-coloured **sambar** (*cervus unicolor*) is also well represented, despite succumbing to diseases spread by domestic cattle during the 1970s and 1980s. Two types of deer you're less likely to come across, but which also inhabit the border forests, are the **barking deer** (*muntiacus muntjack*), or *bhenkaro*, whose call closely resembles that of a domestic dog, and the timid **mouse deer** (*Tragulus meminna*), or *pisoi*: a speckled-grey member of the *Tragulidae* family that is India's smallest deer, growing to a mere thirty centimetres in height. Both of these are highly secretive and nocturnal; they are also the preferred snack of Goa's smaller predators: the **striped hyena** (*Hyaena hyaena*) or *yeul*, **jackal** (*Canis aureus*) or *colo*, and **wild dog** (*Cuon alpinus*) or *deucolo*, which hunts in packs.

Long-beaked **dolphins** are regular visitors to the shallow waters of South Goa's more secluded bays and beaches. They are traditionally regarded as a pest by local villagers, who believe they eat scarce stocks of fish. However, this long-standing antipathy is gradually eroding as local people realize the tourist-pulling potential of the dolphins: Palolem beach, in Canacona (see p.199), is where you're most likely to see one, although "Dolphin-Spotting" boat trips also operate out of Colva (see p.182).

Finally, no rundown of Goan wildlife would be complete without some mention of **monkeys**. The most ubiquitous species is the mangy pink-bottomed **macaque** (*Macaca mulatta*), or *makad*, which hangs out anywhere scraps may be scavenged or snatched from unwary humans: temples and picnic spots such as Dudhsagar Falls in the Western Ghats (see p.110) are good places to watch them in action. The black-faced **Hanuman langur**, by contrast, is less audacious, retreating to the trees if threatened. It is much larger than the macaque, with pale grey fur and long limbs and tail. In forest areas, the langur's distinctive call is an effective early-warning system against big cats and other predators, which is why you often come across herds of cheetal grazing under trees inhabited by large colonies.

Goa's wildlife parks

Of the state's main wildlife parks, the **Bhagwan Mahaveer Sanctuary**, 56km east of Panjim (see p.107), harbours the most impressive scenery and diverse fauna, with the **Cotigao Sanctuary** in south Goa (see p.205) coming a close second. **Bondla** (see p.106), near Ponda in central Goa, is more a zoo than wildlife park – a depressing spectacle of small cages and enclosures – although the variety of birdlife in this area can be astonishing. Ornithologists should also make time to take in the **Salim Ali Sanctuary** on Chorao Island (see p.95), a short way upriver from Panjim, whose mangrove swamps and mud flats teem with waders and other water birds.

The **best time of year** for viewing wildlife is immediately after the monsoons, between October and January, when water levels are still high and temperatures cool enough for hiking. However, during the rainy season – roughly late June to September – off-track transport is frequently disrupted by flooding, and the larger reserves are closed to visitors. If you plan to do any serious wildlife spotting, bring with you a pair of sturdy waterproof shoes or boots, a set of binoculars and a good field guide (those available in Goa are not so great; recommended titles are listed on p.263).

Reptiles

Reptiles are well represented in the region, with more than forty species of **snakes**, **lizards**, **turtles** and **crocodiles** recorded. The best places to spot them are not the interior forests, whose dense foliage makes observation difficult, but open cultivated areas: paddy fields and village ponds provide abundant fresh water, nesting sites and prey (frogs, insects and small birds) to feed on.

Your house or hotel room, however, is where you are most likely to come across Goa's most common reptile, the **gecko** (*Hemidactylus*), which clings to walls and ceilings with its widely splayed toes. Deceptively static most of the time, these small yellow-brown lizards will dash at lightning speed for cracks and holes if you try to catch one, or if an unwary mosquito, fly or cockroach scuttles within striking distance. The much rarer **chameleon** is even more elusive, mainly because its constantly changing camouflage makes it virtually impossible to spot. They'll have no problem seeing you, though: independently moving eyes allow them to pin-point approaching predators, while prey is slurped up with their fast-moving forty-centimetre-long tongues. The other main lizard to look out for is the **Bengal monitor**. This giant brown speckled reptile looks like a refugee from *Jurassic Park*, growing to well over a metre in length, and used to be a common sight in coastal areas, where they basked on roads and rocks. However, monitors are often killed and eaten by villagers (not that you'll find monitor *vindaloo* on many menus), and have become increasingly rare.

The monsoon period is when you're most likely to encounter **turtles**. Two varieties paddle around village ponds and wells while water is plentiful: the **flap-shell** (*Lissemys punctata*) and **black-pond** (*Melanochelys trijuga*) turtles, neither of which are endangered. Numbers of **marine turtles** (*Lepidochelys olivacea*), by contrast, have plummeted over the past few decades because villagers raid their nests when they crawl on to the beach to lay their eggs. This amazing natural spectacle occurs each year in Morgim and Cabo da Rama. Local coastguards and scientists from the Institute of Oceanography in Dona Paula monitor the migration, patrolling the beaches to deter poachers, but the annual egg binge remains a highlight of the local gastronomic calendar, eagerly awaited by fisher families, who sell the illegal harvest in local markets. Only in Orissa, in eastern India, where a special wildlife sanctuary has been set up to protect them, have the sea turtles (also known as **olive ridleys**) survived the seasonal slaughter to reproduce in healthy numbers.

An equally rare sight nowadays is the **crocodile**. Populations have dropped almost to the point of extinction, although the Cambarjua Canal near Old Goa, and more remote stretches of the Mandovi and Zuari estuaries, support vestigial colonies of **salt-water** crocs, which bask on mud flats and river rocks. Dubbed "salties", they occasionally take calves and goats, and will snap at the odd human if given half a chance. The more ominously named **mugger crocodile**, however, is harmless, inhabiting unfrequented freshwater streams and riversides around Devil's Canyon, near Molem (see p.108).

Snakes

Twenty-three species of **snake** are found in Goa, ranging from the gigantic **Indian python** (*Python molurus*, or *har* in Konkani) – a forest-dwelling constrictor that grows up to four metres in length – to the innocuous **worm snake** (*Typhlops braminus*) or *sulva*, which is tiny, completely blind and often mistaken for an earthworm.

The eight **poisonous snakes** present in the region include India's four most deadly species: the cobra, the krait, the Russel's viper and saw-scaled viper. Though these are relatively common in coastal and cultivated areas, even the most aggressive snake will slither off at the first sign of an approaching human. Nevertheless, ten thousand Indians die from snake bites each year, and if you regularly cut across paddy fields or plan to do any hiking, it makes sense to familiarize yourself with the following four or five species just in case: their bites nearly always prove fatal if not treated immediately with anti-venom serum, available at most clinics and hospitals.

Present in most parts of the state and an important character in Hindu mythology, the **Indian cobra** (*naja naja*), or *naga*, is the most common of the venomous species. Wheat-brown or grey in colour, it is famed for the "hood" it unfurls when confronted and whose rear side usually bears the snake's characteristic spectacle markings. Its big brother, the **king cobra** (*Naja hannah*), or *Raj nag*, is much less often encountered. Inhabiting the remote forest regions along the Karnatakan border, this beautiful brown, yellow and black snake, which grows to a length of four metres or more, is very rare, although the itinerant snake charmers that perform in markets occasionally keep one. Defanged, they rear up and "dance" when provoked by the handler, or are set against mongooses in ferocious (and often fatal) fights. The king cobra is also the only snake in the world known to make its own nest.

Distinguished by their steel-blue colour and faint white cross markings, **kraits** (*Bungarus coerulus*), locally known as *kaner* or *maniar*, are twice as deadly as the Indian cobra: even the bite of a new'y hatched youngster is lethal. **Russel's viper** (*Viperi Russeli*), or *mandol*, is another one to watch out for. Distinguished by the three bands of elliptical markings that extend

down its brown body, the Russel hisses at its victims before darting at them and burying its centimetre-long fangs into their flesh. The other common poisonous snake in Goa is the **saw-scaled viper** (*Echis carinatus*), or *phurshem*. Grey with an arrow-shaped mark on its triangular head, it hangs around in the cracks between stone walls, feeding on scorpions, lizards, frogs, rodents and smaller snakes. *Phurshems* also hiss when threatened; they produce the sound by rubbing together serrated scales located on the side of their head. Finally, **sea snakes** (*Enhdrina schistosa*), called *kusada* in Konkani, are common in coastal areas and potentially lethal, although rarely encountered by swimmers as they lurk only in deep water off the shore.

Harmless snakes are far more numerous than their killer cousins and frequently more attractive. The beautiful **golden tree snake** (*Chrysopelea ormata*) or *kalingin*, for example, sports an exquisitely intricate geometric pattern of red, yellow and black markings, while the **green whip snake** (*Dryhopis nasutus*) or *sarpatol*, is stunning parakeet green with a whip-like tail extending more than a metre behind it. The ubiquitous **Indian rat snake**, often mistaken for a cobra, also has beautiful markings, although it leaves behind it a foul stench of decomposing flesh. Other common non-poisonous snakes include the **wolf snake** (*Lycodon aulicus*) or *kaidya*, the **Russel sand boa** (*Eryx conicus*) or *malun*, the **kukri snake** (*Oligodon taeniolatus*) or *pasko*, the **cat snake** (*Boiga trigonata*) or *manjra*, and the **keelbacks** (*Natrix*).

Birds

You don't have to be an aficionado to enjoy Goa's abundant **birdlife**. Travelling around the state, breathtaking birds regularly flash between the branches of trees or appear on overhead wires at the roadside.

Thanks to the internationally popular brand of Goan beer, the **kingfisher** has become the state's unofficial mascot: it's not hard to see why the brewers chose it as their logo. Three common species of kingfisher frequently crop up amid the paddy fields and wetlands of the coastal plains, where they feed on small fish and tadpoles. With its enormous bill and pale green-blue wing feathers, the **stork-billed kingfisher** (*Perargopis capensis*) is the largest and most distinctive member of the family, although the **white-**

breasted kingfisher (*Halcyon smyrnensis*) – which has iridescent turquoise plumage and a coral-red bill – and the common, or **small-blue kingfisher** (*Aalcedo althis*), are more alluring.

Other common and brightly coloured species include the grass-green, blue and yellow **bee-eaters** (*Merops*), the stunning **golden oriole** (*Oriolus oriolus*), and the **Indian roller** (*Coracius bengalensis*), famous for its brilliant blue flight feathers and exuberant aerobatic mating displays. **Hoopes** (*Upupa epops*), recognizable by their elegant black-and-white tipped crests, fawn plumage and distinctive "hoo...po...po" call, also flit around fields and villages, as do **purple sunbirds** (*Nectarina asiatica*), and several kinds of bulbuls, babblers and drongos (*Dicrurus*), including the fork-tailed black drongo (*Dicrurus adsimilis*) – a winter visitor that can often be seen perched on telegraph wires. If you're lucky, you may also catch a glimpse of the **paradise flycatcher** (*Tersiphone paradisi*), which is widespread in Goa and among the region's most exquisite birds, with a thick black crest and long silver tail streamers.

Goa's paddy fields, ponds and saline mud flats are teeming with **water birds**. The most ubiquitous of these is the snowy white **cattle egret** (*Bubulcus ibis*), which can usually be seen wherever there are cows and buffalo, feeding off the grubs, insects and other parasites that live on them. The **large egret** (*Ardea alba*) is also pure white, although lankier and with a long yellow bill, while the third member of this family, the **little egret** (*Egretta garzetta*), sports a short black bill and, during the mating season, two long tail feathers. Look out too for the mud-brown **paddy bird**, India's most common heron. Distinguished by its pale green legs, speckled breast and hunched posture, it stands motionless for hours in water waiting for fish or frogs to feed on.

The hunting technique of the beautiful **white-bellied fish eagle** (*Haliaeetus leucogaster*), by contrast, is truly spectacular. Cruising twenty to thirty metres above the surface of the water, this black and white osprey stoops at high speed to snatch its prey – usually sea snakes and mackerel – from the waves with its fierce yellow talons: an everyday sight in the more secluded coves of south Goa. More common birds of prey such as the **brahminy kite** (*Haliastur indus*) – recognizable by its white breast and chestnut head markings – and the **pariah kite** (*Milvus migrans govinda*) – a dark-brown buzzard with a fork tail

– are widespread around towns and fishing villages, where they vie with raucous gangs of house **crows** (*Corvus splendens*) and white-eyed **jackdaws** (*Corvus monedula*) for scraps. Gigantic pink-headed **king vultures** (*Sarcogyps clavus*) and the **white-backed vulture** (*Gyps bengallensis*), which has a white ruff around its bare neck and head, also show up whenever there are carcasses to pick clean.

Other birds of prey to keep an eye open for, especially around open farmland, are the white-eyed buzzard (*Butastur teesa*), the honey buzzard (*Pernis ptilorhyncus*), the black-winged kite (*Elanus caeruleus*) – famous for its blood red eyes – and shikra (*Accipiter badius*), which closely resembles the European sparrowhawk.

Forest Birds

The region's **forests** may have lost many of their larger animals, but they still offer exciting possibilities for bird-watchers. One species every enthusiast hopes to glimpse while in the woods is the magnificent **hornbill**, of which three species have been spotted in the region: the **grey hornbill** (*Tockus birostris*), with its blue-brown plumage and long curved beak, is the most common, although the **Indian pied hornbill** (*Anthracoceros malabaricus*), distinguished by its white wing and tail tips and the pale patch on its face, often flies into villages in search of fruit and lizards. The magnificent **great pied hornbill** (*Buceors bicornis*), however, is more elusive, limited to the forest areas around Molem and Canacona where it may occasionally be spotted flitting through the dense canopy. Growing to 130 centimetres in length, it has a black-and-white striped body and wings, and a huge yellow beak with a long curved casque on top.

Several species of **woodpecker** also inhabit the interior forests, among them two types of golden-backed woodpecker: the lesser golden-back, *Dinopium bengalensis*, is the most colourful of the pair, with a crimson crown and bright splashes of yellow across its back. The Cotigao sanctuary in south Goa (see p.205) is also one of the last remaining strongholds of the **Indian great black woodpecker**, which has completely disappeared from the more heavily deforested hill areas further north. In spite of its bright red head and white rump, this shy bird is more often heard than seen, making loud drumming noises on tree trunks between December and March.

Another bird whose call is a regular feature of the Goan forest, particularly in teak areas, is the wild ancestor of the domestic chicken – the **jungle fowl**. The more common variety of the two found in Goa is the secretive but vibrantly coloured red junglefowl (*Gallus gallus*), which sports golden neck feathers and a metallic black tail. Its larger cousin, the grey or sonnerat's jungle fowl (*Galolus sommeratii*), has darker plumage scattered with yellow spots and streaks. Both inhabit clearings, and are most often seen scavenging for food on the verges of forest roads.

Goan music and dance

With reggae and techno blaring out of so many beach bars, you'd be forgiven for thinking Goa's music and dance scene started with the invention of the synthesizer. However, the state boasts a vibrant musical tradition of its own: a typically syncretic blend of east and west that is as spicy and distinctive as the region's cuisine. You won't hear the calypso-like rhythms of Konkani pop or haunting Kunbi folk songs at the full-moon parties, though. Rooted in village and religious life, Goan music is primarily for domestic consumption, played at temple festivals, harvest celebrations, as an accompaniment to popular theatre, and, most noticeably, on the crackly cassette machines of local buses. If you're keen to sample and understand a little more about the state's music and dance, the following account should provide some useful pointers.

Devotional Music and Dance

Devotional music and dance have played an important part in Hindu temple worship in Goa for at least one thousand years. Traditionally, wealthier temples employed permanent groups of musicians to regale the deity and participate in the annual *Zatra* processions (see p.92). Singers, accompanied by the harmonium, *tabla*, and other percussion instruments, led the performances, which were usually held in the hall in front of the shrine, or in a special musician's tower erected above the main entrance to the temple precinct. For important festivals, the congregation would also assemble in front of the sanctum to intone devotional songs, known as **kirtans** and **bhajans**.

While music still features in many temple rituals, sacred dance is seldom performed these days. Up until the turn of the century, however, most of the larger shrines boasted troupes of specially trained dancers, known as **Devadasis**, literally "wives of the god". Gifted or sold to the temple authorities by their parents at a young age (either as an offering, or in fulfilment of a thanksgiving vow), these women were symbolically married to the deity in a ritual known as *sessa*, after which they effectively became slaves, expected to grant sexual favours to the temple priests and wealthy visitors as well as to fulfil their ritual responsibilities. Formerly an act of worship and regarded as one of the highest classical art forms, this kind of dance degenerated over time into a kind of crude commercial entertainment.

Among the more illustrious descendants of the Devadasis caste is the playback singer **Lata**

Mangeshkar, who appears in the *Guinness Book of Records* as the world's most recorded artist. With over 30,000 songs and more than 2000 films to her credit, her high vibrato voice has become the hallmark of the Hindi movie soundtrack. Lata was born in Pune, Maharashtra, in 1928, but her father, Dinanath Mangeshkar (also a famous actor and singer) originally came from Mangeshki in Ponda *taluka*. During a visit to her father's village, the star was not allowed to approach the deity in the local temple because of her Devadasi roots. As a result of this snub, Lata has refused ever to return to Goa, despite repeated invitations to perform in the state.

The licentious associations of temple dance also account for the rarity with which recitals are given in *devuls* today. You can, however, catch performances of classical Indian dance at secular **venues** around the state, notably the Kala Academy in Panjim (see p.75), and Calangute's *Kerkar Art Gallery* (see p.131). These two places also host regular recitals of Indian **classical** music by students, teachers, and visiting artistes from elsewhere in India.

Folk music and dance

Wander into almost any Hindu village on the eve of an important *puja*, particularly around harvest time after the monsoons, and you'll experience Goan roots music and dance at its most authentic. The torchbearers of the region's thriving **folk tradition** are the Kunbi class of landless labourers, most often seen bent double in rice paddy, the women with garish coloured cotton *saris* tied *dhoti*-style around their legs. Agricultural work – planting, threshing and grinding grain, raking salt pans, and fixing fishing nets – provide the essential rhythms for Konkani songs, known as **Kunbi geet**.

More rehearsed performances take place during the Hindu month of Paush (late Feb), when groups of women gather in the village square-cum-dance ground (*mannd*) to sing *dhalos* and *fugdis*. The singing may run over seven or more

Remo

Ask anyone in Goa to name you a famous Goan and they'll probably say "**Remo**". The state's most acclaimed musician, singer-songwriter and local hero Remo Fernandes, is unknown in the west, but enjoys mega-star status among India's young English-speaking middle classes. The secret of his success is his eccentric flair for **fusion**. Dressed in a cotton *dhoti* and twelve-hole *Doc Martens*, Remo blends Western rock with traditional Indian sounds, spiced up with South American rhythms and overscored by punchy issues-based lyrics. He's also staunchly proud of his Goan heritage, and is as happy crooning *fados* and Konkani folk tunes at local *festas* as performing electric sets in the concert halls of Delhi and Bombay.

Born in 1953 in the picturesque riverside village of Siolim, near Chapora in north Goa, Remo's earliest musical influence was his father's collection of Portuguese, Latin-American and Goan records. A spell with a college rock band in Bombay during the 1970s, followed by a couple of years hitching around Europe and North Africa, added new ingredients to this musical melting pot, and in 1980 he founded the ground-breaking fusion band

"Indiana", whose extravagant stage costumes and hybrid style would later become hallmarks of the Goan's own career.

Remo's big break, though, came in 1983 with the release of his first solo album, *Goan Crazy*. Recorded and mixed at his family home in Siolim, its syncretic sound and acerbic social commentary showcased Remo's talents as a multi-instrumentalist and lyric writer, finally bringing him to the attention of Bombay's movie moguls and record companies. A series of hit film scores and a major record deal followed, culminating with his two best-selling albums, *Pack That Smack* and *Bombay City*, which both shot straight to the top of the rock/pop charts.

Since the late 1980s, Remo has enjoyed continued success, alternating between bouts of recording in Goa and touring the country with his band. Living locally also means he often gets to perform in front of a home crowd. So if you see a gig advertised, check it out. Whether backed by his own "troupe" or just a solo acoustic guitar, Remo's songs, with their satirical lyrics and catchy rhythms, are both entertaining and provocative.

nights, culminating with outbreaks of spirit possession and trances.

The most famous Goan folk song and dance form, though, has to be the **mando**. Originally, this slow and expressive dance (whose name derives from the Sanskrit *mandala*, meaning circular pattern) was traditionally performed in circles, but these days tends to be danced by men and women standing opposite each other in parallel lines, waving fans and coloured handkerchiefs. *Mandos* gather pace as they progress and are usually followed by a series of **dulpods**, quick-time tunes whose lyrics are traditionally satirical, exposing village gossip about errant housewives, lapsed priests and so on. *Dulpods*, in turn, merge into the even jauntier rhythms of **deknis**, bringing the set dances to a tumultuous conclusion.

The basic rhythmic cycles, or *ovis*, of Goan folk songs were exploited by early Christian missionaries in their work. Overlaid with improving lyrics inspired by Bible stories, many were eventually assimilated into the local Catholic tradition: today, the *mando*, for example, is usually danced by Christians on church *festas* and wedding days. It also became the favourite dance of the Goan gentry, who, dressed in ball gowns and dinner suits with fans and flamboyant handkerchiefs, used to perform it during the glittering functions held in the reception rooms of the territory's top houses.

Fados

The most European-influenced of all the Goan folk idioms is the **fado**. Rendered in a turgid mock operatic style, these melancholic songs epitomize the colonial predeliction for nostalgia or longing for the home country, known in Portuguese as *saudades*. Ironically, though, few *fadistas* actually laid eyes on the fabled lights of Lisbon or Coimbra they eulogized in their lyrics, and today the *fado* is a dying art form. However, a couple of renowned folk singers, notably the band leader **Oslando** and singer-guitarist **Lucio Miranda**, invariably include a couple of old *fado* numbers on their albums. Lucio, the greatest living exponent of the form, also gives the odd performance in the five-star hotels around Panjim.

Konkani Pop

Rave music aside, most of the sounds you hear around Goa these days are either *filmi* hits from the latest blockbuster Hindi movies, or a mishmash of folk tunes and calypso rhythms known as **Konkani pop**. Backed by groups of women singers and fanfaring mariachi-style brass sections, Konkani lead vocalists croon away with the

---

Recommended cassettes

Virtually every music store and street stall in Goa stocks a representative selection of **audio cassettes** by Goan artists. Costing between Rs20 and Rs50, they're usually cheap enough to risk buying on spec, although most retailers will let you listen to them if they are not sealed in plastic. The following are among the safest bets:

Agostinho's Trio *Soul of Music* (*Goa Productions*). Whacky Konkani covers of popular Latin and Western numbers accompanied by accordions, mandolins, violas and conga percussion.

Gavana *Souvenirs1–3*. The only *conjunto* still using exclusively acoustic instruments, and these three albums are all the richer for it. Pick of the *Souvenir* trio is No. 3, which features several beautiful *fados* and a side of lyrical Konkani classics. If you leave Goa with only one cassette, let it be this.

Lucio *Forwards into the Past* (*Remo Presents*). A string of sombre Portuguese ballads and *bossa novas* by Goa's master *fadista*. Some fine flute-playing by Remo, too.

Oslando *Goa Meu Amor* (*VP Sinari*). One of several soundalike albums by the bespectacled grandfather of Goan folk; this one features a side of Portuguese songs followed by a selection of *Kunbi geets*, *dekhnis*, and *dulpods*.

Remo *Goan Crazy*. The most "Goan" of Remo's rock albums includes his cheeky single "Hello, Mr Rajiv Gandhi", and other Indo-Western hits.

Remo *Goan Gold*. Remo's arrangements of Portuguese and Konkani classics are somewhat marred by incongruous synthesizer sounds, but one track – the hauntingly beautiful *Panch Vorsad* – is outstanding.

---

reverb cranked up against a cacophony of electric guitar and keyboard accompaniment.

Konkani pop is best experienced live (the costumes tend to be as lurid as the music), but if you don't manage to get to a gig, every kerbside cassette-*wallah* stocks a range of popular tapes. No particular artist is worth singling out; nor are many likely to find fans among Western visitors. However, world-music aficionados should definitely check out a couple of cassettes to sample the sometimes surreal blend of musical influences. Underpinning the Portuguese-style melodies are conga-driven African and Caribbean rhythms, Brazilian syncopations, and almost Polynesian-sounding harmonies. The only part of the world Konkani pop sounds like it doesn't come from is India.

Books

There's a surprising dearth of books on Goa, particularly when you consider the reams of printed matter devoted to regions of India formerly colonized by the British. This neglect may well be reversed as the state's tourist boom gathers momentum, but in the meantime most titles are, with a few notable exceptions, either specialist tomes on history and architecture, or else travelogues that feature accounts of short sojourns in the territory.

While many of the titles listed below are stocked by high-street bookshops in Western countries, those published in India tend only to be available in Goa itself, usually at a fraction of what they would cost back home: Panjim's five-star hotels are the best place to start searching. For rare out-of-print books, as well as current publications, check *Amazon Books'* web site on the internet (http://www.amazon.com), through which you can order several of the more obscure titles listed below. Serious students of art and architecture should also scour the shelves of academic libraries, which are a rich source of out-of-print material, including some of the acknowledged classics on the region. Bona fide Goan literature is in very short supply, mainly because Konkani was suppressed for centuries by the Portuguese. If you want to sample the state's contemporary fiction, dip into the short-story pages of the monthly magazine *Goa Today*, available at most Goan newsagents.

Wherever a book is in print, the UK publisher is listed first, followed by the publishers in the US and India, where applicable. Where books are out of print, they are annotated o/p.

History, society and architecture

Teresa Albuquerque *Anjuna: Profile of a Village in Goa* (S Asia, US/Promilla & Co, New Delhi). A fascinating village study by one of Goa's most renowned social historians. Crammed full of fine-grain detail on local legends, celebrities, shrines, traditions and other curiosities.

Teresa Albuquerque *Santa Cruz* (Fernandes Publications, Panjim). Albuquerque tackles her home patch, a large village near Panjim, in the same style as her previous offering. This one's equally rich, although too detailed for a casual read.

José Nicolau da Fonseca *A Historical and Architectural Sketch of the City of Old Goa* (S. Asia, US). An affordable facsimile edition of an old gazetteer-style guide, with lithographic prints and meticulously detailed accounts of Goa's economy and environment around the turn of the century.

James Leasor *Boarding Party* (Heinemann, UK, o/p). A vivid account of the sinking of the German spy ship, *Ehrenfels*, in Mormugao harbour by British veterans of the Calcutta Light Horse regiment (see p.162). The melodramatic "faction" style grates after a while, but this is a rip-roaring yarn.

Marg VIII No. 1 (Marg, Bombay). A special edition of India's premier art and architecture periodical devoted to Goa. Well worth hunting out.

Judiha Nunes *The Monuments in Old Goa* (New Delhi). The most meticulously detailed rundown of the site's monuments, architectural background and historical context.

R.G. Pereira *Goa: Hindu Temples and Deities* (Goa, Panjim). An erudite overview of the state's Hindu heritage with detailed accounts of its monuments and traditions. Tough going at times, though.

Ariant Kakba Priolkar *The Goa Inquisition* (New Delhi). First-hand accounts of the dreaded *autos da fé* and torture techniques employed by the Holy Office, framed with a very accessible history.

Elaine Sanceau *Indies Adventure: the Amazing Career of Alfonso de Albuquerque* (Blackie and Sons, UK). A lengthy but highly readable biography of Goa's first Portuguese governor, who wrested the territory from its former Muslim overlords in 1510.

Georg Schurhammer *Francis Xavier: His Life and Times* (Loyola, US). This definitive biography of Goa's wandering patron saint includes a graphic rundown of the decapitations inflicted on his corpse (see p.92).

P.P. Shirodkhar and H.K. Mandal *People of India: Goa* (Anthropological Society of India). This outline of the region's tribal and caste divisions is cringingly old-fashioned, with mugshots of "A Lamani female" and "Velip males" and the like, but is strong on village customs. Widely available in Goa.

Other guides

David Abram, Devdan Sen, Harriet Sharkey and Gareth John Williams *Rough Guide: India* (Rough Guides, UK). Obviously we're biased, but we think this guide, described by *Condé Nast Traveler* as "the Bible for any visitor to India", is the most comprehensive ever published, and an indispensable travelling companion if you plan to venture far outside Goa. The second edition includes expanded coverage of Kerala, Karnataka, Maharashtra and Bombay, with nearly 1300 pages of candid accounts and cultural background, backed up by solid practical information. But don't believe us: check it out for yourself at the *Rough Guides*' website (see inside cover).

Mario Cabral e Sa *Goa* (Lustre Press). The best of the coffee-table souvenir tomes on sale in the five-star hotels, with excellent colour photos by Jean-Louis Nou.

Maurice Hall *Window on Goa: A History and Guide* (Quiller Press, UK). Published posthumously and widely available, this work, completed during the author's retirement after a career as a steel engineer in India, was clearly a labour of love. Covering every conceivable site of historic interest, it offers a concise, highly readable background on all aspects of Goan life, enlivened by dozens of colour photographs that will whet your appetite before you leave, and revive memories after returning.

Anthony Hutt *Goa: A Traveller's Historical and Architectural Guide* (Scorpion Publishing, UK). A detailed and scholarly overview of Goa's past and present, with accounts of the main monuments, illustrations and a good index. Ideal if you want to deepen your understanding of the region without getting tangled in nit-picking academic prose.

J.M. Richards *Goa* (C. Hurst, UK/Vikas, New Delhi). Now only printed in India, this retired architecture journalist's wide-ranging little book touches on most aspects of Goan life, making a better armchair read than field companion.

Travel

Clive Anderson *Our Man In . . .* (BBC Books, UK). In the second of six chapters on different parts of the world, television presenter and barrister Anderson takes a typically wry look at the way Goa is being threatened by mass tourism, interviewing wealthy local developers, dispossessed villagers and even a couple of naked hippies in his witty whistle-stop trip of the coast.

Alexander Frater *Chasing the Monsoon* (Penguin/H Holt and Co). Frater's wet-season jaunt across the subcontinent took him through a Goa of grey skies and muddy puddles: an evocative account of the region as few visitors see it.

Gita Mehta *Karma Cola* (Mandarin/Fawcett). Satirical look at the psychedelic 1970s freak scene that winds up, appropriately enough, at the Anjuna flea market. Now somewhat dated, but with some hilarious anecdotes and many a telling observation on the excesses of spiritual tourism in India.

Cleo Odzer *Goa Freaks: My Hippie Years in India* (Blue Moon Books, US). A cloyingly self-indulgent account of an American woman's youthful hippy odyssey, revolving around Goa and Bombay. In more skilled hands, the subject matter might have yielded an entertaining neo-Beat novel, but as it is, the total absence of irony and tone of barely suppressed excitement with which Odzer narrates her brush with destitution (*"Sleeping on the street with beggars! Could that happen to me?"*) leaves us cold – a far cry indeed from Kerouac. (An extract from *Goa Freaks*, and an interview with the author, appear on the internet at http://www.well.com/user/patpong).

François Pryard *Voyage to the East Indies, the Maldives, the Moluccas and Brazil* (Hakkluyt Society, India). Albert Gray's translation of the famous French chronicler's travelogue includes a vivid first-hand description of the Portuguese colony during its decadent heyday. Goa was Pryard's first port of call after being shipwrecked in the Maldives in 1608.

Frank Simoes *Glad Seasons in Goa* (Viking). An affectionate portrait of Goa and its inhabitants by a local author, with a particularly memorable evocation of the joys of *feni* drinking. Widely available in Goa, but harder to find abroad.

Cookery

Madhur Jaffrey *Flavours of India* (BBC Books, UK). Accompanying the popular BBC TV series, the uncrowned *rani* of Indian cookery's latest tome features a couple of dozen Goan dishes, with enlightening background notes and some mouthwatering colour photos.

Wildlife and the environment

Salim Ali, Dillon and Ripley *The Handbook of the Birds of India and Pakistan* (OUP, UK). Covers all of South Asia's birds in a single volume, with plates and maps: the definitive work, although hard to come by.

Claude Alvares (editor) *Fish Curry and Rice: A Citizens' Report on the Goan Environment* (Ecoforum, India). The most thorough overview of Goan green issues ever compiled in a single volume, giving a region-by-region rundown of the state's natural habitats, followed by articles outlining the principal threats to the environment from tourism, transport policy, changes in local farming practices, and a host of other eco evils.

PV Bole and Yogini Vaghini *Field Guide to the Common Trees of India* (OUP, UK/US). A handy-sized, indispensable tome for serious tree spotters.

Bikram Grewal *Birds of India, Bangladesh, Nepal, Pakistan and Sri Lanka* (Odyssey, UK). Five hundred species are detailed in this glossy but practical field guide, most with excellent colour photographs. Based on Salim Ali & Co's authoritative work, and the best of the bunch available in UK and US high-street bookshops.

Insight Guides *Indian Wildlife* (APA Publications, UK). An excellent all-round introduction to India's wildlife, with scores of superb colour photographs, features on different animals and habitats, and a thorough bibliography. Recommended.

S Prater *The Book of Indian Animals* (OUP, UK/Bombay Natural History Society). The most comprehensive single-volume reference book on the subject, although only available in India.

Romulus Whitaker *Common Indian Snakes* (Macmillan, UK). A detailed illustrated guide to the subcontinent's snakes, with all the Goan species included.

Martin Woodcock *Handguide to the Birds of the Indian Subcontinent* (Collins, UK). For years the market leader, although now superceded by Grewal's guide. Available in light-weight, pocket-sized paperback form, and very user-friendly, with nearly every species illustrated (some in black and white).

Language

Konkani, an Indo-Aryan offshoot of Sanskrit that took root in the region more than two thousand years ago, is the mother tongue of most Goans, spoken by virtually all of its native inhabitants. Only in 1976, however, was it recognized by Delhi as more than a minor dialect; another decade elapsed before the Indian government, bowing to popular opinion, named it the state's official language. Before then, Maharathi, the language of Goa's politically and economically powerful neighbour, Maharashtra, was the principal medium of government and education.

Portuguese has these days all but died out, in spite of concerted attempts by the old colonial regime to eradicate Konkani. The only people who still speak it tend to be elderly, well-educated members of upper-class families, and the odd household in the staunchly pro-Portuguese neighbourhood of Fontainhas, Panjim. **English**, by contrast, is very widespread, especially in the coastal resorts where you can easily get by without a word of Konkani or Maharathi. Even fluent English speakers, though, will be flattered if you attempt a few words of their native tongue.

The following list of words and phrases is intended as an aid to meeting people and travelling independently around more off-the-beaten track areas of the state, where English is less commonly spoken. Konkani has no script of its own (Christians use Roman, and Hindus write with Devanagiri) so we've transcribed the expressions phonetically, indicating the correct syllable stress in italics.

A BRIEF GUIDE TO KONKANI

Talking to people

Hello/good morning good evening	Dio boro *dees* diun
Goodbye	Miochay
How are you?	*Kos*-o-asaee?
What is your name?	Tu Chay Nau Kit*ay*?
My name is (David)	Majay Nau (David)
Where do you come from?	Tu Koyee-sau Yat-ee?
I come from . . .	Mau Zo Gao . . .
Thank you	Dio *Boray* Kor*unc*
Happy Christmas	Kooshal Bhoo*reet* Nat*a*la
Happy *Holi*	Holi Moo*ba*rak
May I take your photograph?	Au eek *foto* kardung?
I am hungry	Maka bhook *lag*leah
I am thirsty	Maka taan *lag*leah
I am tired	Aoo tsod *tok*la
I am happy	Aoo tsaud *koo*shi
I love Goa	Maka Goeya boray *lak*ta
The food is good	Jon boray ha
I understand a little Konkani	*Ma*ka *to*ree *Kon*kani saz*ma*ta
I speak a little Konkani	Aoo *to*ree *Kon*kani oo*lay*ta
How much?	Kitlay?

Useful vocabulary

Father	Pai (Christian), Bapui (Hindu)
Mother	Maee (Christian), Avoi (Hindu)
Grandmother	Shamai
Grandfather	Shapai

Continues...

Continued...

Daughter	Dhoo	How many kilometres	(Kongotchi) kitley
Son	Phoot	is it to (Calangute)?	pois asa?
Wife	Bhai	Turn left/right	Dai-an/ooj-an wot.
Husband	Ghoo	Drive more slowly!	Sossegarde so*lay*!
Beach	*Pray*ia	Do you have a room/	Tu jay shee room/
Cave	Bhuher	house to rent?	gora asa?
Church	Ig*roz*		
Hill	*Don*goor	**Numbers**	
Moon	Tson*drim*	1 Ek	20 Vees
Palm tree	Mard	2 Dohn	30 Tees
River	Wow	3 Teen	40 Cha-*ees*
Road	*Ros*to	4 Char	50 Po-*nas*
Sea	*Dor*ia	5 Pants	100 Chem-*bor*
Sun	Wot	6 Soh	150 Dher-chen
Temple	Day-*vool*	7 Saht	200 Dho-chen
Village	Gao	8 Ahrt	1000 Ek-azar
		9 Nou	2000 Dhon-azar
		10 Dha	

Getting around and finding accommodation

Where can I catch the bus to (Calangute)?	(Kon*got*chi) bus ko-ee *tam*ta
Does this bus go to (Calagute)?	Ee Kon*got*chi bus?
When does the bus leave?	Bus kitley-anc *so*-ta?

Note: A hundred thousand is a *lakh* (written 1,00,000); ten million is a *crore* (1,00,00,000). Millions, billions and the like are not in common usage.

Glossary

ANTARALHAYA Temple vestibule.

ARGASHALLAS Pilgrims' hostels in Hindu temples.

AVATAR Reincarnation of Vishnu on earth, in human or animal form.

AZULEJO White ceramic tiles hand-painted in blue and yellow: a traditional Portuguese art form.

BALCÃO Deep verandah of Goan villas with stone benches where residents relax during siesta and the evenings.

BEDEES Tiny Indian cigarettes hand-rolled in brown eucalyptus leaves and tied with cotton thread. The aroma they give off is one of India's quintessential smells.

BRAHMAPURI Hindu religious centre.

BRAHMINS Caste made up of priests and teachers.

BURQA Enveloping black veil worn by Muslim women.

CARAVELA Portuguese galleon with a triangular sail derived from the Arab *dhow*.

CHAI Indian tea; usually boiled with lots of milk and sugar.

CHARAS Cannabis resin (hashish).

CHOWKIDAR Watchman/caretaker.

DARSHAN Ritual viewing of a deity or saint; receiving religious teachings.

DEEP STAMBHAS Lamp tower positioned outside Hindu temples – a feature introduced to Goa by the Marathas.

DEEPMAL Lamp tower (see above).

DEVTA Deity.

DEVUL Temple.

DHABA Roadside food stall selling local dishes.

DHARAMSALA Rest house for pilgrims.

DHOBI Man or woman who washes clothes.

DHOTI White ankle-length cloth worn by men, tied around the waist, and sometimes hitched up through the legs.

DWARPALAS Guardian deities; in Goa, these feature on the embossed silver doors flanking the temple shrine rooms.

FENI Clear liquor distilled from cashew fruit or coconut sap (*toddi*).

FESTA Christian feast day connected with a patron saint.

GARBHAGRIHA Sanctum or shrine room of a Hindu temple.

GAUR Indian bison.

GHAT Literally "step"; usually refers to the Sahyadri Hills lining the Goan border.

GOPURA Ornamental gateway to a temple enclosure, surmounted by a multi-tiered tower (often decorated with statues).

HARIJANS Literally "Children of God"; a term introduced by Mahatma Gandhi to designate those outside, or below, the four principal Hindu castes.

HIDALGOS Portuguese nobles.

KOTT Fort.

KSHATRIYAS The second-highest caste, made up of rulers and warriors.

LANGUR Black-faced monkey.

LINGAM Phallic symbol in places of worship representing the god Shiva.

LUNGHI Male garment; long wrap-around cloth, like a *dhoti*, but coloured (usually plaid).

MANDAPA Assembly hall tacked onto the front of a temple, often with many pillars.

MANDIR Temple.

MIHRAB Niche in the wall of a mosque indicating the direction of prayer (to Mecca). In India, the *mihrab* is normally in the west wall.

MOKSHA Spiritual release from the cycle of rebirth.

NACRE Rectangles of polished fish scales (often mistakenly referred to as 'oyster shells') traditionally used instead of glass to make windows.

NAUBHAT KHANNA Musician's gallery in a Goan temple.

NOVAS CONQUISTAS The "New Conquests" area of Pernem, Satari, Canacona and Sanguem *talukas*, acquired by the Portuguese in the eighteenth century.

PARIWAR DEVTA Accessory *devtas.*

PRADAKSHENA Circumambulatory passage around a temple shrine.

PUJA Worship.

PUJARI Priest.

PURIS Deep-fried flat breads.

RATH Processional temple chariot.

SATI One who sacrifices her life on her husband's funeral pyre in emulation of Shiva's wife. No longer a common practice, and officially illegal.

SATYAGRAHAS Goan Ghandhi-ites: non-violent protestors against colonial occupation.

SESSO Martel wood.

SHALWA-CAMISES Long shirts and pyjama trousers worn by women and Muslim men.

SHIKHARA Temple tower or spire.

SHIVALINGAM See *lingam.*

SHUDRAS The lowest of the four castes, designating menial workers.

SONDDIOS Galleries for storing musical instruments in temples.

SOSSEGARDE A typically Goan phrase, meaning "laid-back"; something like the Spanish "mañana".

TALUKA Administrative district.

THALI Combination of dishes: chutneys, pickles, rice and bread served on a large round metal plate.

TILAK Vermillion paste smeared on the forehead by Hindu worshippers.

TIRTHA Holy water.

TULSI VRINDAVAN Ornamental pot (*vrindavan*) containing the sacred shrub *tulsi,* representing a former mistress of Vishnu.

VADDO/WADDO Ward, or area of a village.

VAHANA The vehicle of a deity: the bull Nandi is Shiva's *vahana.*

VAISHYAS Third-highest of the Hindu castes made up of merchants and cultivators.

VELHAS CONQUISTAS The Old Conquests area of Bardez, Tiswadi and Salcete.

WALLAH/WALLI Suffix implying occupation or purveyor of something, eg *dhobi wallah* (laundry man), *rickshaw wallah* (rickshaw driver), *flower walli* (lady flower seller).

Index

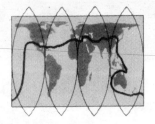

TROPICAL PLACES

Tropical Places are the specialists for exotic holidays and offer good-quality hotels at big savings on standard brochure prices. Featured destinations include:

CARIBBEAN: Antigua, Barbados, Grenada, Jamaica, St Lucia, Tobago.

AFRICA: Egypt, Kenya, South Africa, Zimbabwe

INDIAN OCEAN: Goa, Seychelles, Sri Lanka, Maldives, Mauritius

FAR EAST: Bali, Hong Kong, Malaysia, Singapore, Thailand.

For details of the latest special offers from Tropical Places see ITV Teletext page 259.

For a free colour brochure, call the 24-hr brochure line on 01342 825599.

Tropical Places Ltd.
Freshfield House, Lewes Road
Forest Row, East Sussex
RH18 5ES
Tel 01342 825123
Fax 01342 822364